⑤

Love&Lies

LOVE and LIES by MUSAWO

CONTENTS

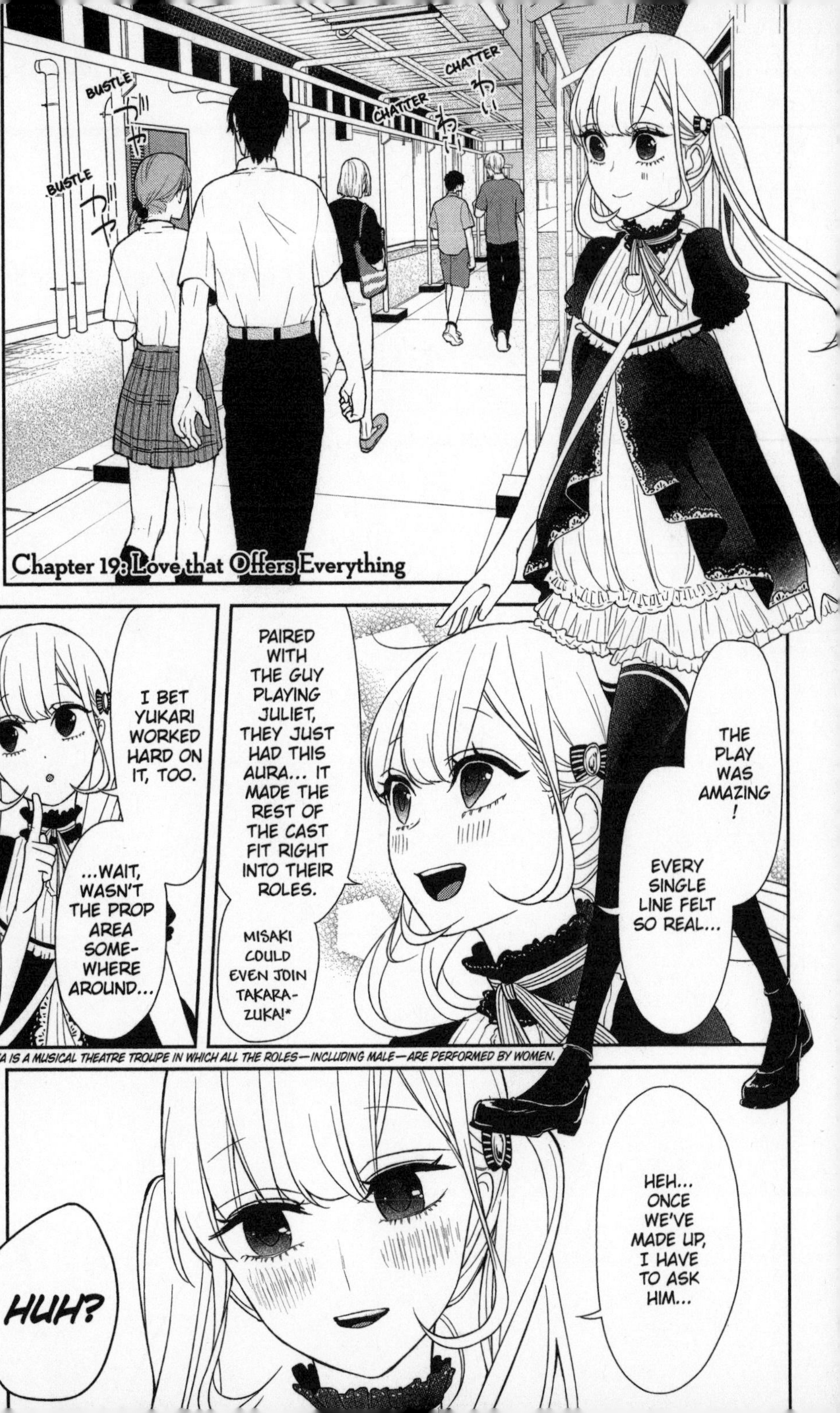
Chapter 19: Love that Offers Everything
CHATTER
CHATTER
BUSTLE
BUSTLE
THE PLAY WAS AMAZING!
EVERY SINGLE LINE FELT SO REAL...
PAIRED WITH THE GUY PLAYING JULIET, THEY JUST HAD THIS AURA... IT MADE THE REST OF THE CAST FIT RIGHT INTO THEIR ROLES.
MISAKI COULD EVEN JOIN TAKARA-ZUKA!*
I BET YUKARI WORKED HARD ON IT, TOO.
...WAIT, WASN'T THE PROP AREA SOME-WHERE AROUND...
HERE?
?
*TAKARAZUKA IS A MUSICAL THEATRE TROUPE IN WHICH ALL THE ROLES—INCLUDING MALE—ARE PERFORMED BY WOMEN.
HEH... ONCE WE'VE MADE UP, I HAVE TO ASK HIM...
HUH?

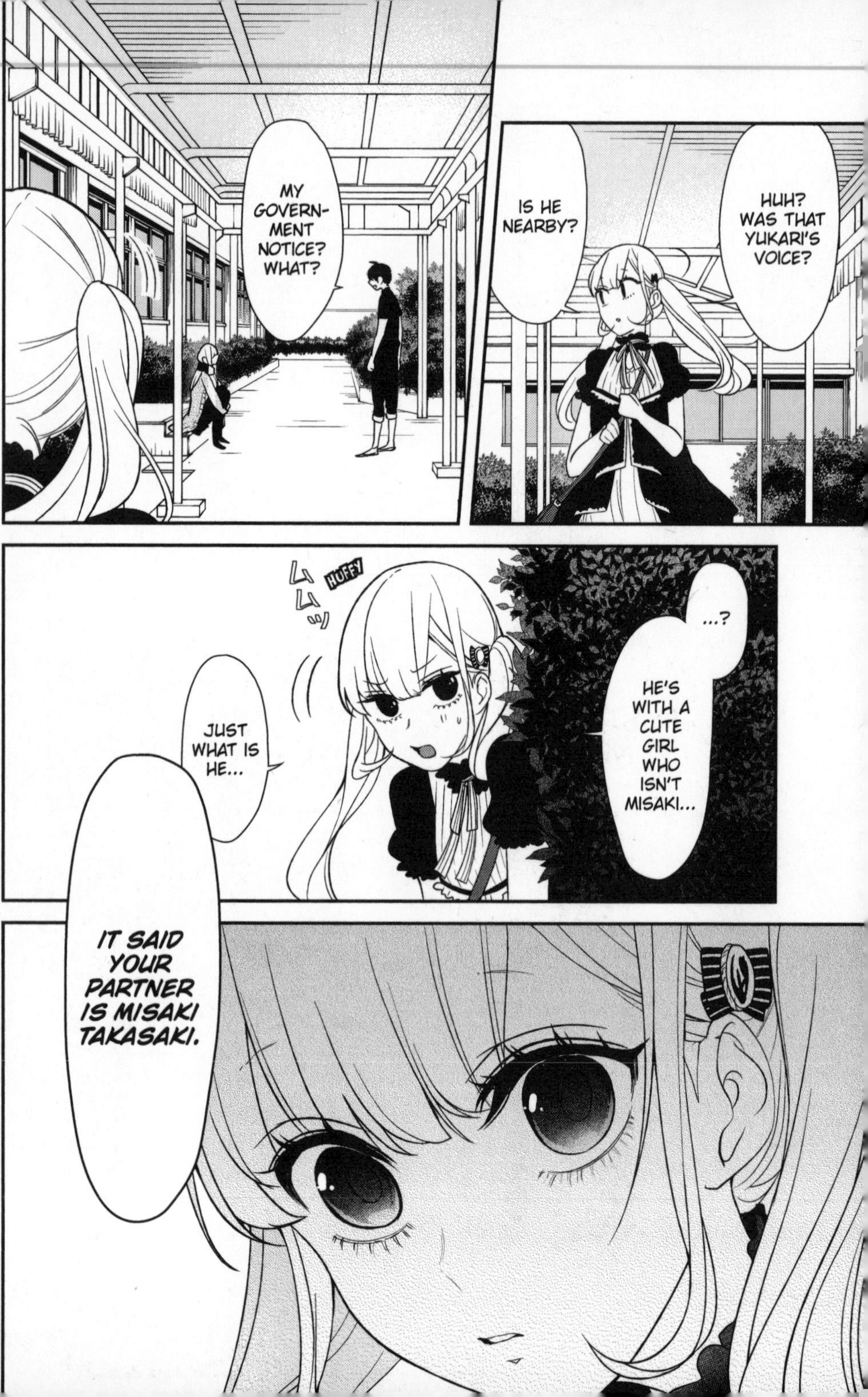
HUH? WAS THAT YUKARI'S VOICE?
IS HE NEARBY?
MY GOVERN-MENT NOTICE? WHAT?
...?
HE'S WITH A CUTE GIRL WHO ISN'T MISAKI...
ムムッ
HUFFY
JUST WHAT IS HE...
IT SAID YOUR PARTNER IS MISAKI TAKASAKI.

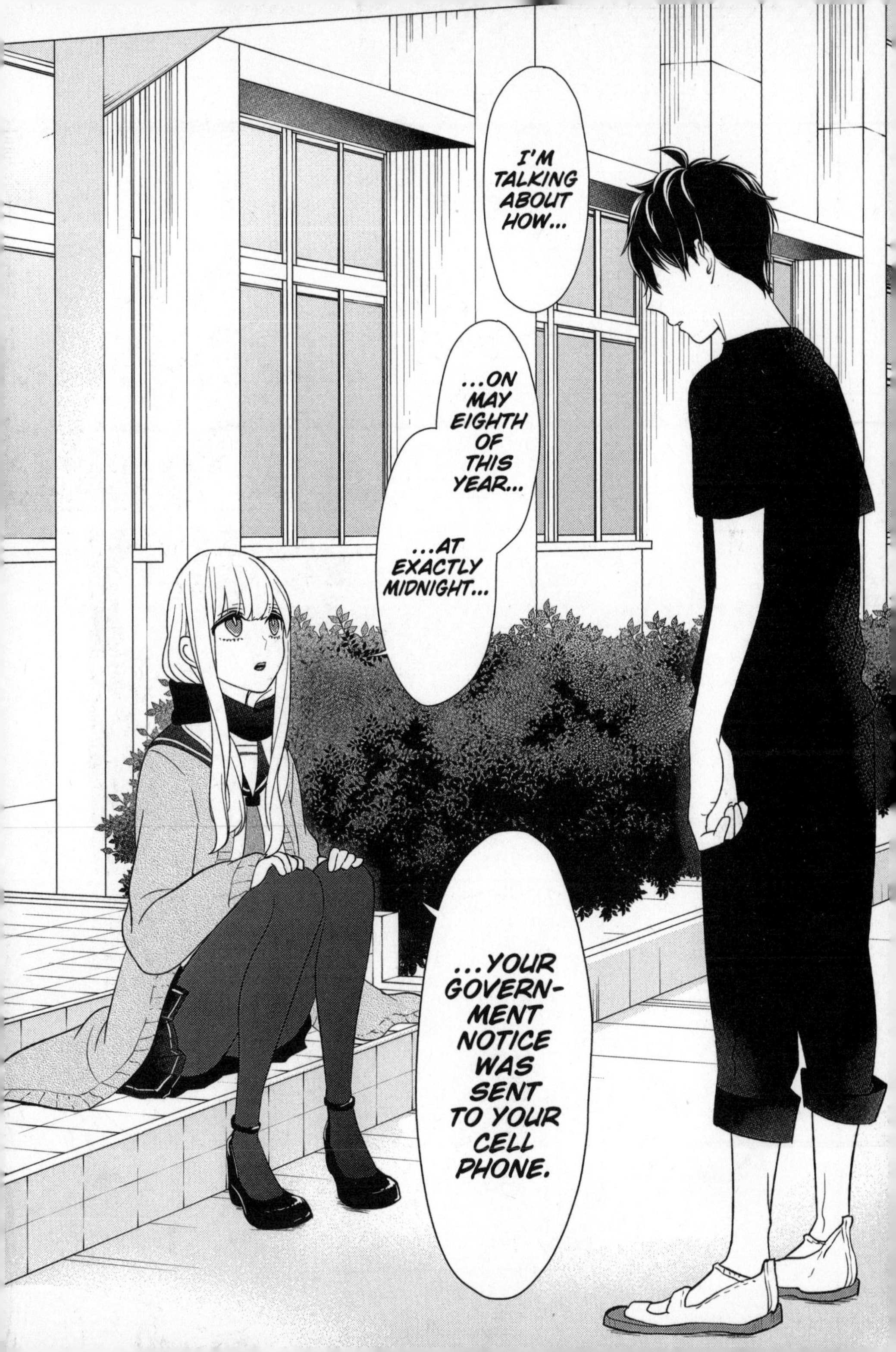
I'M TALKING ABOUT HOW...
...ON MAY EIGHTH OF THIS YEAR...
...AT EXACTLY MIDNIGHT...
...YOUR GOVERN-MENT NOTICE WAS SENT TO YOUR CELL PHONE.

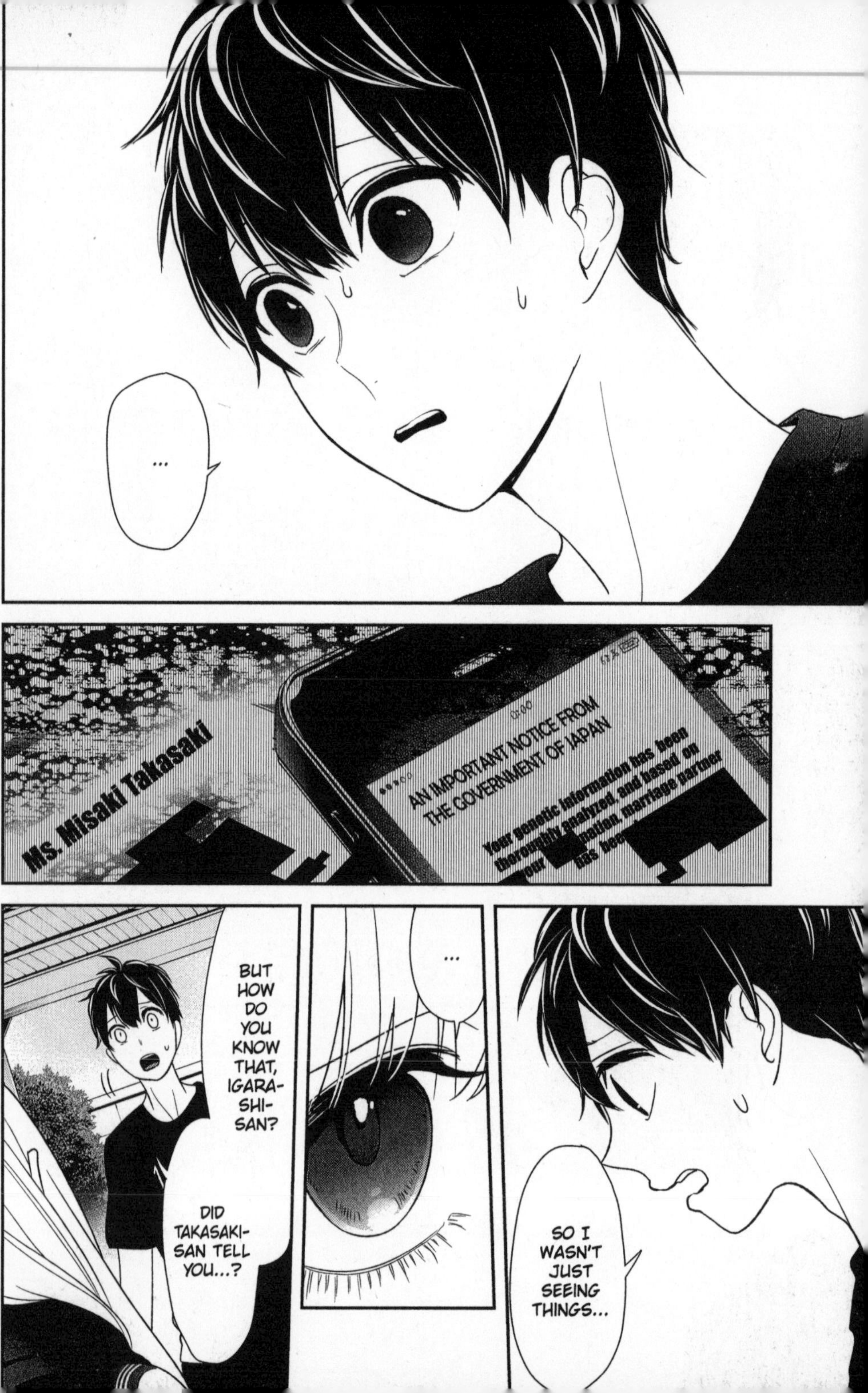
...
AN IMPORTANT NOTICE FROM THE GOVERNMENT OF JAPAN
Your genetic information has been thoroughly analyzed, and based on your [redacted]nation, marriage partner has bee [redacted]
Ms. Misaki Takasaki [redacted]
SO I WASN'T JUST SEEING THINGS...
...
BUT HOW DO YOU KNOW THAT, IGARASHI-SAN?
DID TAKASAKI-SAN TELL YOU...?

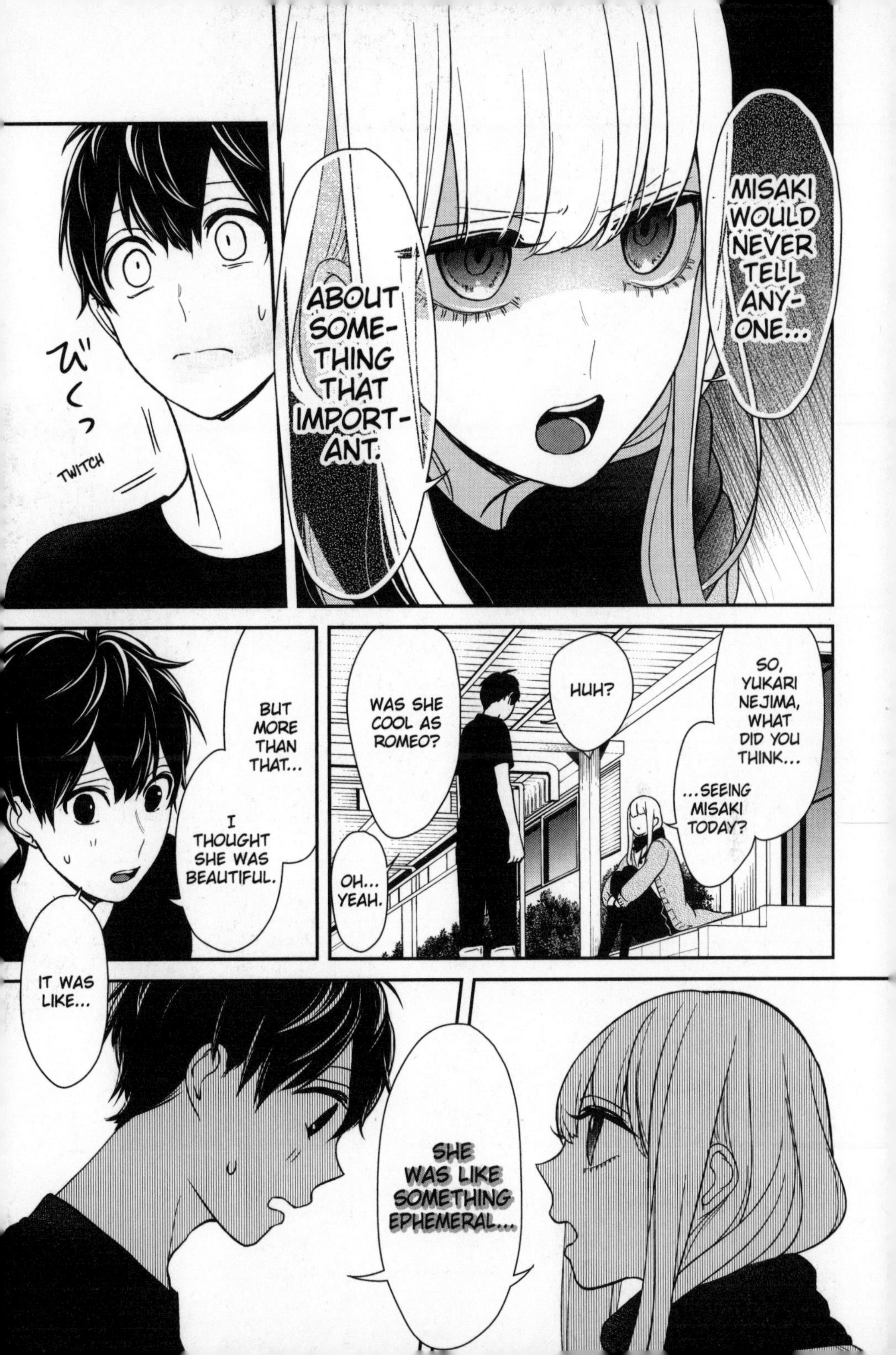
MISAKI WOULD NEVER TELL ANY-ONE...
ABOUT SOME-THING THAT IMPORT-ANT.
びくっ
TWITCH
SO, YUKARI NEJIMA, WHAT DID YOU THINK...
...SEEING MISAKI TODAY?
HUH?
WAS SHE COOL AS ROMEO?
OH... YEAH.
BUT MORE THAN THAT...
I THOUGHT SHE WAS BEAUTIFUL.
IT WAS LIKE...
SHE WAS LIKE SOMETHING EPHEMERAL...

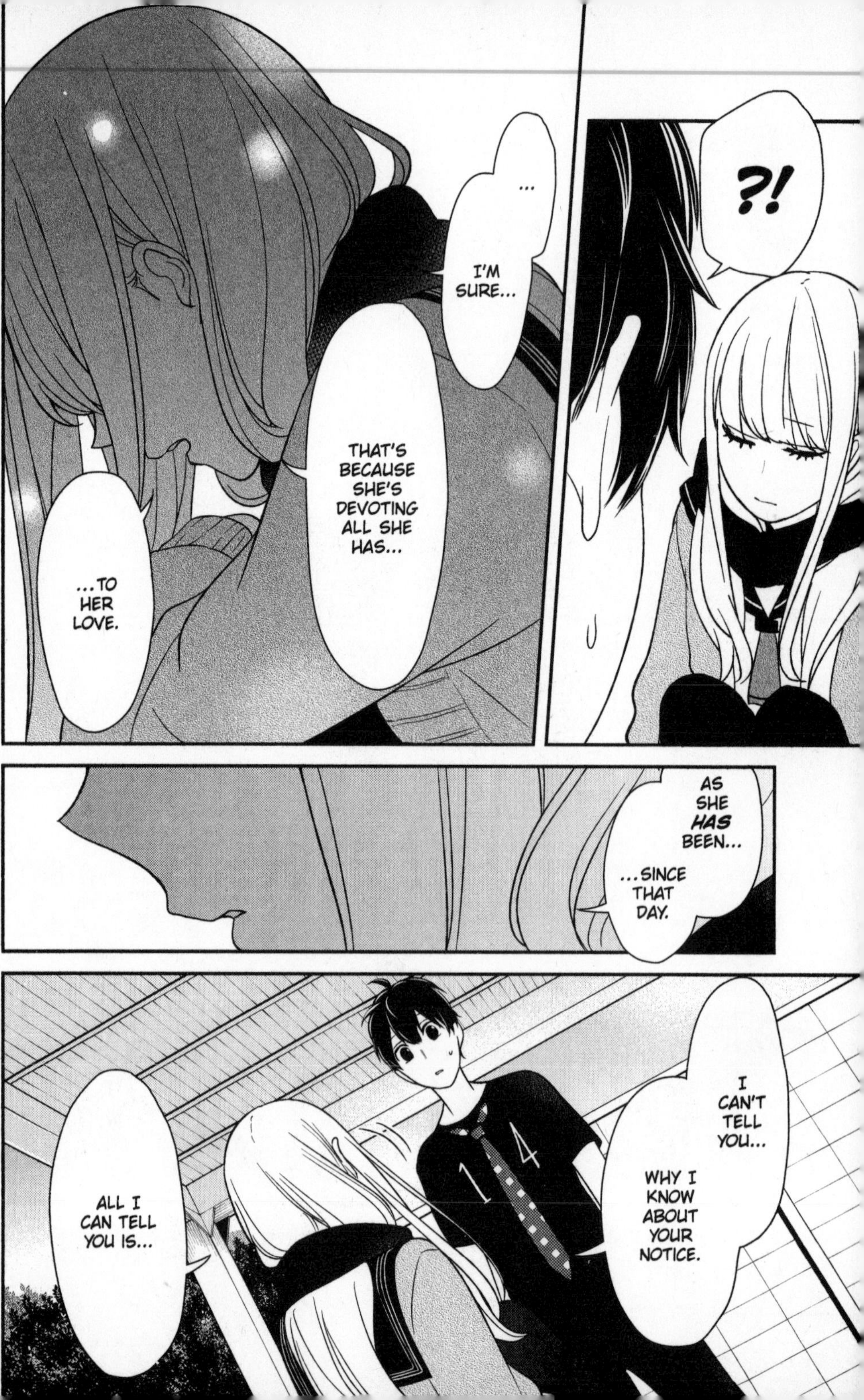
?!
...
I'M SURE...
THAT'S BECAUSE SHE'S DEVOTING ALL SHE HAS...
...TO HER LOVE.
AS SHE *HAS* BEEN...
...SINCE THAT DAY.
I CAN'T TELL YOU...
WHY I KNOW ABOUT YOUR NOTICE.
ALL I CAN TELL YOU IS...

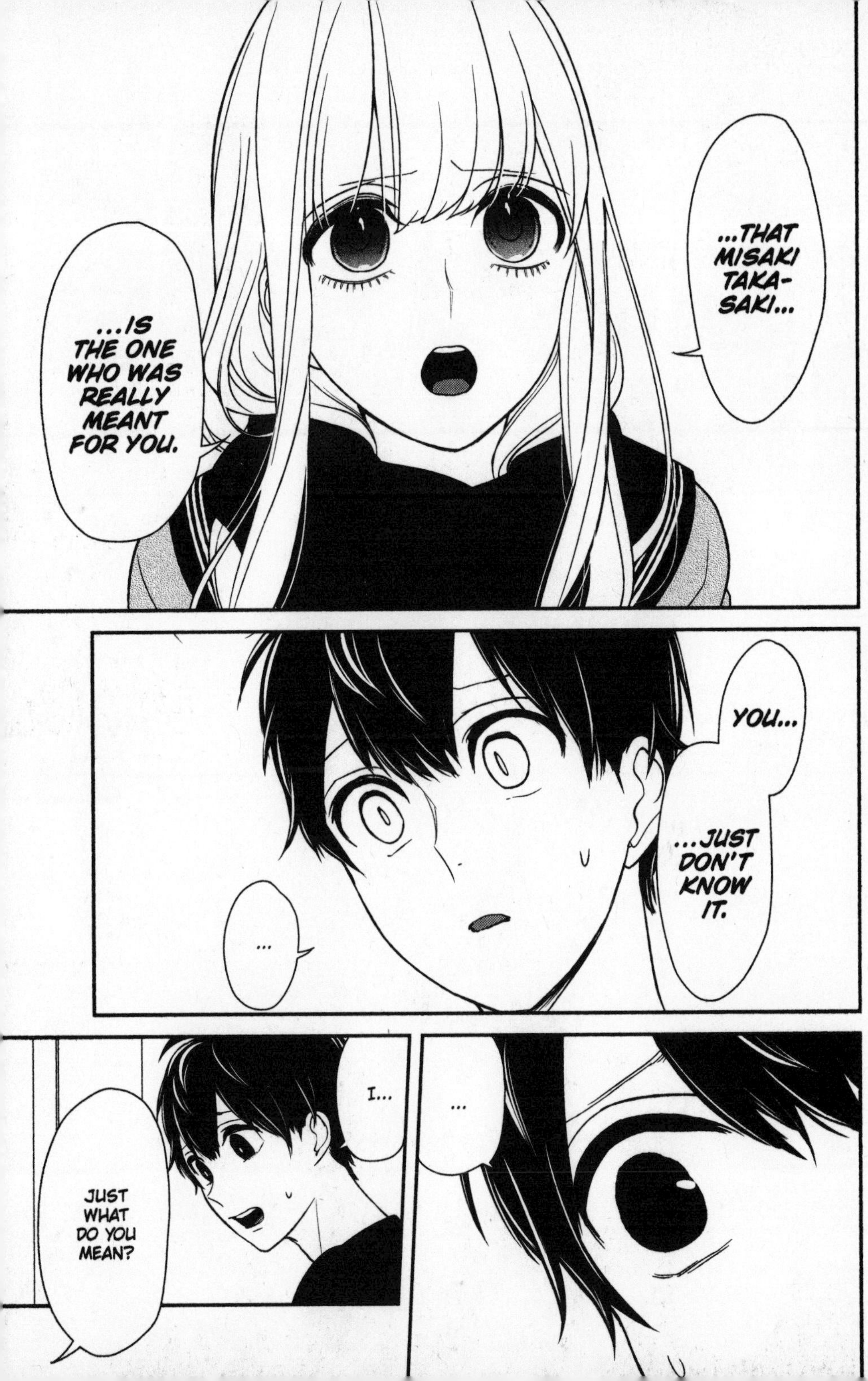
...THAT MISAKI TAKA-SAKI...
...IS THE ONE WHO WAS REALLY MEANT FOR YOU.
YOU...
...JUST DON'T KNOW IT.
...
...
I...
JUST WHAT DO YOU MEAN?

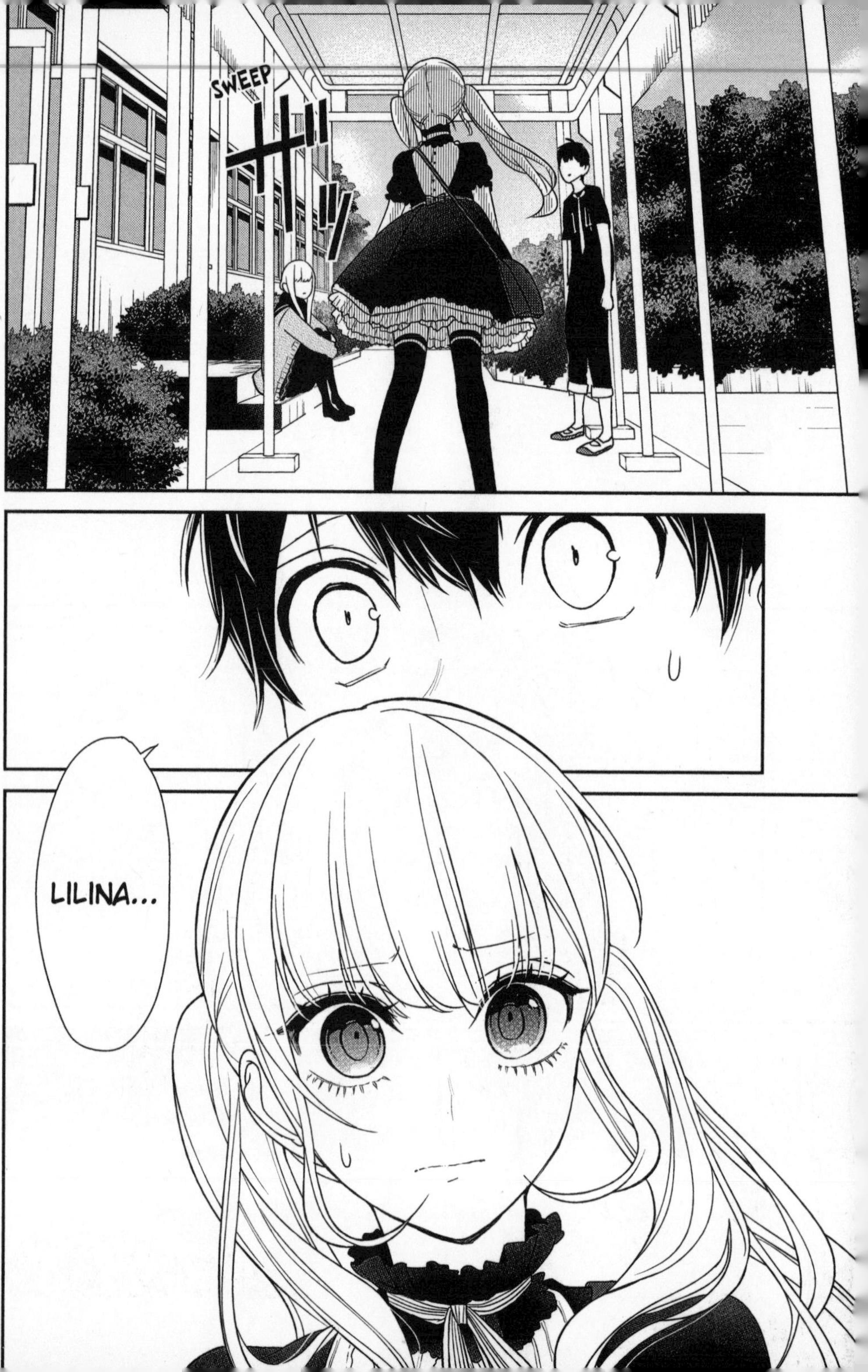
SWEEP
LILINA...

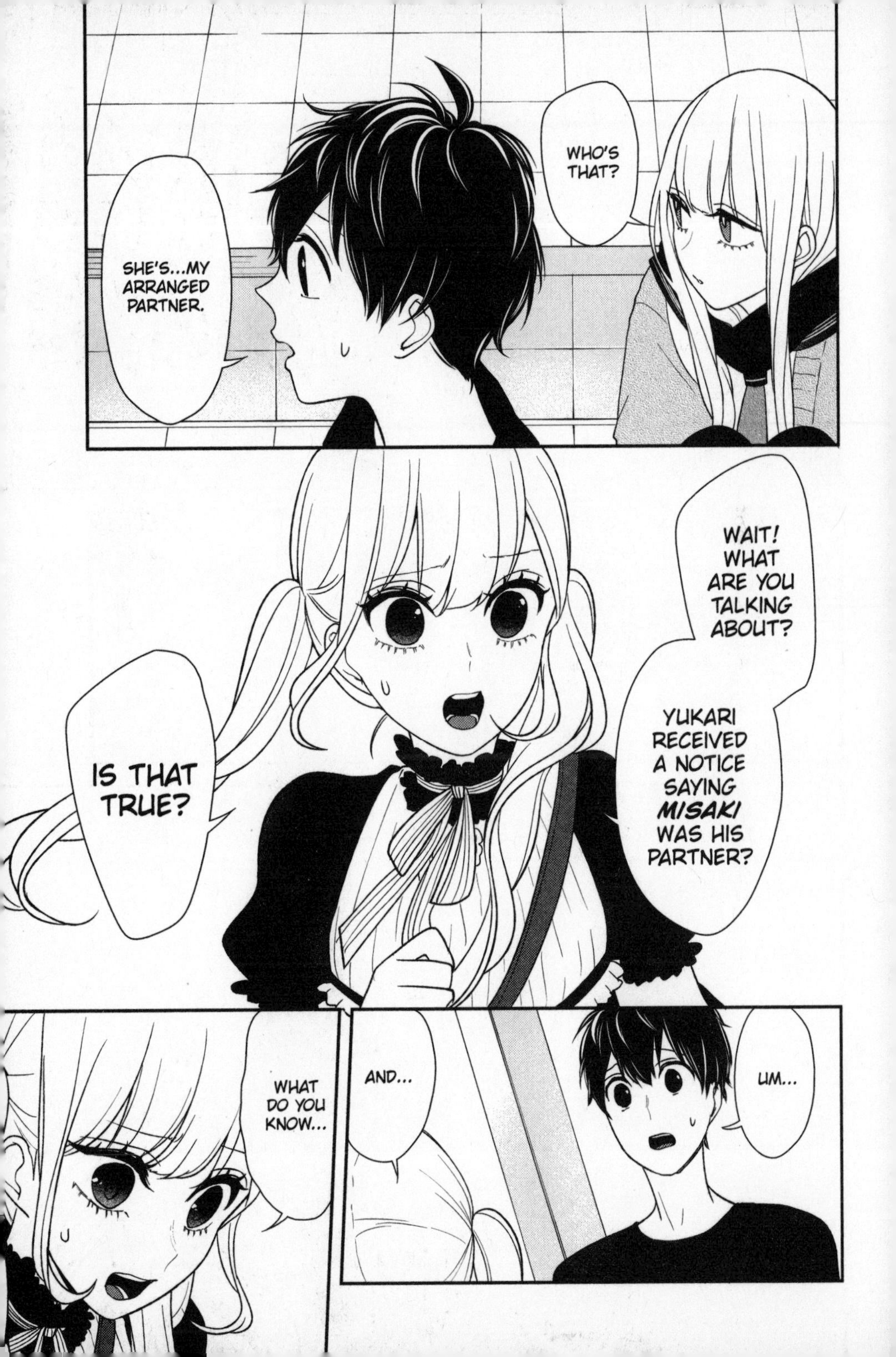
WHO'S THAT?
SHE'S...MY ARRANGED PARTNER.
WAIT! WHAT ARE YOU TALKING ABOUT?
YUKARI RECEIVED A NOTICE SAYING *MISAKI* WAS HIS PARTNER?
IS THAT TRUE?
UM...
AND...
WHAT DO YOU KNOW...

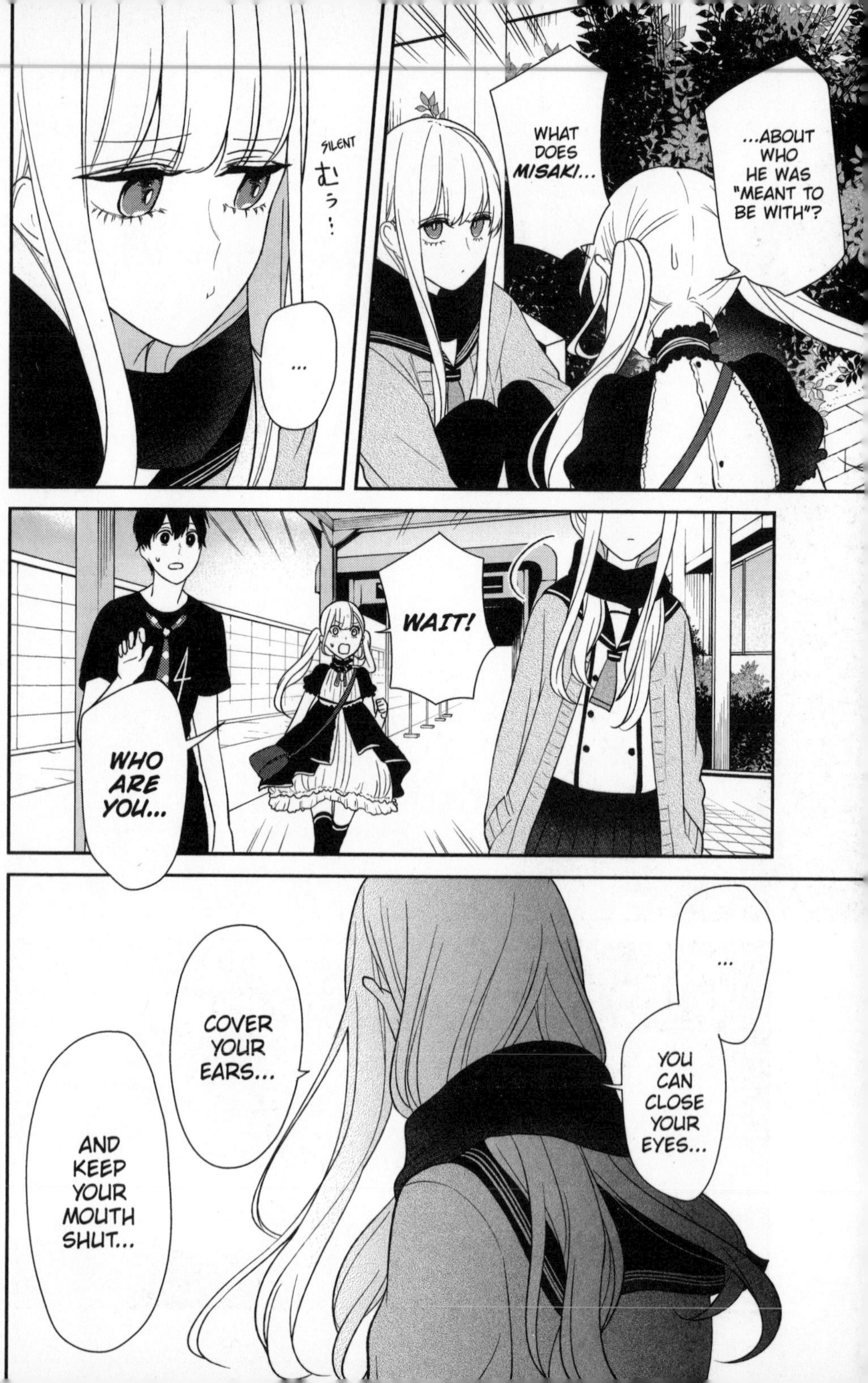

WHAT DOES MISAKI...
...ABOUT WHO HE WAS "MEANT TO BE WITH"?
SILENT
むぅ…
...
WAIT!
WHO ARE YOU...
...
YOU CAN CLOSE YOUR EYES...
COVER YOUR EARS...
AND KEEP YOUR MOUTH SHUT...

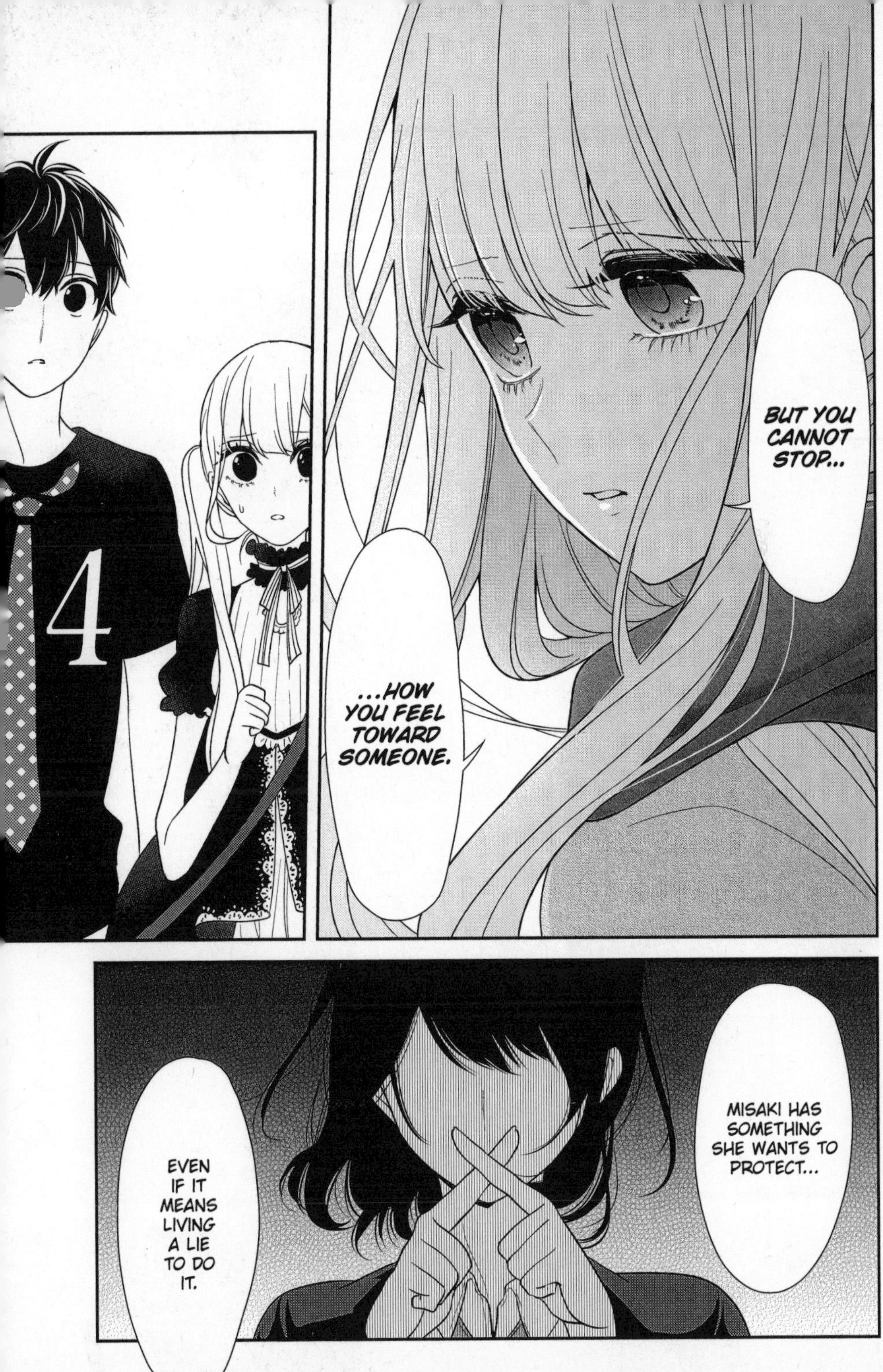
BUT YOU CANNOT STOP...
...HOW YOU FEEL TOWARD SOMEONE.
MISAKI HAS SOMETHING SHE WANTS TO PROTECT...
EVEN IF IT MEANS LIVING A LIE TO DO IT.

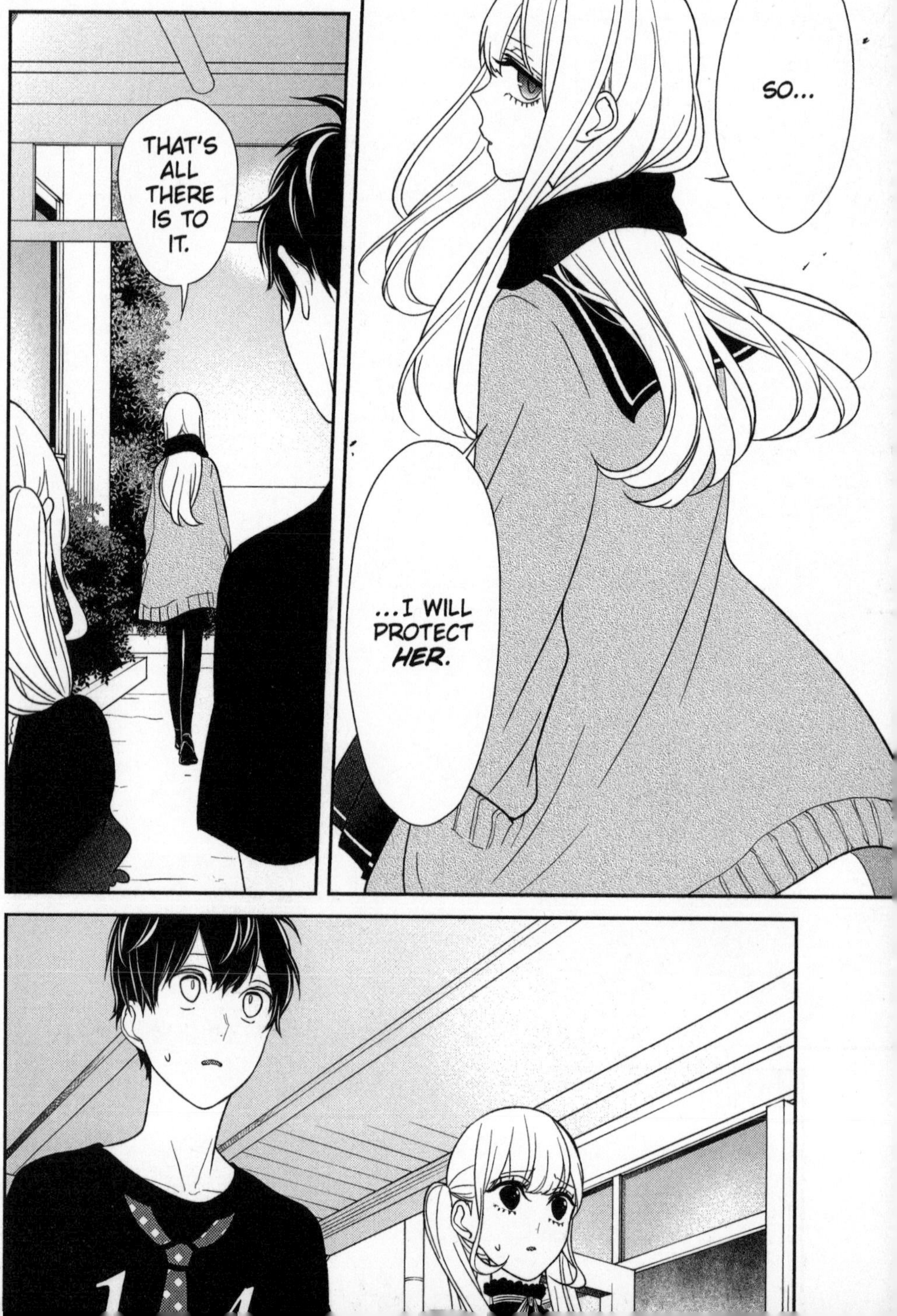
SO...
...I WILL PROTECT HER.
THAT'S ALL THERE IS TO IT.

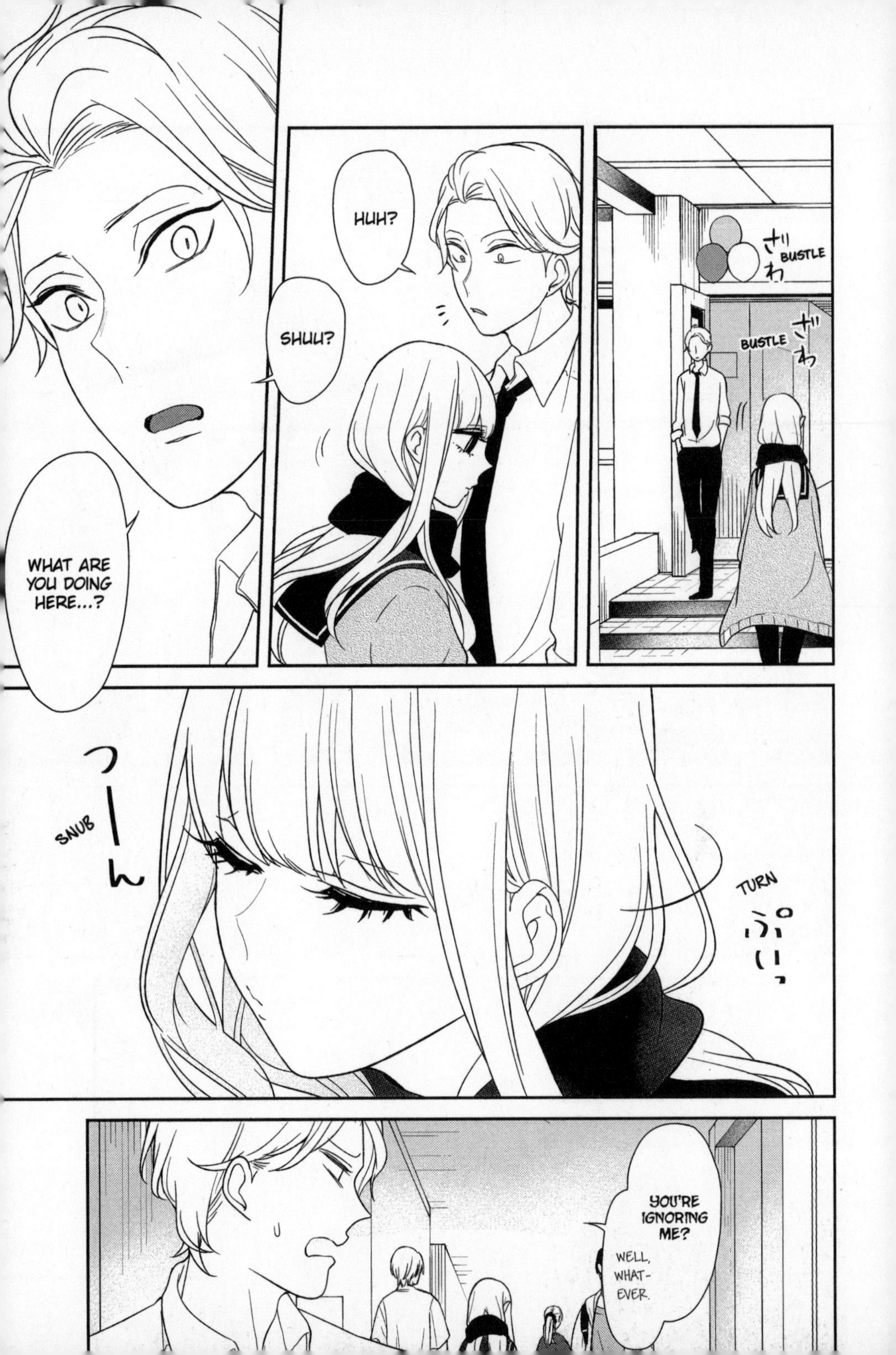

ざわ BUSTLE
BUSTLE ざわ
HUH?
SHUU?
WHAT ARE YOU DOING HERE...?
TURN ぷいっ
SNUB つーん
YOU'RE IGNORING ME?
WELL, WHAT-EVER.

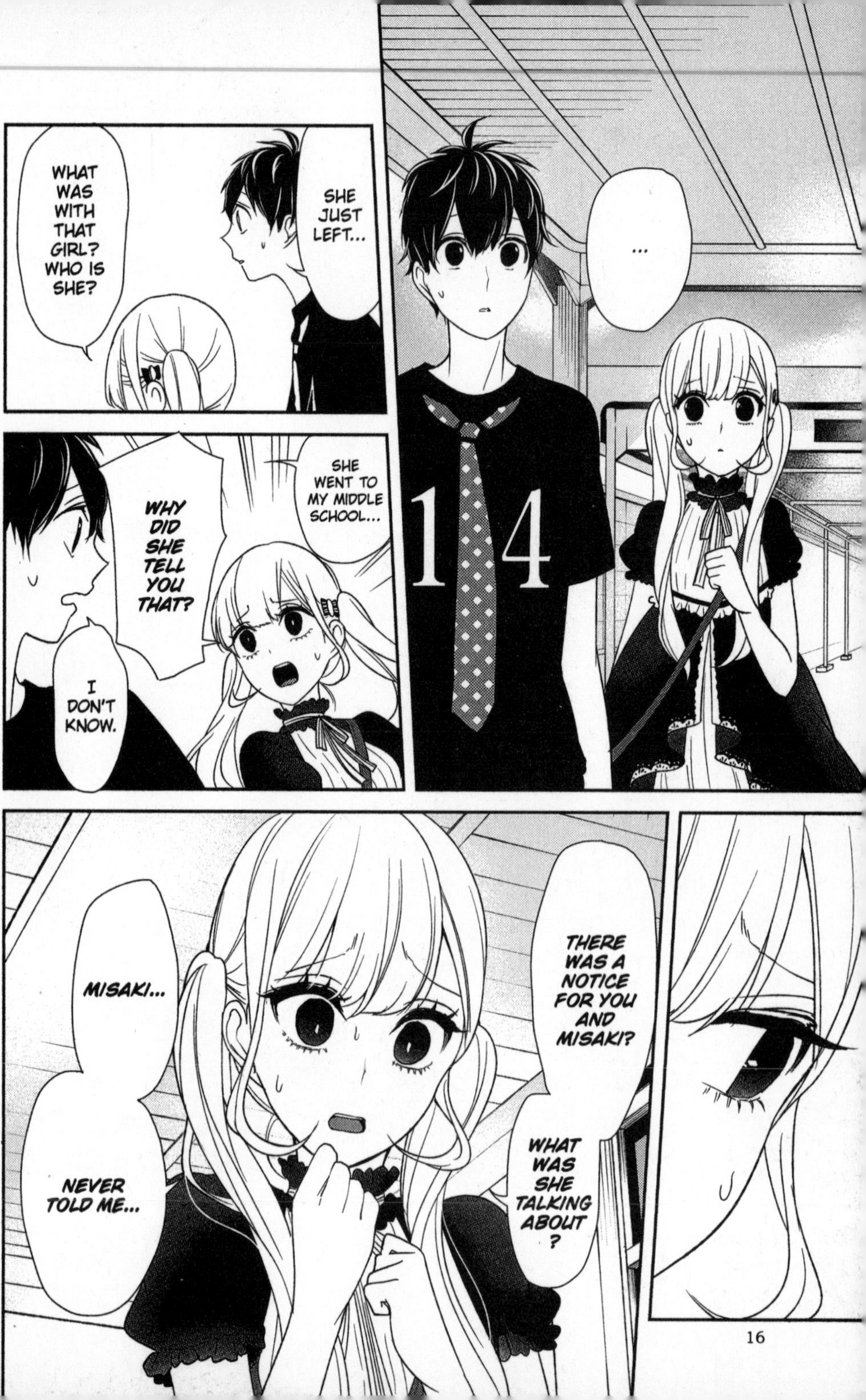
...
SHE JUST LEFT...
WHAT WAS WITH THAT GIRL? WHO IS SHE?
SHE WENT TO MY MIDDLE SCHOOL...
WHY DID SHE TELL YOU THAT?
I DON'T KNOW.
THERE WAS A NOTICE FOR YOU AND MISAKI?
WHAT WAS SHE TALKING ABOUT?
MISAKI...
NEVER TOLD ME...

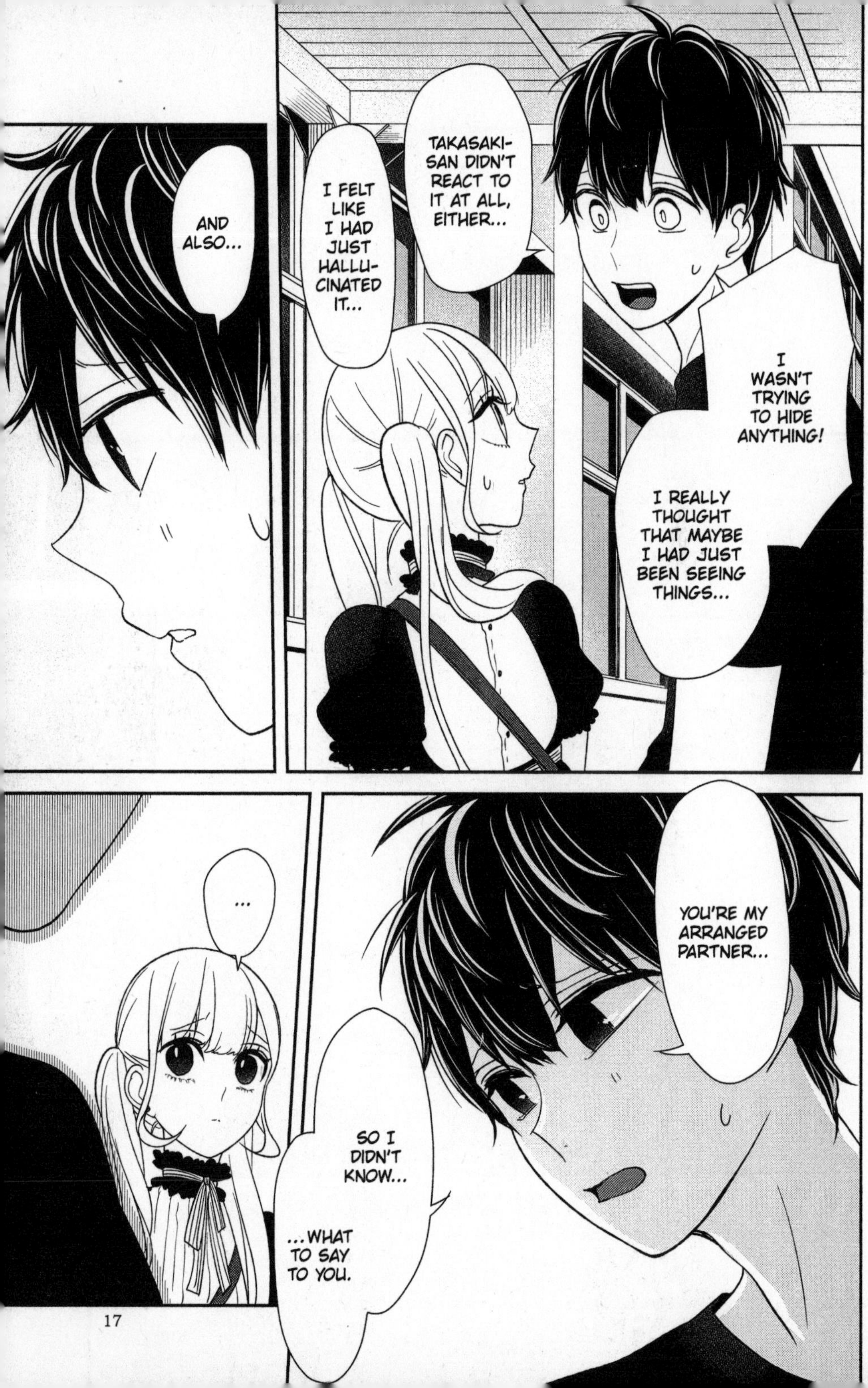
I WASN'T TRYING TO HIDE ANYTHING!
I REALLY THOUGHT THAT MAYBE I HAD JUST BEEN SEEING THINGS...
TAKASAKI-SAN DIDN'T REACT TO IT AT ALL, EITHER...
I FELT LIKE I HAD JUST HALLU-CINATED IT...
AND ALSO...
YOU'RE MY ARRANGED PARTNER...
SO I DIDN'T KNOW...
...WHAT TO SAY TO YOU.
...

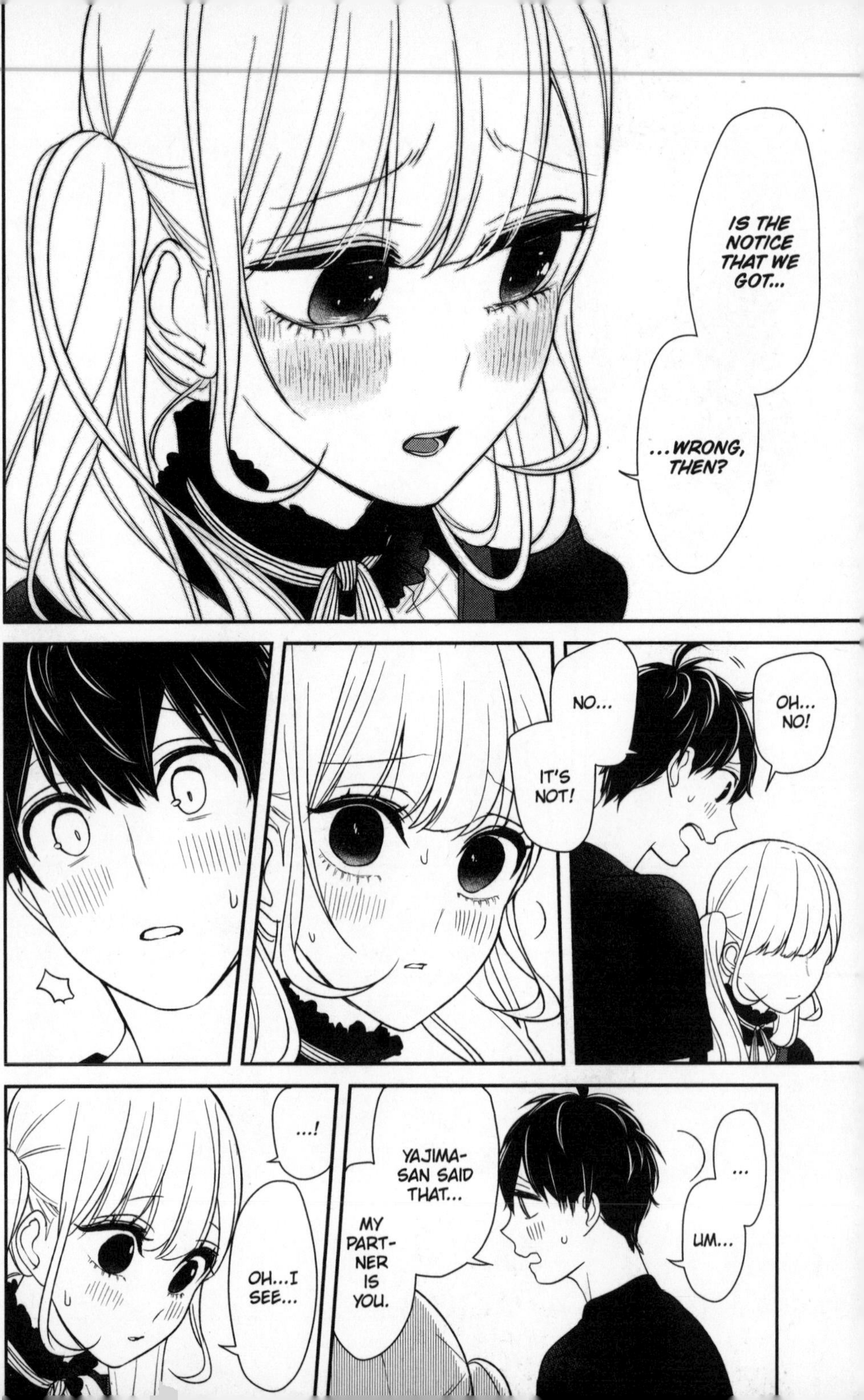
IS THE NOTICE THAT WE GOT...
...WRONG, THEN?
OH... NO!
NO...
IT'S NOT!
...
UM...
YAJIMA-SAN SAID THAT...
MY PARTNER IS YOU.
...!
OH...I SEE...

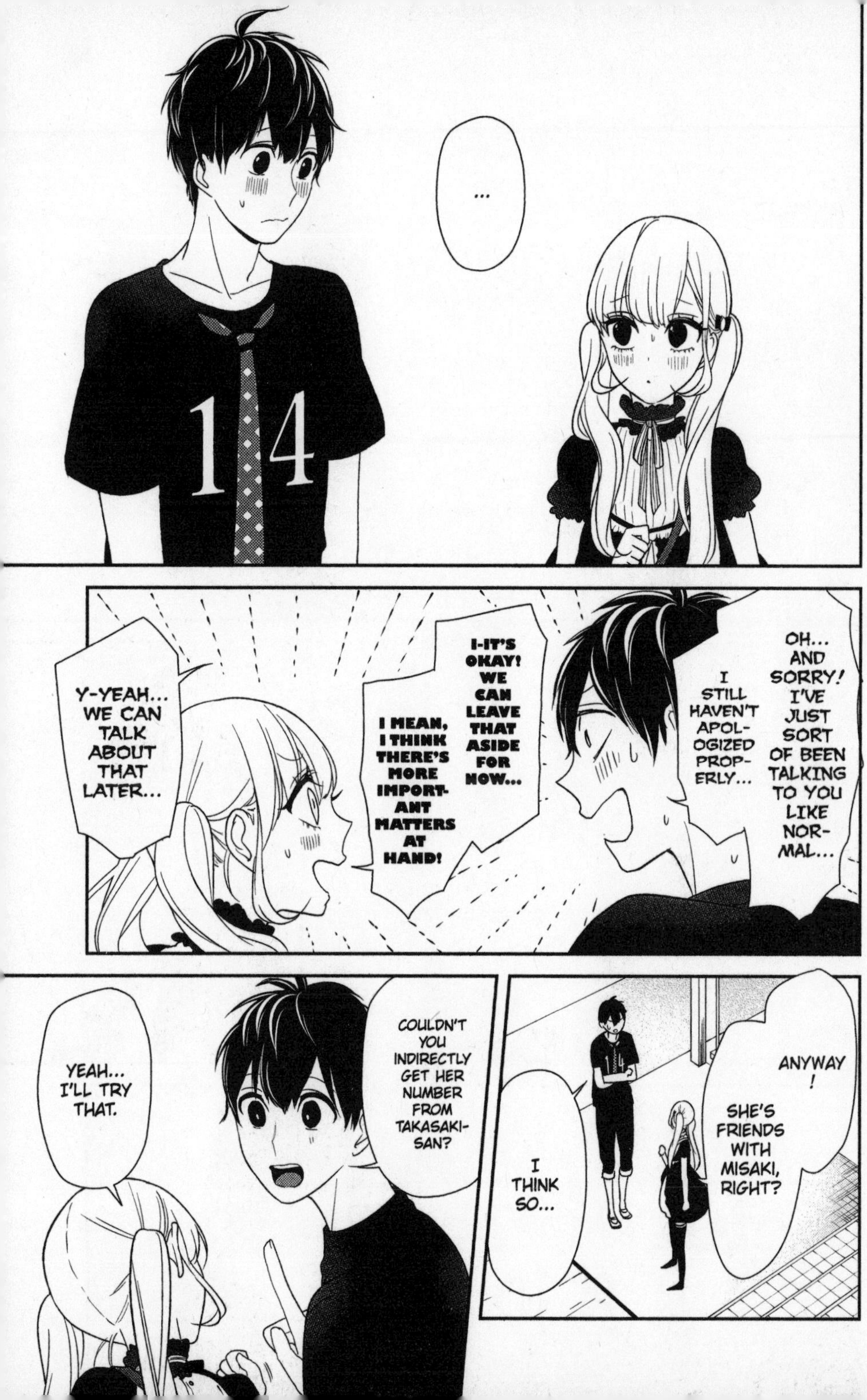
...
OH... AND SORRY! I'VE JUST SORT OF BEEN TALKING TO YOU LIKE NORMAL...
I STILL HAVEN'T APOLOGIZED PROPERLY...
I-IT'S OKAY! WE CAN LEAVE THAT ASIDE FOR NOW...
I MEAN, I THINK THERE'S MORE IMPORTANT MATTERS AT HAND!
Y-YEAH... WE CAN TALK ABOUT THAT LATER...
ANYWAY!
SHE'S FRIENDS WITH MISAKI, RIGHT?
I THINK SO...
COULDN'T YOU INDIRECTLY GET HER NUMBER FROM TAKASAKI-SAN?
YEAH... I'LL TRY THAT.

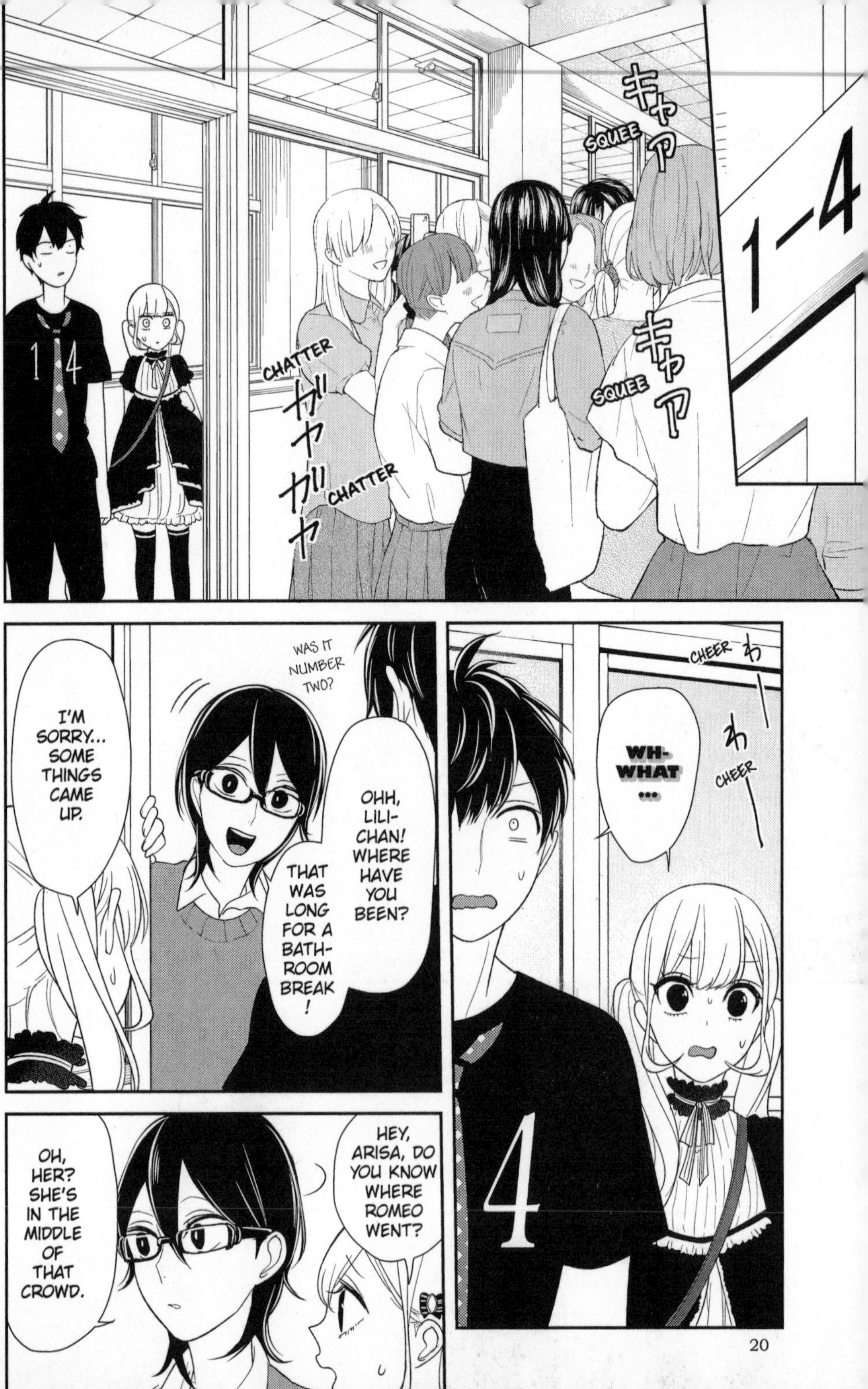
キャア
SQUEE
キャア
SQUEE
1-4
ガヤガヤ
CHATTER
CHATTER
わーわー
CHEER
CHEER
WH-WHAT...
WAS IT NUMBER TWO?
OHH, LILI-CHAN! WHERE HAVE YOU BEEN?
THAT WAS LONG FOR A BATHROOM BREAK!
I'M SORRY... SOME THINGS CAME UP.
HEY, ARISA, DO YOU KNOW WHERE ROMEO WENT?
OH, HER? SHE'S IN THE MIDDLE OF THAT CROWD.

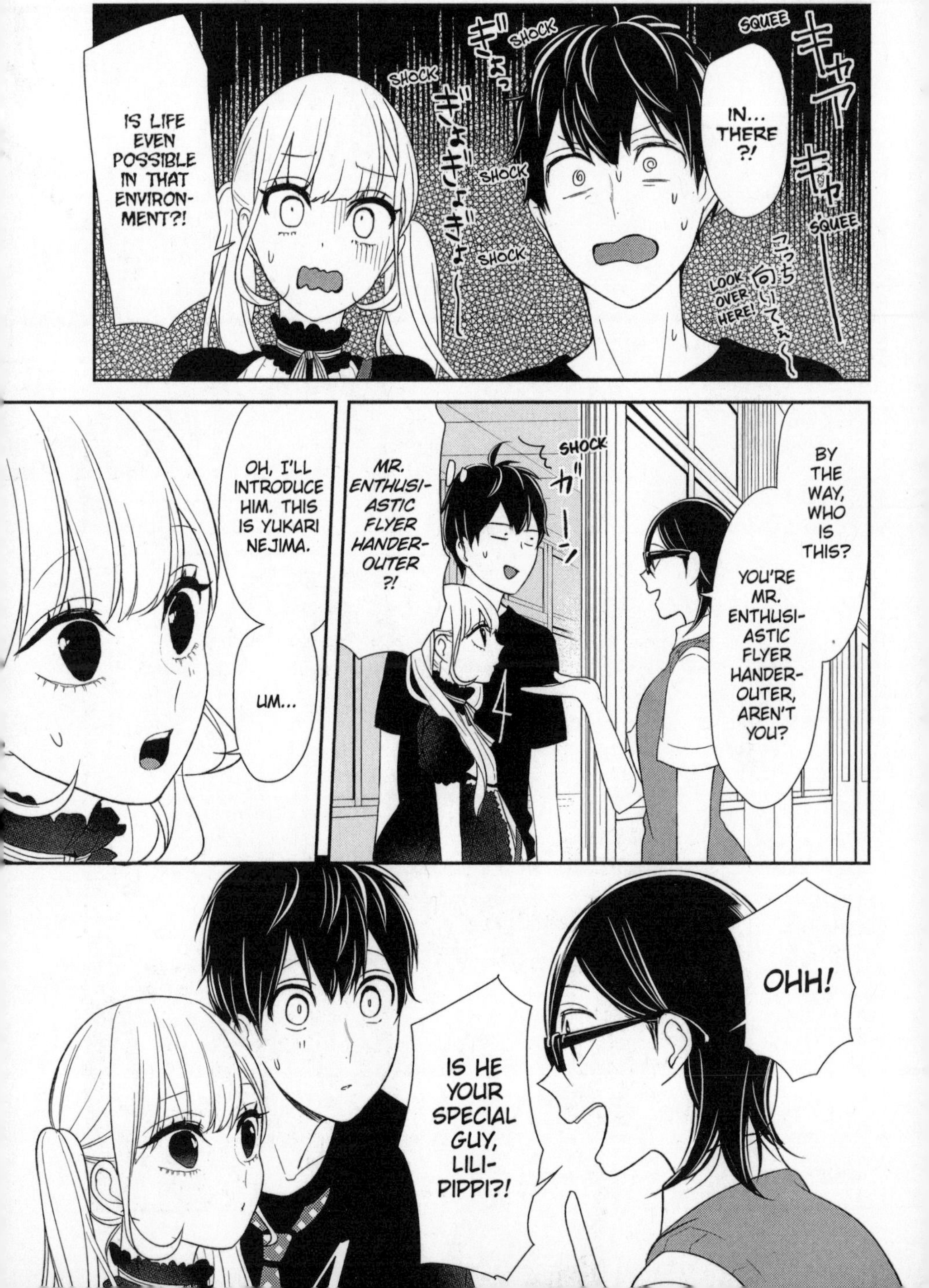
SQUEE
SQUEE
LOOK OVER HERE!
IN... THERE?!
SHOCK
SHOCK
SHOCK
SHOCK
IS LIFE EVEN POSSIBLE IN THAT ENVIRONMENT?!
BY THE WAY, WHO IS THIS?
YOU'RE MR. ENTHUSI-ASTIC FLYER HANDER-OUTER, AREN'T YOU?
SHOCK
MR. ENTHUSI-ASTIC FLYER HANDER-OUTER?!
OH, I'LL INTRODUCE HIM. THIS IS YUKARI NEJIMA.
UM...
OHH!
IS HE YOUR SPECIAL GUY, LILI-PIPPI?!

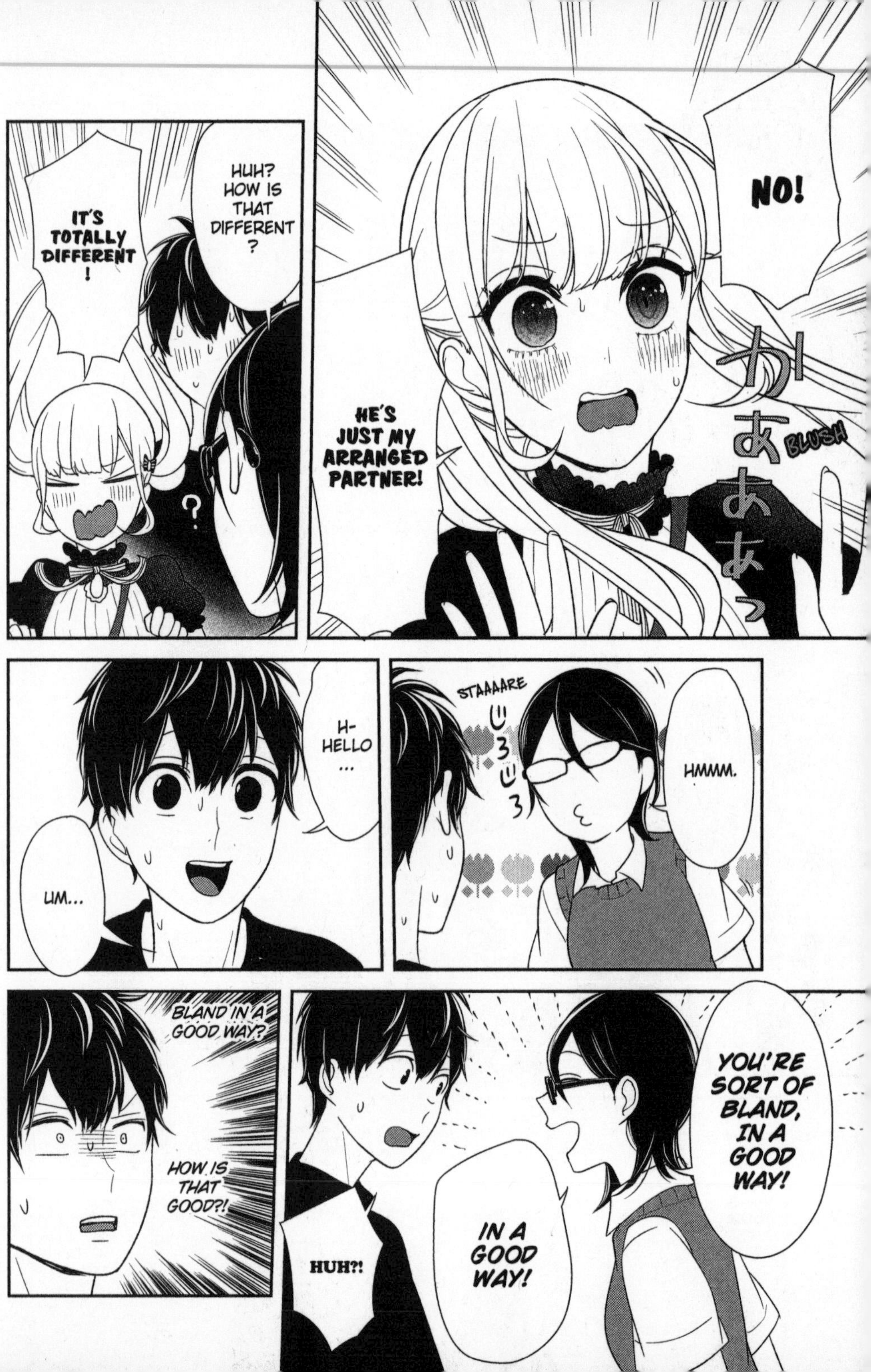
NO!
HE'S JUST MY ARRANGED PARTNER!
かあああっ
BLUSH
HUH? HOW IS THAT DIFFERENT?
IT'S TOTALLY DIFFERENT!
?
HMMM.
STAAAARE
じろじろ
H-HELLO...
UM...
YOU'RE SORT OF BLAND, IN A GOOD WAY!
IN A GOOD WAY!
HUH?!
BLAND IN A GOOD WAY?
HOW IS THAT GOOD?!

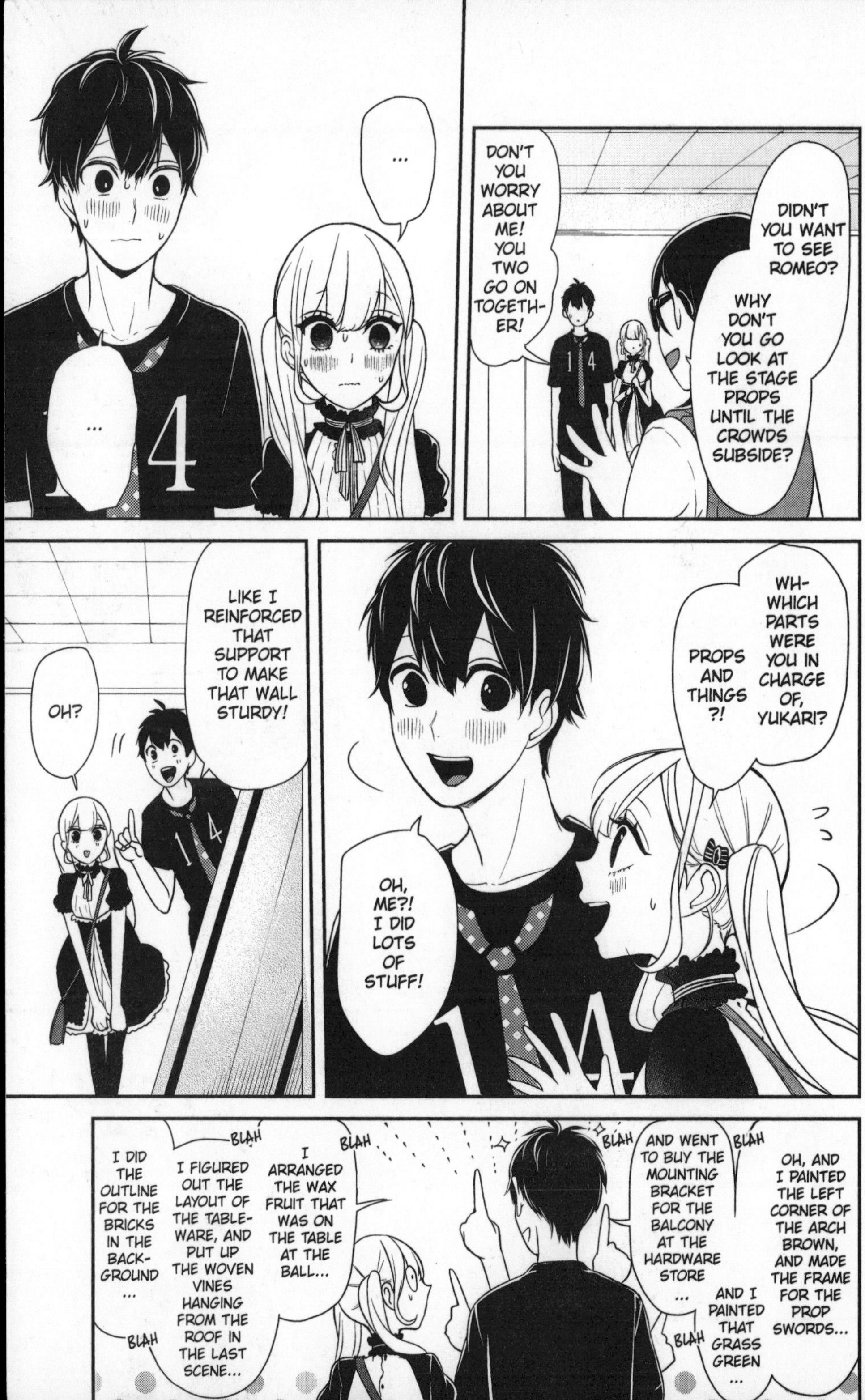
DIDN'T YOU WANT TO SEE ROMEO?
WHY DON'T YOU GO LOOK AT THE STAGE PROPS UNTIL THE CROWDS SUBSIDE?
DON'T YOU WORRY ABOUT ME! YOU TWO GO ON TOGETH-ER!
...
...
WH-WHICH PARTS WERE YOU IN CHARGE OF, YUKARI?
PROPS AND THINGS?!
OH, ME?! I DID LOTS OF STUFF!
LIKE I REINFORCED THAT SUPPORT TO MAKE THAT WALL STURDY!
OH?
BLAH
OH, AND I PAINTED THE LEFT CORNER OF THE ARCH BROWN, AND MADE THE FRAME FOR THE PROP SWORDS...
AND I PAINTED THAT GRASS GREEN ...
BLAH
BLAH
AND WENT TO BUY THE MOUNTING BRACKET FOR THE BALCONY AT THE HARDWARE STORE ...
BLAH
I ARRANGED THE WAX FRUIT THAT WAS ON THE TABLE AT THE BALL...
BLAH
I FIGURED OUT THE LAYOUT OF THE TABLE-WARE, AND PUT UP THE WOVEN VINES HANGING FROM THE ROOF IN THE LAST SCENE...
I DID THE OUTLINE FOR THE BRICKS IN THE BACK-GROUND ...
BLAH

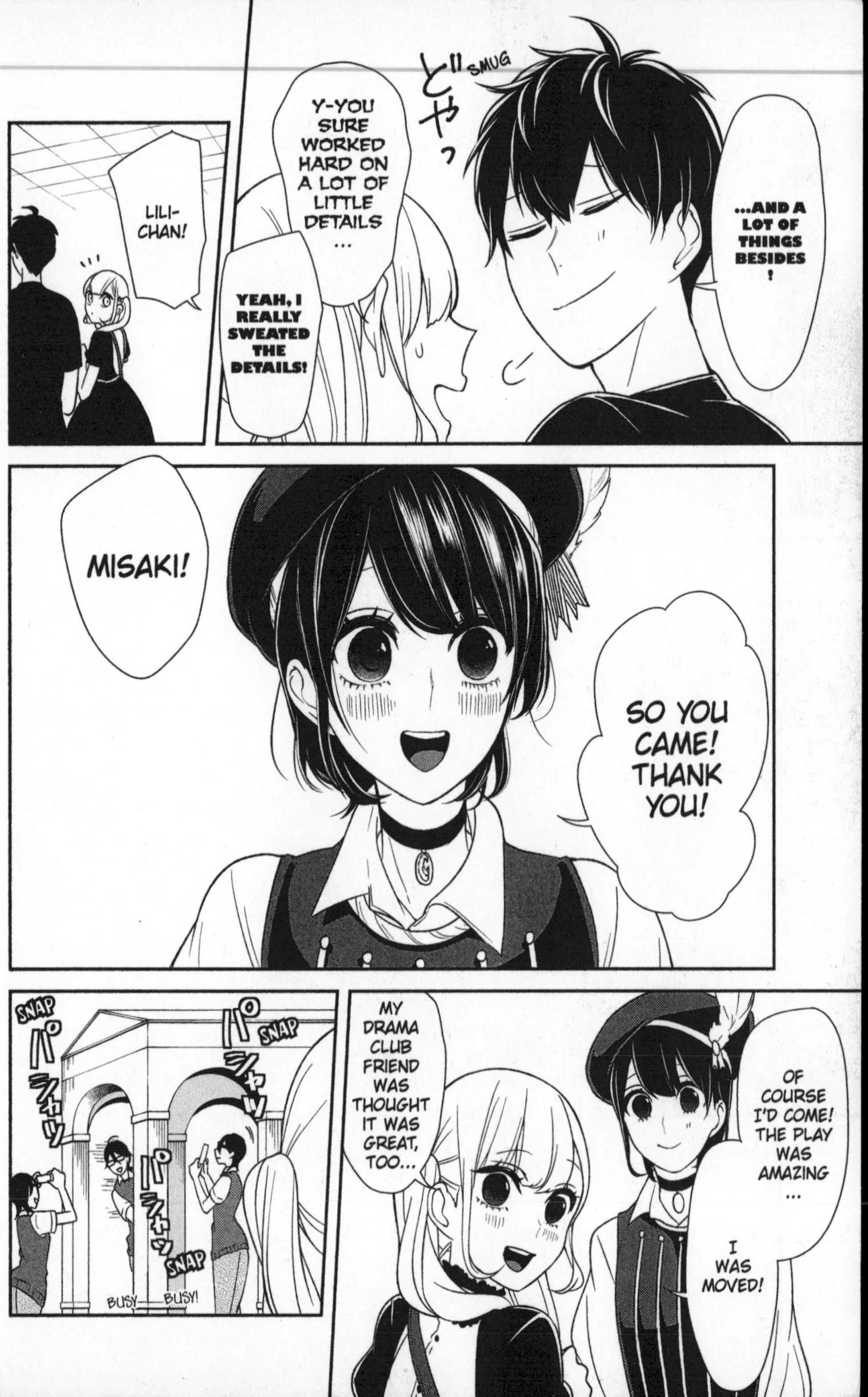
とやっ SMUG
Y-YOU SURE WORKED HARD ON A LOT OF LITTLE DETAILS…
...AND A LOT OF THINGS BESIDES!
YEAH, I REALLY SWEATED THE DETAILS!
LILI-CHAN!
MISAKI!
SO YOU CAME! THANK YOU!
OF COURSE I'D COME! THE PLAY WAS AMAZING…
I WAS MOVED!
MY DRAMA CLUB FRIEND WAS THOUGHT IT WAS GREAT, TOO…
パシャッ SNAP
パシャッ SNAP
パシャッ SNAP
BUSY BUSY!

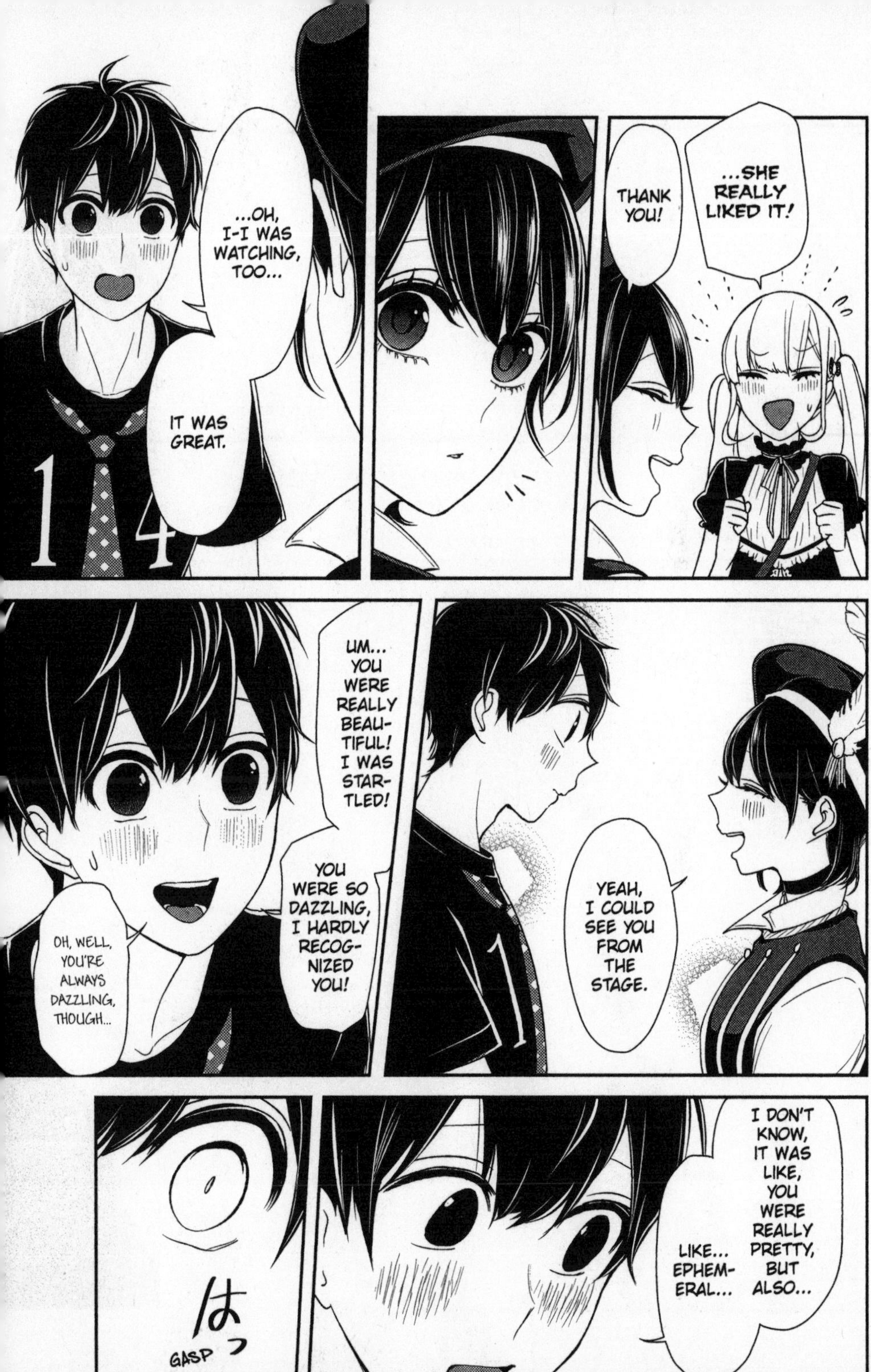

...SHE REALLY LIKED IT!
THANK YOU!
...OH, I-I WAS WATCHING, TOO...
IT WAS GREAT.
YEAH, I COULD SEE YOU FROM THE STAGE.
UM... YOU WERE REALLY BEAUTIFUL! I WAS STARTLED!
YOU WERE SO DAZZLING, I HARDLY RECOGNIZED YOU!
OH, WELL, YOU'RE ALWAYS DAZZLING, THOUGH...
I DON'T KNOW, IT WAS LIKE, YOU WERE REALLY PRETTY, BUT ALSO...
LIKE... EPHEMERAL...
はっ
GASP

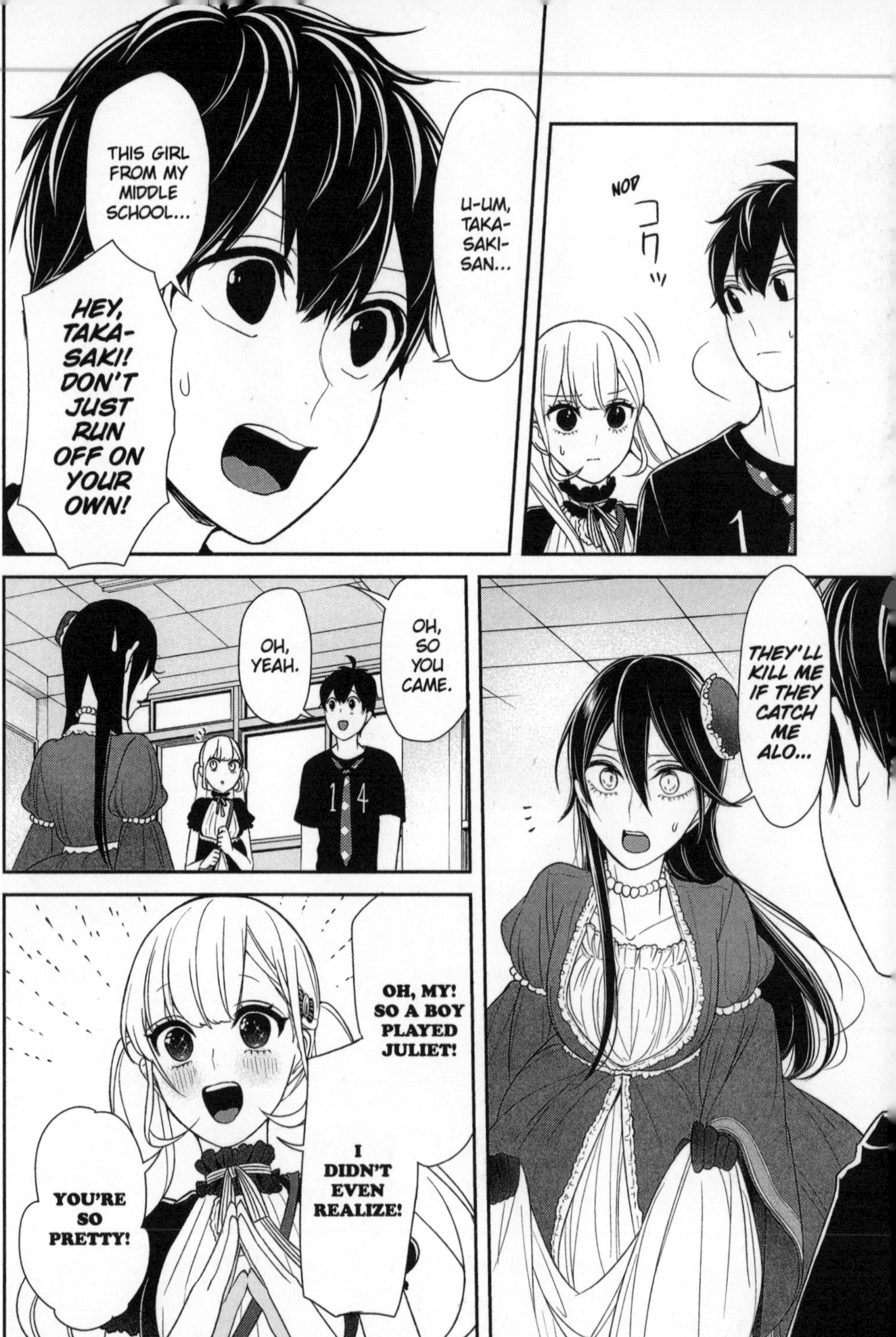
NOD
コクッ
U-UM, TAKA-SAKI-SAN...
THIS GIRL FROM MY MIDDLE SCHOOL...
HEY, TAKA-SAKI! DON'T JUST RUN OFF ON YOUR OWN!
THEY'LL KILL ME IF THEY CATCH ME ALO...
OH, SO YOU CAME.
OH, YEAH.
OH, MY! SO A BOY PLAYED JULIET!
I DIDN'T EVEN REALIZE!
YOU'RE SO PRETTY!

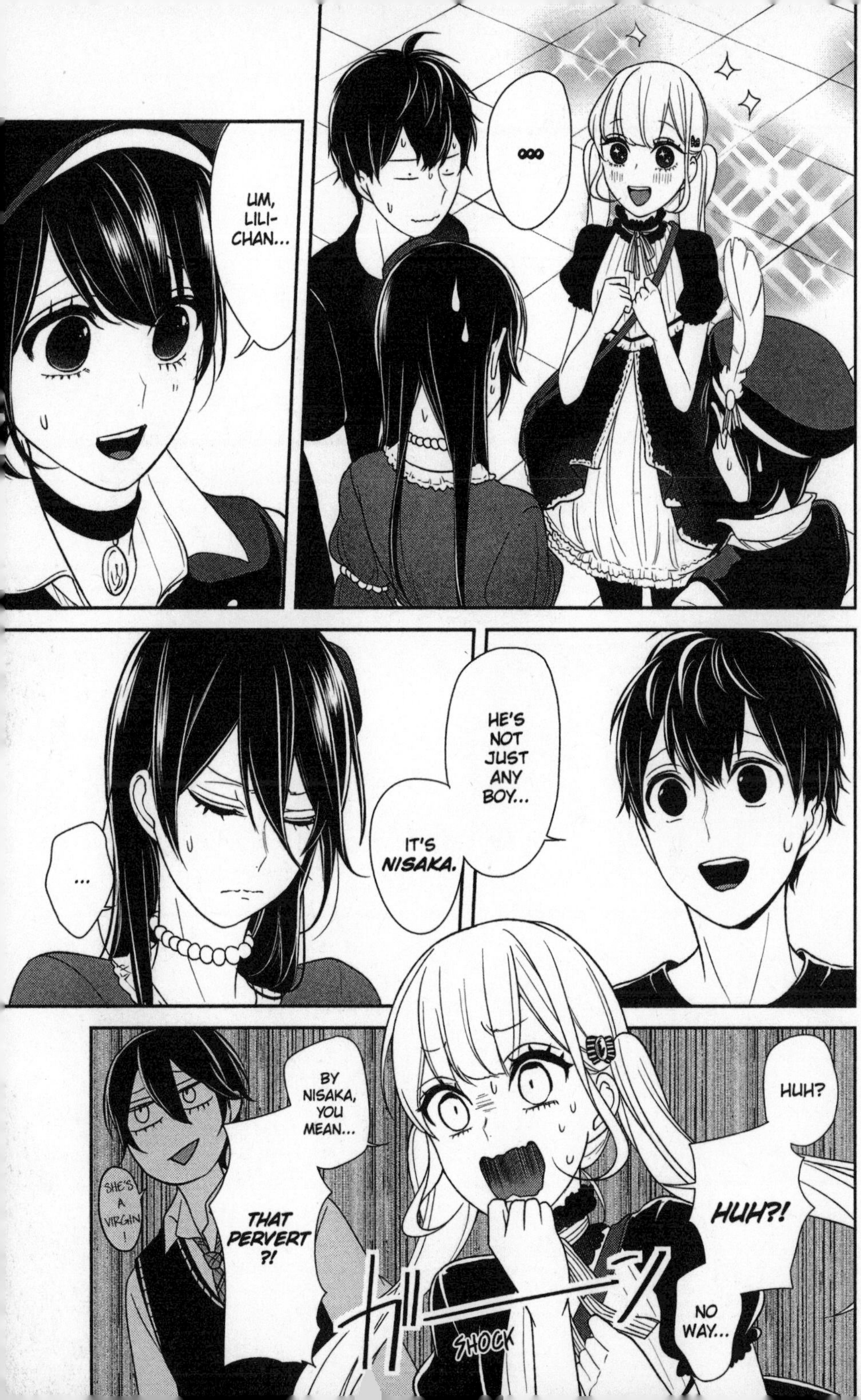
...
UM, LILI-CHAN...
HE'S NOT JUST ANY BOY...
IT'S NISAKA.
...
HUH?
HUH?!
NO WAY...
BY NISAKA, YOU MEAN...
THAT PERVERT?!
SHE'S A VIRGIN!
SHOCK

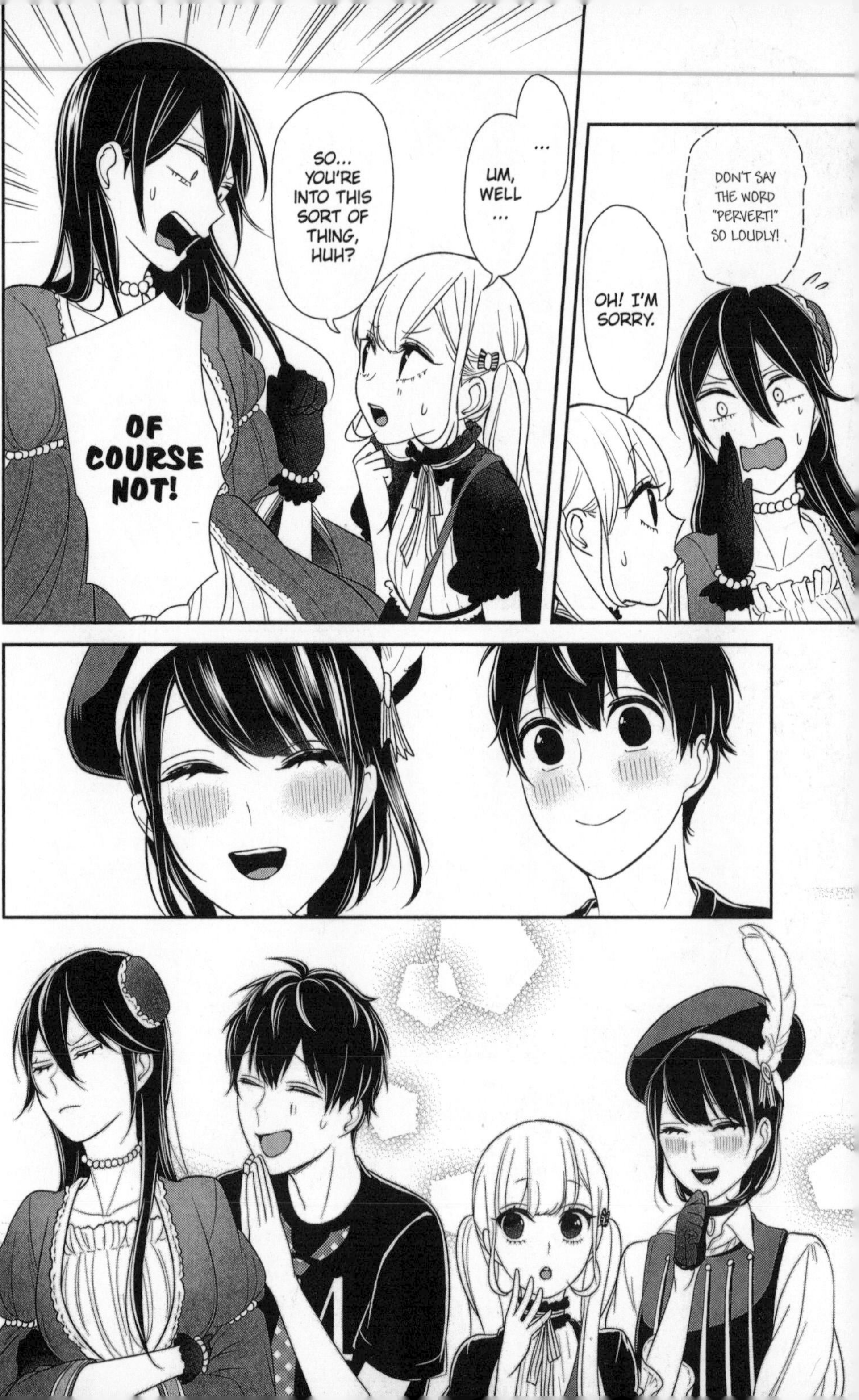
DON'T SAY THE WORD "PERVERT!" SO LOUDLY!
OH! I'M SORRY.
... UM, WELL ...
SO... YOU'RE INTO THIS SORT OF THING, HUH?
OF COURSE NOT!

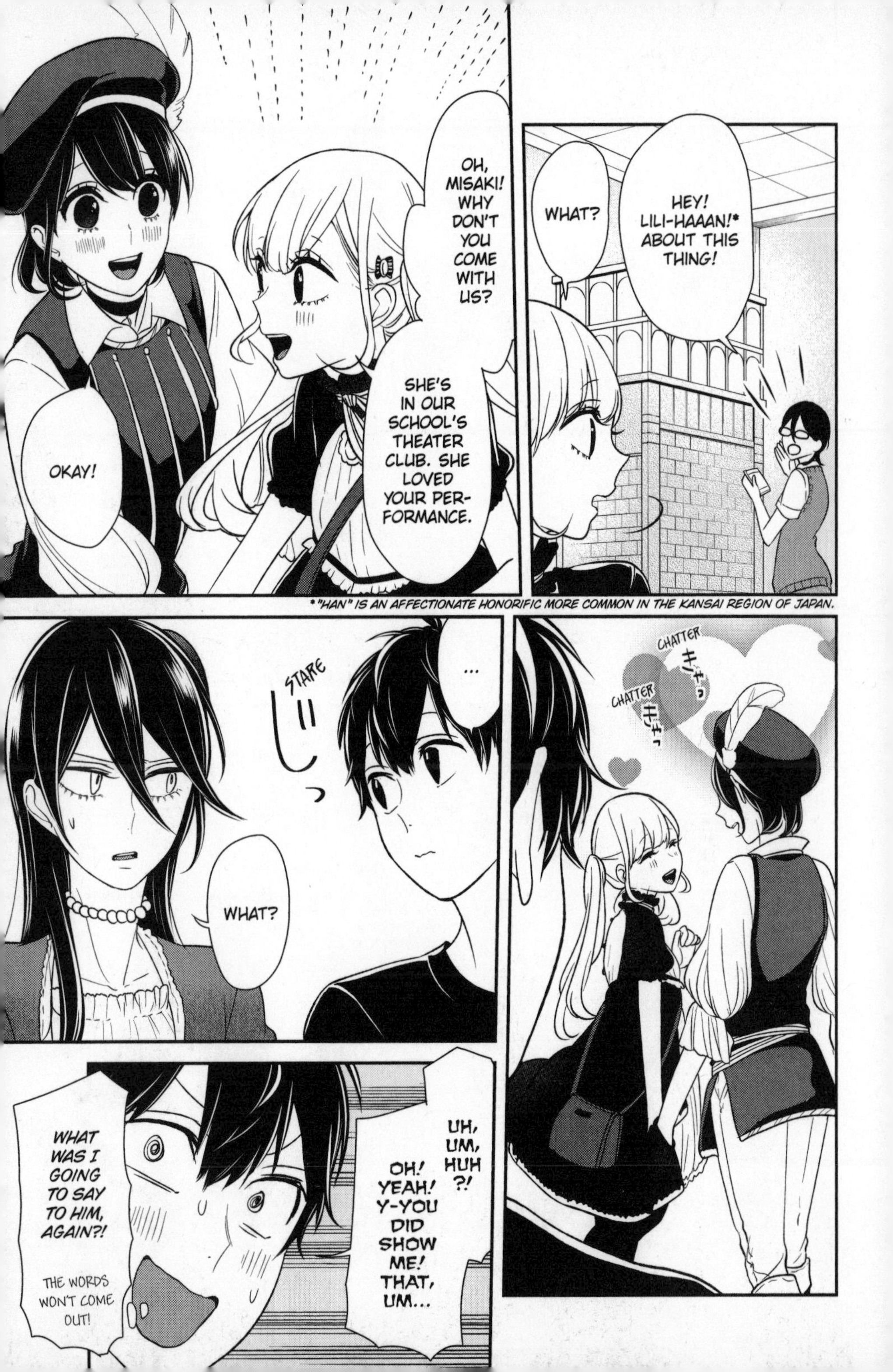
HEY! LILI-HAAAN!* ABOUT THIS THING!
WHAT?
OH, MISAKI! WHY DON'T YOU COME WITH US?
SHE'S IN OUR SCHOOL'S THEATER CLUB. SHE LOVED YOUR PER-FORMANCE.
OKAY!
CHATTER
CHATTER
...
STARE
WHAT?
UH, UM, HUH?!
OH! YEAH! Y-YOU DID SHOW ME! THAT, UM...
WHAT WAS I GOING TO SAY TO HIM, AGAIN?!
THE WORDS WON'T COME OUT!

*"HAN" IS AN AFFECTIONATE HONORIFIC MORE COMMON IN THE KANSAI REGION OF JAPAN.

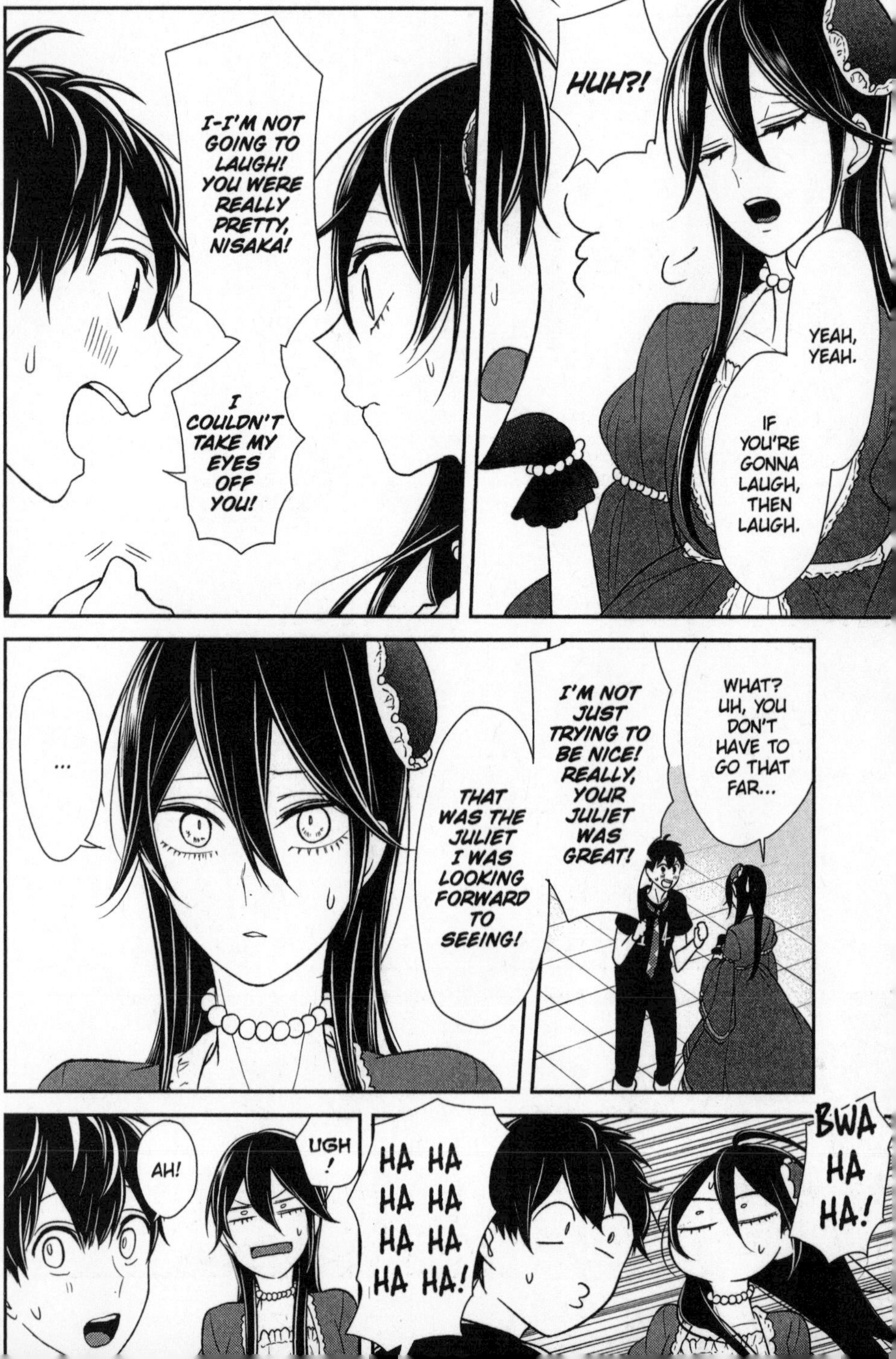
YEAH, YEAH.
IF YOU'RE GONNA LAUGH, THEN LAUGH.
HUH?!
I-I'M NOT GOING TO LAUGH! YOU WERE REALLY PRETTY, NISAKA!
I COULDN'T TAKE MY EYES OFF YOU!
WHAT? UH, YOU DON'T HAVE TO GO THAT FAR...
I'M NOT JUST TRYING TO BE NICE! REALLY, YOUR JULIET WAS GREAT!
THAT WAS THE JULIET I WAS LOOKING FORWARD TO SEEING!
...
BWA HA HA!
HA HA HA HA HA HA HA HA!
UGH!
AH!

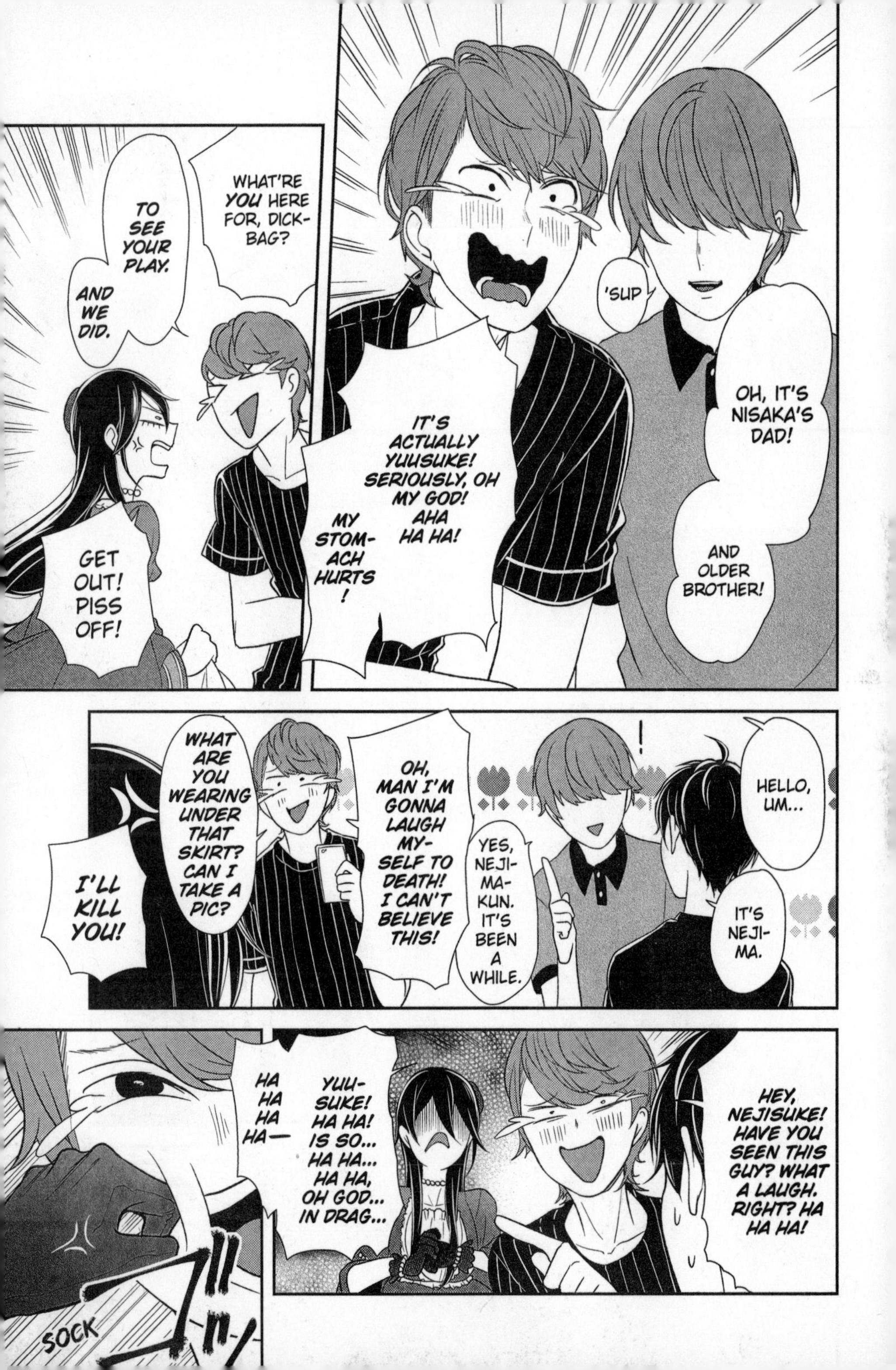
'SUP
OH, IT'S NISAKA'S DAD!
AND OLDER BROTHER!
IT'S ACTUALLY YUUSUKE! SERIOUSLY, OH MY GOD! AHA HA HA!
MY STOMACH HURTS!
WHAT'RE YOU HERE FOR, DICKBAG?
TO SEE YOUR PLAY.
AND WE DID.
GET OUT! PISS OFF!
HELLO, UM...
IT'S NEJIMA.
YES, NEJIMA-KUN. IT'S BEEN A WHILE.
!
OH, MAN I'M GONNA LAUGH MYSELF TO DEATH! I CAN'T BELIEVE THIS!
WHAT ARE YOU WEARING UNDER THAT SKIRT? CAN I TAKE A PIC?
I'LL KILL YOU!
HEY, NEJISUKE! HAVE YOU SEEN THIS GUY? WHAT A LAUGH. RIGHT? HA HA HA!
YUUSUKE! HA HA! IS SO... HA HA... HA HA, OH GOD... IN DRAG...
HA HA HA HA—
SOCK

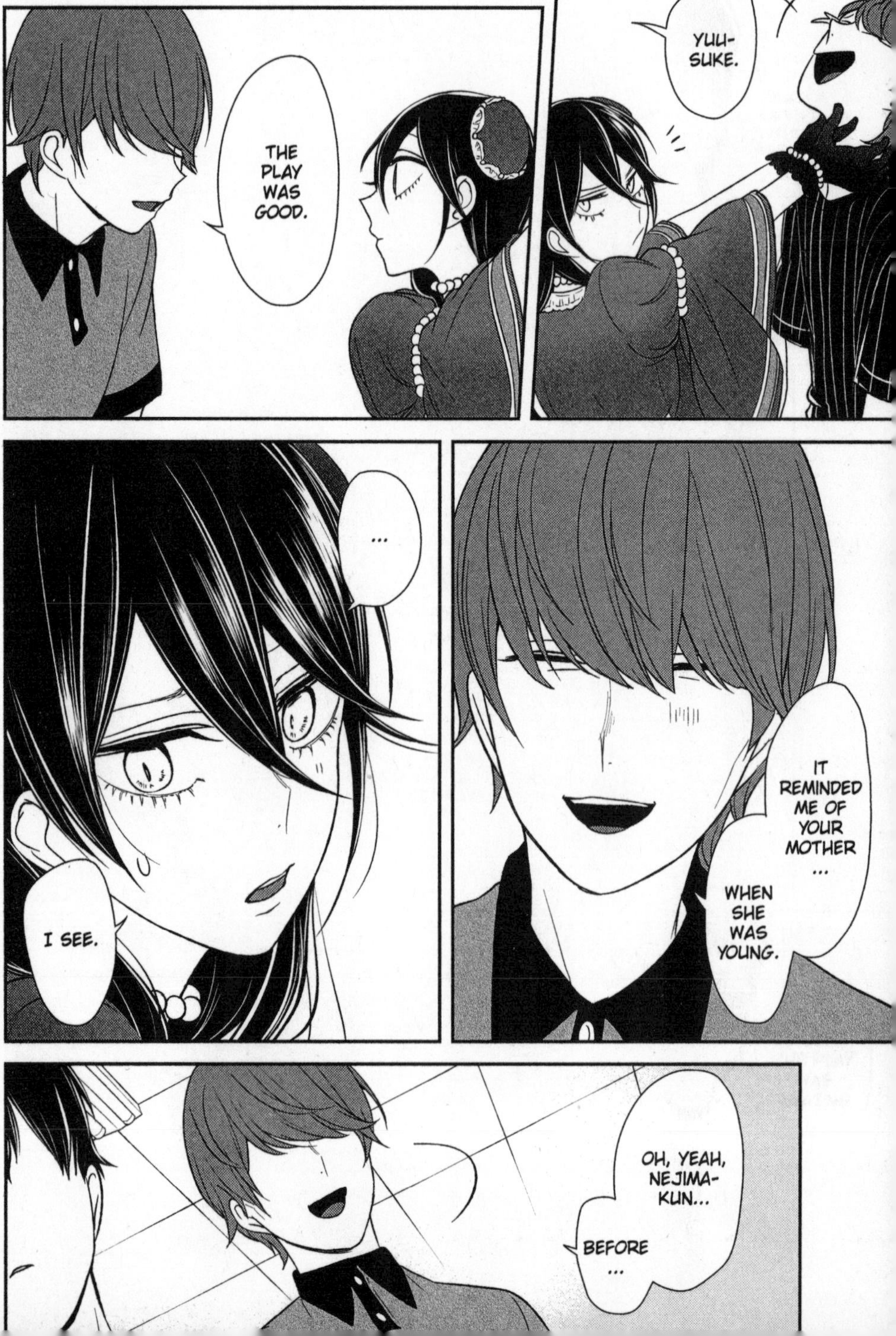
YUU-SUKE.
THE PLAY WAS GOOD.
IT REMINDED ME OF YOUR MOTHER... WHEN SHE WAS YOUNG.
...
I SEE.
OH, YEAH, NEJIMA-KUN... BEFORE...

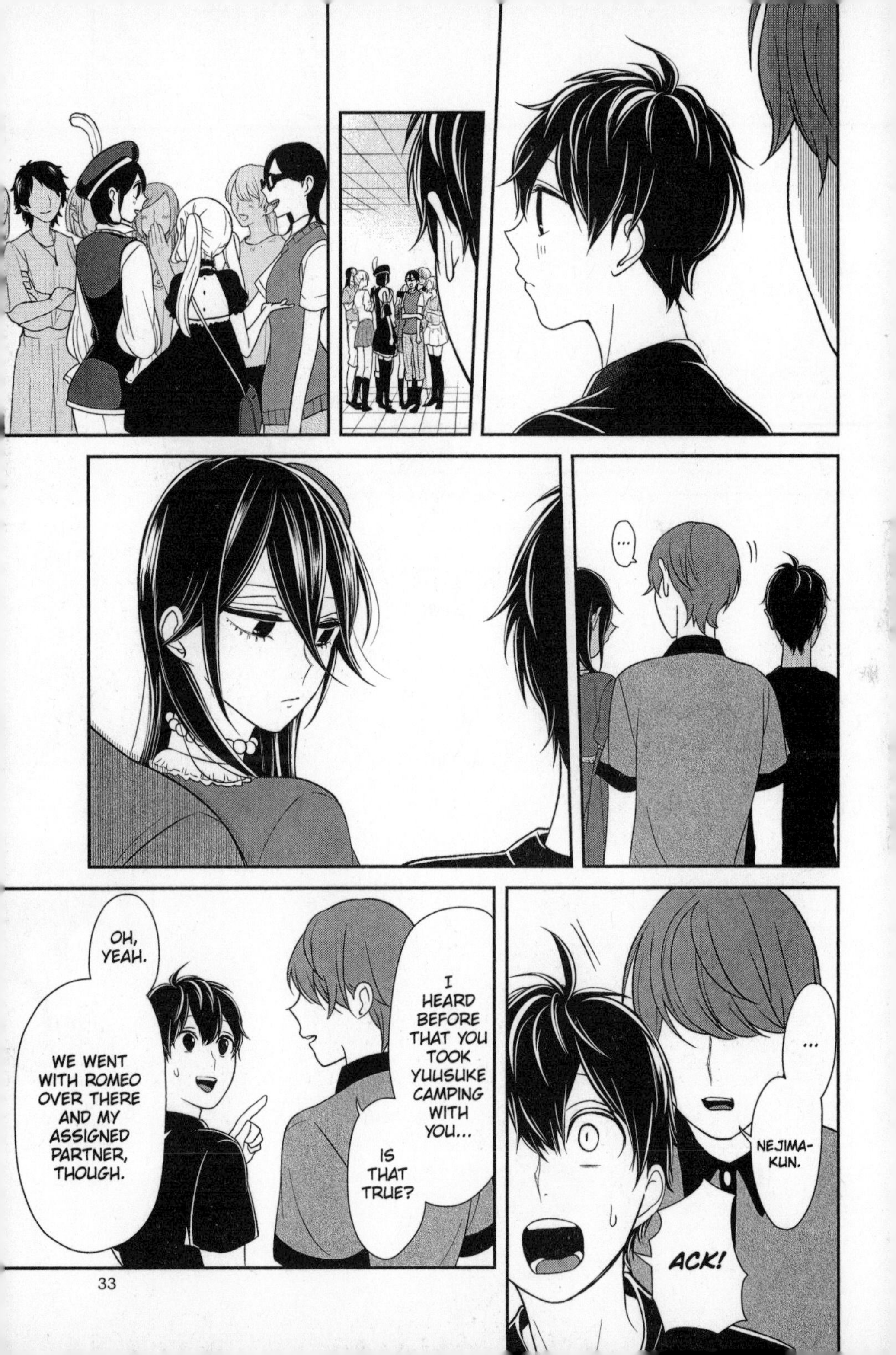
...
...
NEJIMA-KUN.
ACK!
I HEARD BEFORE THAT YOU TOOK YUUSUKE CAMPING WITH YOU...
IS THAT TRUE?
OH, YEAH.
WE WENT WITH ROMEO OVER THERE AND MY ASSIGNED PARTNER, THOUGH.

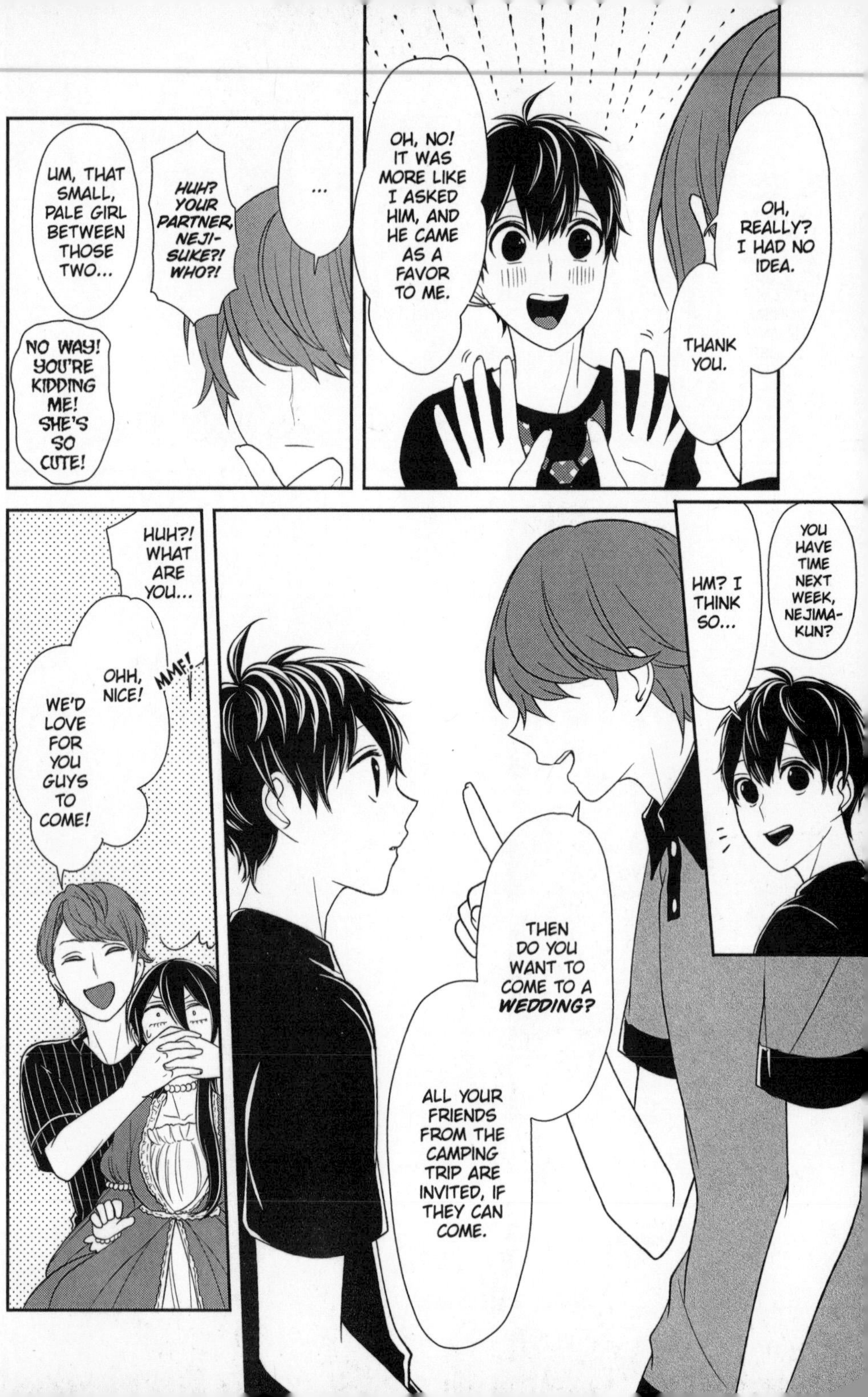
OH, REALLY? I HAD NO IDEA.
THANK YOU.
OH, NO! IT WAS MORE LIKE I ASKED HIM, AND HE CAME AS A FAVOR TO ME.
...
HUH? YOUR PARTNER, NEJI-SUKE?! WHO?!
UM, THAT SMALL, PALE GIRL BETWEEN THOSE TWO...
NO WAY! YOU'RE KIDDING ME! SHE'S SO CUTE!
YOU HAVE TIME NEXT WEEK, NEJIMA-KUN?
HM? I THINK SO...
THEN DO YOU WANT TO COME TO A *WEDDING*?
ALL YOUR FRIENDS FROM THE CAMPING TRIP ARE INVITED, IF THEY CAN COME.
HUH?! WHAT ARE YOU...
OHH, NICE!
MMF!
WE'D LOVE FOR YOU GUYS TO COME!

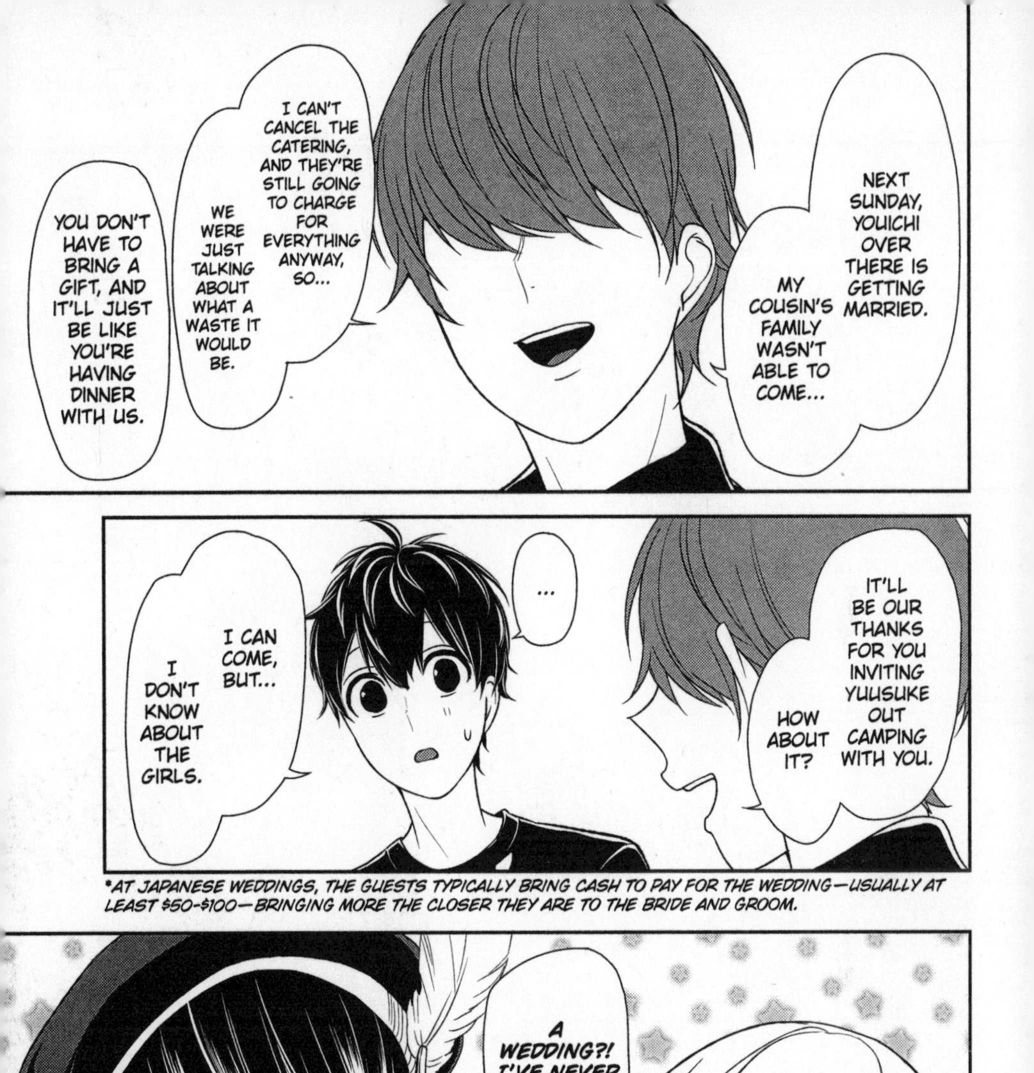
NEXT SUNDAY, YOUICHI OVER THERE IS GETTING MARRIED.
MY COUSIN'S FAMILY WASN'T ABLE TO COME...
I CAN'T CANCEL THE CATERING, AND THEY'RE STILL GOING TO CHARGE FOR EVERYTHING ANYWAY, SO...
WE WERE JUST TALKING ABOUT WHAT A WASTE IT WOULD BE.
YOU DON'T HAVE TO BRING A GIFT, AND IT'LL JUST BE LIKE YOU'RE HAVING DINNER WITH US.
IT'LL BE OUR THANKS FOR YOU INVITING YUUSUKE OUT CAMPING WITH YOU.
HOW ABOUT IT?
...
I CAN COME, BUT...
I DON'T KNOW ABOUT THE GIRLS.

*AT JAPANESE WEDDINGS, THE GUESTS TYPICALLY BRING CASH TO PAY FOR THE WEDDING—USUALLY AT LEAST $50-$100—BRINGING MORE THE CLOSER THEY ARE TO THE BRIDE AND GROOM.

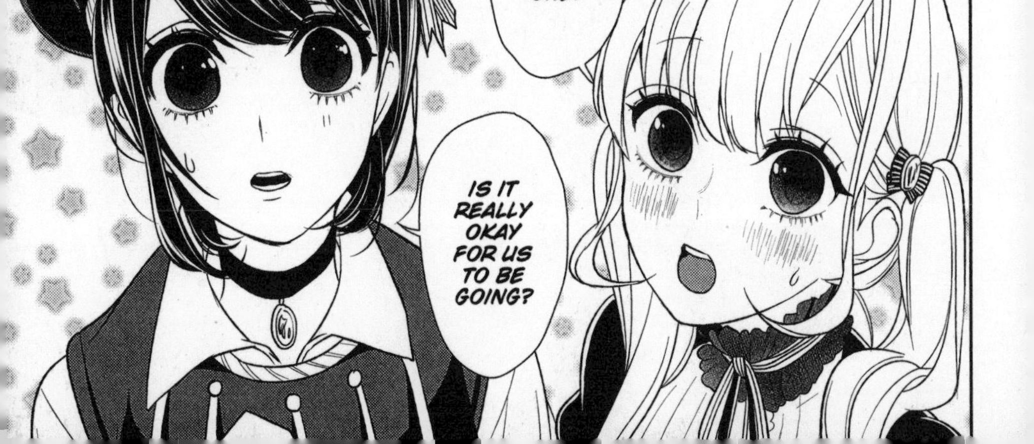
A WEDDING?! I'VE NEVER BEEN TO ONE!
IS IT REALLY OKAY FOR US TO BE GOING?

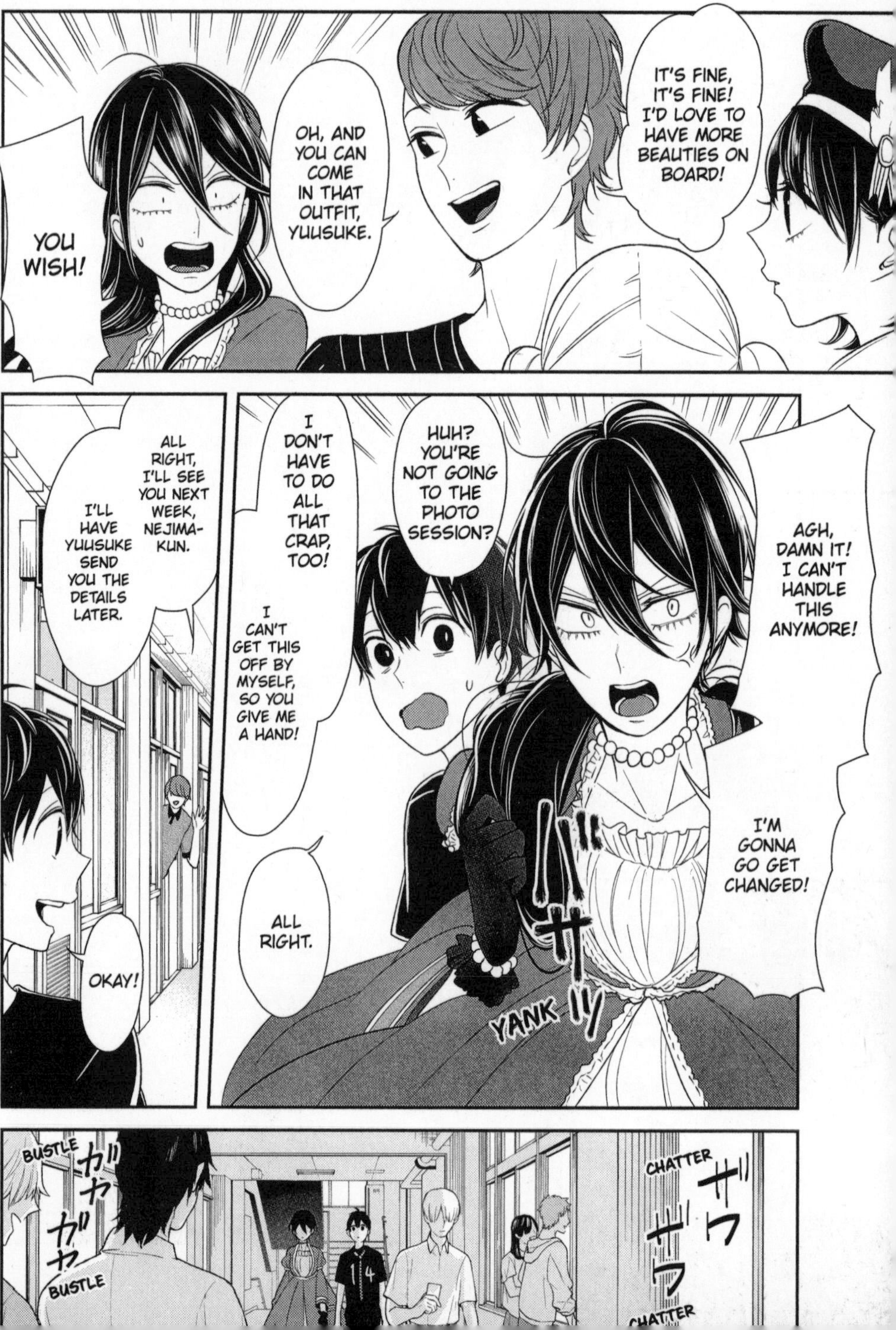
IT'S FINE, IT'S FINE! I'D LOVE TO HAVE MORE BEAUTIES ON BOARD!
OH, AND YOU CAN COME IN THAT OUTFIT, YUUSUKE.
YOU WISH!
AGH, DAMN IT! I CAN'T HANDLE THIS ANYMORE!
I'M GONNA GO GET CHANGED!
HUH? YOU'RE NOT GOING TO THE PHOTO SESSION?
I DON'T HAVE TO DO ALL THAT CRAP, TOO!
I CAN'T GET THIS OFF BY MYSELF, SO YOU GIVE ME A HAND!
ALL RIGHT.
YANK
ALL RIGHT, I'LL SEE YOU NEXT WEEK, NEJIMA-KUN.
I'LL HAVE YUUSUKE SEND YOU THE DETAILS LATER.
OKAY!
CHATTER
CHATTER
BUSTLE
BUSTLE

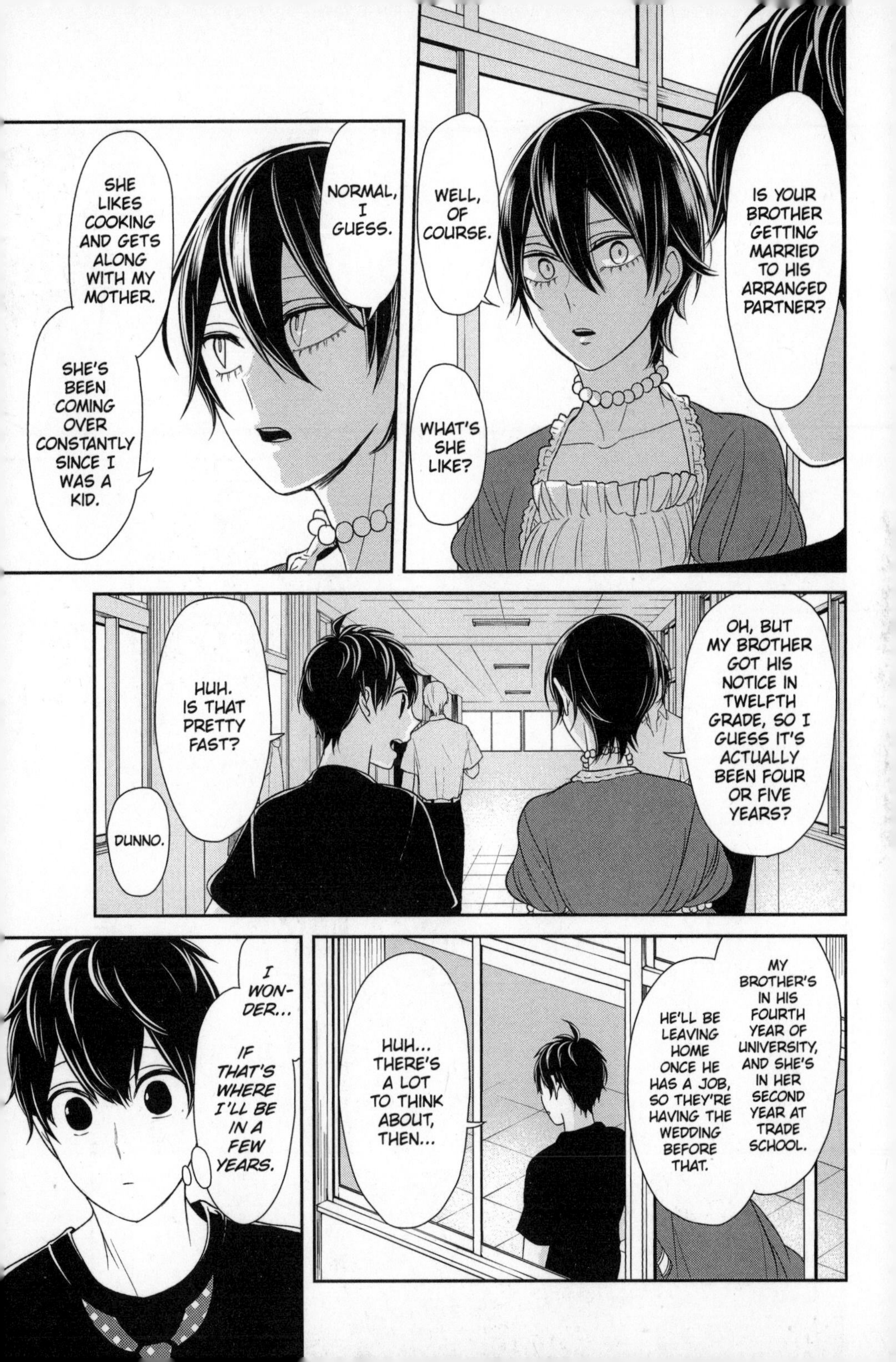
IS YOUR BROTHER GETTING MARRIED TO HIS ARRANGED PARTNER?
WELL, OF COURSE.
WHAT'S SHE LIKE?
NORMAL, I GUESS.
SHE LIKES COOKING AND GETS ALONG WITH MY MOTHER.
SHE'S BEEN COMING OVER CONSTANTLY SINCE I WAS A KID.
OH, BUT MY BROTHER GOT HIS NOTICE IN TWELFTH GRADE, SO I GUESS IT'S ACTUALLY BEEN FOUR OR FIVE YEARS?
HUH. IS THAT PRETTY FAST?
DUNNO.
MY BROTHER'S IN HIS FOURTH YEAR OF UNIVERSITY, AND SHE'S IN HER SECOND YEAR AT TRADE SCHOOL.
HE'LL BE LEAVING HOME ONCE HE HAS A JOB, SO THEY'RE HAVING THE WEDDING BEFORE THAT.
HUH... THERE'S A LOT TO THINK ABOUT, THEN...
I WONDER...
IF THAT'S WHERE I'LL BE IN A FEW YEARS.

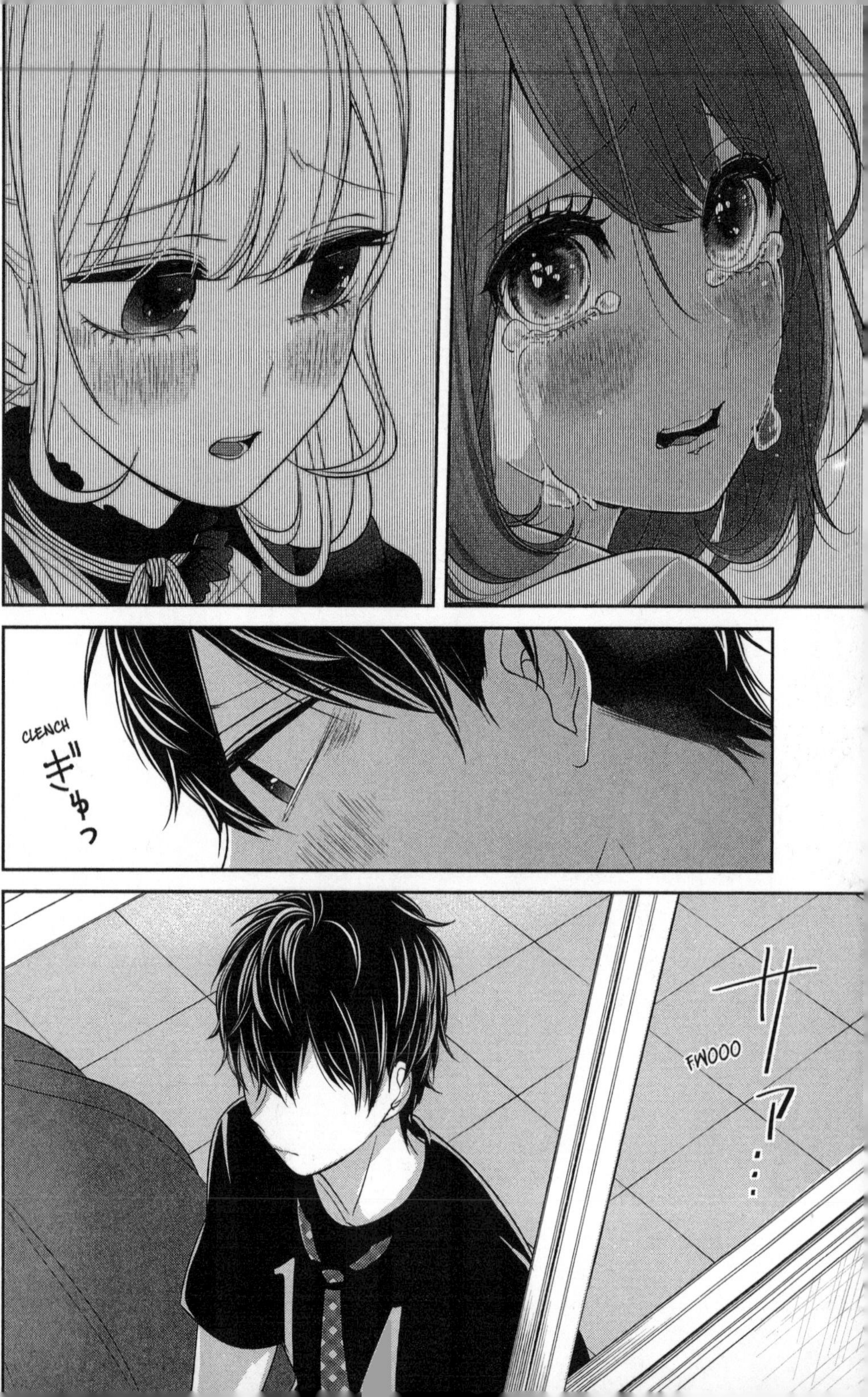
CLENCH
ぎゅっ
サァ…
FWOOO

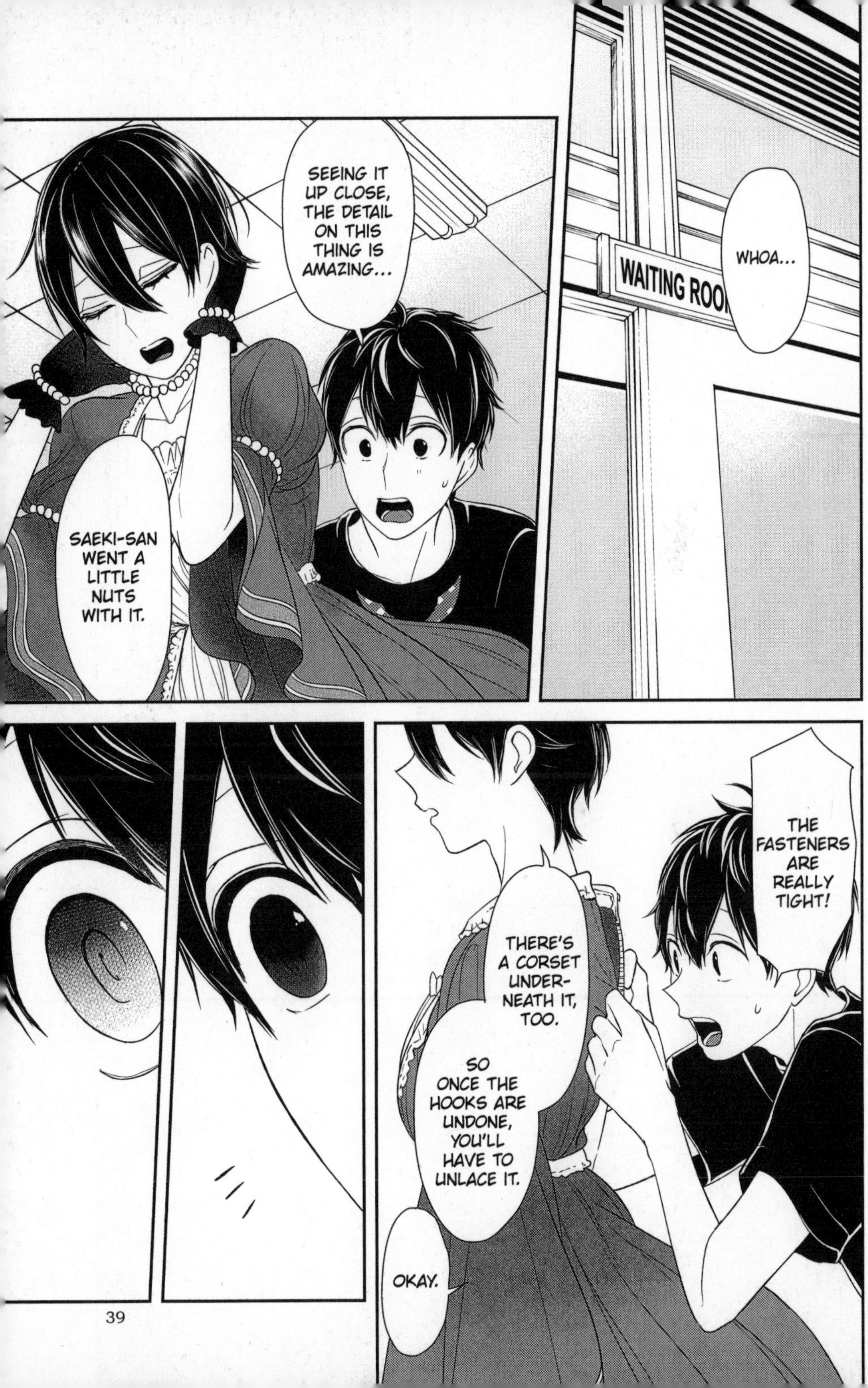
WAITING ROOM
WHOA...
SEEING IT UP CLOSE, THE DETAIL ON THIS THING IS AMAZING...
SAEKI-SAN WENT A LITTLE NUTS WITH IT.
THE FASTENERS ARE REALLY TIGHT!
THERE'S A CORSET UNDER-NEATH IT, TOO.
SO ONCE THE HOOKS ARE UNDONE, YOU'LL HAVE TO UNLACE IT.
OKAY.

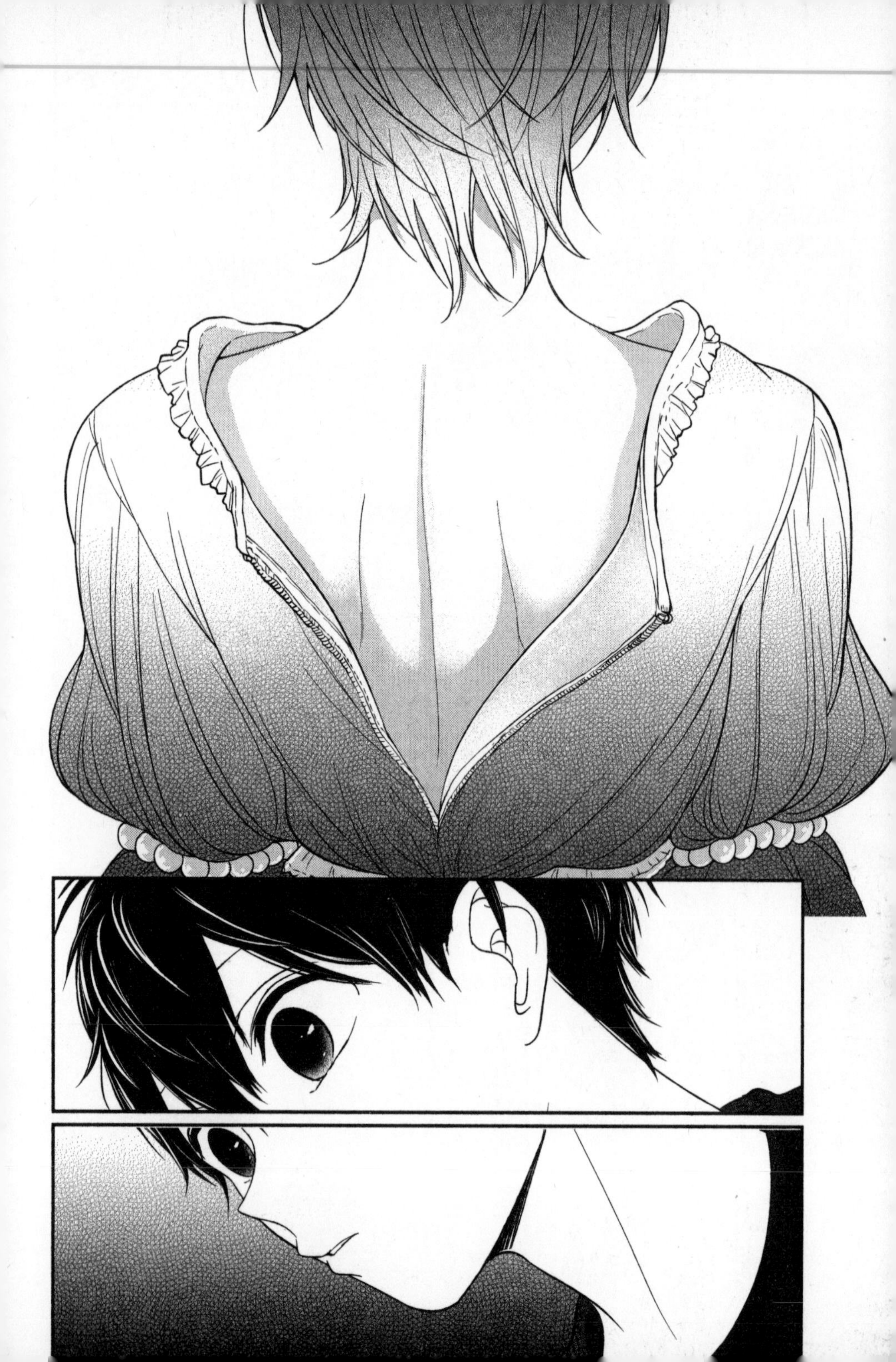

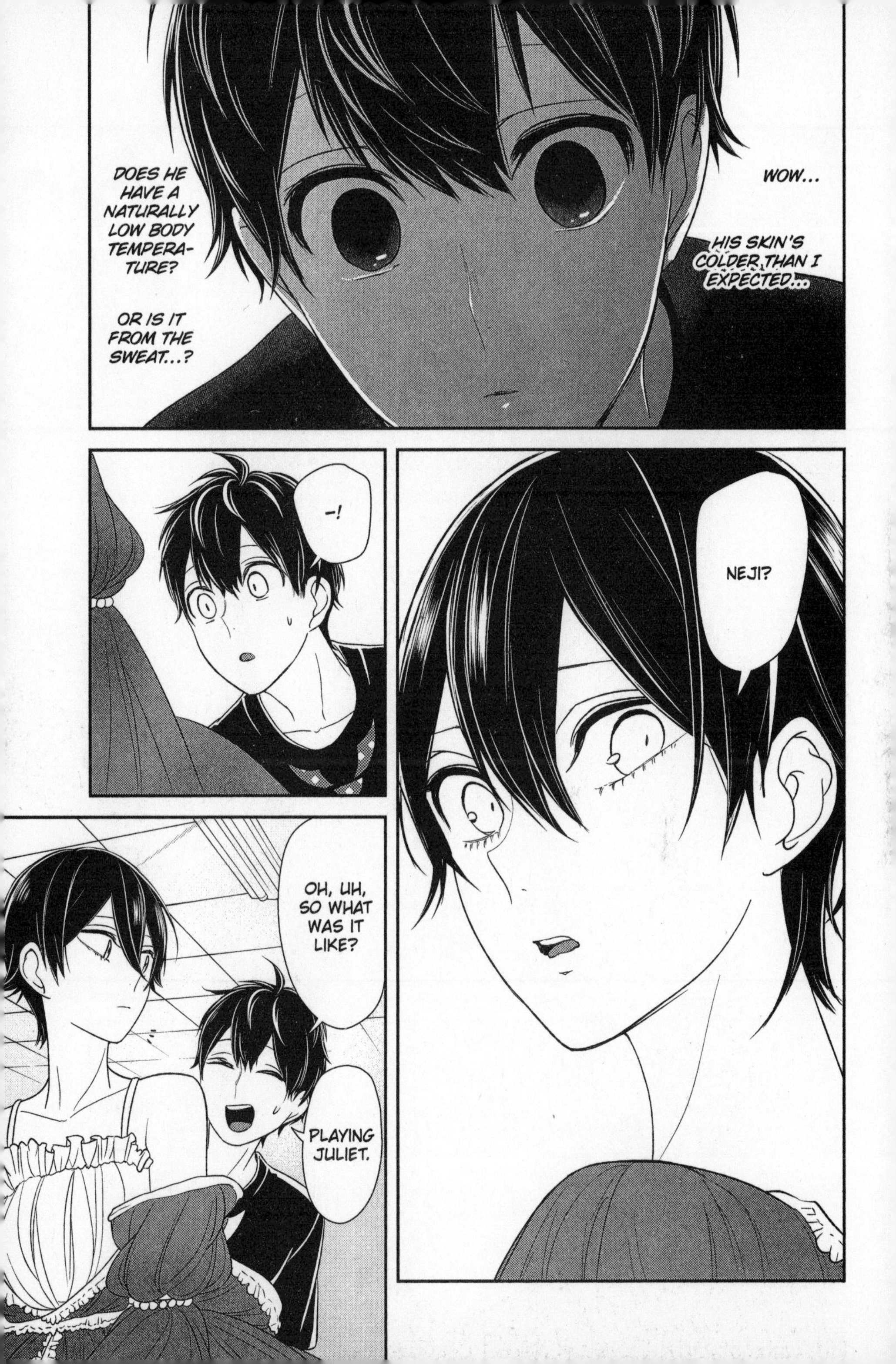
WOW...
HIS SKIN'S COLDER THAN I EXPECTED...
DOES HE HAVE A NATURALLY LOW BODY TEMPERA-TURE?
OR IS IT FROM THE SWEAT...?
NEJI?
–!
OH, UH, SO WHAT WAS IT LIKE?
PLAYING JULIET.

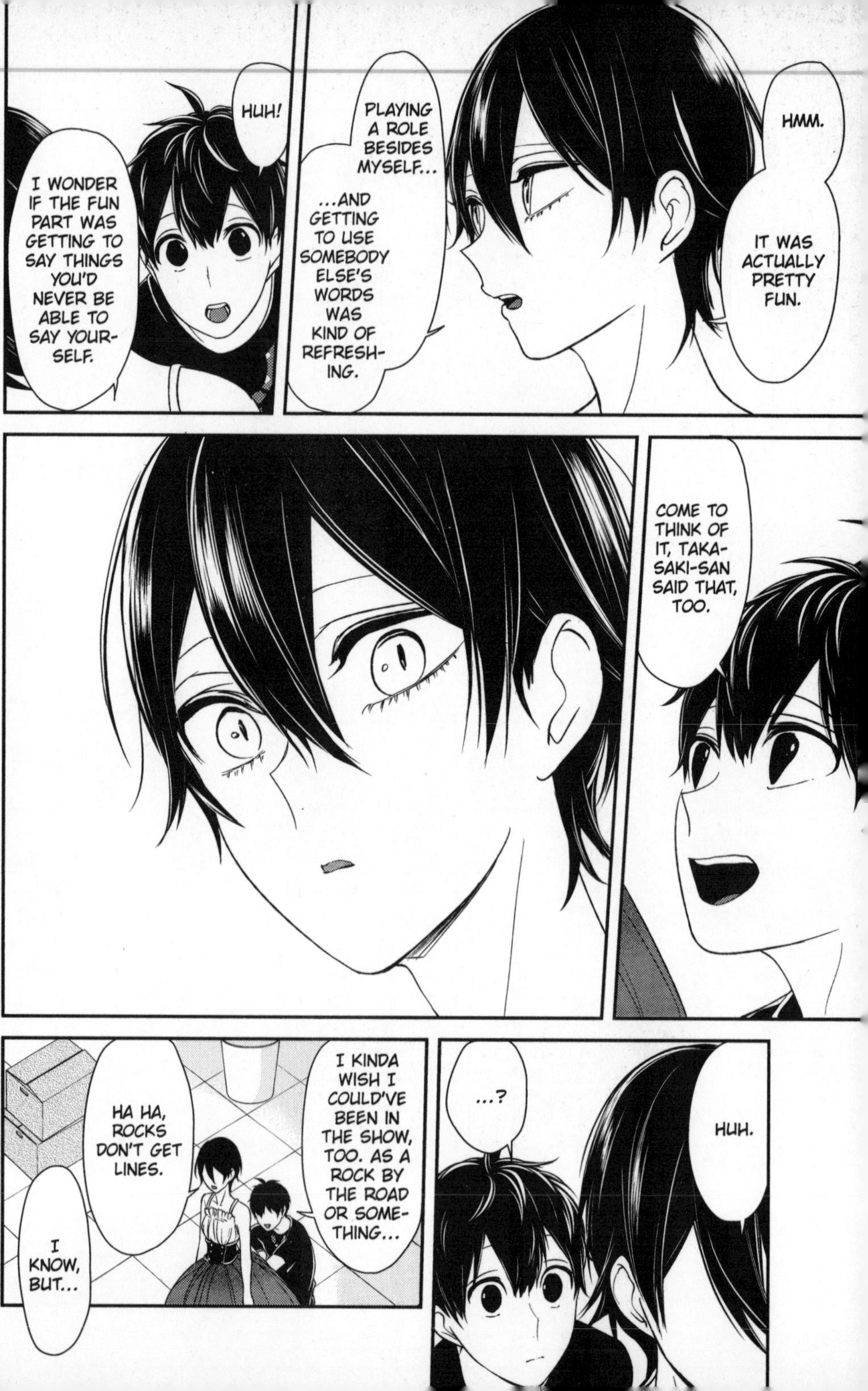
HMM.
IT WAS ACTUALLY PRETTY FUN.
PLAYING A ROLE BESIDES MYSELF...
...AND GETTING TO USE SOMEBODY ELSE'S WORDS WAS KIND OF REFRESHING.
HUH!
I WONDER IF THE FUN PART WAS GETTING TO SAY THINGS YOU'D NEVER BE ABLE TO SAY YOURSELF.
COME TO THINK OF IT, TAKASAKI-SAN SAID THAT, TOO.
HUH.
...?
I KINDA WISH I COULD'VE BEEN IN THE SHOW, TOO. AS A ROCK BY THE ROAD OR SOMETHING...
HA HA, ROCKS DON'T GET LINES.
I KNOW, BUT...

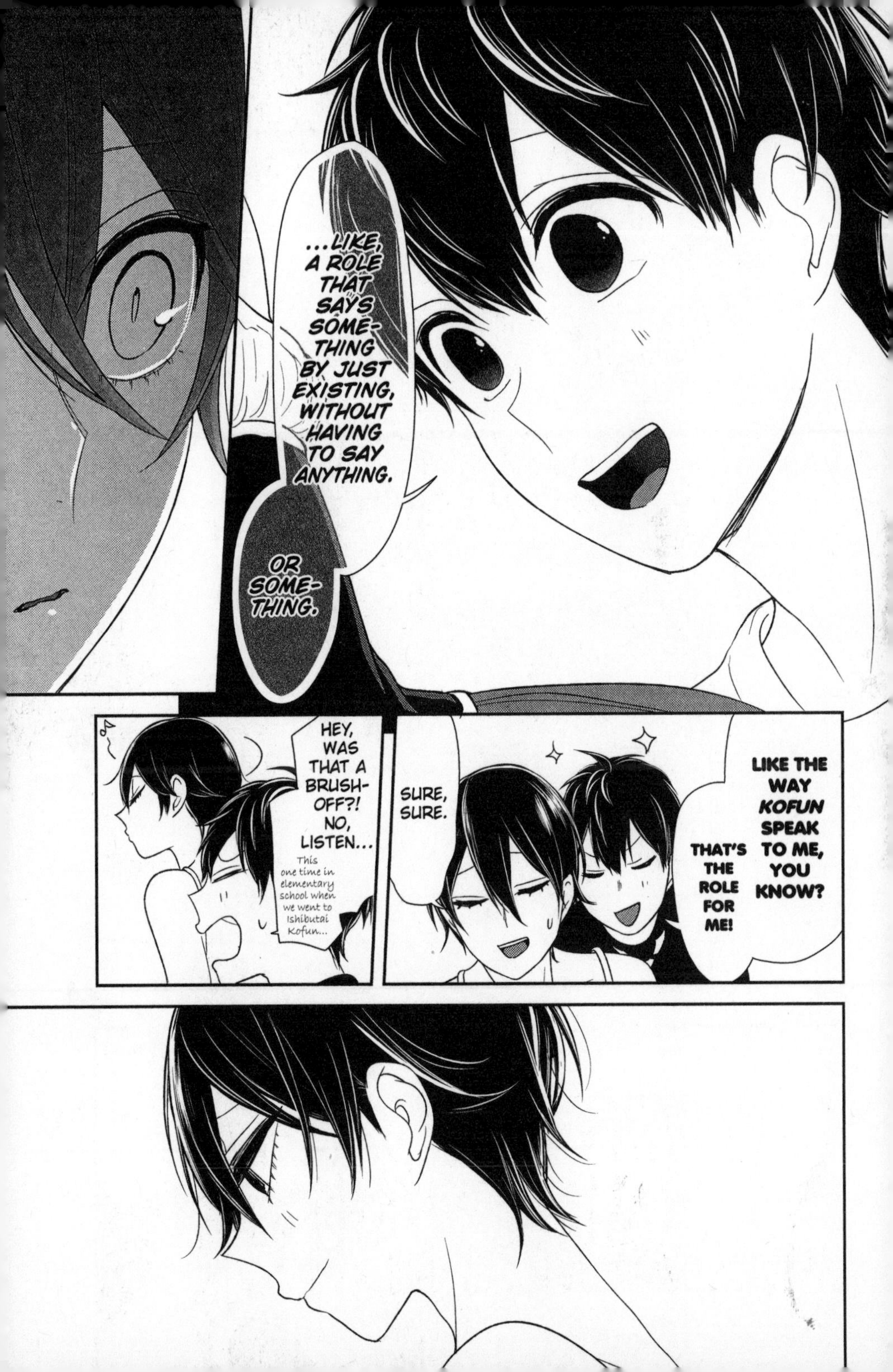
...LIKE, A ROLE THAT SAYS SOME-THING BY JUST EXISTING, WITHOUT HAVING TO SAY ANYTHING.
OR SOME-THING.
LIKE THE WAY KOFUN SPEAK TO ME, YOU KNOW?
THAT'S THE ROLE FOR ME!
SURE, SURE.
HEY, WAS THAT A BRUSH-OFF?! NO, LISTEN...
This one time in elementary school when we went to Ishibutai Kofun...

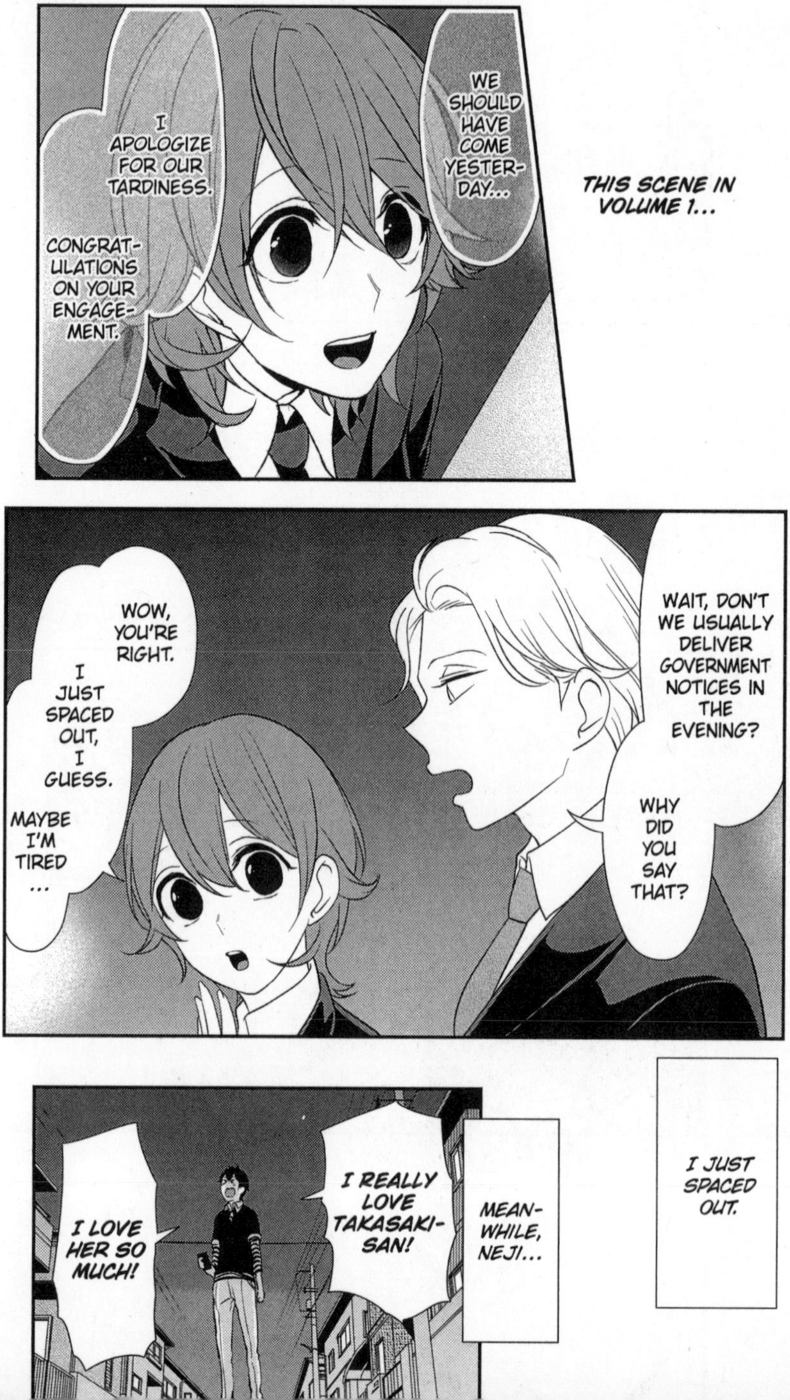
THIS SCENE IN VOLUME 1...
WE SHOULD HAVE COME YESTER-DAY...
I APOLOGIZE FOR OUR TARDINESS.
CONGRAT-ULATIONS ON YOUR ENGAGE-MENT.
WAIT, DON'T WE USUALLY DELIVER GOVERNMENT NOTICES IN THE EVENING?
WHY DID YOU SAY THAT?
WOW, YOU'RE RIGHT.
I JUST SPACED OUT, I GUESS.
MAYBE I'M TIRED...
I JUST SPACED OUT.
MEAN-WHILE, NEJI...
I REALLY LOVE TAKASAKI-SAN!
I LOVE HER SO MUCH!

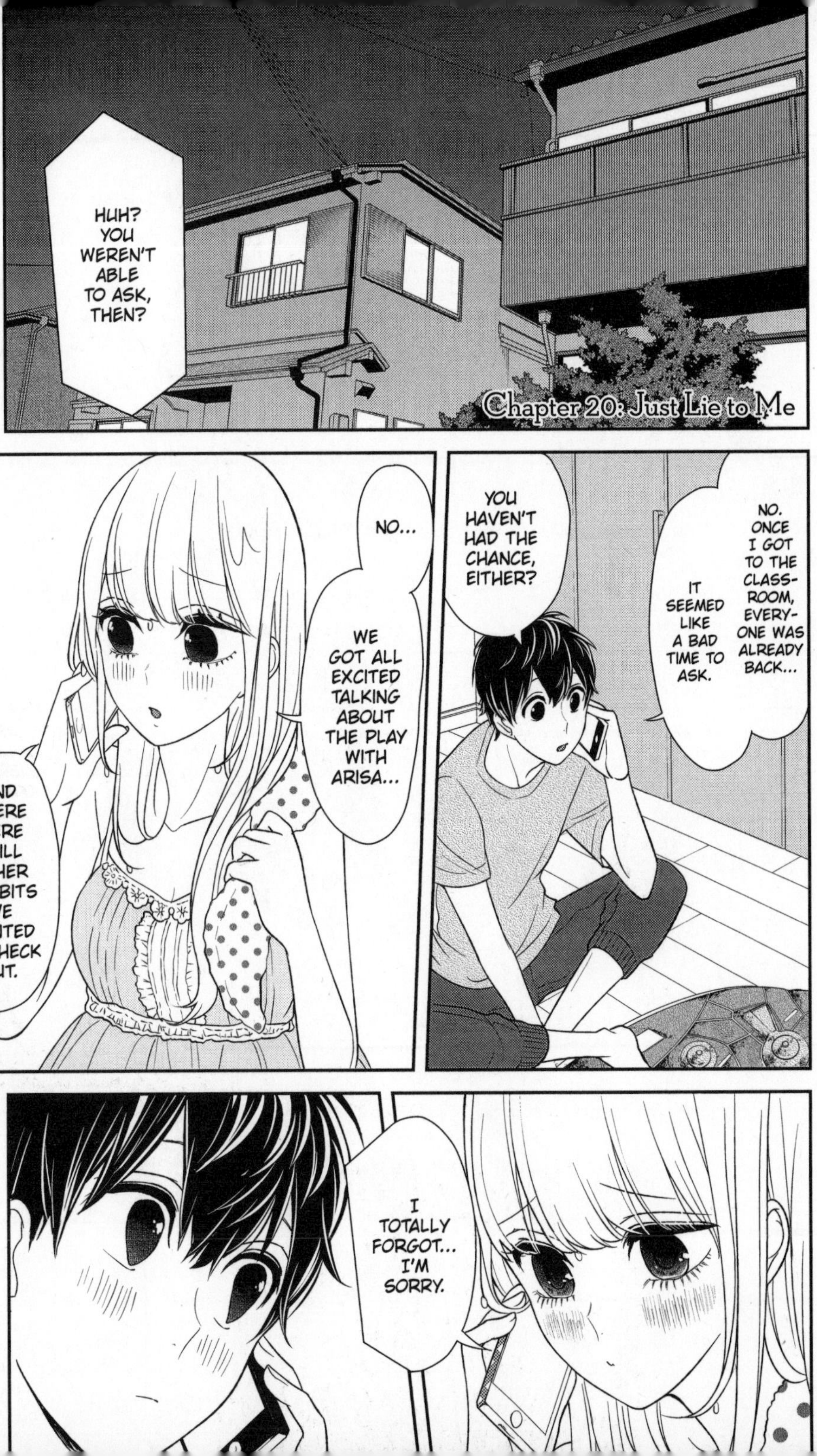
HUH? YOU WEREN'T ABLE TO ASK, THEN?
Chapter 20: Just Lie to Me
NO. ONCE I GOT TO THE CLASSROOM, EVERYONE WAS ALREADY BACK...
IT SEEMED LIKE A BAD TIME TO ASK.
YOU HAVEN'T HAD THE CHANCE, EITHER?
NO...
WE GOT ALL EXCITED TALKING ABOUT THE PLAY WITH ARISA...
AND THERE WERE STILL OTHER EXHIBITS WE WANTED TO CHECK OUT.
I TOTALLY FORGOT... I'M SORRY.

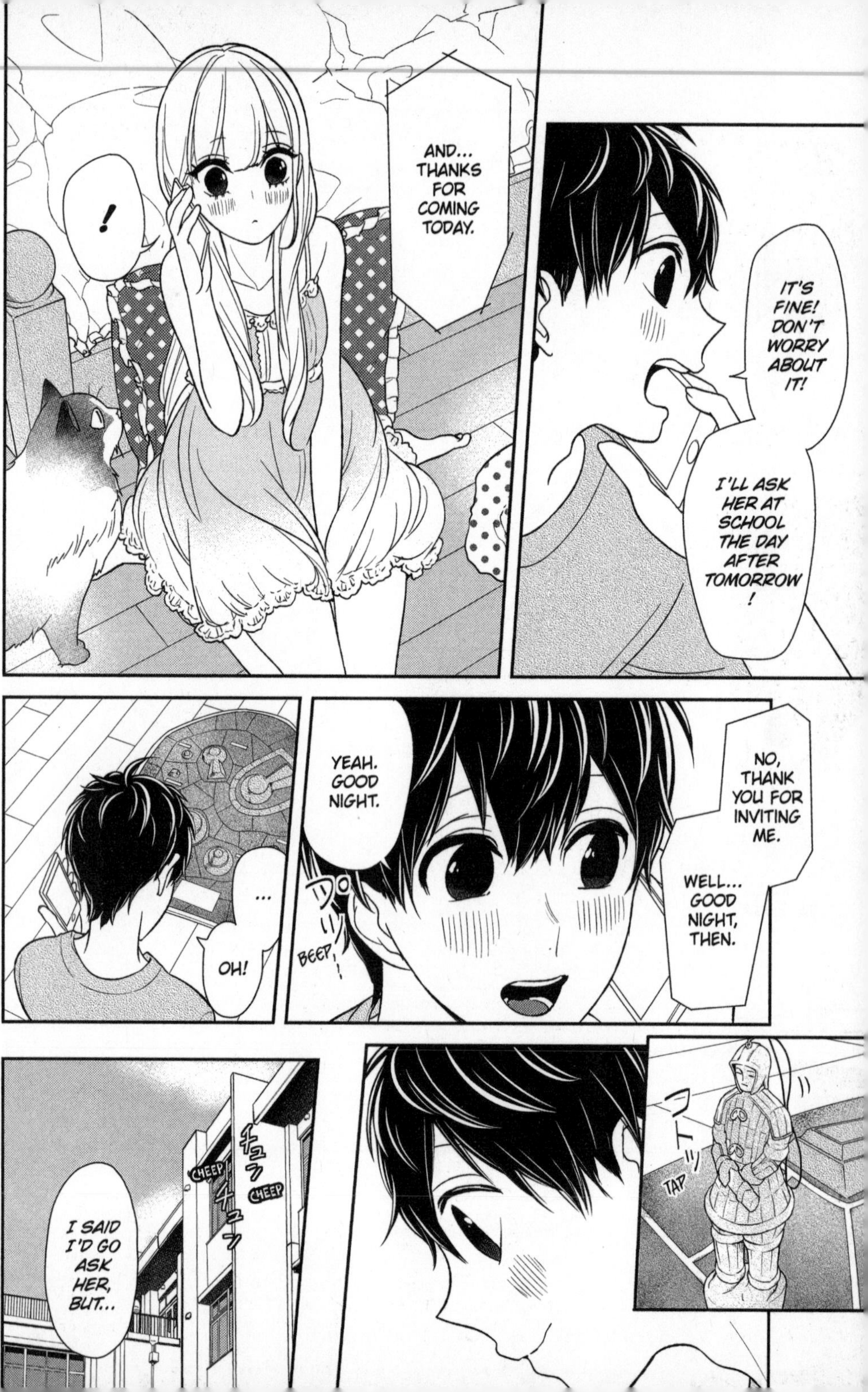
IT'S FINE! DON'T WORRY ABOUT IT!
I'LL ASK HER AT SCHOOL THE DAY AFTER TOMORROW!
AND... THANKS FOR COMING TODAY.
!
NO, THANK YOU FOR INVITING ME.
WELL... GOOD NIGHT, THEN.
YEAH. GOOD NIGHT.
BEEP
...
OH!
TAP
CHEEP
CHEEP
I SAID I'D GO ASK HER, BUT...

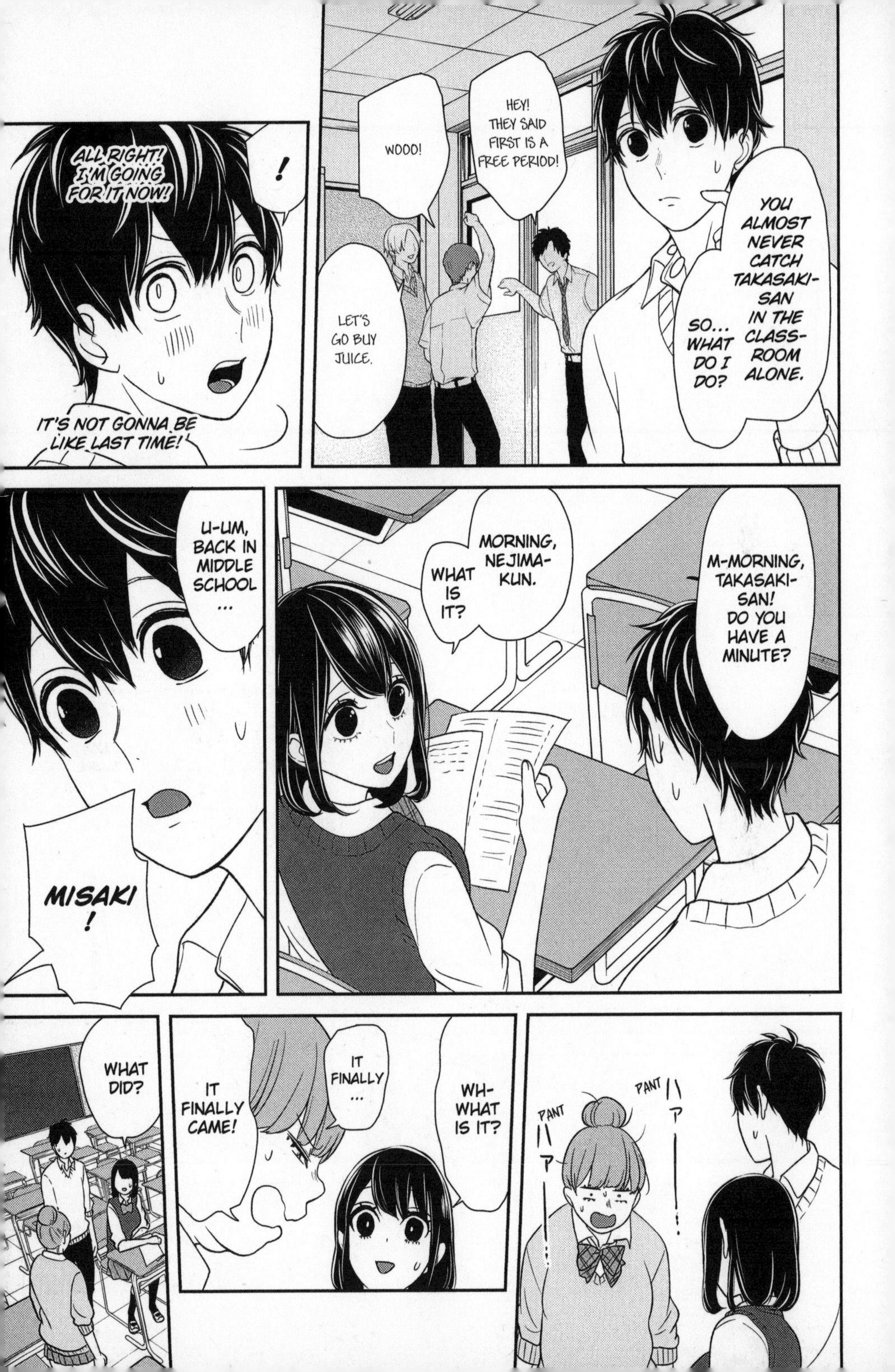

YOU ALMOST NEVER CATCH TAKASAKI-SAN IN THE CLASSROOM ALONE.
SO... WHAT DO I DO?
HEY! THEY SAID FIRST IS A FREE PERIOD!
WOOO!
LET'S GO BUY JUICE.
!
ALL RIGHT! I'M GOING FOR IT NOW!
IT'S NOT GONNA BE LIKE LAST TIME!
M-MORNING, TAKASAKI-SAN! DO YOU HAVE A MINUTE?
MORNING, NEJIMA-KUN.
WHAT IS IT?
U-UM, BACK IN MIDDLE SCHOOL ...
MISAKI!
PANT
ハァー
PANT
ハァー
WH-WHAT IS IT?
IT FINALLY ...
IT FINALLY CAME!
WHAT DID?

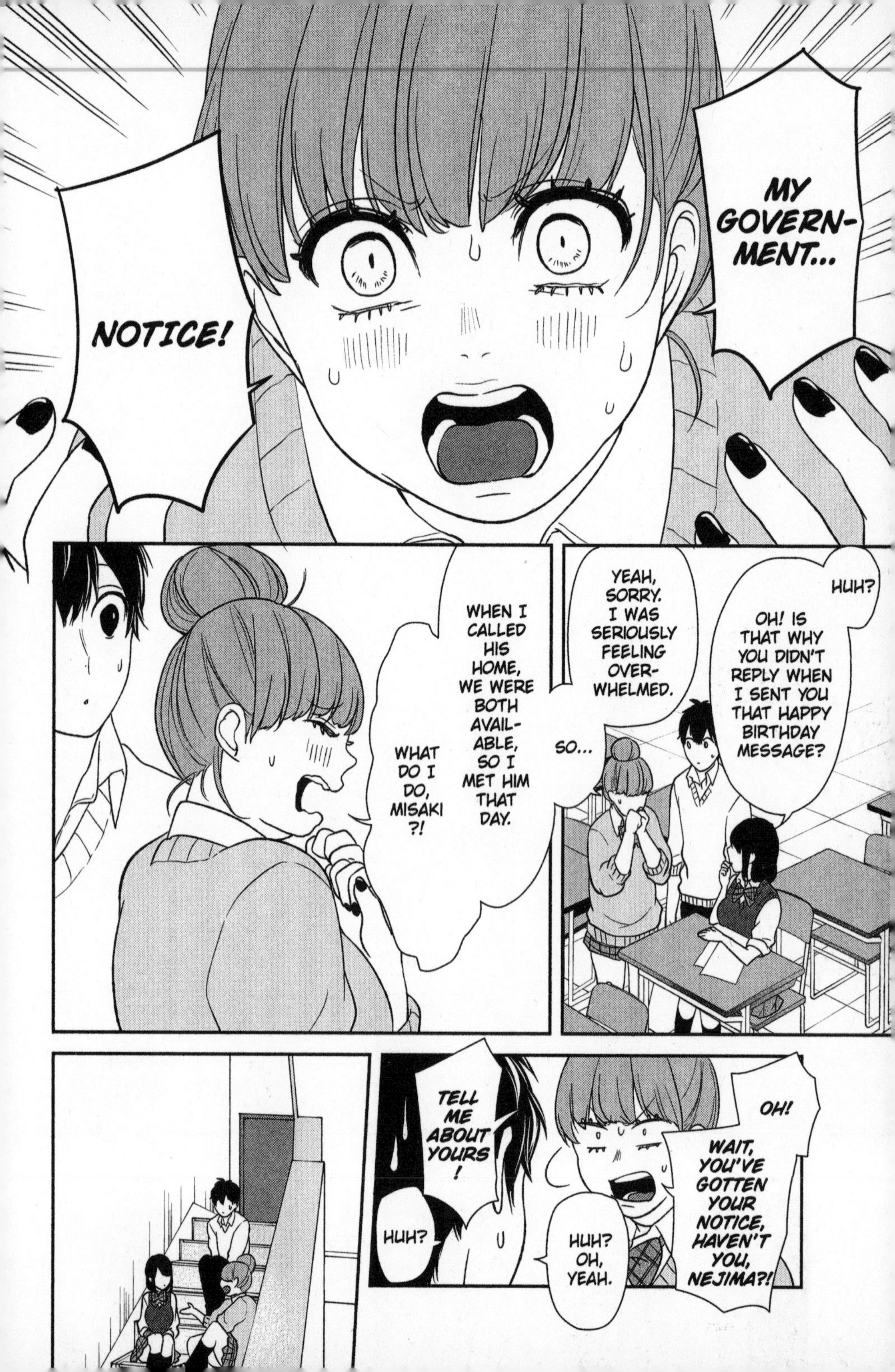
MY GOVERNMENT...
NOTICE!
HUH?
OH! IS THAT WHY YOU DIDN'T REPLY WHEN I SENT YOU THAT HAPPY BIRTHDAY MESSAGE?
YEAH, SORRY. I WAS SERIOUSLY FEELING OVERWHELMED.
SO...
WHEN I CALLED HIS HOME, WE WERE BOTH AVAILABLE, SO I MET HIM THAT DAY.
WHAT DO I DO, MISAKI?!
OH!
WAIT, YOU'VE GOTTEN YOUR NOTICE, HAVEN'T YOU, NEJIMA?!
HUH? OH, YEAH.
TELL ME ABOUT YOURS!
HUH?

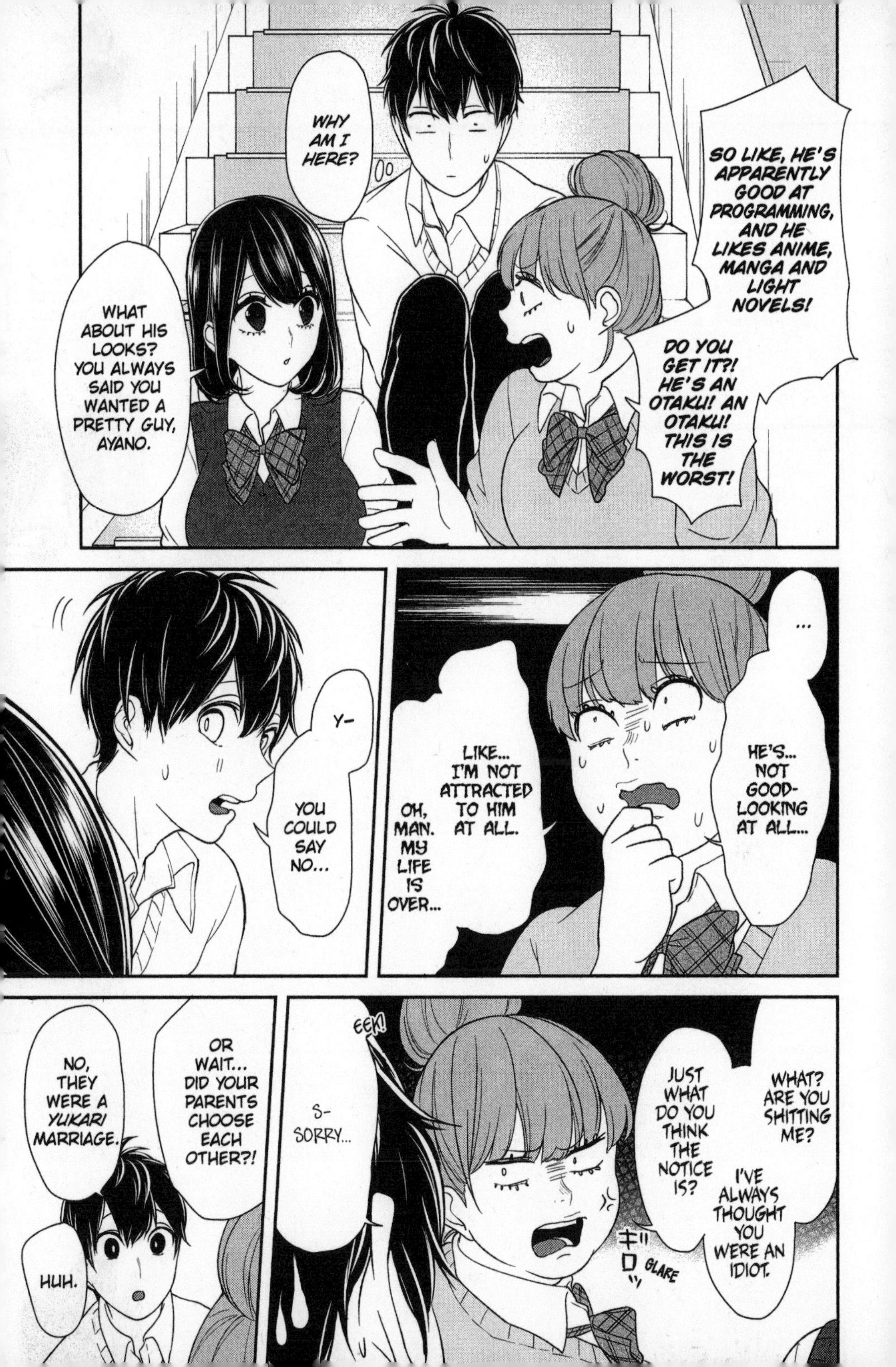
SO LIKE, HE'S APPARENTLY GOOD AT PROGRAMMING, AND HE LIKES ANIME, MANGA AND LIGHT NOVELS!
DO YOU GET IT?! HE'S AN OTAKU! AN OTAKU! THIS IS THE WORST!
WHY AM I HERE?
WHAT ABOUT HIS LOOKS? YOU ALWAYS SAID YOU WANTED A PRETTY GUY, AYANO.
...
HE'S... NOT GOOD-LOOKING AT ALL...
LIKE... I'M NOT ATTRACTED TO HIM AT ALL.
OH, MAN. MY LIFE IS OVER...
Y-
YOU COULD SAY NO...
WHAT? ARE YOU SHITTING ME?
JUST WHAT DO YOU THINK THE NOTICE IS?
I'VE ALWAYS THOUGHT YOU WERE AN IDIOT.
ギロッ GLARE
EEK!
S-SORRY...
OR WAIT... DID YOUR PARENTS CHOOSE EACH OTHER?!
NO, THEY WERE A *YUKARI* MARRIAGE.
HUH.

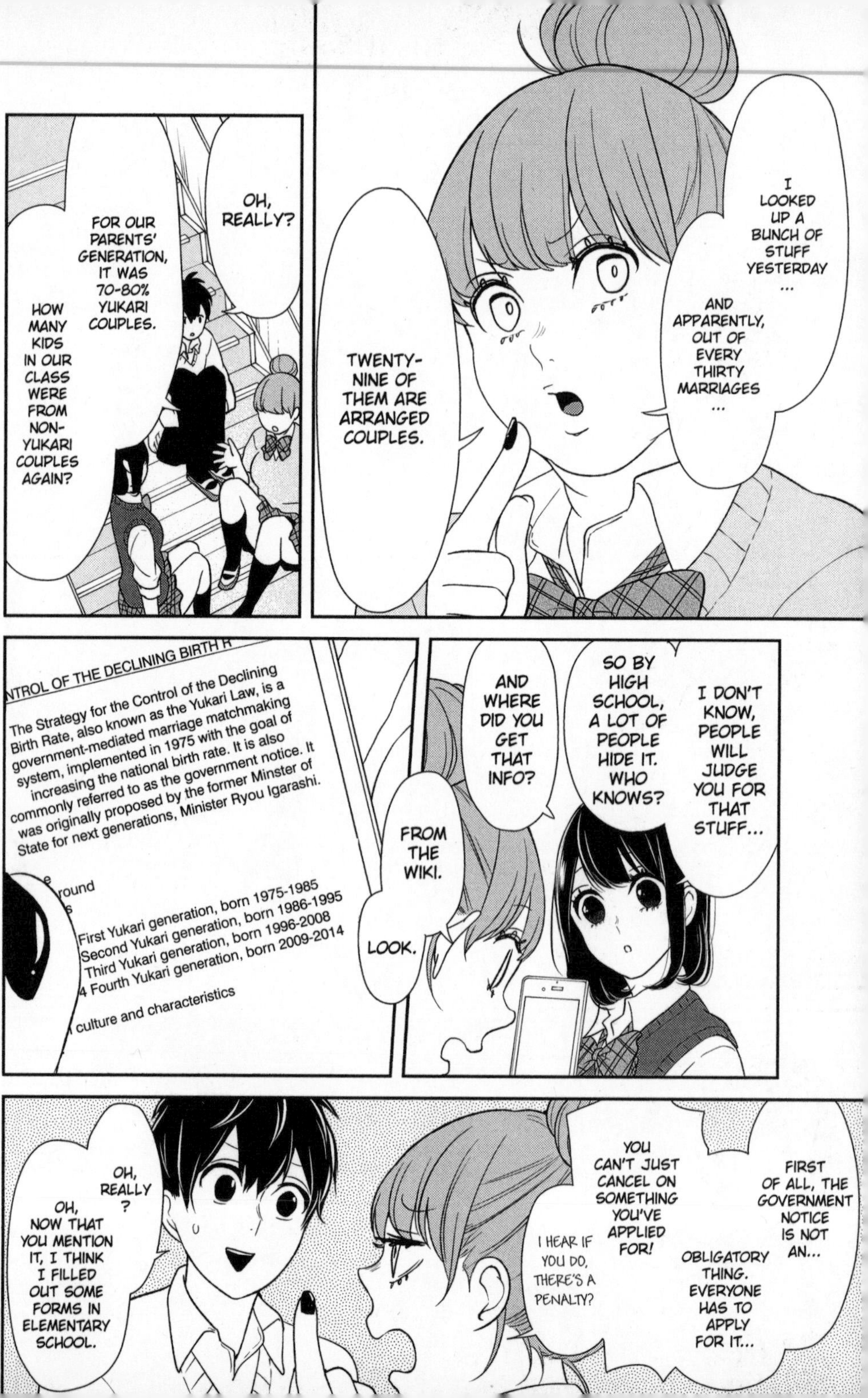
I LOOKED UP A BUNCH OF STUFF YESTERDAY ...
AND APPARENTLY, OUT OF EVERY THIRTY MARRIAGES ...
TWENTY-NINE OF THEM ARE ARRANGED COUPLES.
OH, REALLY?
FOR OUR PARENTS' GENERATION, IT WAS 70-80% YUKARI COUPLES.
HOW MANY KIDS IN OUR CLASS WERE FROM NON-YUKARI COUPLES AGAIN?
I DON'T KNOW, PEOPLE WILL JUDGE YOU FOR THAT STUFF...
SO BY HIGH SCHOOL, A LOT OF PEOPLE HIDE IT. WHO KNOWS?
AND WHERE DID YOU GET THAT INFO?
FROM THE WIKI.
LOOK.
NTROL OF THE DECLINING BIRTH R
The Strategy for the Control of the Declining Birth Rate, also known as the Yukari Law, is a government-mediated marriage matchmaking system, implemented in 1975 with the goal of increasing the national birth rate. It is also commonly referred to as the government notice. It was originally proposed by the former Minster of State for next generations, Minister Ryou Igarashi.
First Yukari generation, born 1975-1985
Second Yukari generation, born 1986-1995
Third Yukari generation, born 1996-2008
4 Fourth Yukari generation, born 2009-2014
culture and characteristics
FIRST OF ALL, THE GOVERNMENT NOTICE IS NOT AN...
OBLIGATORY THING. EVERYONE HAS TO APPLY FOR IT...
YOU CAN'T JUST CANCEL ON SOMETHING YOU'VE APPLIED FOR!
I HEAR IF YOU DO, THERE'S A PENALTY?
OH, REALLY?
OH, NOW THAT YOU MENTION IT, I THINK I FILLED OUT SOME FORMS IN ELEMENTARY SCHOOL.

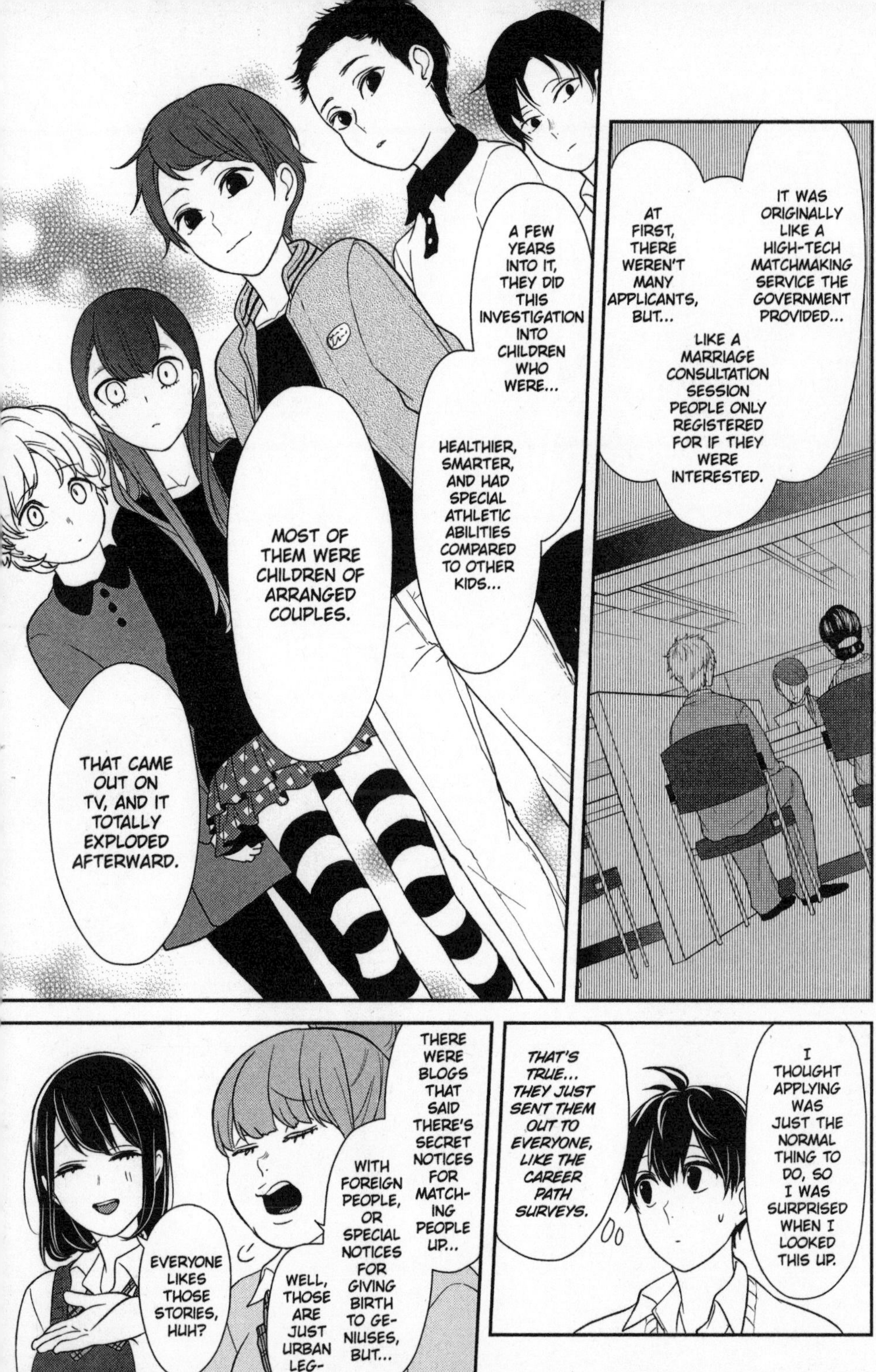
IT WAS ORIGINALLY LIKE A HIGH-TECH MATCHMAKING SERVICE THE GOVERNMENT PROVIDED...
AT FIRST, THERE WEREN'T MANY APPLICANTS, BUT...
LIKE A MARRIAGE CONSULTATION SESSION PEOPLE ONLY REGISTERED FOR IF THEY WERE INTERESTED.
A FEW YEARS INTO IT, THEY DID THIS INVESTIGATION INTO CHILDREN WHO WERE...
HEALTHIER, SMARTER, AND HAD SPECIAL ATHLETIC ABILITIES COMPARED TO OTHER KIDS...
MOST OF THEM WERE CHILDREN OF ARRANGED COUPLES.
THAT CAME OUT ON TV, AND IT TOTALLY EXPLODED AFTERWARD.
I THOUGHT APPLYING WAS JUST THE NORMAL THING TO DO, SO I WAS SURPRISED WHEN I LOOKED THIS UP.
THAT'S TRUE... THEY JUST SENT THEM OUT TO EVERYONE, LIKE THE CAREER PATH SURVEYS.
THERE WERE BLOGS THAT SAID THERE'S SECRET NOTICES FOR MATCH-ING PEOPLE UP...
WITH FOREIGN PEOPLE, OR SPECIAL NOTICES FOR GIVING BIRTH TO GE-NIUSES, BUT...
WELL, THOSE ARE JUST URBAN LEG-ENDS.
EVERYONE LIKES THOSE STORIES, HUH?

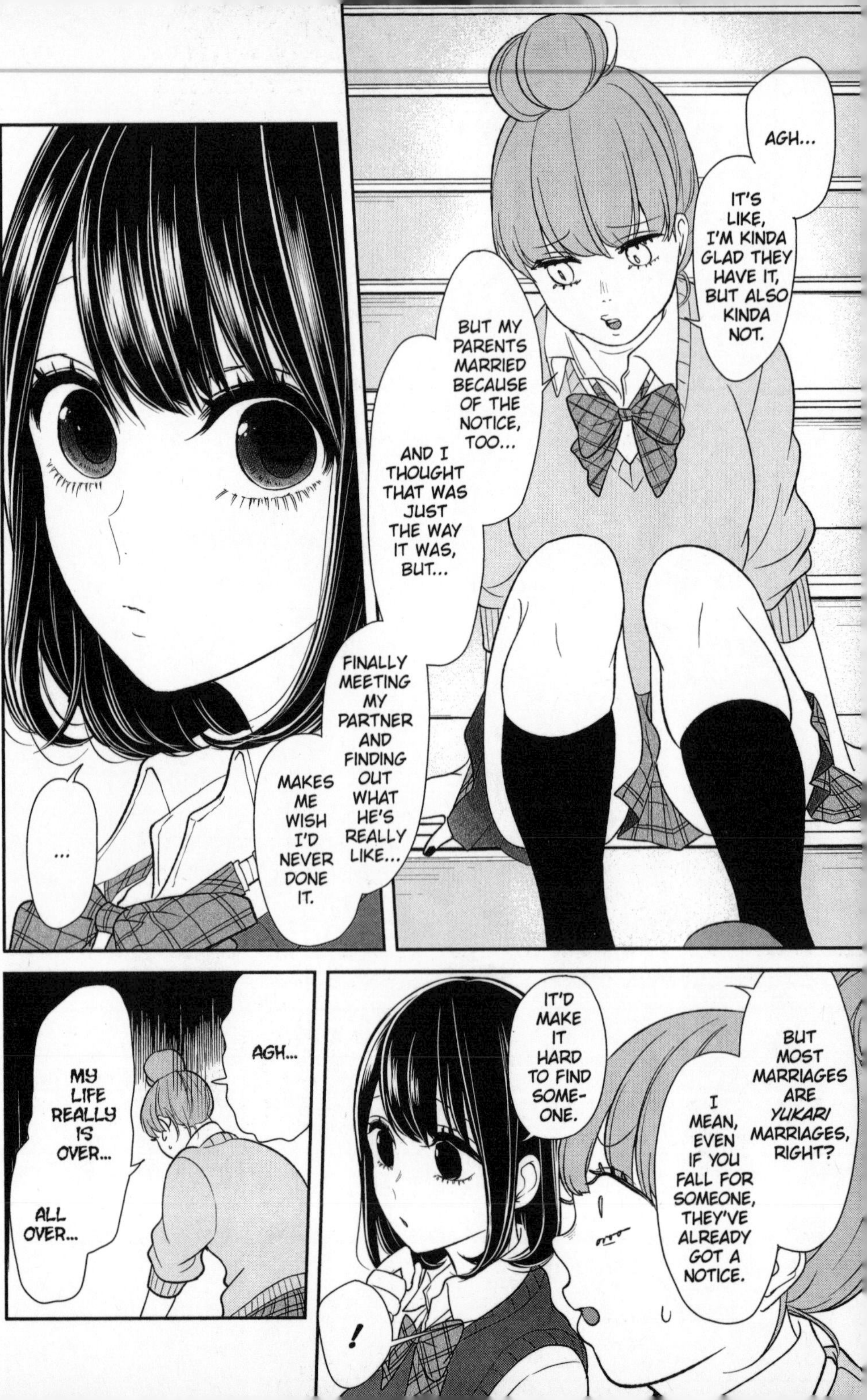
AGH...
IT'S LIKE, I'M KINDA GLAD THEY HAVE IT, BUT ALSO KINDA NOT.
BUT MY PARENTS MARRIED BECAUSE OF THE NOTICE, TOO...
AND I THOUGHT THAT WAS JUST THE WAY IT WAS, BUT...
FINALLY MEETING MY PARTNER AND FINDING OUT WHAT HE'S REALLY LIKE...
MAKES ME WISH I'D NEVER DONE IT.
...
BUT MOST MARRIAGES ARE *YUKARI* MARRIAGES, RIGHT?
I MEAN, EVEN IF YOU FALL FOR SOMEONE, THEY'VE ALREADY GOT A NOTICE.
IT'D MAKE IT HARD TO FIND SOME-ONE.
!
AGH...
MY LIFE REALLY IS OVER...
ALL OVER...

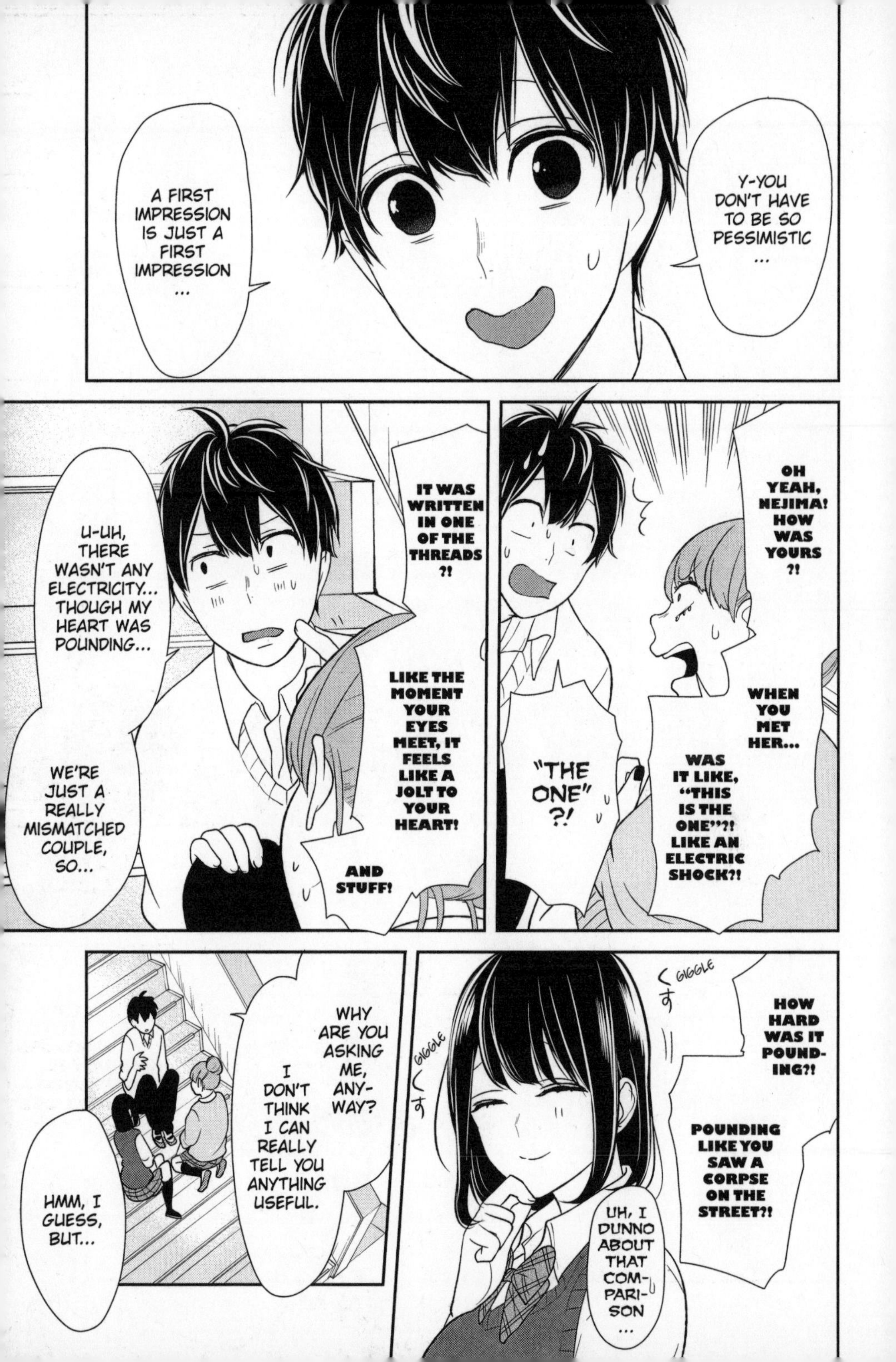
Y-YOU DON'T HAVE TO BE SO PESSIMISTIC ...
A FIRST IMPRESSION IS JUST A FIRST IMPRESSION ...
OH YEAH, NEJIMA! HOW WAS YOURS ?!
WHEN YOU MET HER... WAS IT LIKE, "THIS IS THE ONE"?! LIKE AN ELECTRIC SHOCK?!
"THE ONE" ?!
IT WAS WRITTEN IN ONE OF THE THREADS ?!
LIKE THE MOMENT YOUR EYES MEET, IT FEELS LIKE A JOLT TO YOUR HEART! AND STUFF!
U-UH, THERE WASN'T ANY ELECTRICITY... THOUGH MY HEART WAS POUNDING...
WE'RE JUST A REALLY MISMATCHED COUPLE, SO...
HOW HARD WAS IT POUNDING?!
POUNDING LIKE YOU SAW A CORPSE ON THE STREET?!
くす GIGGLE
くす GIGGLE
UH, I DUNNO ABOUT THAT COMPARISON ...
WHY ARE YOU ASKING ME, ANYWAY?
I DON'T THINK I CAN REALLY TELL YOU ANYTHING USEFUL.
HMM, I GUESS, BUT...

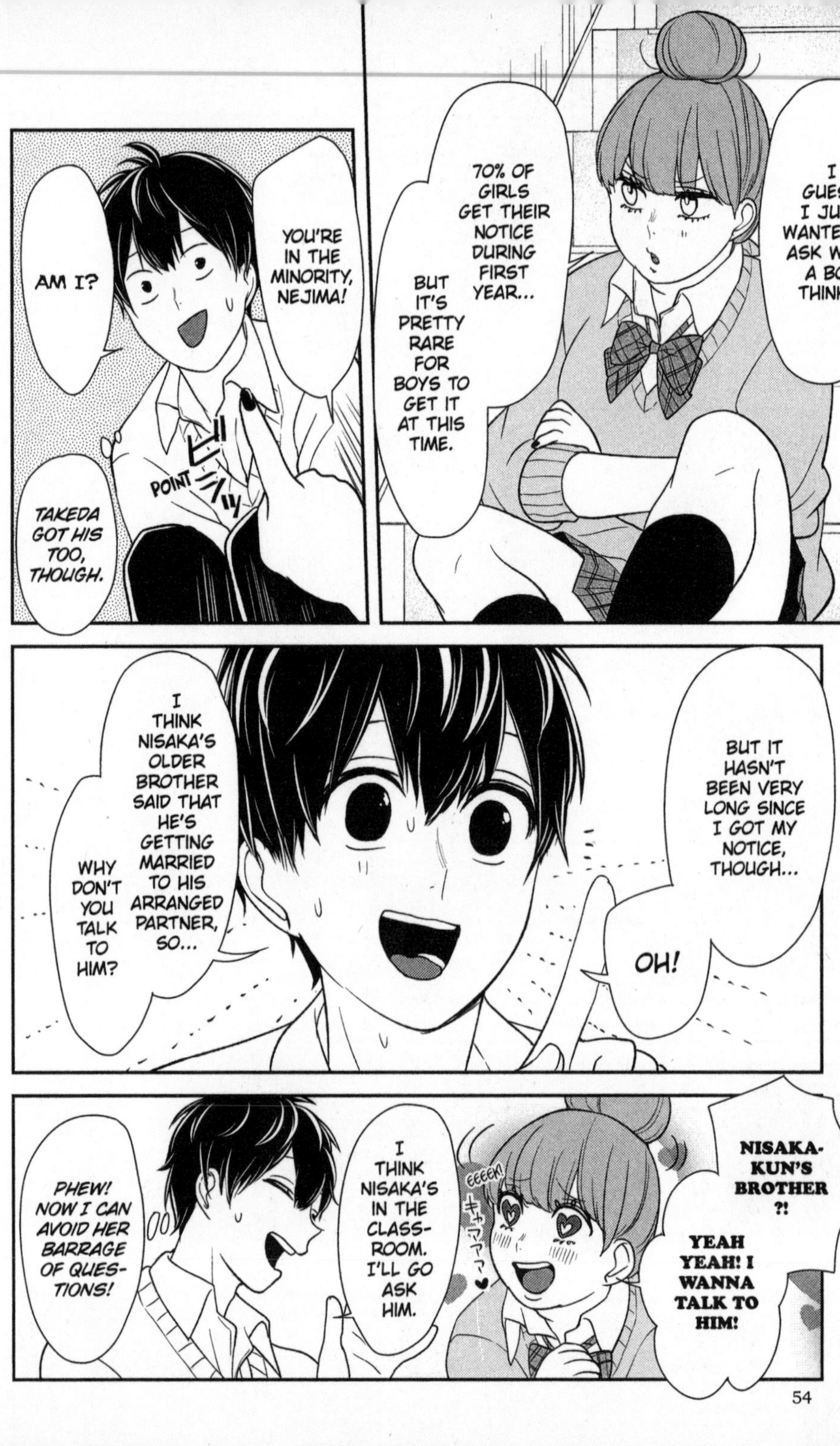
I GUESS I JUST WANTED TO ASK WHAT A BOY THINKS.
70% OF GIRLS GET THEIR NOTICE DURING FIRST YEAR...
BUT IT'S PRETTY RARE FOR BOYS TO GET IT AT THIS TIME.
YOU'RE IN THE MINORITY, NEJIMA!
POINT
AM I?
TAKEDA GOT HIS TOO, THOUGH.
BUT IT HASN'T BEEN VERY LONG SINCE I GOT MY NOTICE, THOUGH...
OH!
I THINK NISAKA'S OLDER BROTHER SAID THAT HE'S GETTING MARRIED TO HIS ARRANGED PARTNER, SO...
WHY DON'T YOU TALK TO HIM?
NISAKA-KUN'S BROTHER?!
YEAH YEAH! I WANNA TALK TO HIM!
EEEEK!
I THINK NISAKA'S IN THE CLASSROOM. I'LL GO ASK HIM.
PHEW! NOW I CAN AVOID HER BARRAGE OF QUESTIONS!

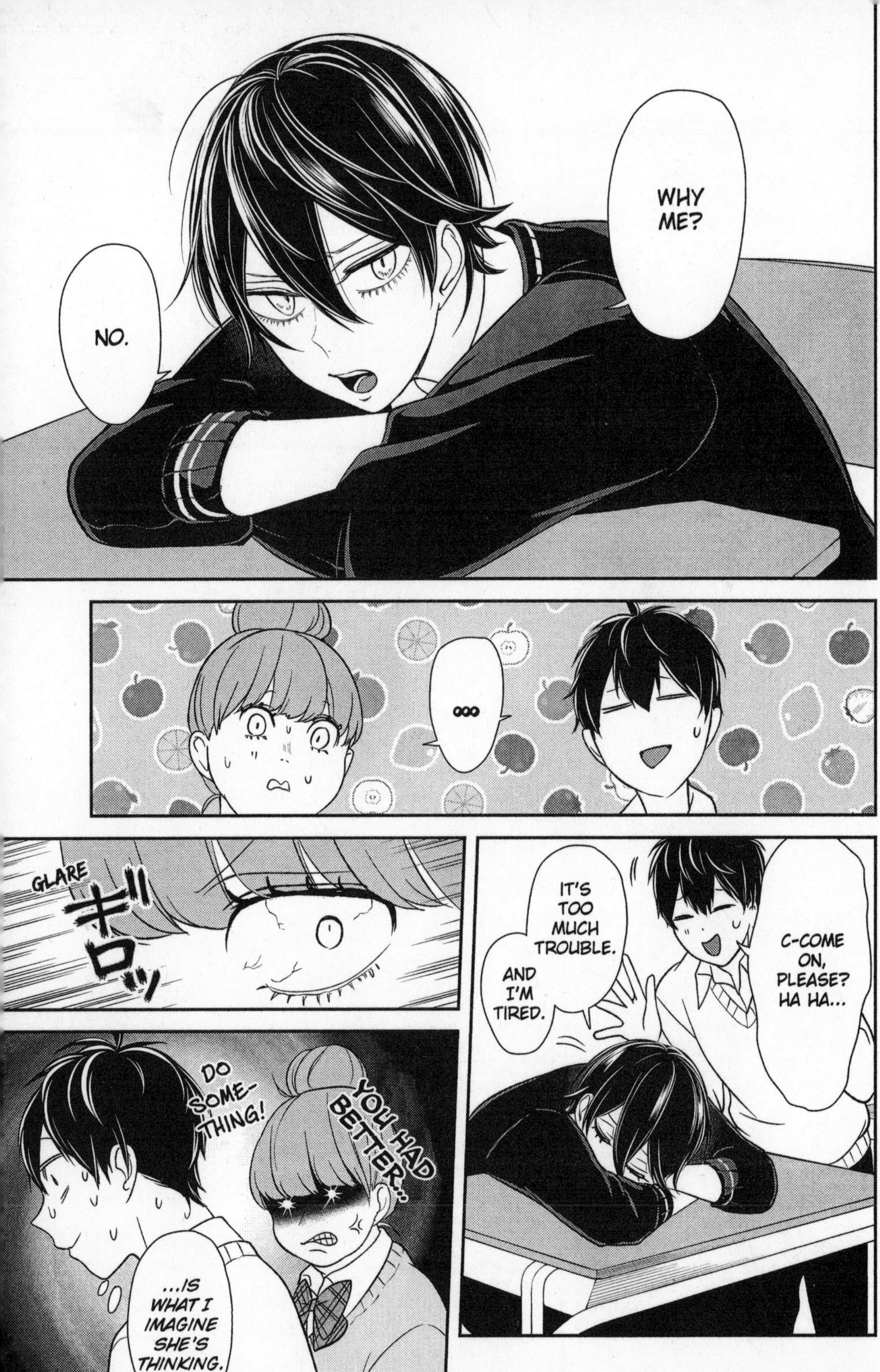
WHY ME?
NO.
...
C-COME ON, PLEASE? HA HA...
IT'S TOO MUCH TROUBLE.
AND I'M TIRED.
GLARE
YOU HAD BETTER...
DO SOME-THING!
...IS WHAT I IMAGINE SHE'S THINKING.

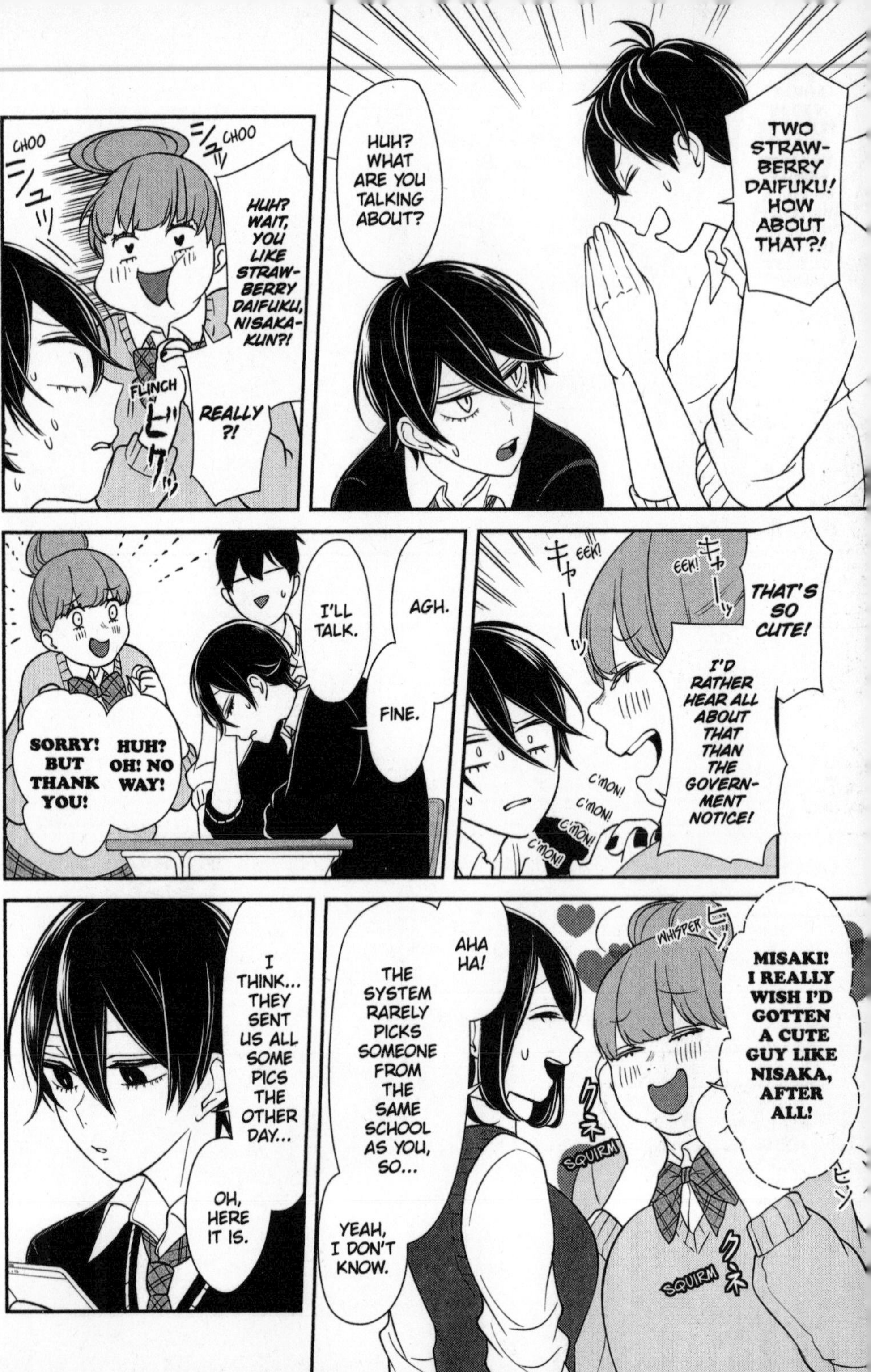
TWO STRAWBERRY DAIFUKU! HOW ABOUT THAT?!
HUH? WHAT ARE YOU TALKING ABOUT?
CHOO
CHOO
HUH? WAIT, YOU LIKE STRAWBERRY DAIFUKU, NISAKA-KUN?!
FLINCH
REALLY?!
EEK!
EEK!
THAT'S SO CUTE!
I'D RATHER HEAR ALL ABOUT THAT THAN THE GOVERNMENT NOTICE!
C'MON!
C'MON!
C'MON!
C'MON!
AGH.
FINE.
I'LL TALK.
HUH? OH! NO WAY!
SORRY! BUT THANK YOU!
WHISPER
MISAKI! I REALLY WISH I'D GOTTEN A CUTE GUY LIKE NISAKA, AFTER ALL!
SQUIRM
SQUIRM
AHA HA!
THE SYSTEM RARELY PICKS SOMEONE FROM THE SAME SCHOOL AS YOU, SO...
YEAH, I DON'T KNOW.
I THINK... THEY SENT US ALL SOME PICS THE OTHER DAY...
OH, HERE IT IS.

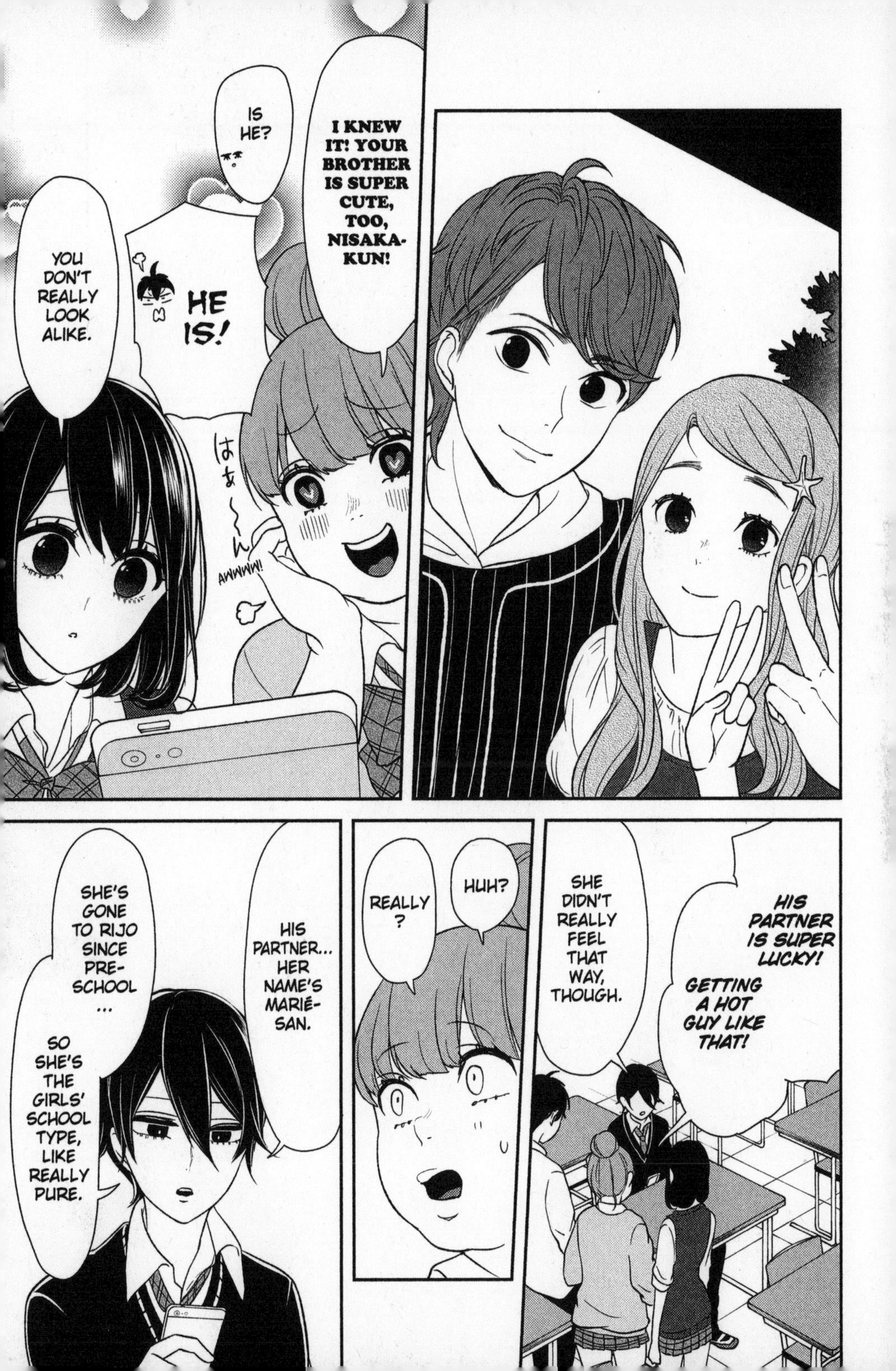
I KNEW IT! YOUR BROTHER IS SUPER CUTE, TOO, NISAKA-KUN!
IS HE?
HE IS!
YOU DON'T REALLY LOOK ALIKE.
はぁ〜ん
AWWWW!!
HIS PARTNER IS SUPER LUCKY!
GETTING A HOT GUY LIKE THAT!
SHE DIDN'T REALLY FEEL THAT WAY, THOUGH.
HUH?
REALLY?
HIS PARTNER... HER NAME'S MARIÉ-SAN.
SHE'S GONE TO RIJO SINCE PRE-SCHOOL...
SO SHE'S THE GIRLS' SCHOOL TYPE, LIKE REALLY PURE.

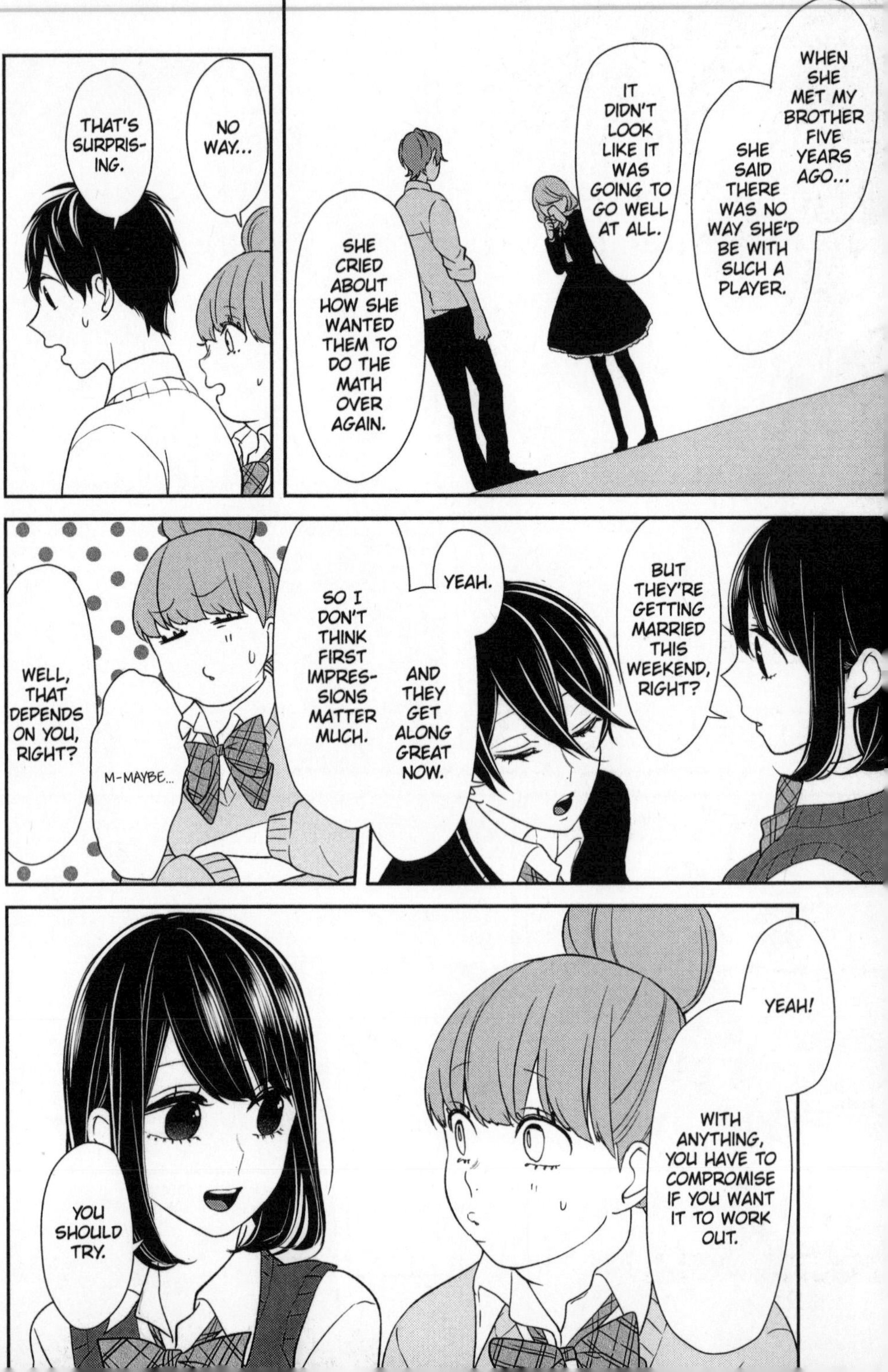
WHEN SHE MET MY BROTHER FIVE YEARS AGO...
SHE SAID THERE WAS NO WAY SHE'D BE WITH SUCH A PLAYER.
IT DIDN'T LOOK LIKE IT WAS GOING TO GO WELL AT ALL.
SHE CRIED ABOUT HOW SHE WANTED THEM TO DO THE MATH OVER AGAIN.
NO WAY...
THAT'S SURPRIS-ING.
BUT THEY'RE GETTING MARRIED THIS WEEKEND, RIGHT?
YEAH.
AND THEY GET ALONG GREAT NOW.
SO I DON'T THINK FIRST IMPRES-SIONS MATTER MUCH.
WELL, THAT DEPENDS ON YOU, RIGHT?
M-MAYBE...
YEAH!
WITH ANYTHING, YOU HAVE TO COMPROMISE IF YOU WANT IT TO WORK OUT.
YOU SHOULD TRY.

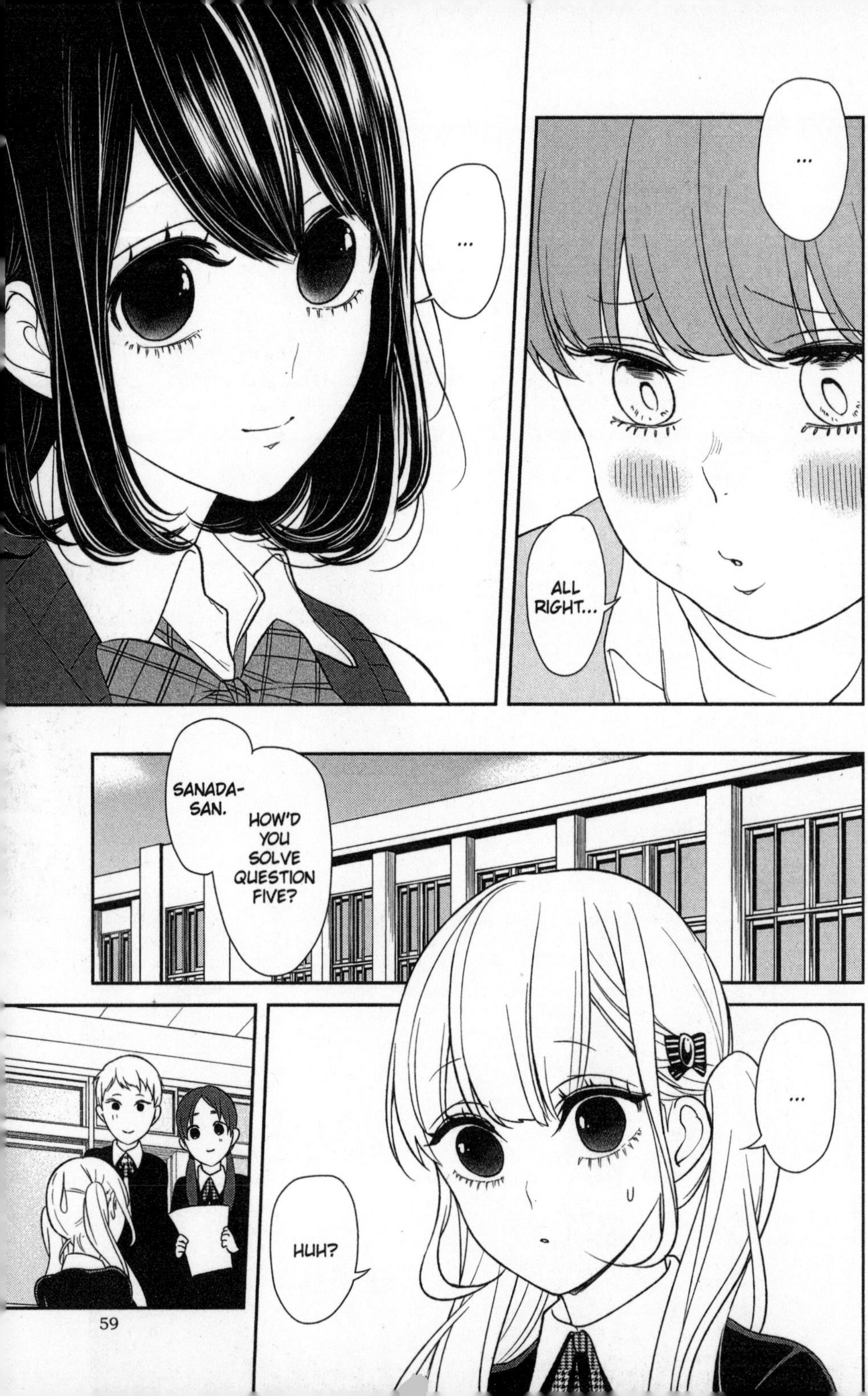
...
ALL RIGHT...
...
SANADA-SAN.
HOW'D YOU SOLVE QUESTION FIVE?
...
HUH?

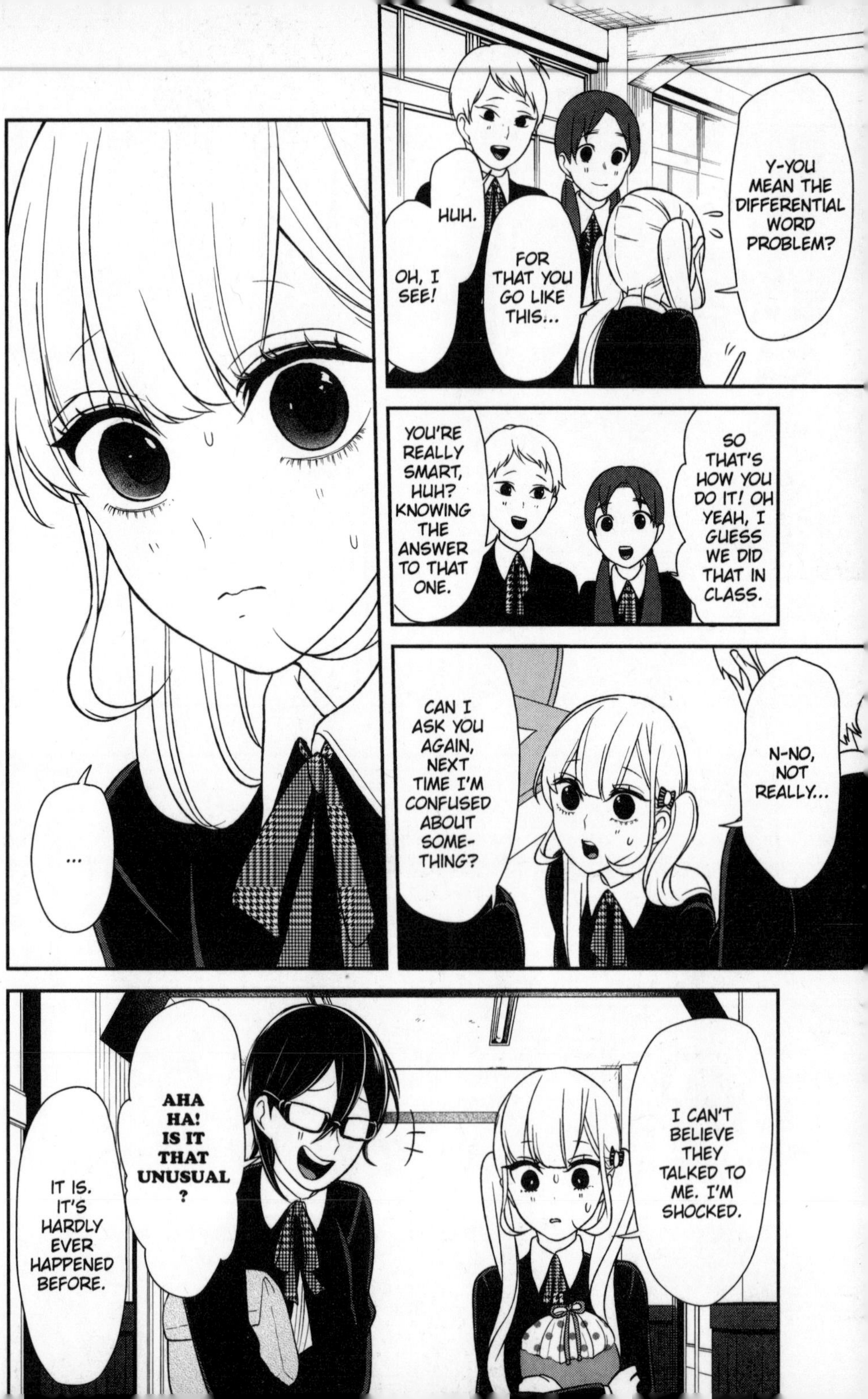
Y-YOU MEAN THE DIFFERENTIAL WORD PROBLEM?
FOR THAT YOU GO LIKE THIS...
HUH.
OH, I SEE!
SO THAT'S HOW YOU DO IT! OH YEAH, I GUESS WE DID THAT IN CLASS.
YOU'RE REALLY SMART, HUH? KNOWING THE ANSWER TO THAT ONE.
N-NO, NOT REALLY...
CAN I ASK YOU AGAIN, NEXT TIME I'M CONFUSED ABOUT SOMETHING?
...
I CAN'T BELIEVE THEY TALKED TO ME. I'M SHOCKED.
AHA HA! IS IT THAT UNUSUAL?
IT IS. IT'S HARDLY EVER HAPPENED BEFORE.

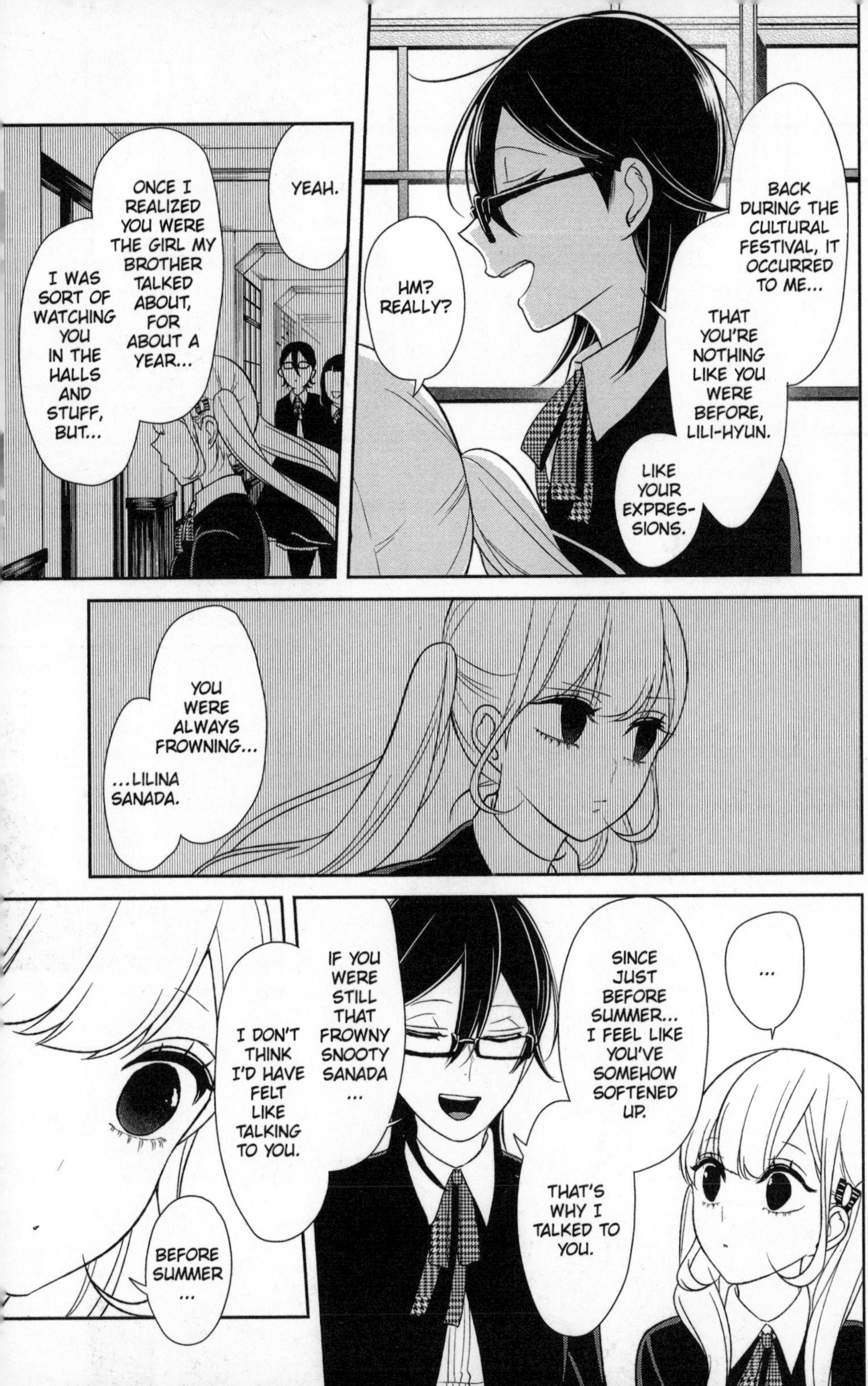
BACK DURING THE CULTURAL FESTIVAL, IT OCCURRED TO ME...
THAT YOU'RE NOTHING LIKE YOU WERE BEFORE, LILI-HYUN.
LIKE YOUR EXPRESSIONS.
HM? REALLY?
YEAH.
ONCE I REALIZED YOU WERE THE GIRL MY BROTHER TALKED ABOUT, FOR ABOUT A YEAR...
I WAS SORT OF WATCHING YOU IN THE HALLS AND STUFF, BUT...
YOU WERE ALWAYS FROWNING...
...LILINA SANADA.
...
SINCE JUST BEFORE SUMMER... I FEEL LIKE YOU'VE SOMEHOW SOFTENED UP.
THAT'S WHY I TALKED TO YOU.
IF YOU WERE STILL THAT FROWNY SNOOTY SANADA...
I DON'T THINK I'D HAVE FELT LIKE TALKING TO YOU.
BEFORE SUMMER...

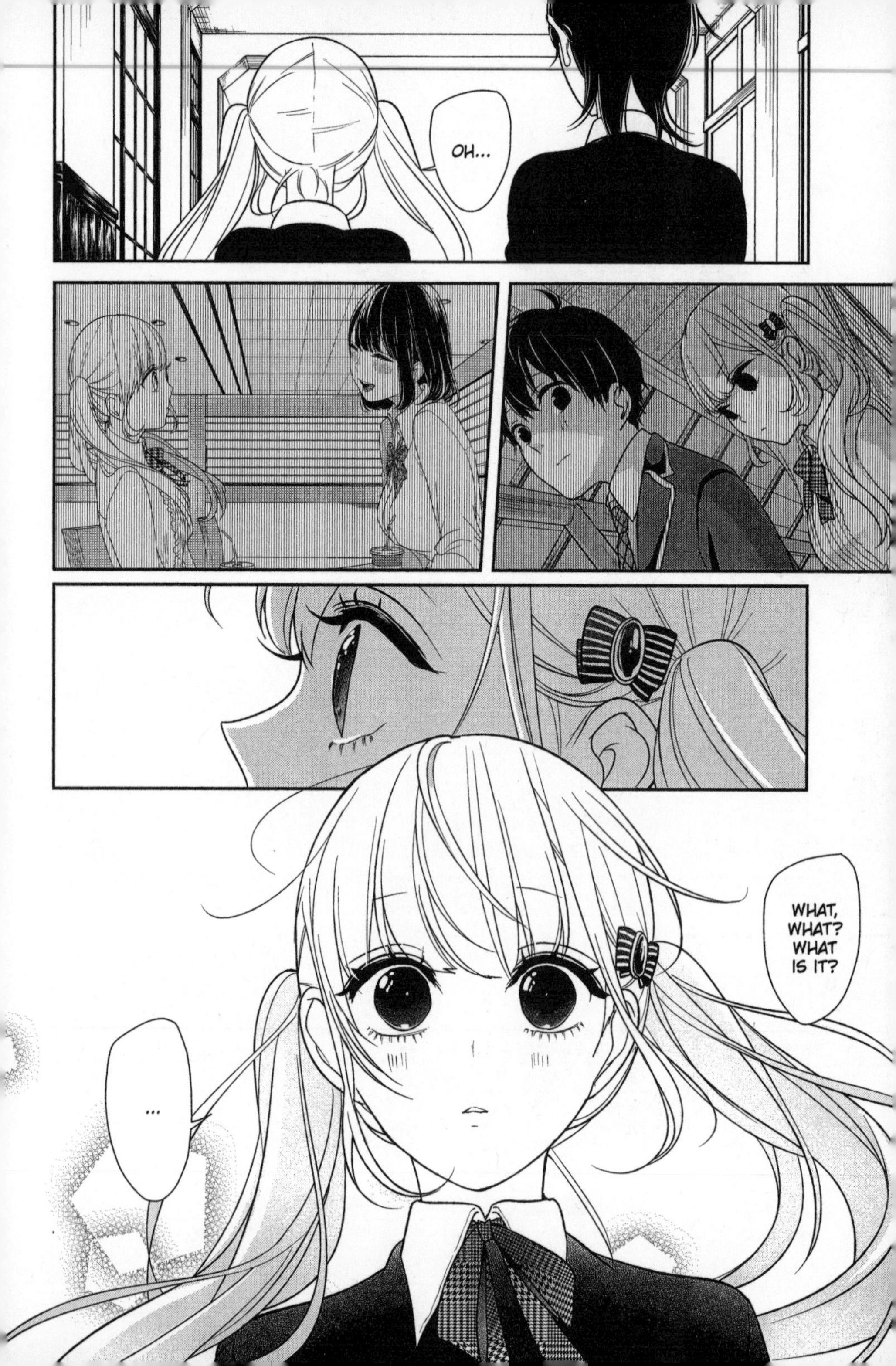
OH...
WHAT, WHAT? WHAT IS IT?
...

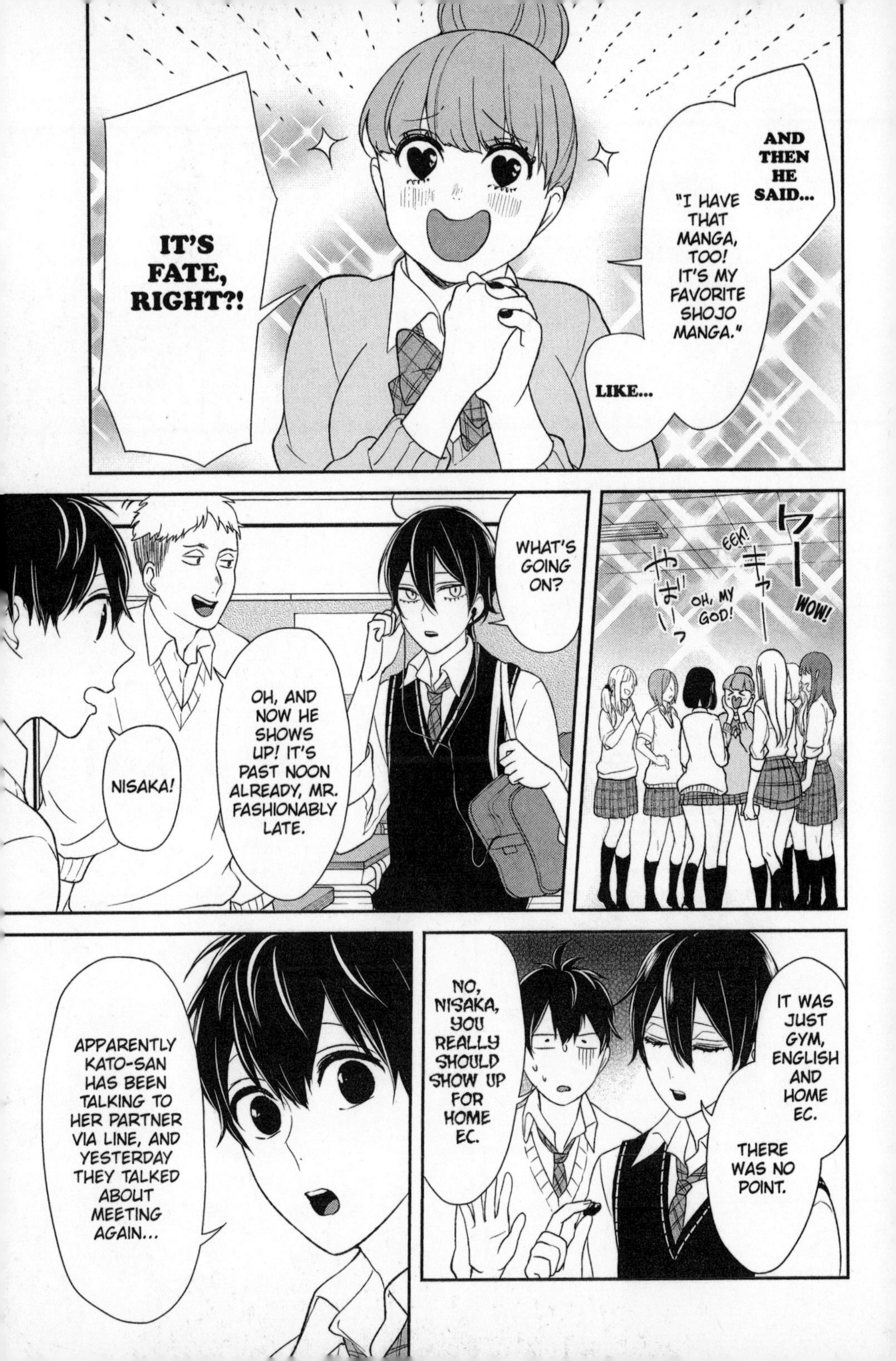
AND THEN HE SAID...
"I HAVE THAT MANGA, TOO! IT'S MY FAVORITE SHOJO MANGA."
LIKE...
IT'S FATE, RIGHT?!
ワー
WOW!
キャー
EEK!
やばいっ
OH, MY GOD!
WHAT'S GOING ON?
OH, AND NOW HE SHOWS UP! IT'S PAST NOON ALREADY, MR. FASHIONABLY LATE.
NISAKA!
IT WAS JUST GYM, ENGLISH AND HOME EC.
THERE WAS NO POINT.
NO, NISAKA, YOU REALLY SHOULD SHOW UP FOR HOME EC.
APPARENTLY KATO-SAN HAS BEEN TALKING TO HER PARTNER VIA LINE, AND YESTERDAY THEY TALKED ABOUT MEETING AGAIN...

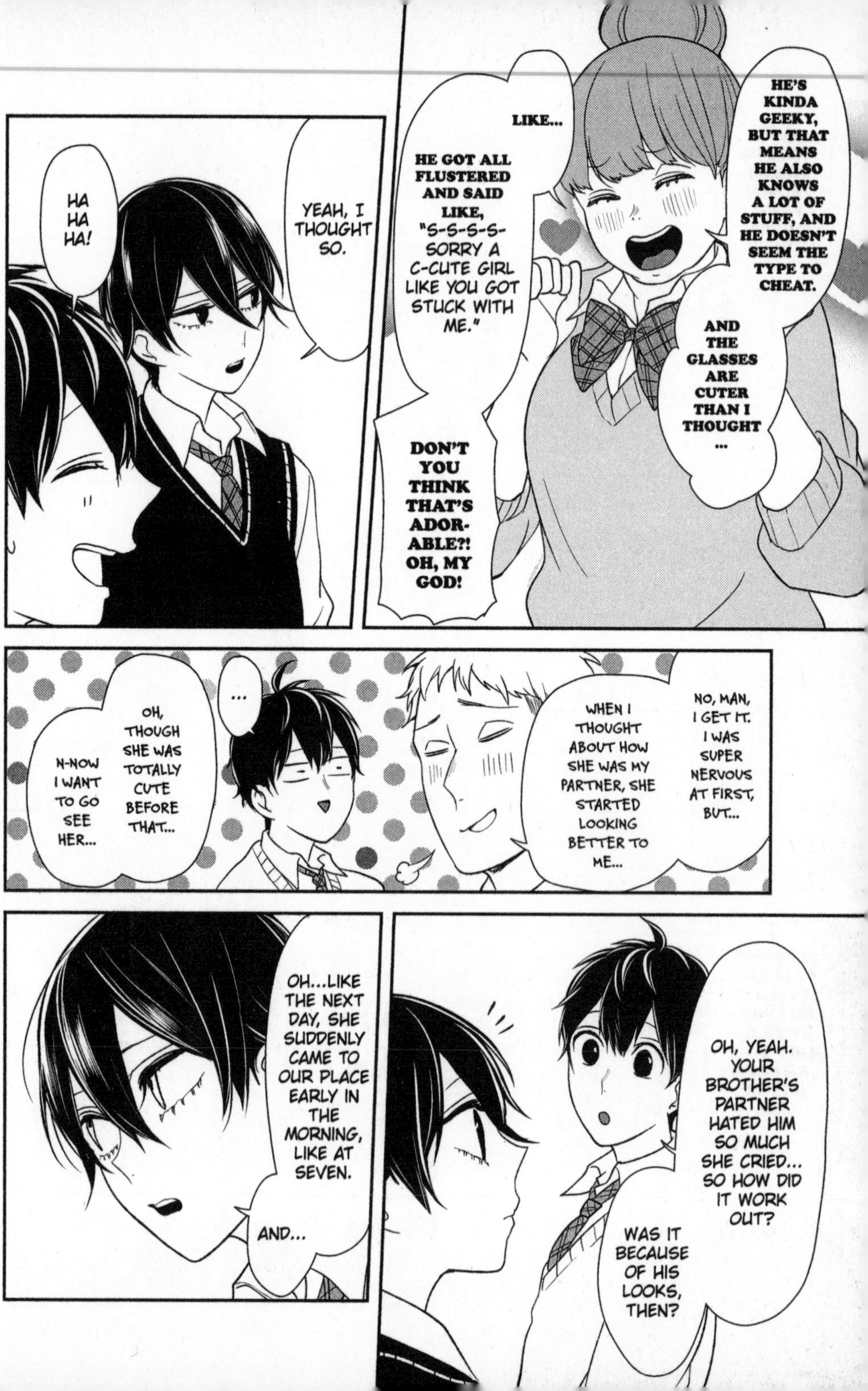
HE'S KINDA GEEKY, BUT THAT MEANS HE ALSO KNOWS A LOT OF STUFF, AND HE DOESN'T SEEM THE TYPE TO CHEAT.
AND THE GLASSES ARE CUTER THAN I THOUGHT...
LIKE...
HE GOT ALL FLUSTERED AND SAID LIKE, "S-S-S-S-SORRY A C-CUTE GIRL LIKE YOU GOT STUCK WITH ME."
DON'T YOU THINK THAT'S ADOR-ABLE?! OH, MY GOD!
YEAH, I THOUGHT SO.
HA HA HA!
NO, MAN, I GET IT. I WAS SUPER NERVOUS AT FIRST, BUT...
WHEN I THOUGHT ABOUT HOW SHE WAS MY PARTNER, SHE STARTED LOOKING BETTER TO ME...
...
OH, THOUGH SHE WAS TOTALLY CUTE BEFORE THAT...
N-NOW I WANT TO GO SEE HER...
OH, YEAH. YOUR BROTHER'S PARTNER HATED HIM SO MUCH SHE CRIED... SO HOW DID IT WORK OUT?
WAS IT BECAUSE OF HIS LOOKS, THEN?
OH...LIKE THE NEXT DAY, SHE SUDDENLY CAME TO OUR PLACE EARLY IN THE MORNING, LIKE AT SEVEN.
AND...

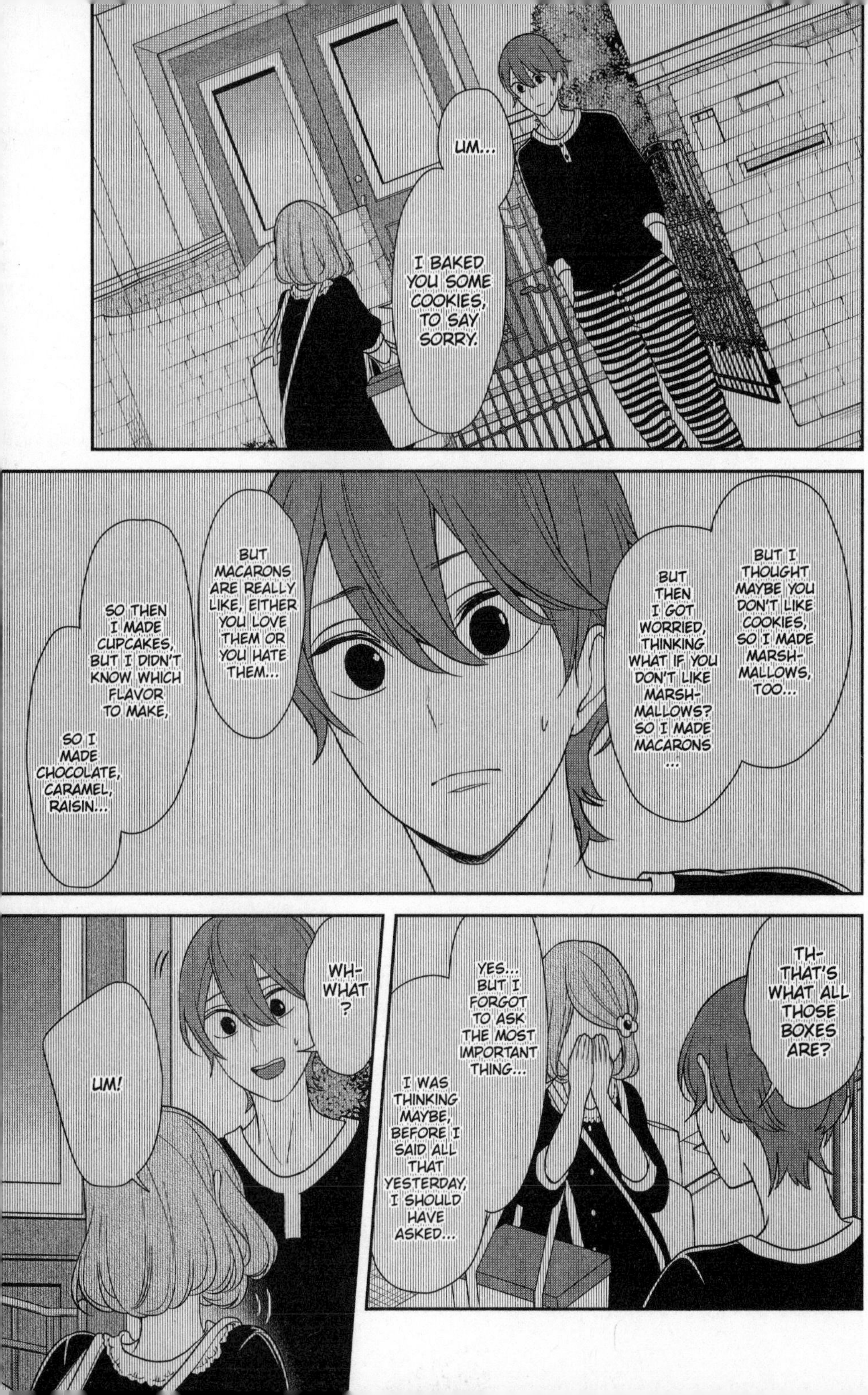
UM...
I BAKED YOU SOME COOKIES, TO SAY SORRY.
BUT I THOUGHT MAYBE YOU DON'T LIKE COOKIES, SO I MADE MARSH-MALLOWS, TOO...
BUT THEN I GOT WORRIED, THINKING WHAT IF YOU DON'T LIKE MARSH-MALLOWS? SO I MADE MACARONS ...
BUT MACARONS ARE REALLY LIKE, EITHER YOU LOVE THEM OR YOU HATE THEM...
SO THEN I MADE CUPCAKES, BUT I DIDN'T KNOW WHICH FLAVOR TO MAKE,
SO I MADE CHOCOLATE, CARAMEL, RAISIN...
TH-THAT'S WHAT ALL THOSE BOXES ARE?
YES... BUT I FORGOT TO ASK THE MOST IMPORTANT THING...
I WAS THINKING MAYBE, BEFORE I SAID ALL THAT YESTERDAY, I SHOULD HAVE ASKED...
WH-WHAT?
UM!

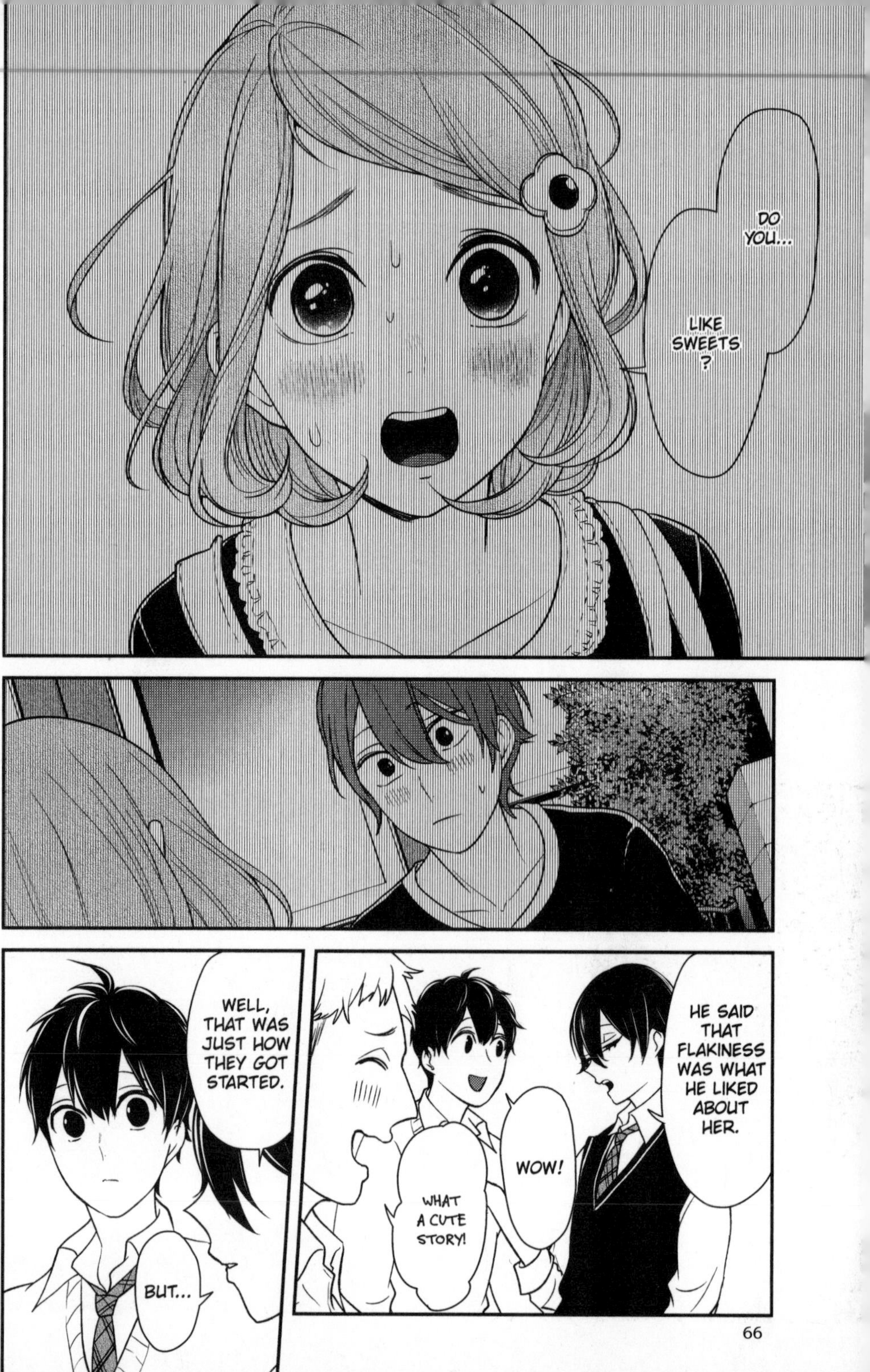
DO YOU...
LIKE SWEETS?
HE SAID THAT FLAKINESS WAS WHAT HE LIKED ABOUT HER.
WOW!
WHAT A CUTE STORY!
WELL, THAT WAS JUST HOW THEY GOT STARTED.
BUT...

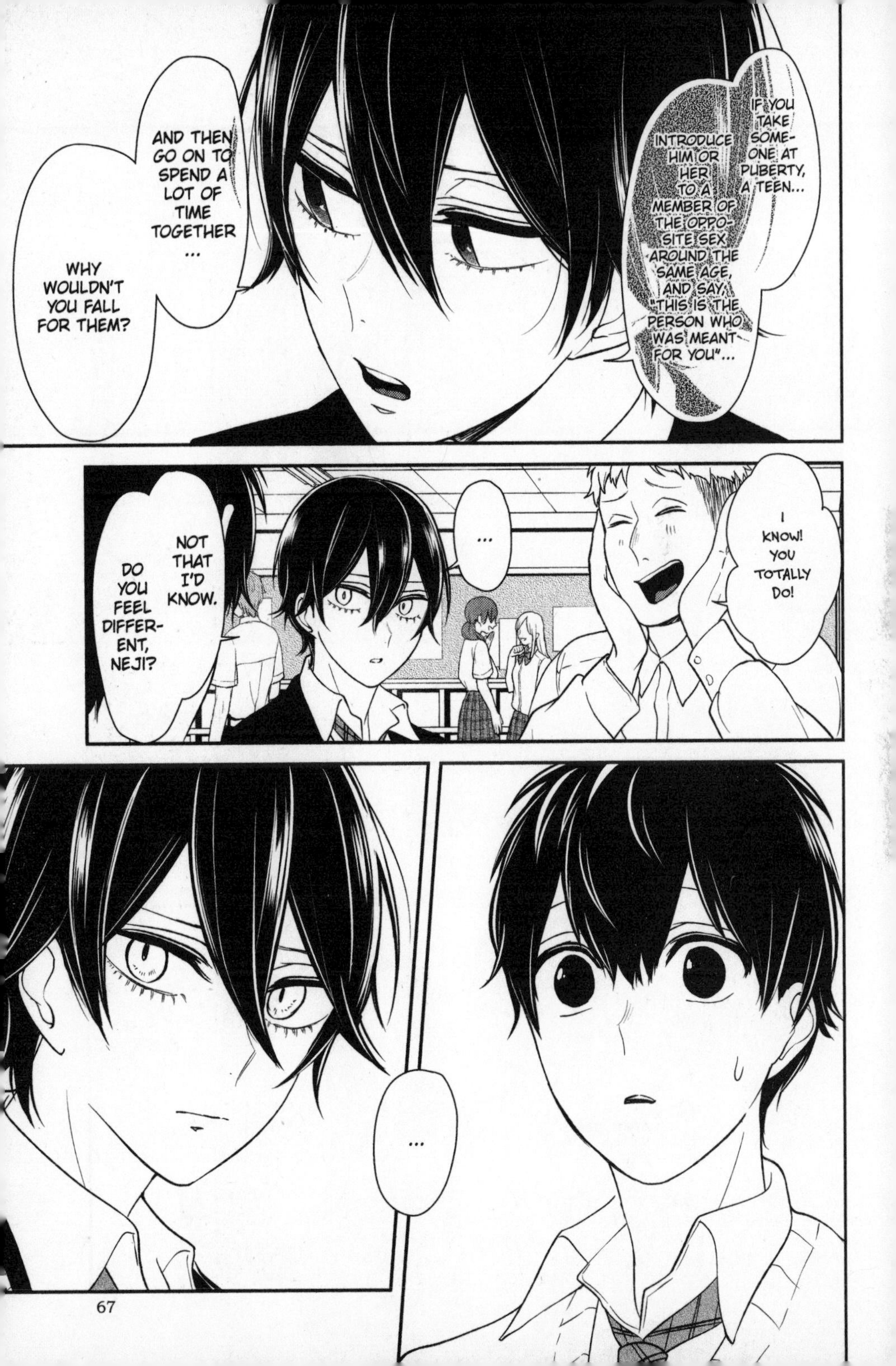
IF YOU TAKE SOME-ONE AT PUBERTY, A TEEN...
INTRODUCE HIM OR HER TO A MEMBER OF THE OPPO-SITE SEX AROUND THE SAME AGE, AND SAY, "THIS IS THE PERSON WHO WAS MEANT FOR YOU"...
AND THEN GO ON TO SPEND A LOT OF TIME TOGETHER ...
WHY WOULDN'T YOU FALL FOR THEM?
I KNOW! YOU TOTALLY DO!
...
NOT THAT I'D KNOW.
DO YOU FEEL DIFFER-ENT, NEJI?
...

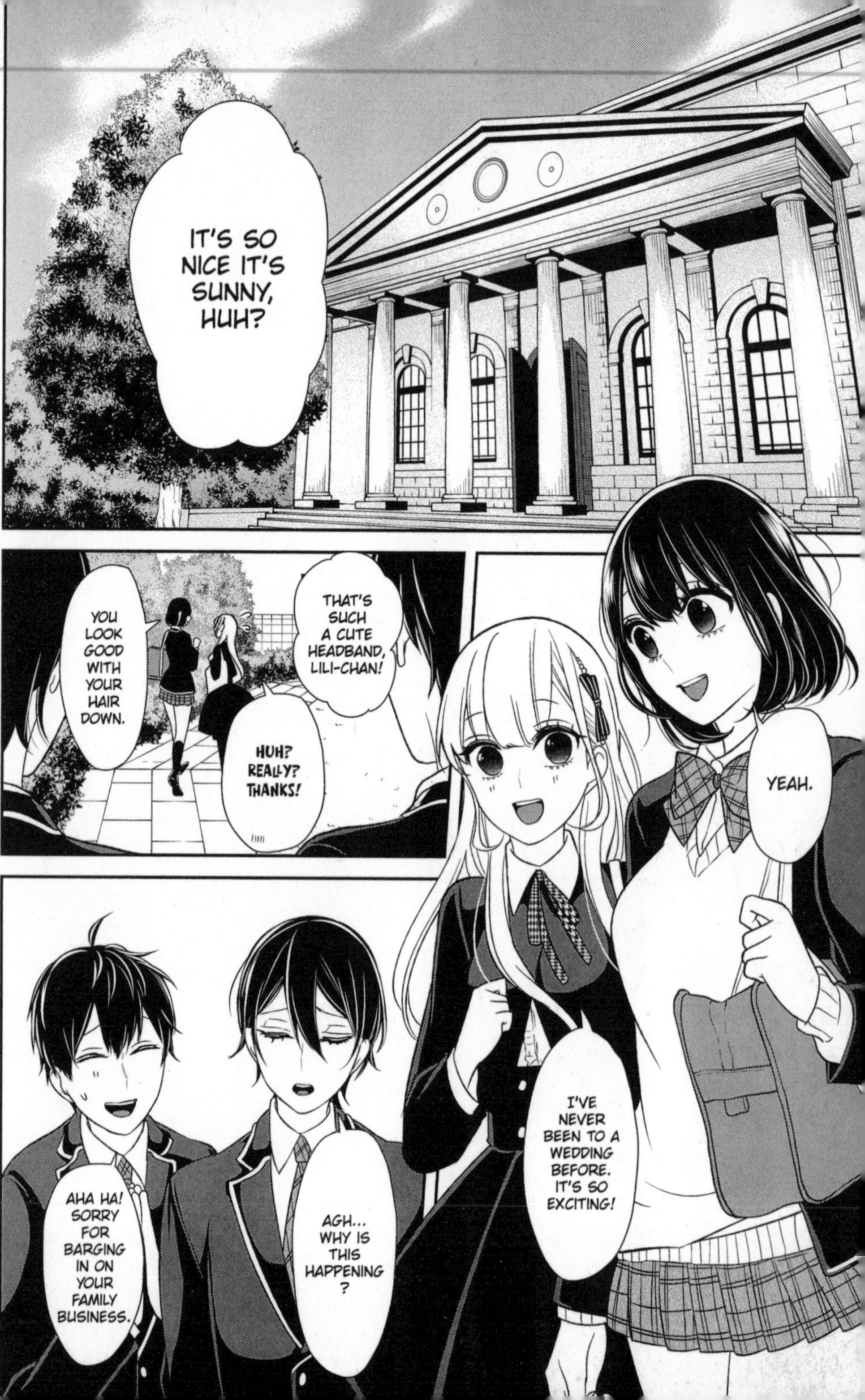
IT'S SO NICE IT'S SUNNY, HUH?
YEAH.
THAT'S SUCH A CUTE HEADBAND, LILI-CHAN!
YOU LOOK GOOD WITH YOUR HAIR DOWN.
HUH? REALLY? THANKS!
I'VE NEVER BEEN TO A WEDDING BEFORE. IT'S SO EXCITING!
AGH... WHY IS THIS HAPPENING?
AHA HA! SORRY FOR BARGING IN ON YOUR FAMILY BUSINESS.

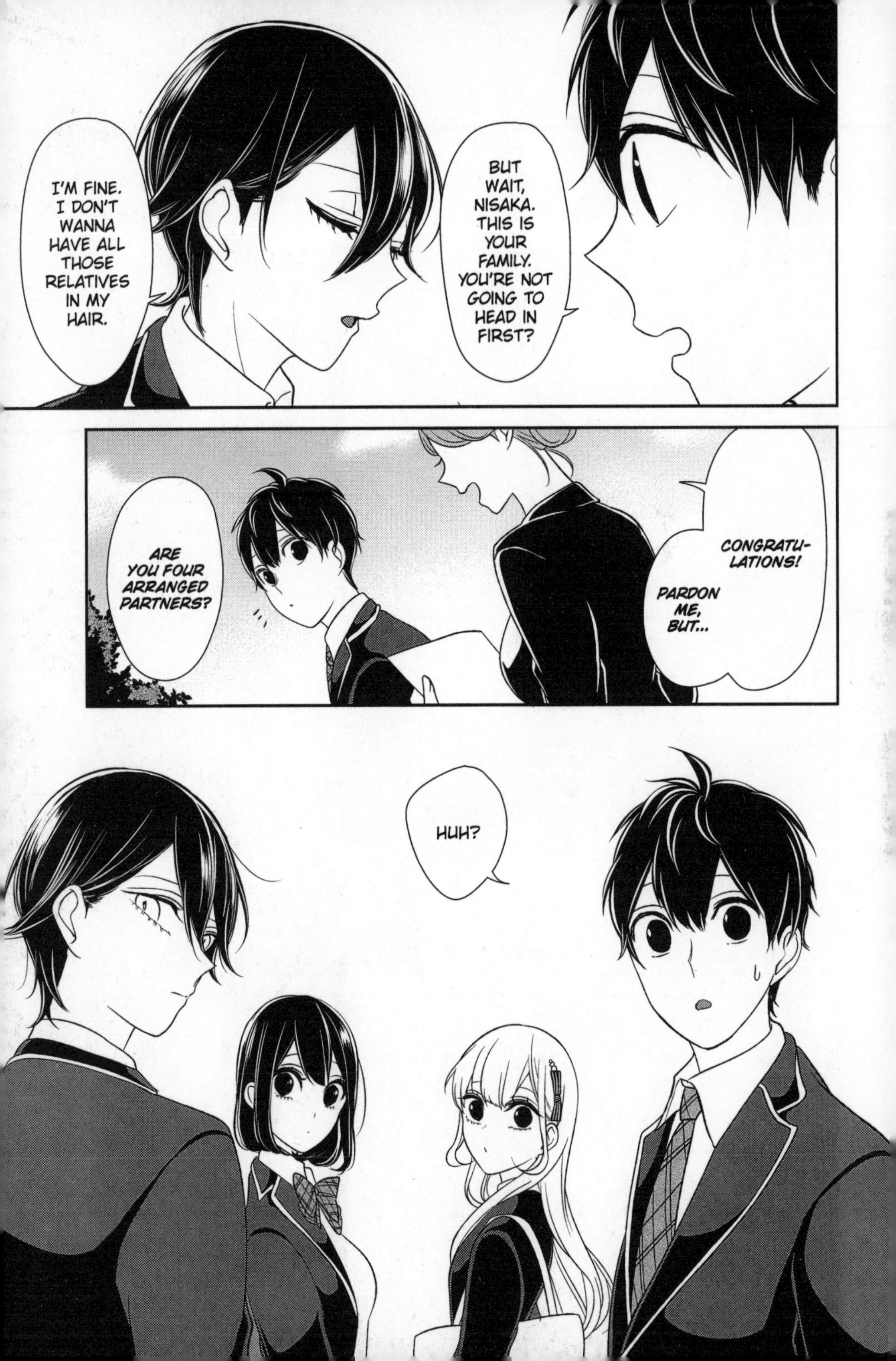
BUT WAIT, NISAKA. THIS IS YOUR FAMILY. YOU'RE NOT GOING TO HEAD IN FIRST?
I'M FINE. I DON'T WANNA HAVE ALL THOSE RELATIVES IN MY HAIR.
CONGRATULATIONS!
PARDON ME, BUT...
ARE YOU FOUR ARRANGED PARTNERS?
HUH?

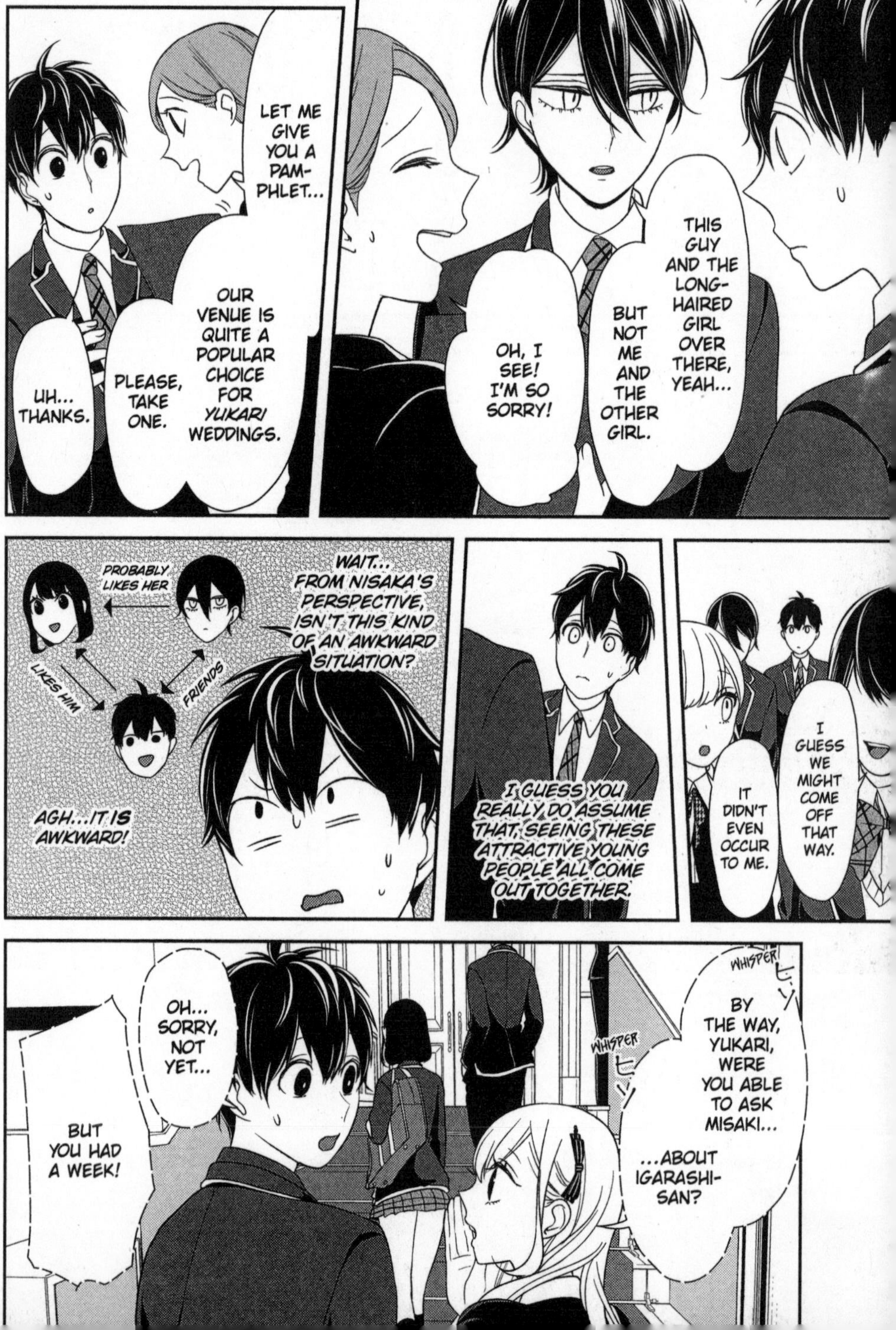
THIS GUY AND THE LONG-HAIRED GIRL OVER THERE, YEAH...
BUT NOT ME AND THE OTHER GIRL.
OH, I SEE! I'M SO SORRY!
LET ME GIVE YOU A PAMPHLET...
OUR VENUE IS QUITE A POPULAR CHOICE FOR *YUKARI* WEDDINGS.
PLEASE, TAKE ONE.
UH... THANKS.
I GUESS WE MIGHT COME OFF THAT WAY.
IT DIDN'T EVEN OCCUR TO ME.
I GUESS YOU REALLY DO ASSUME THAT, SEEING THESE ATTRACTIVE YOUNG PEOPLE ALL COME OUT TOGETHER.
WAIT... FROM NISAKA'S PERSPECTIVE, ISN'T THIS KIND OF AN AWKWARD SITUATION?
PROBABLY LIKES HER
LIKES HIM
FRIENDS
AGH...IT **IS** AWKWARD!
WHISPER
WHISPER
BY THE WAY, YUKARI, WERE YOU ABLE TO ASK MISAKI...
...ABOUT IGARASHI-SAN?
OH... SORRY, NOT YET...
BUT YOU HAD A WEEK!

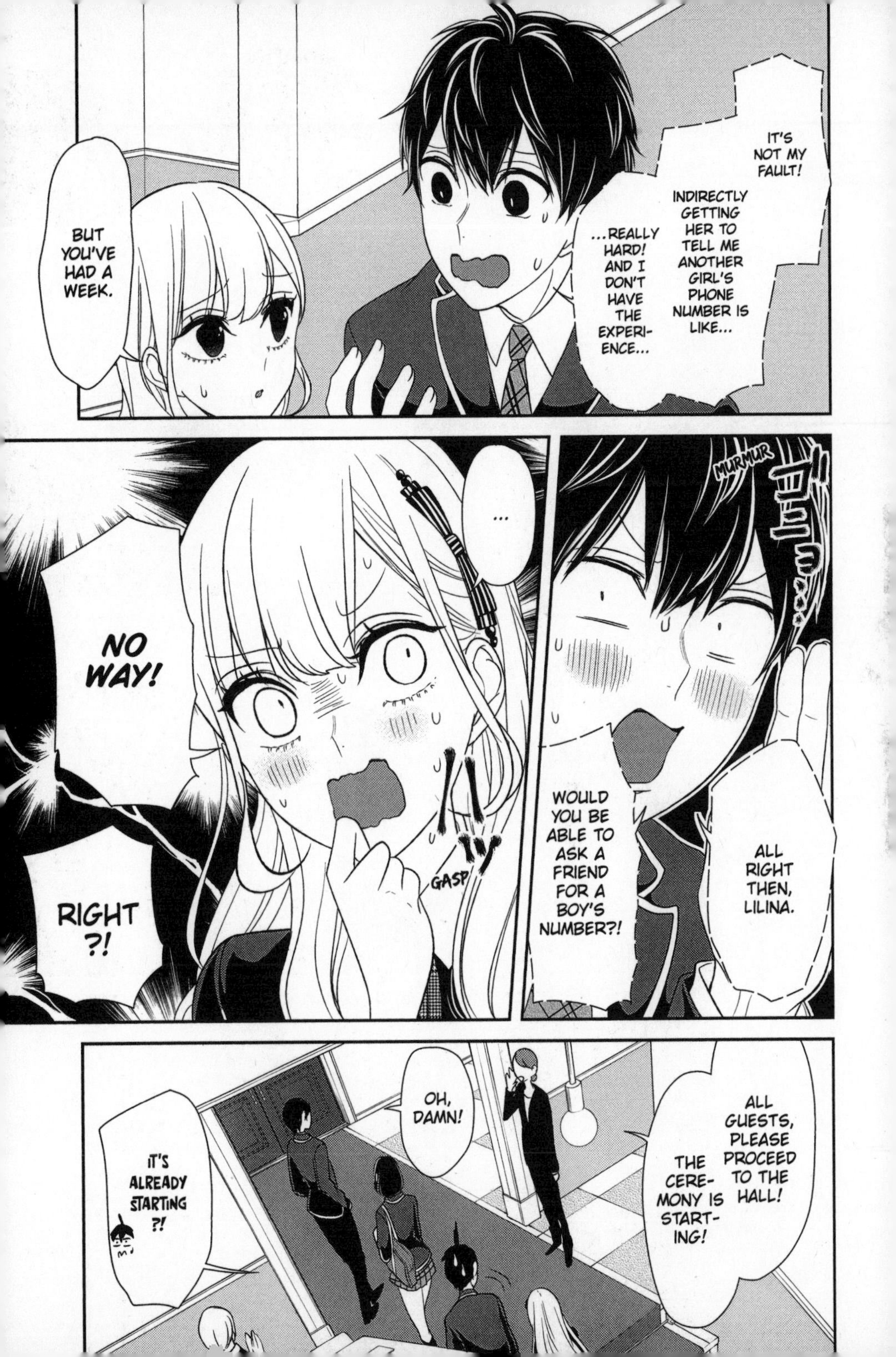
IT'S NOT MY FAULT!
INDIRECTLY GETTING HER TO TELL ME ANOTHER GIRL'S PHONE NUMBER IS LIKE...
...REALLY HARD! AND I DON'T HAVE THE EXPERI- ENCE...
BUT YOU'VE HAD A WEEK.
MURMUR
ALL RIGHT THEN, LILINA.
WOULD YOU BE ABLE TO ASK A FRIEND FOR A BOY'S NUMBER?!
...
GASP
NO WAY!
RIGHT ?!
ALL GUESTS, PLEASE PROCEED TO THE HALL!
THE CERE- MONY IS START- ING!
OH, DAMN!
IT'S ALREADY STARTING ?!

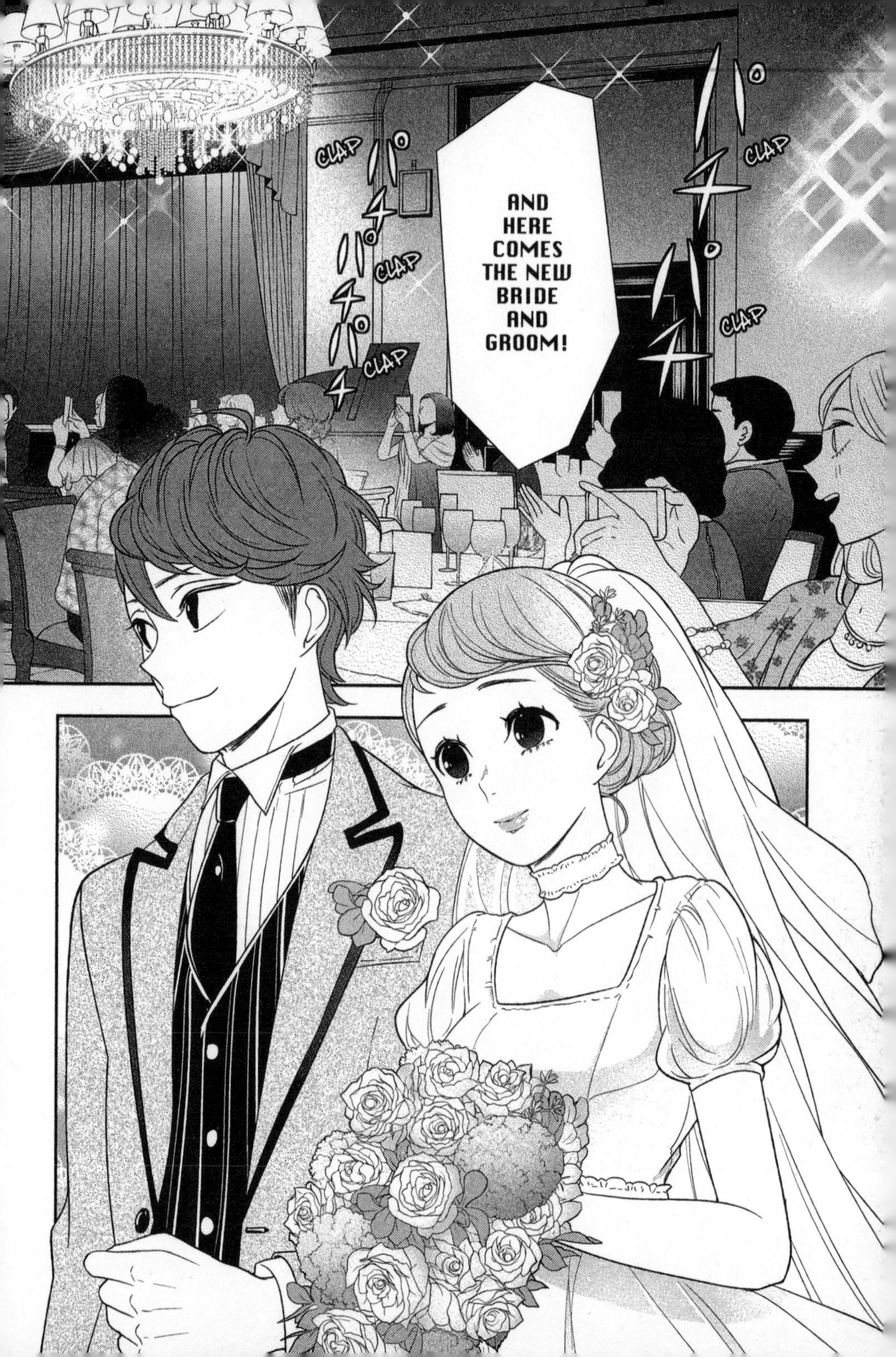
CLAP
CLAP
AND HERE COMES THE NEW BRIDE AND GROOM!
CLAP
CLAP
CLAP
CLAP

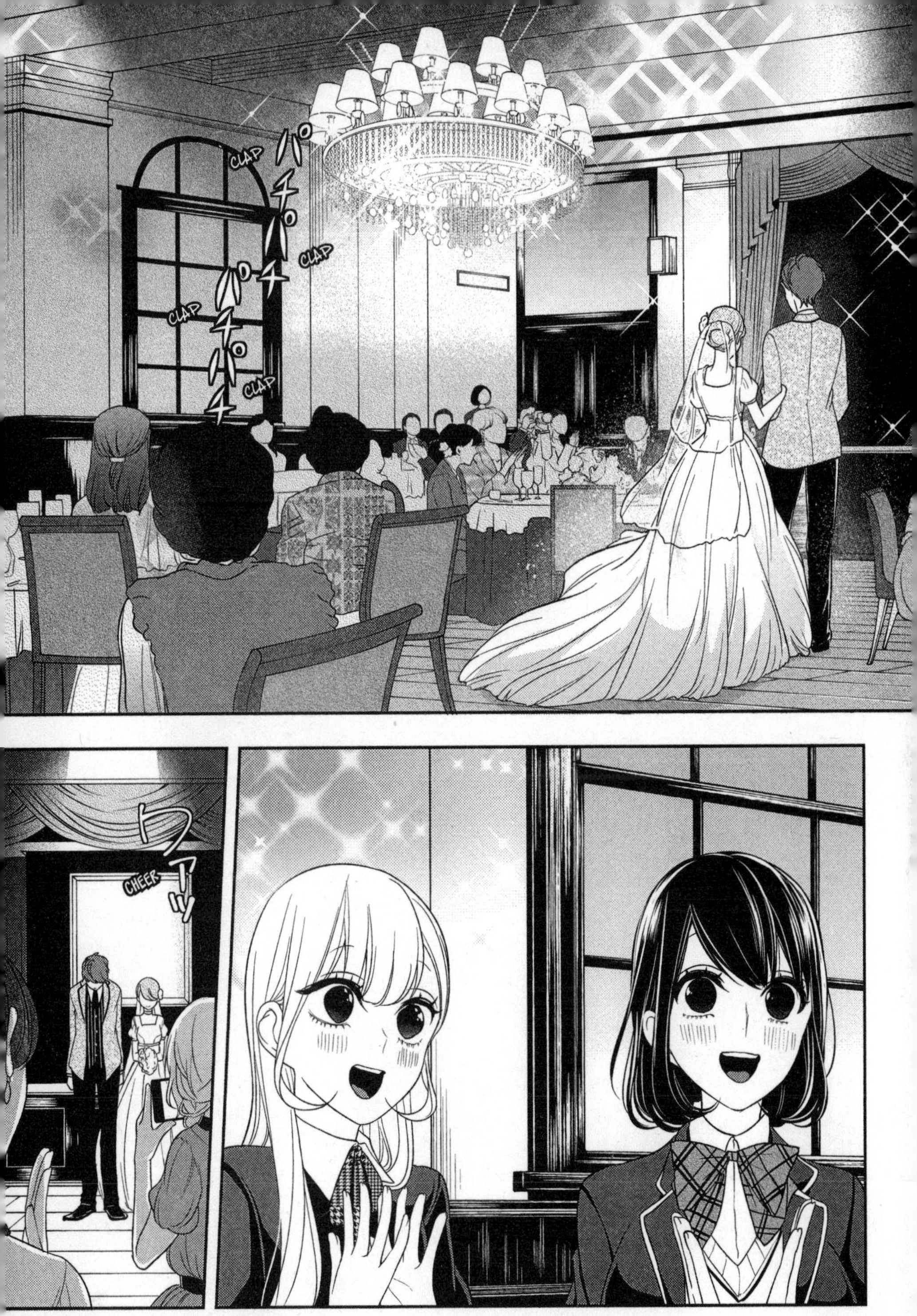
パチパチ
CLAP
パチパチ
CLAP
CLAP
CLAP
ワァッ
CHEER

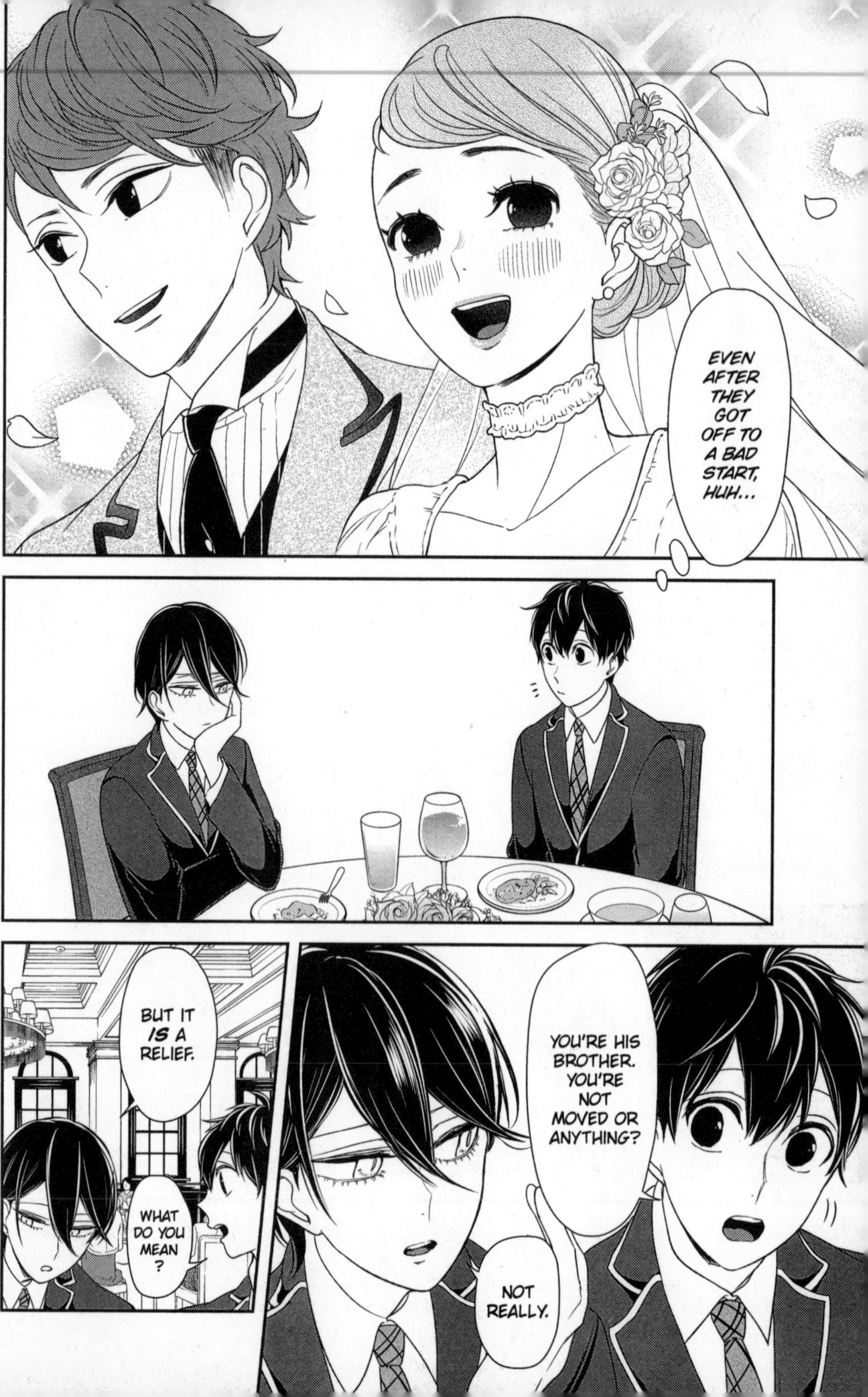
EVEN AFTER THEY GOT OFF TO A BAD START, HUH...
YOU'RE HIS BROTHER. YOU'RE NOT MOVED OR ANYTHING?
NOT REALLY.
BUT IT *IS* A RELIEF.
WHAT DO YOU MEAN?

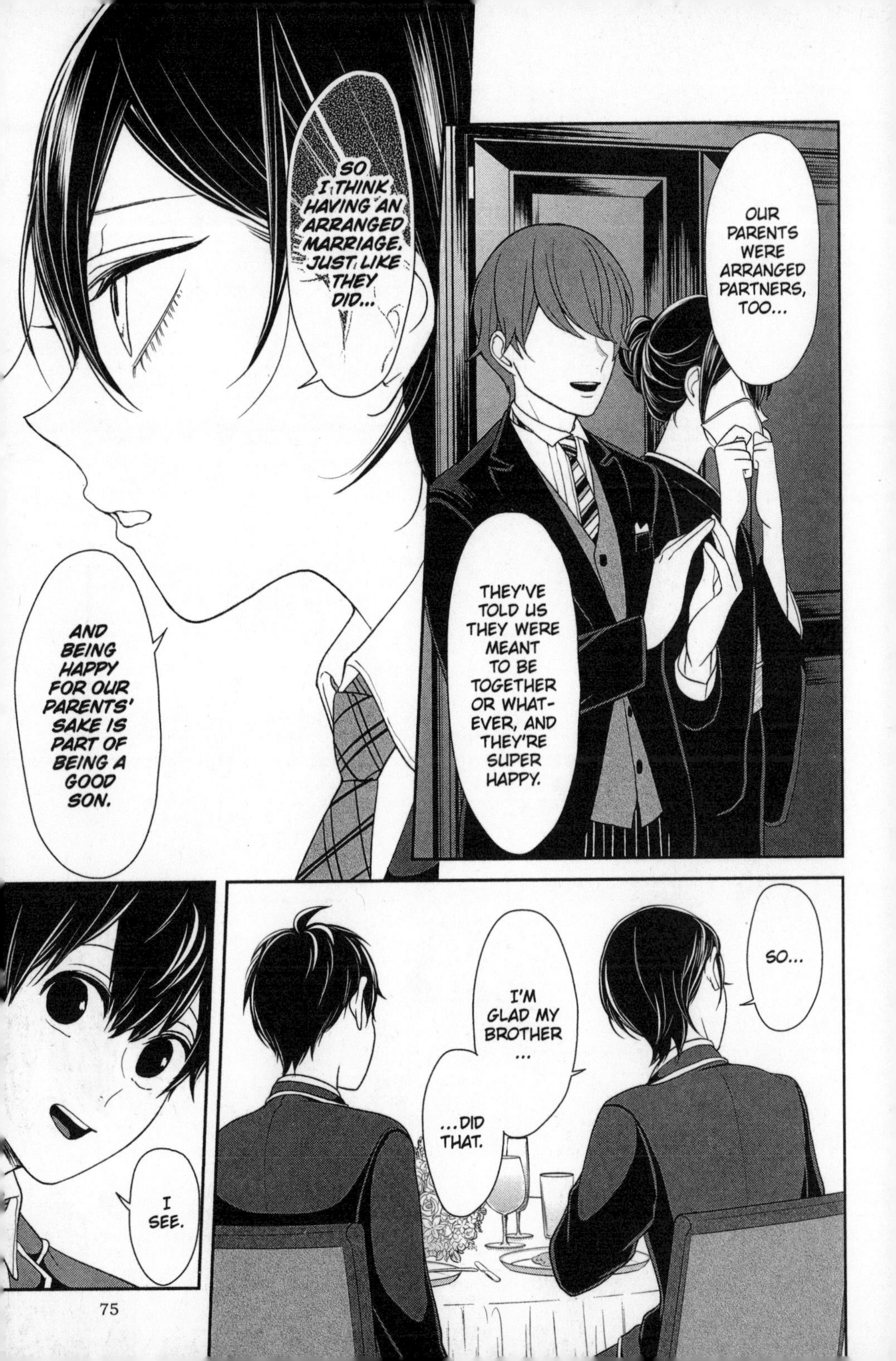
OUR PARENTS WERE ARRANGED PARTNERS, TOO...
THEY'VE TOLD US THEY WERE MEANT TO BE TOGETHER OR WHAT-EVER, AND THEY'RE SUPER HAPPY.
SO I THINK HAVING AN ARRANGED MARRIAGE, JUST LIKE THEY DID...
AND BEING HAPPY FOR OUR PARENTS' SAKE IS PART OF BEING A GOOD SON.
SO...
I'M GLAD MY BROTHER ...
...DID THAT.
I SEE.

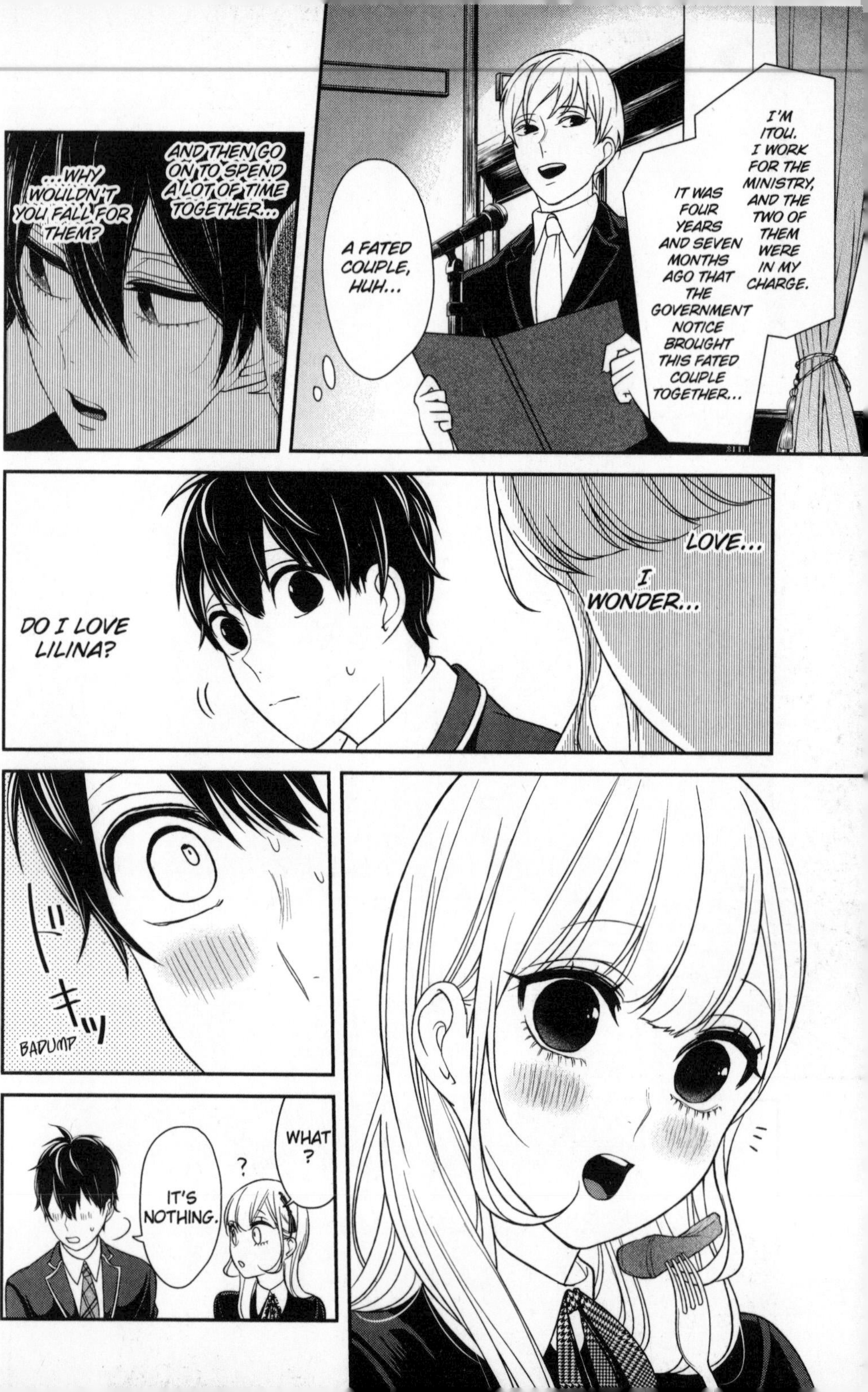
I'M ITOU. I WORK FOR THE MINISTRY, AND THE TWO OF THEM WERE IN MY CHARGE.
IT WAS FOUR YEARS AND SEVEN MONTHS AGO THAT THE GOVERNMENT NOTICE BROUGHT THIS FATED COUPLE TOGETHER...
A FATED COUPLE, HUH...
AND THEN GO ON TO SPEND A LOT OF TIME TOGETHER...
...WHY WOULDN'T YOU FALL FOR THEM?
LOVE...
I WONDER...
DO I LOVE LILINA?
ドキッ
BADUMP
WHAT?
IT'S NOTHING.

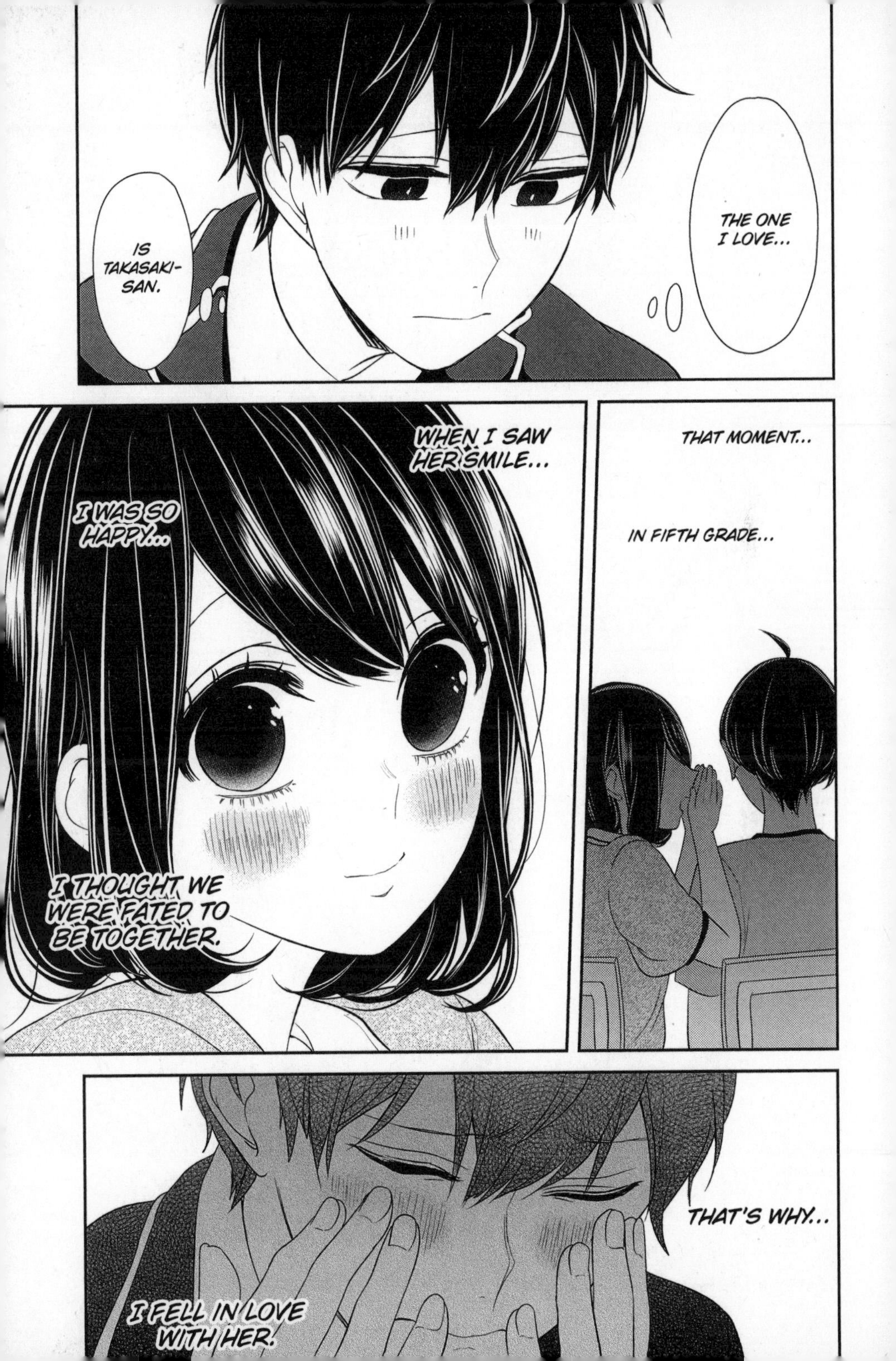
THE ONE I LOVE...
IS TAKASAKI-SAN.
THAT MOMENT...
IN FIFTH GRADE...
WHEN I SAW HER SMILE...
I WAS SO HAPPY...
I THOUGHT WE WERE FATED TO BE TOGETHER.
THAT'S WHY...
I FELL IN LOVE WITH HER.

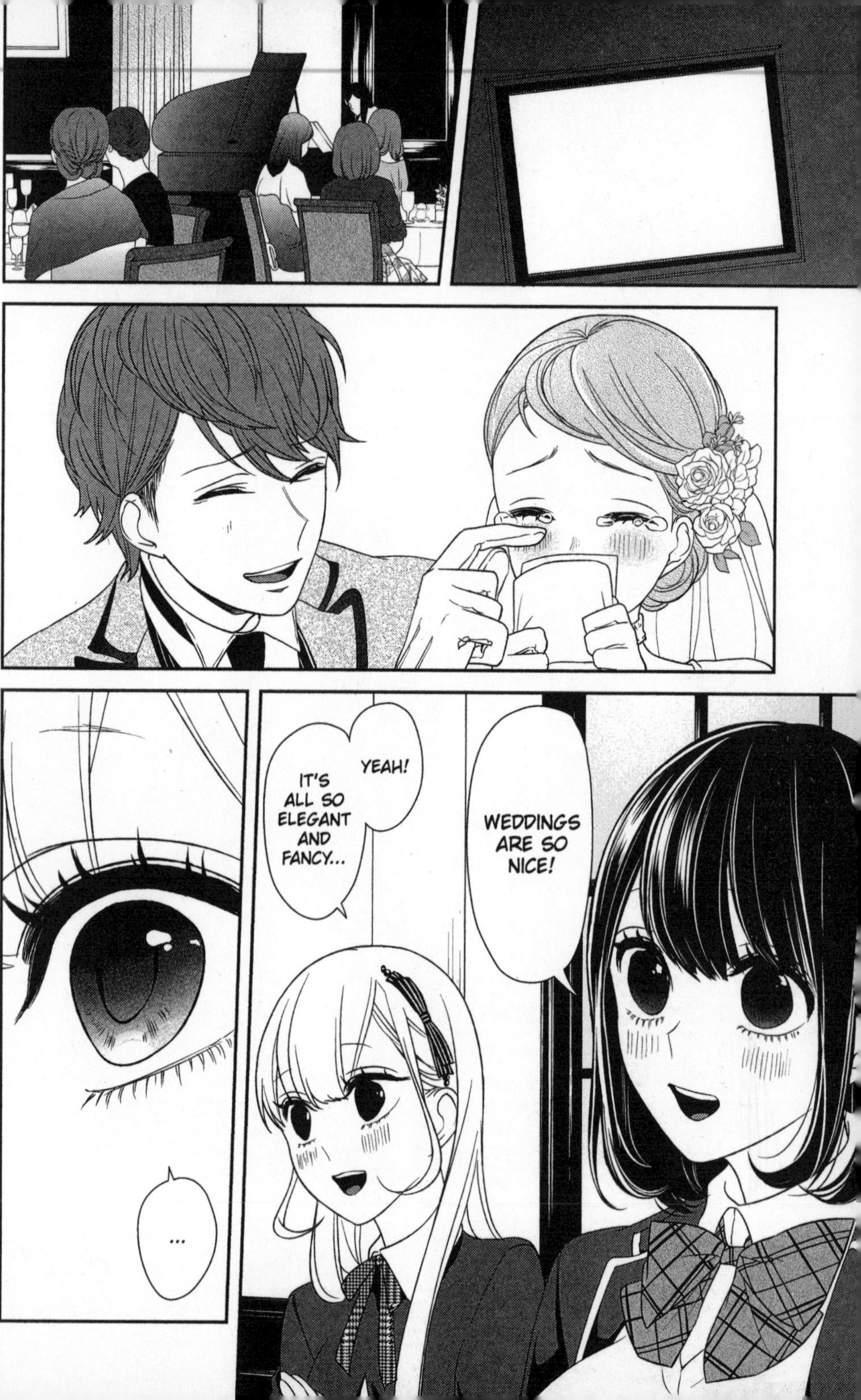
WEDDINGS ARE SO NICE!
YEAH! IT'S ALL SO ELEGANT AND FANCY...
...

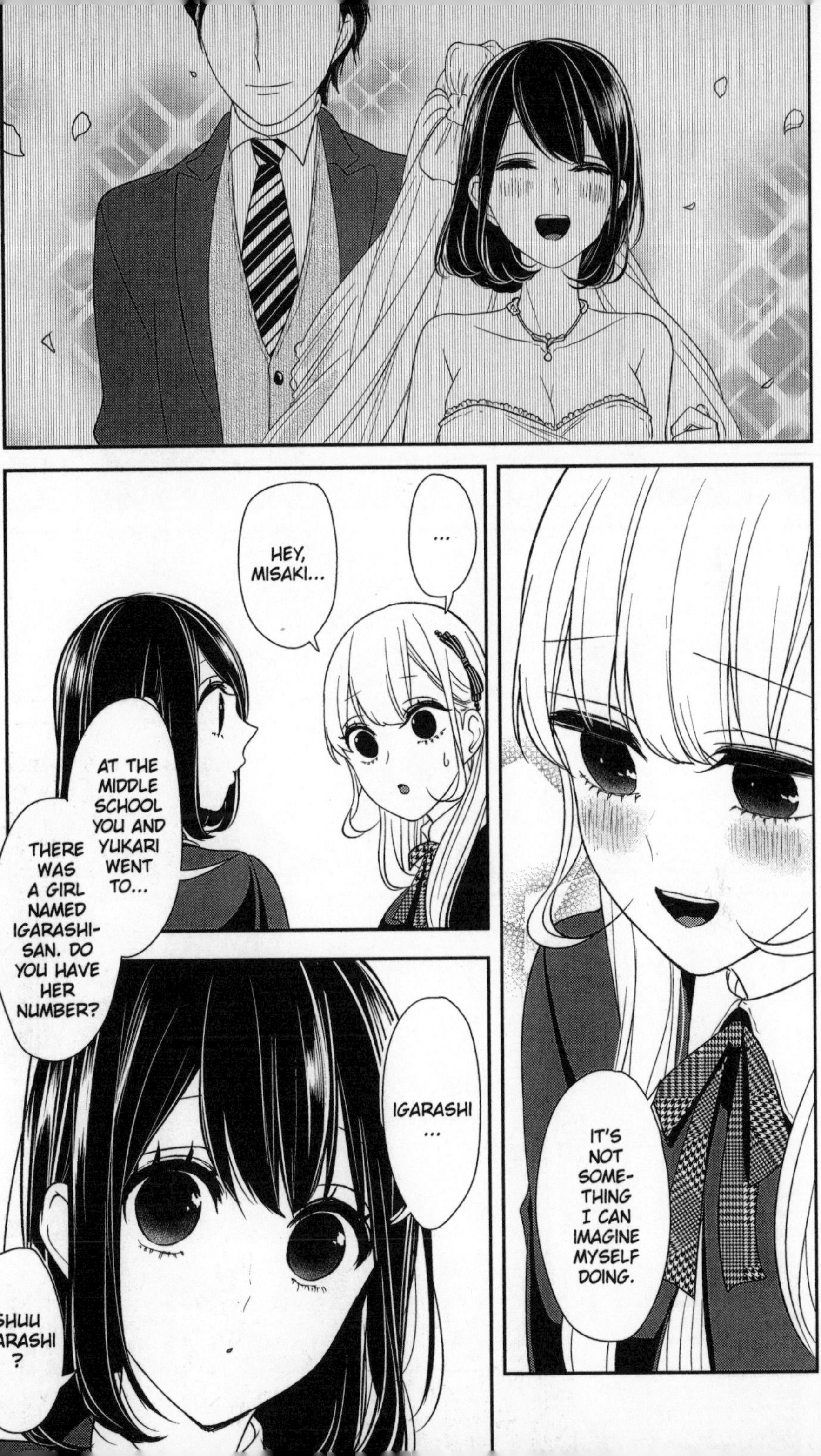
IT'S NOT SOME-THING I CAN IMAGINE MYSELF DOING.
...
HEY, MISAKI...
AT THE MIDDLE SCHOOL YOU AND YUKARI WENT TO...
THERE WAS A GIRL NAMED IGARASHI-SAN. DO YOU HAVE HER NUMBER?
IGARASHI ...
SHUU IGARASHI ?

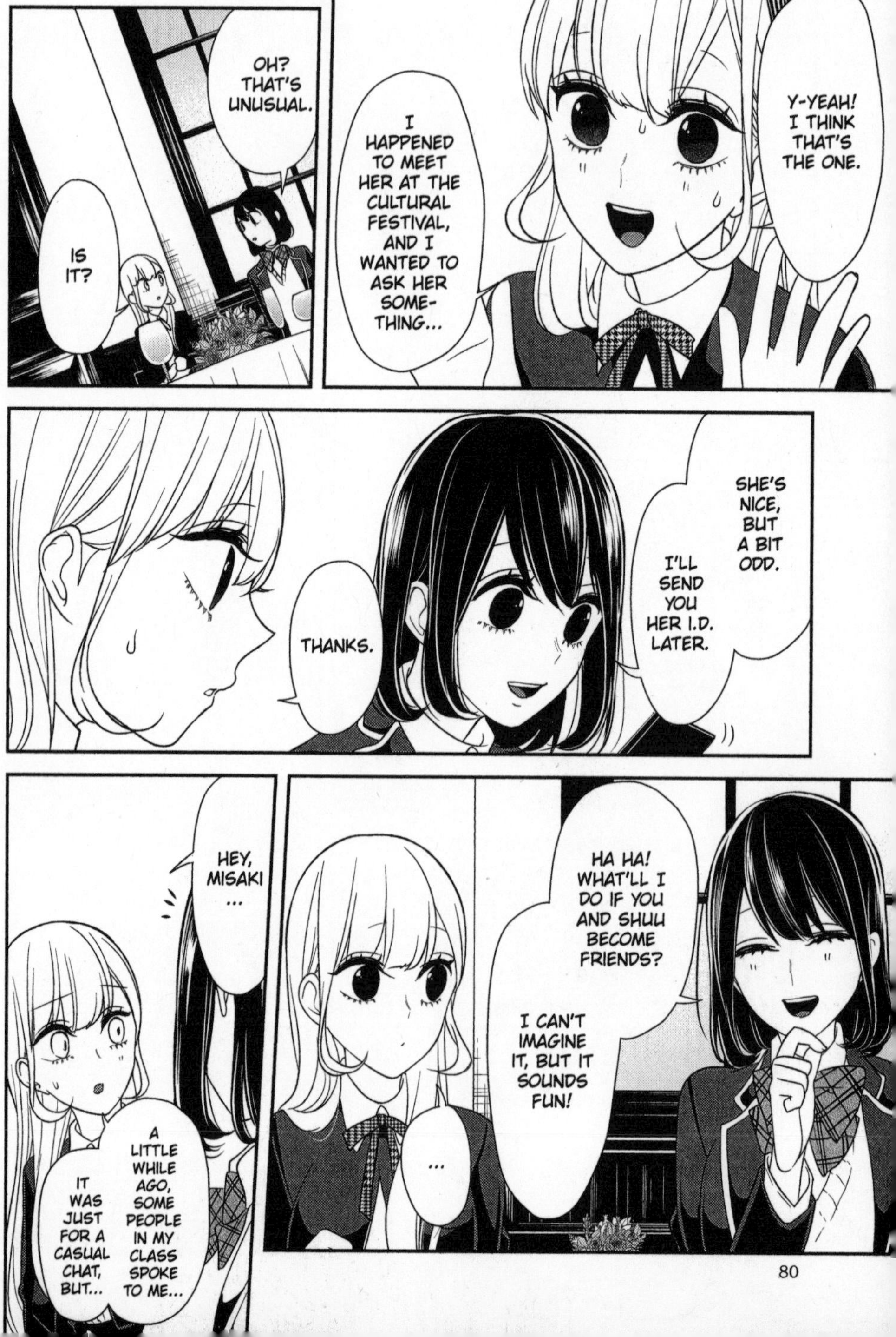
Y-YEAH! I THINK THAT'S THE ONE.
I HAPPENED TO MEET HER AT THE CULTURAL FESTIVAL, AND I WANTED TO ASK HER SOME-THING...
OH? THAT'S UNUSUAL.
IS IT?
SHE'S NICE, BUT A BIT ODD.
I'LL SEND YOU HER I.D. LATER.
THANKS.
HA HA! WHAT'LL I DO IF YOU AND SHUU BECOME FRIENDS?
I CAN'T IMAGINE IT, BUT IT SOUNDS FUN!
...
HEY, MISAKI ...
A LITTLE WHILE AGO, SOME PEOPLE IN MY CLASS SPOKE TO ME...
IT WAS JUST FOR A CASUAL CHAT, BUT...

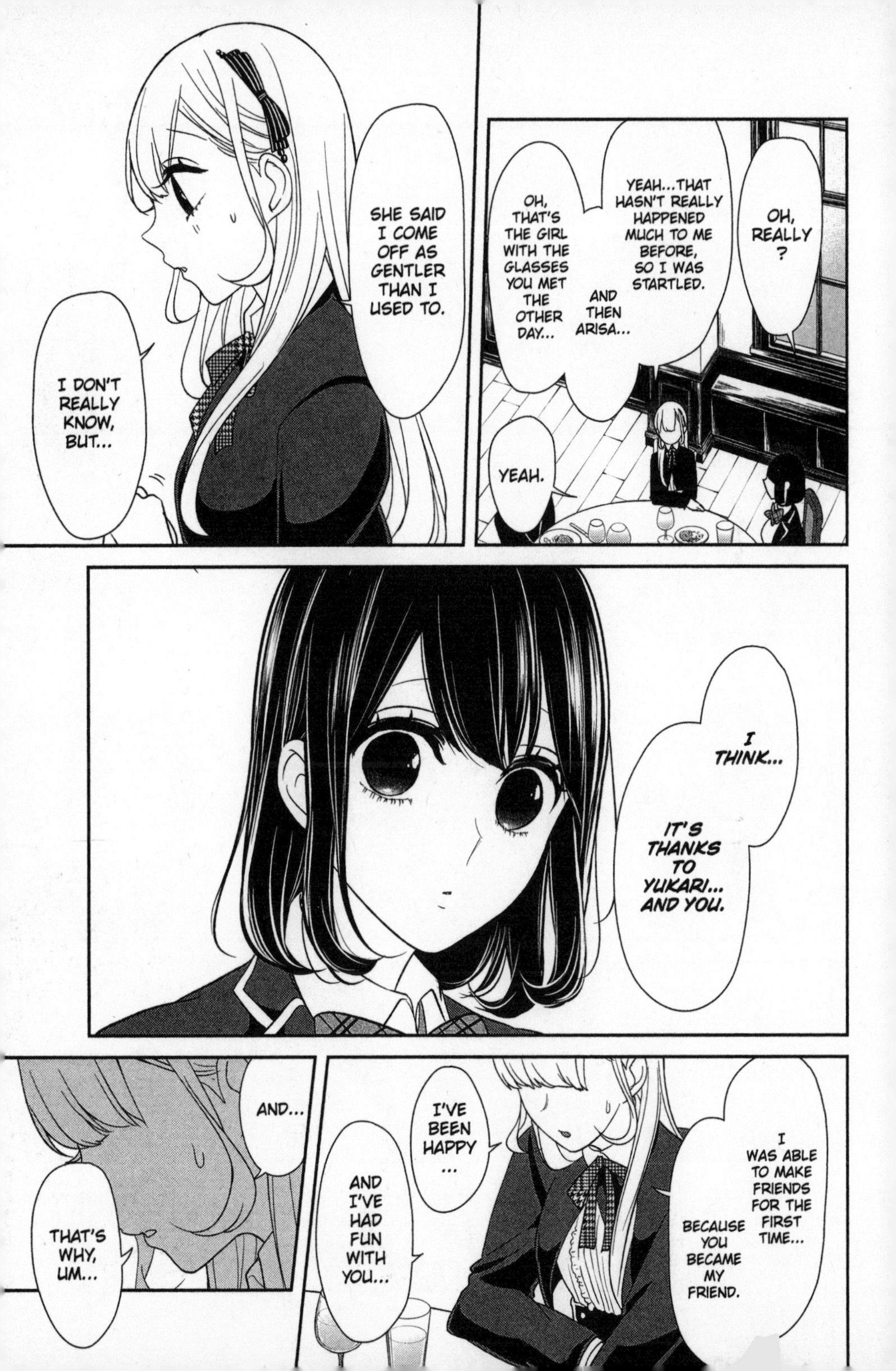
OH, REALLY?
YEAH...THAT HASN'T REALLY HAPPENED MUCH TO ME BEFORE, SO I WAS STARTLED.
AND THEN ARISA...
OH, THAT'S THE GIRL WITH THE GLASSES YOU MET THE OTHER DAY...
YEAH.
SHE SAID I COME OFF AS GENTLER THAN I USED TO.
I DON'T REALLY KNOW, BUT...
I THINK...
IT'S THANKS TO YUKARI... AND YOU.
I WAS ABLE TO MAKE FRIENDS FOR THE FIRST TIME...
BECAUSE YOU BECAME MY FRIEND.
I'VE BEEN HAPPY...
AND I'VE HAD FUN WITH YOU...
AND...
THAT'S WHY, UM...

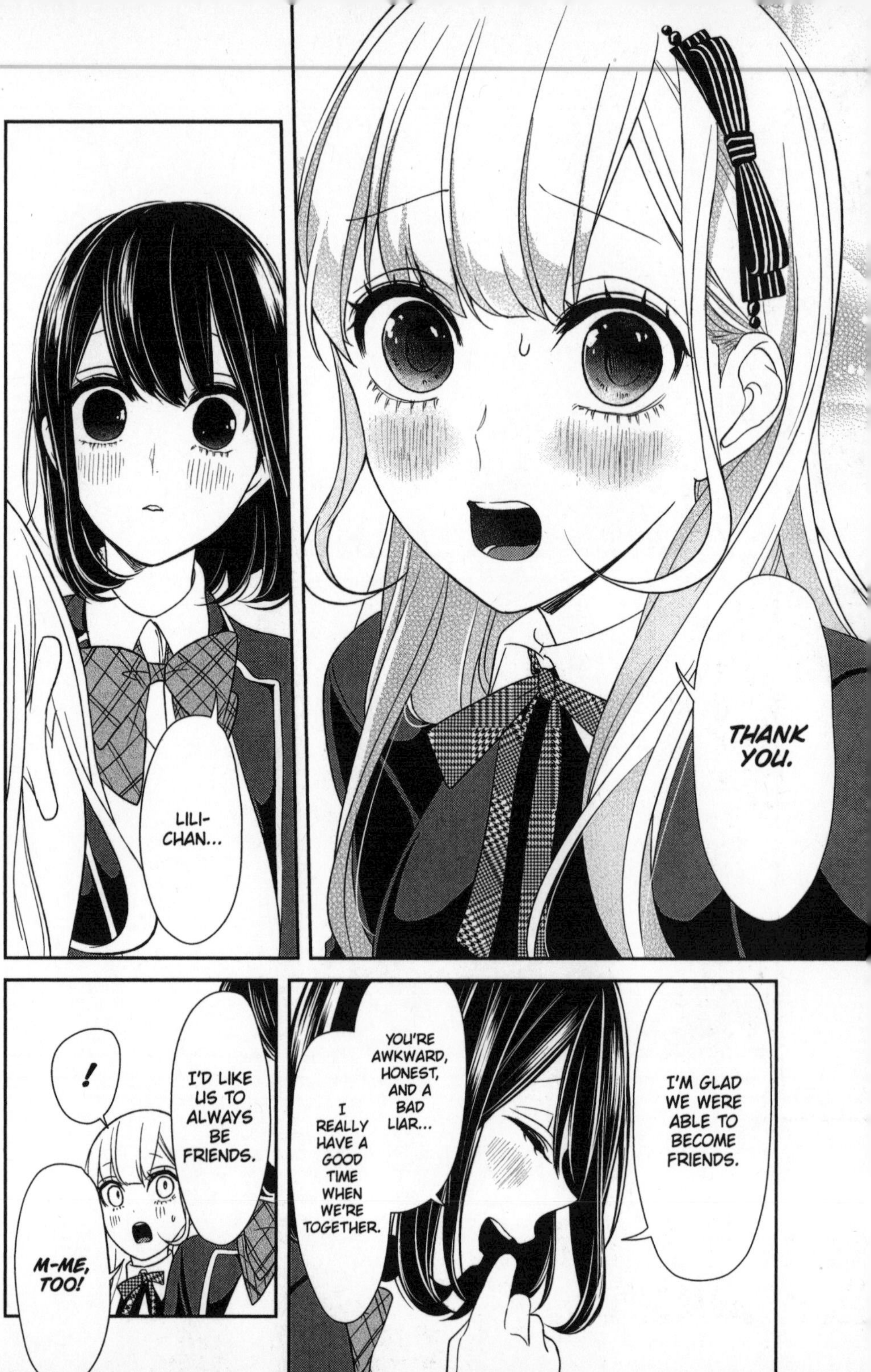
THANK YOU.
LILI-CHAN...
I'M GLAD WE WERE ABLE TO BECOME FRIENDS.
YOU'RE AWKWARD, HONEST, AND A BAD LIAR...
I REALLY HAVE A GOOD TIME WHEN WE'RE TOGETHER.
I'D LIKE US TO ALWAYS BE FRIENDS.
!
M-ME, TOO!

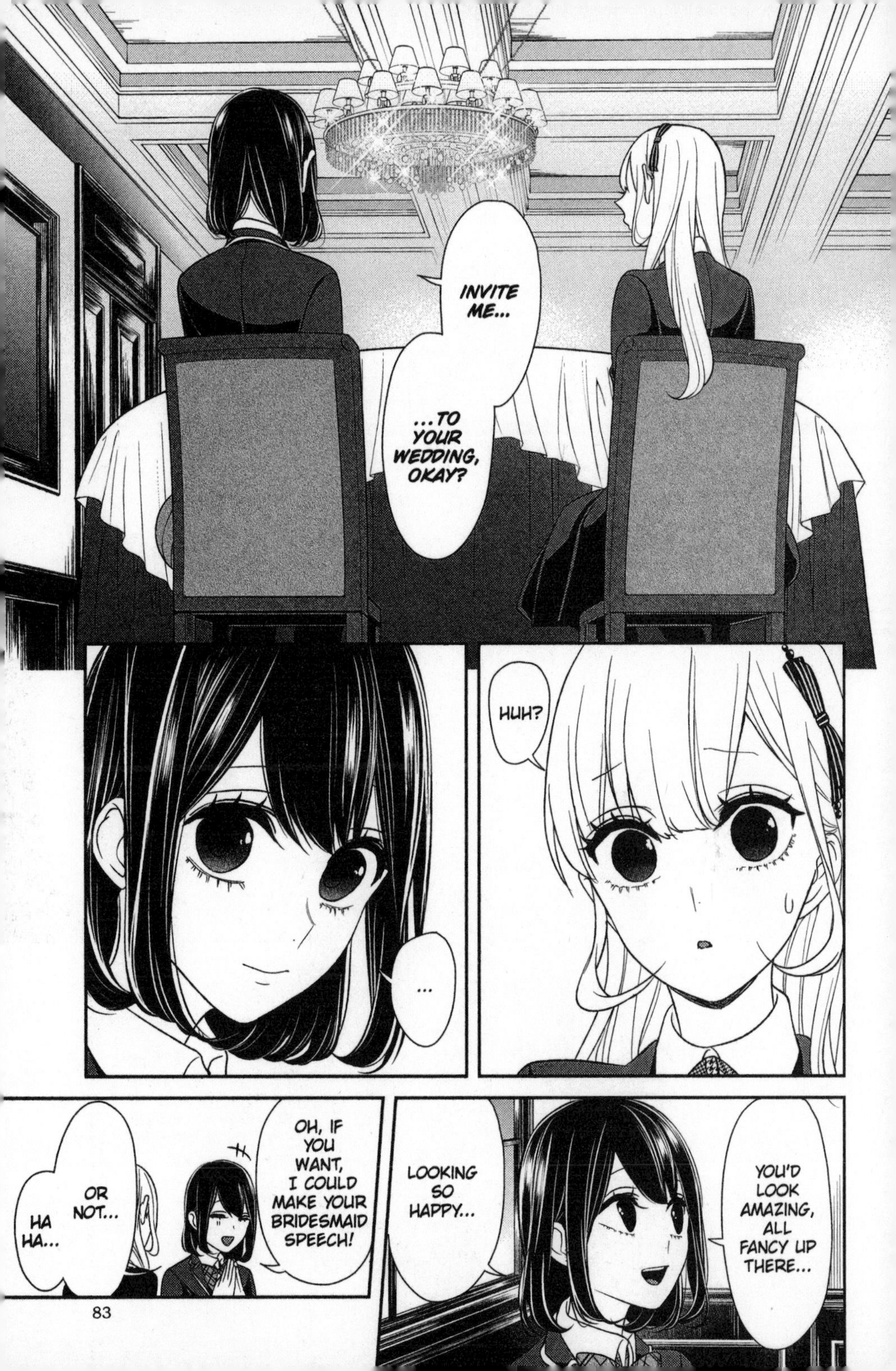
INVITE ME...
...TO YOUR WEDDING, OKAY?
HUH?
...
YOU'D LOOK AMAZING, ALL FANCY UP THERE...
LOOKING SO HAPPY...
OH, IF YOU WANT, I COULD MAKE YOUR BRIDESMAID SPEECH!
OR NOT...
HA HA...

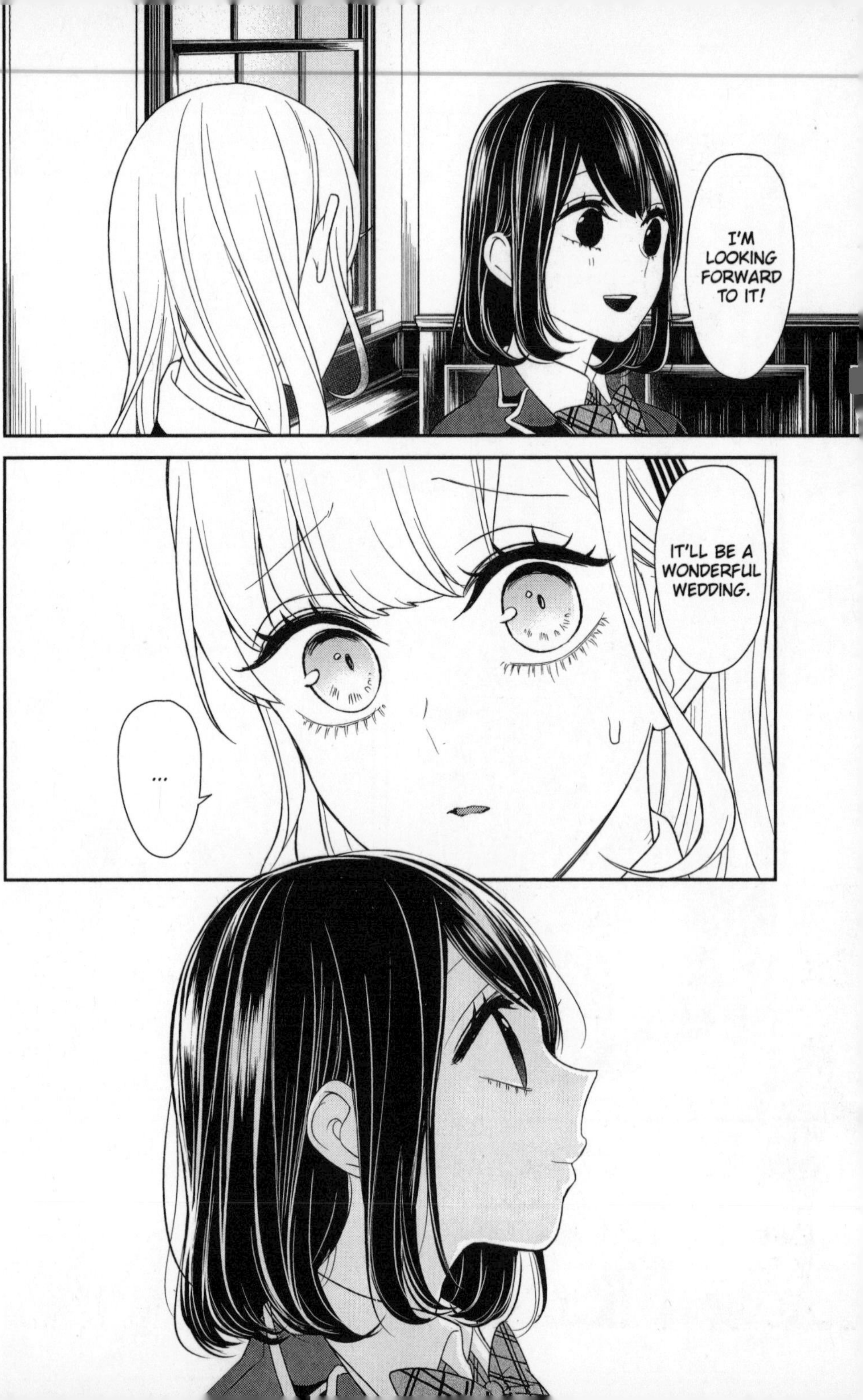
I'M LOOKING FORWARD TO IT!
IT'LL BE A WONDERFUL WEDDING.
...

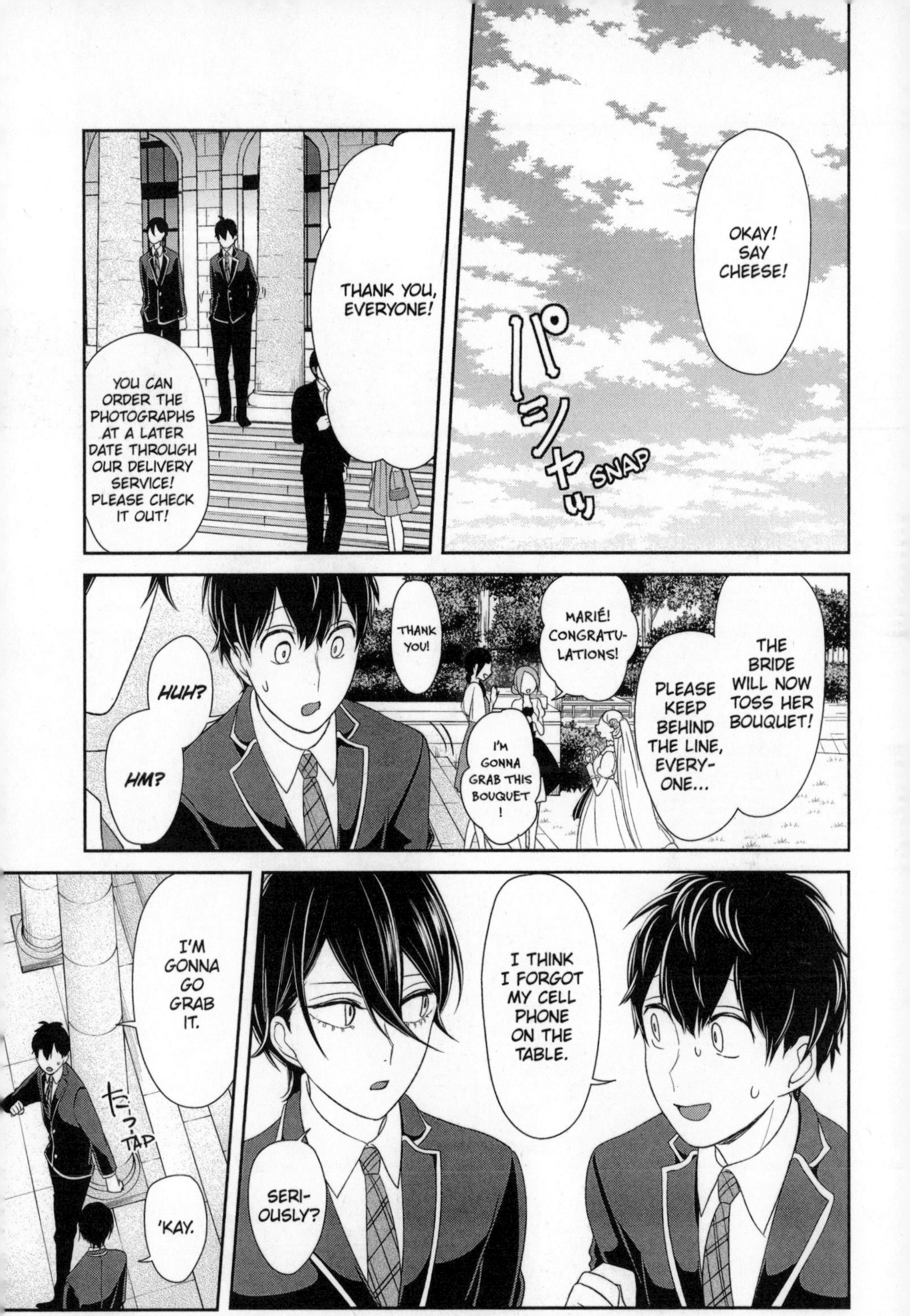
OKAY! SAY CHEESE!
パシャッ SNAP
THANK YOU, EVERYONE!
YOU CAN ORDER THE PHOTOGRAPHS AT A LATER DATE THROUGH OUR DELIVERY SERVICE! PLEASE CHECK IT OUT!
THE BRIDE WILL NOW TOSS HER BOUQUET!
PLEASE KEEP BEHIND THE LINE, EVERY-ONE...
MARIÉ! CONGRATU-LATIONS!
I'M GONNA GRAB THIS BOUQUET!
THANK YOU!
HUH?
HM?
I THINK I FORGOT MY CELL PHONE ON THE TABLE.
SERI-OUSLY?
I'M GONNA GO GRAB IT.
TAP
'KAY.

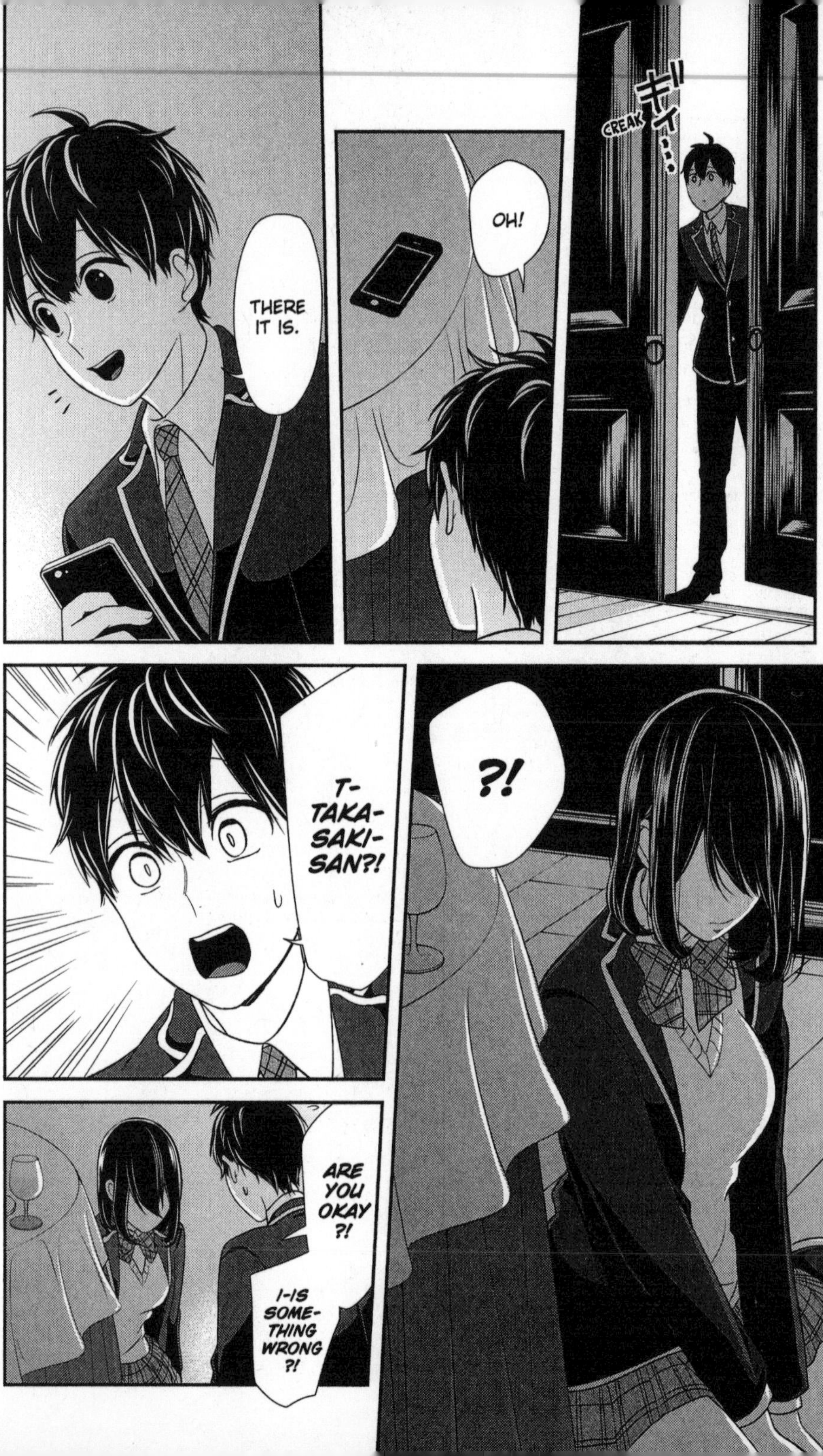

ギィ…
CREAK
OH!
THERE IT IS.
?!
T-TAKASAKI-SAN?!
ARE YOU OKAY?!
I-IS SOMETHING WRONG?!

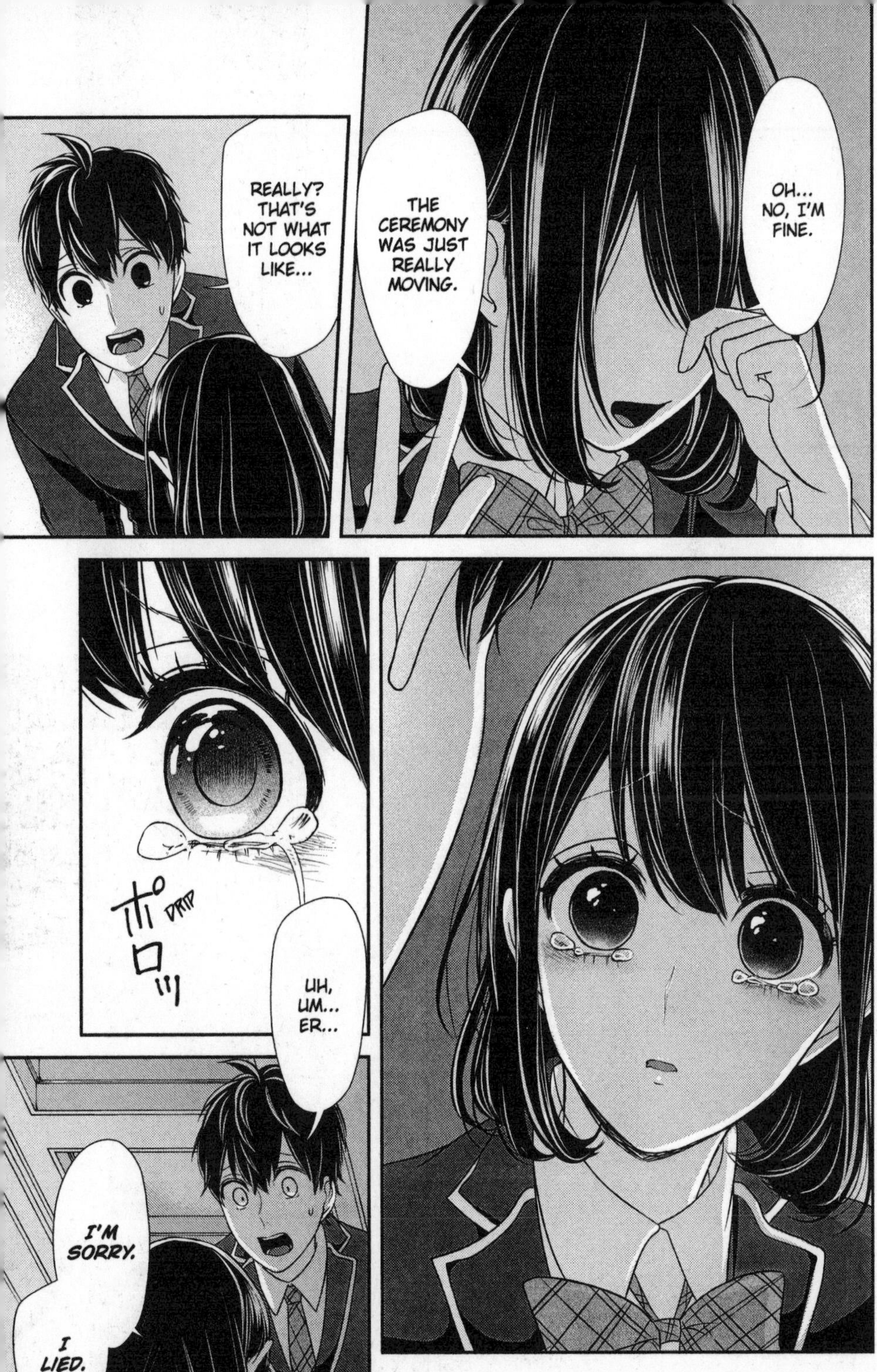
OH... NO, I'M FINE.
THE CEREMONY WAS JUST REALLY MOVING.
REALLY? THAT'S NOT WHAT IT LOOKS LIKE...
ポロッ
DRIP
UH, UM... ER...
I'M SORRY.
I LIED.

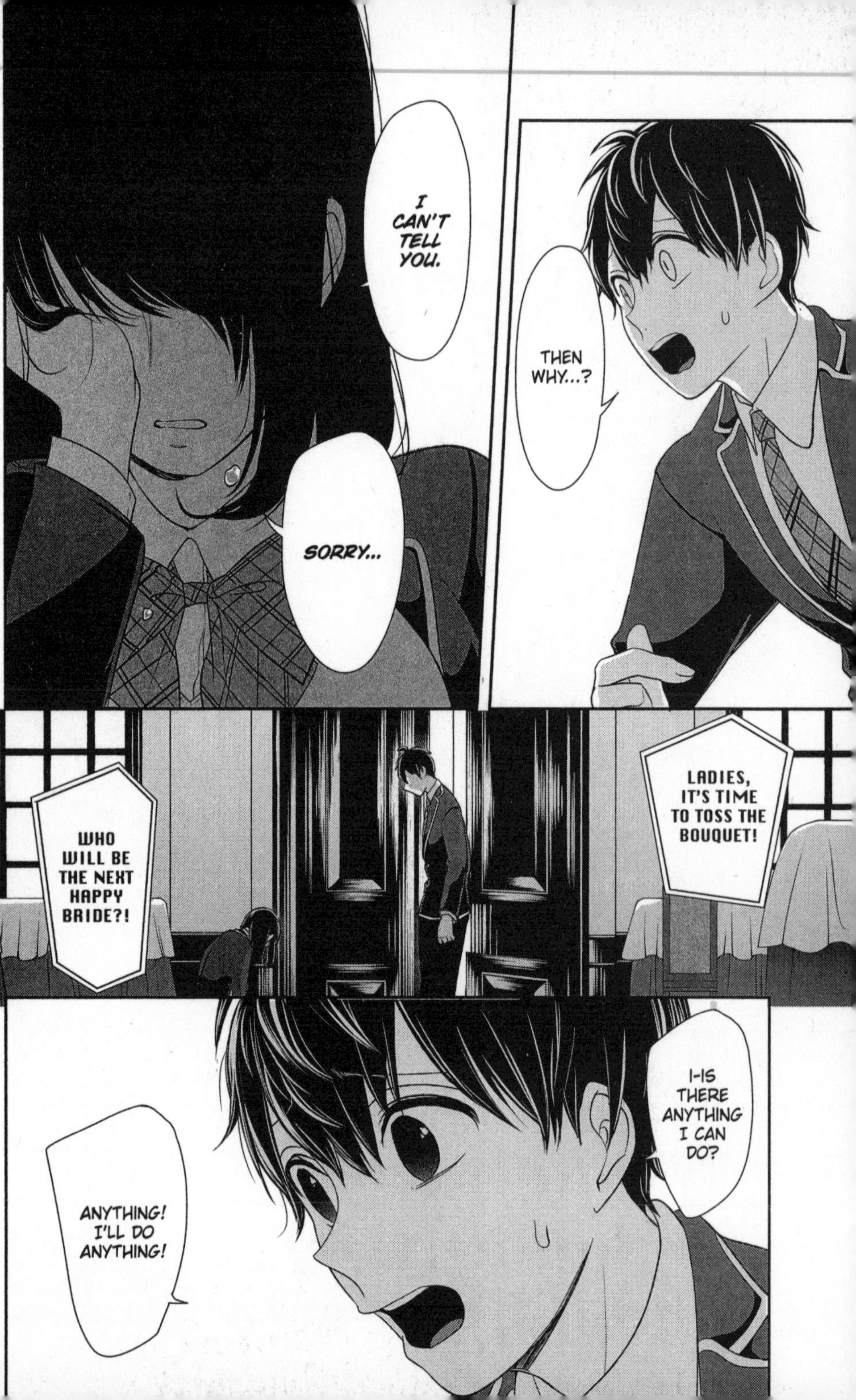
THEN WHY...?
I CAN'T TELL YOU.
SORRY...
LADIES, IT'S TIME TO TOSS THE BOUQUET!
WHO WILL BE THE NEXT HAPPY BRIDE?!
I-IS THERE ANYTHING I CAN DO?
ANYTHING! I'LL DO ANYTHING!

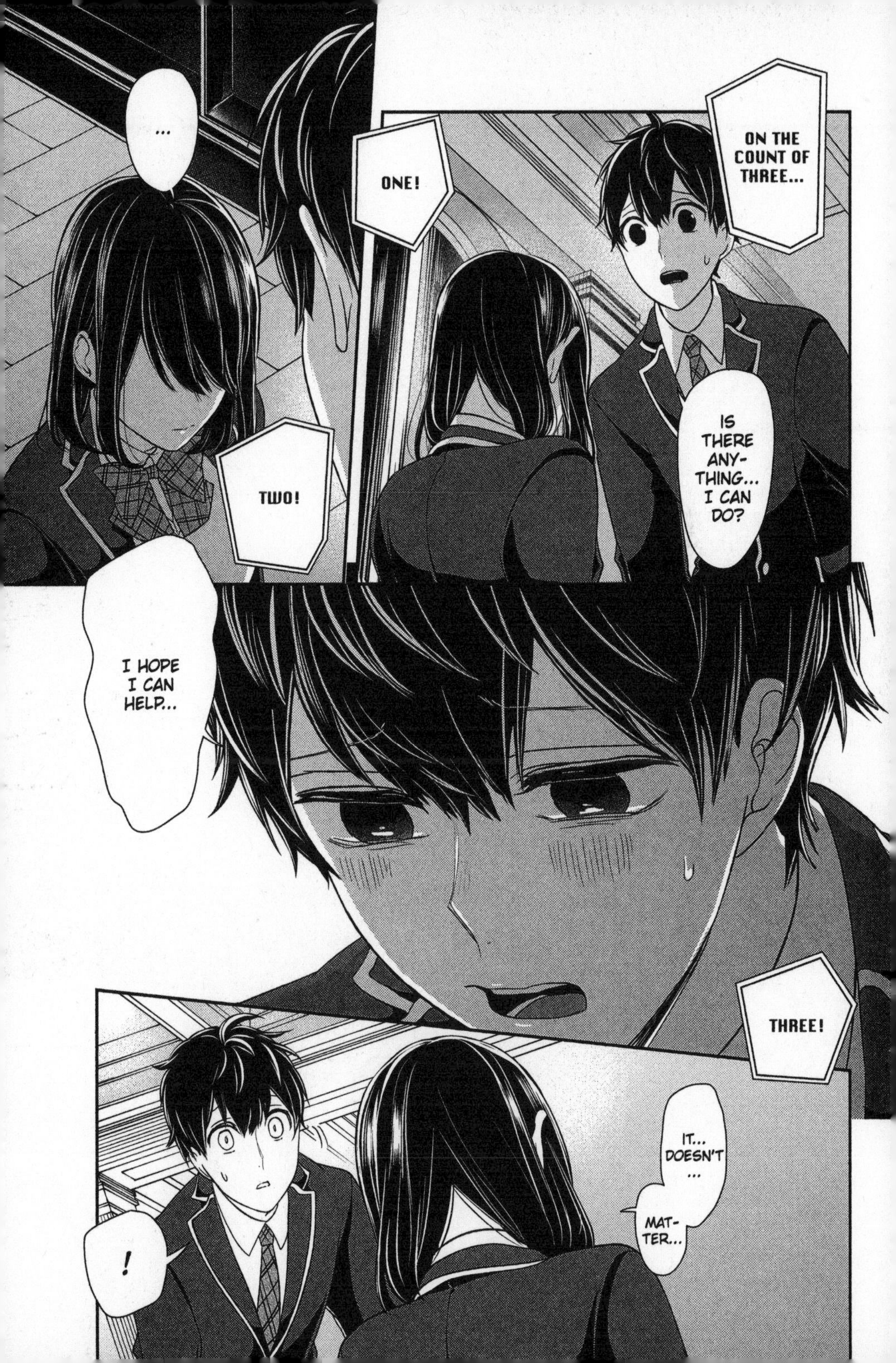

ON THE COUNT OF THREE...
ONE!
IS THERE ANYTHING... I CAN DO?
...
TWO!
I HOPE I CAN HELP...
THREE!
IT... DOESN'T ... MATTER...
!

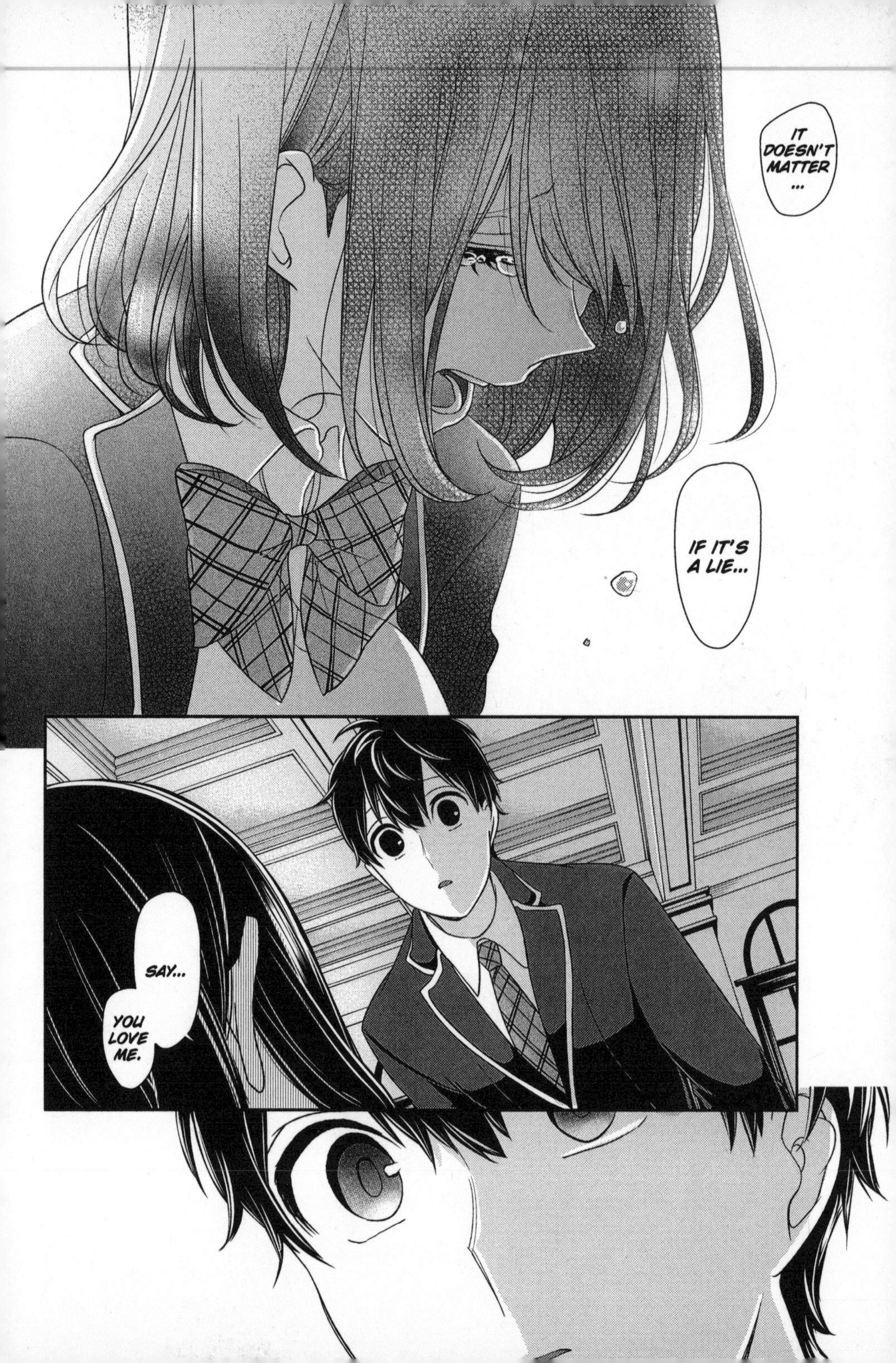
IT DOESN'T MATTER...
IF IT'S A LIE...
SAY... YOU LOVE ME.

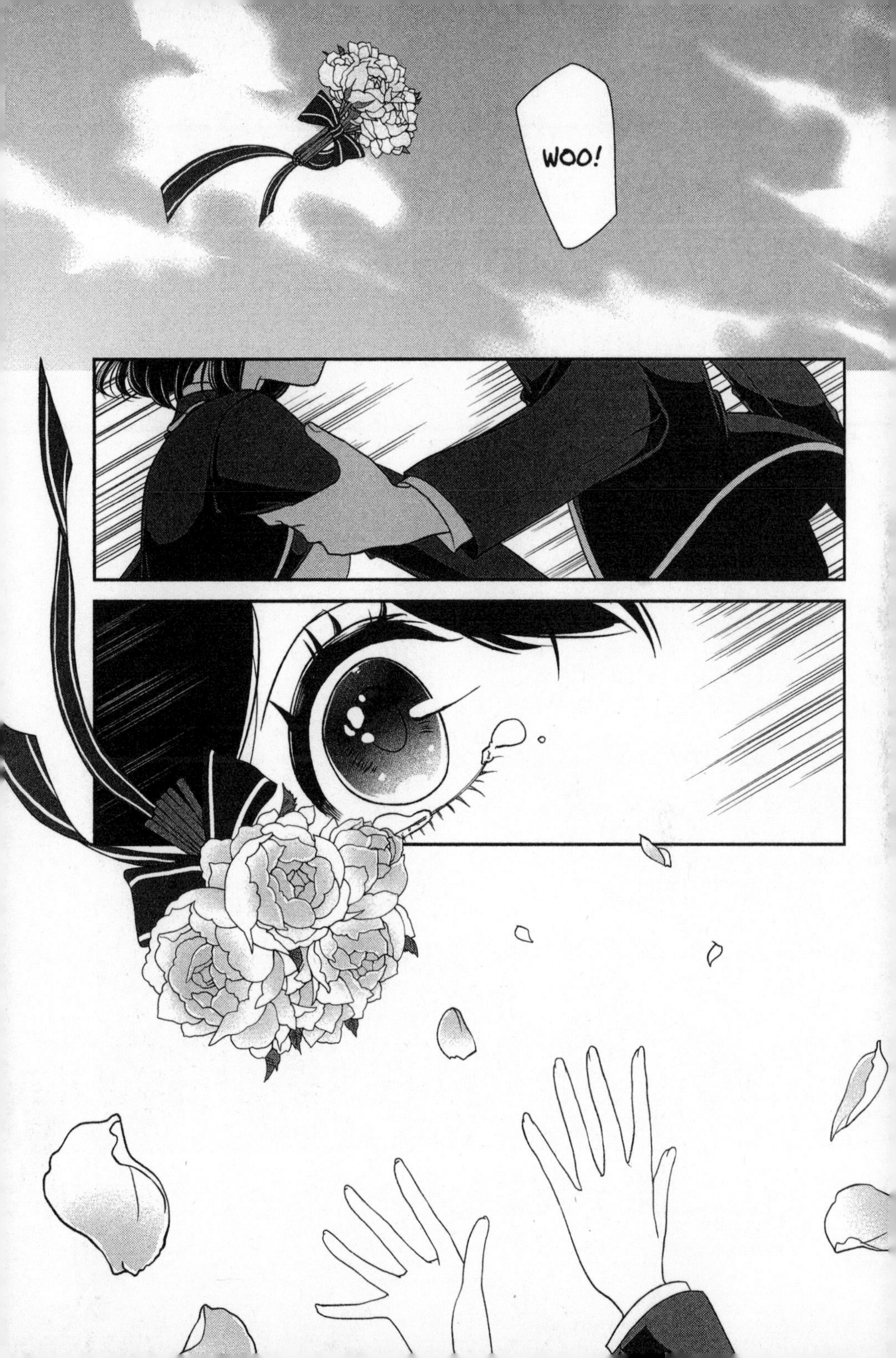
WOO!

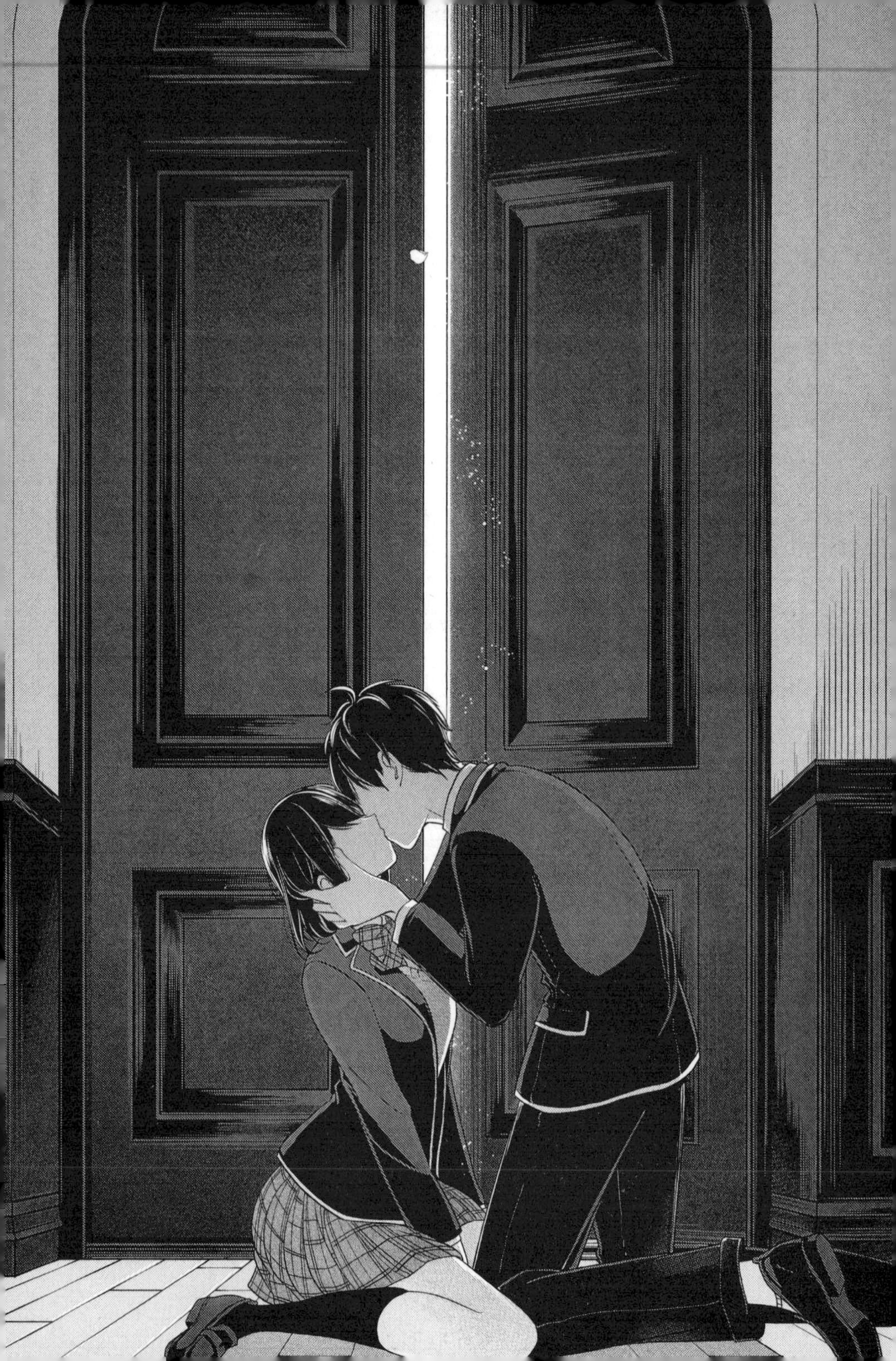

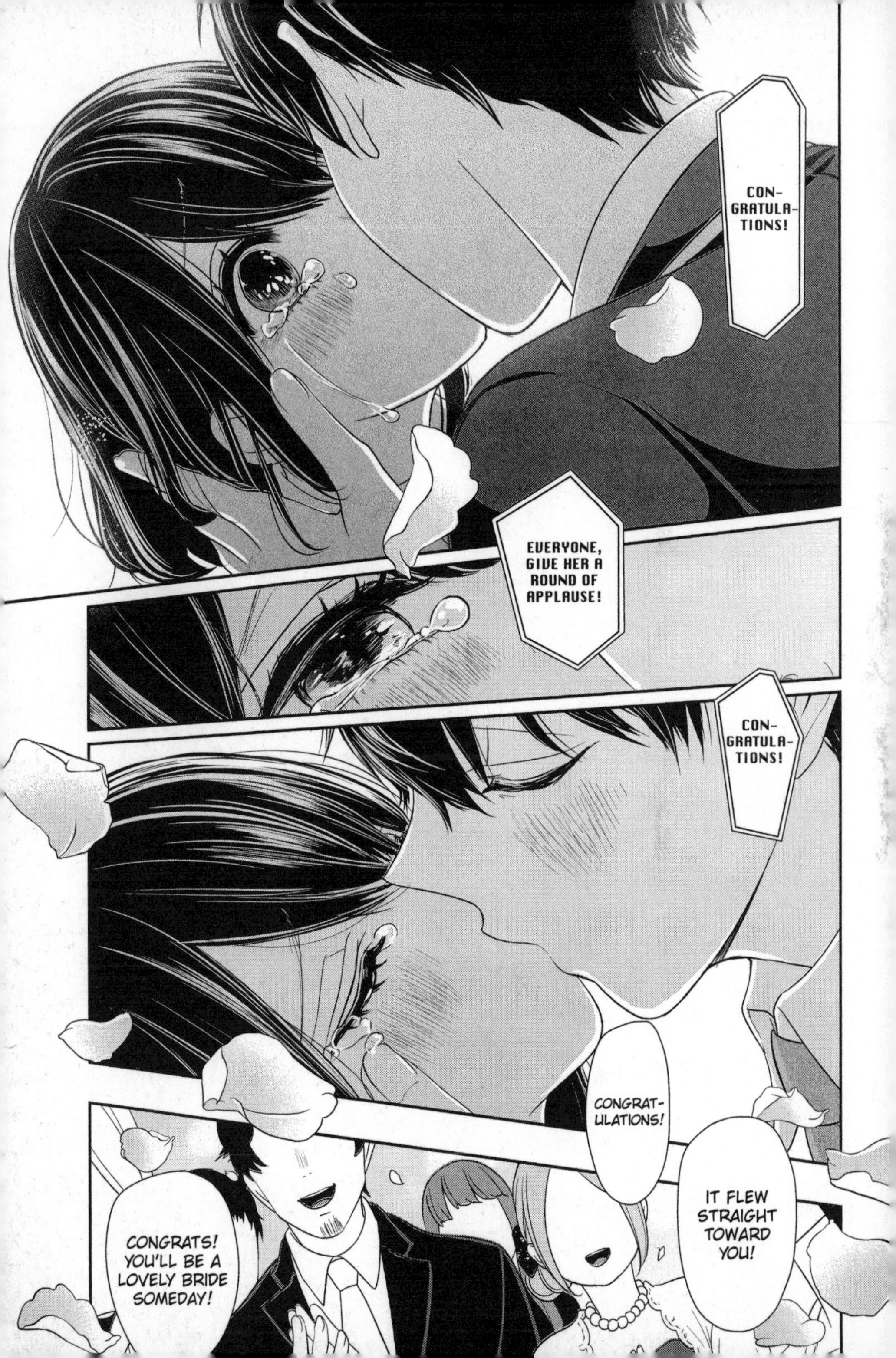
CON-GRATULA-TIONS!
EVERYONE, GIVE HER A ROUND OF APPLAUSE!
CON-GRATULA-TIONS!
CONGRAT-ULATIONS!
IT FLEW STRAIGHT TOWARD YOU!
CONGRATS! YOU'LL BE A LOVELY BRIDE SOMEDAY!

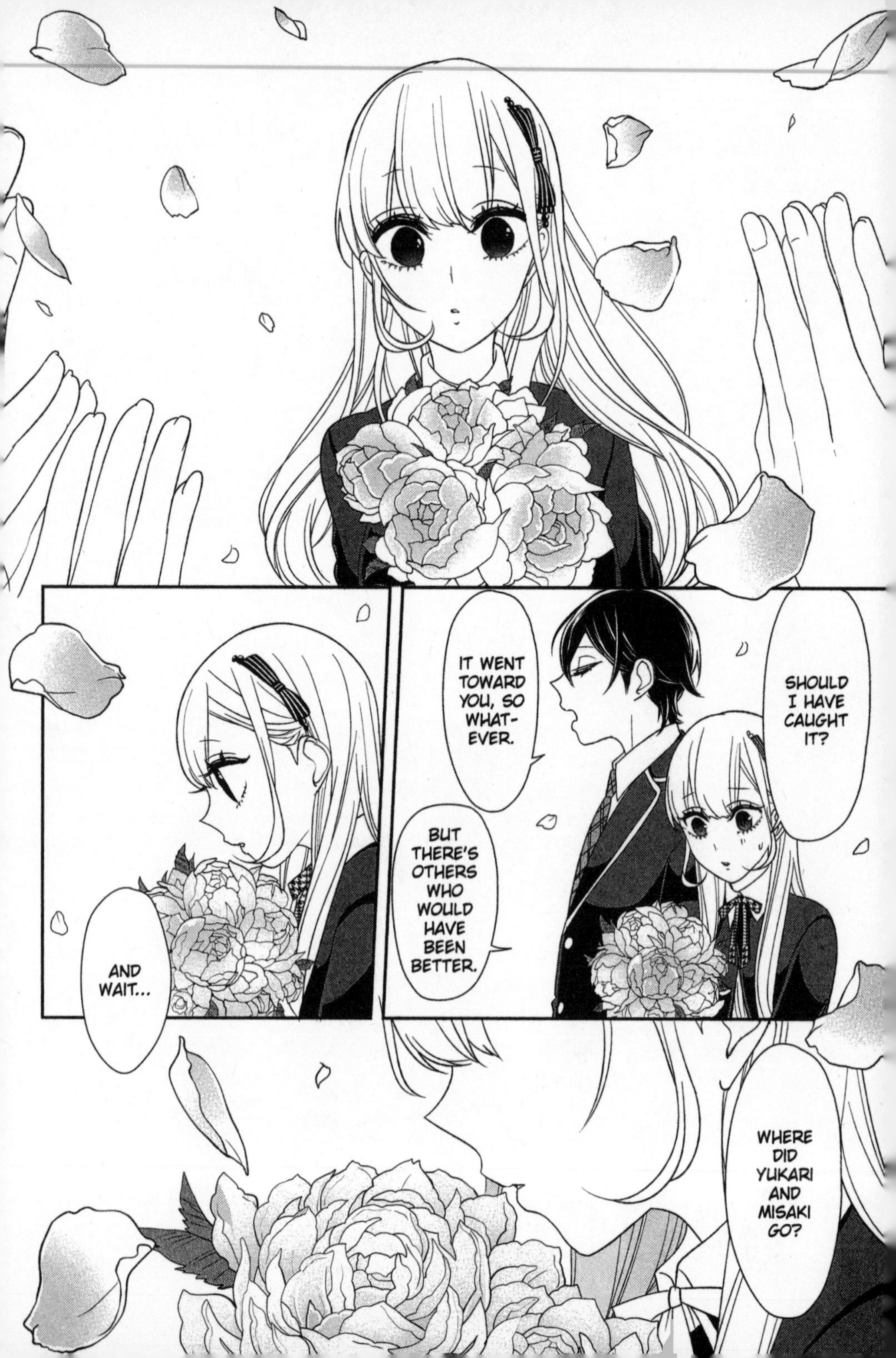
SHOULD I HAVE CAUGHT IT?
IT WENT TOWARD YOU, SO WHAT-EVER.
BUT THERE'S OTHERS WHO WOULD HAVE BEEN BETTER.
AND WAIT...
WHERE DID YUKARI AND MISAKI GO?

Love & Lies

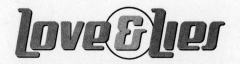

DATE DAY

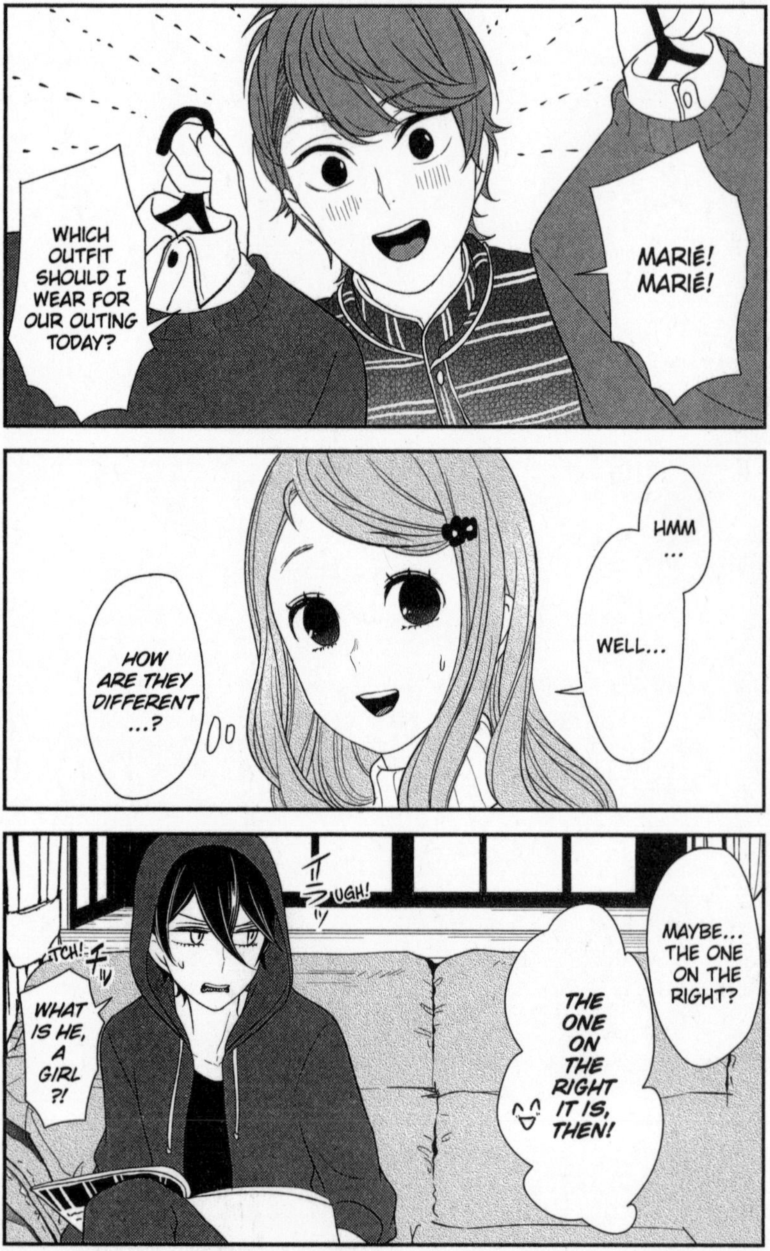
MARIÉ! MARIÉ!
WHICH OUTFIT SHOULD I WEAR FOR OUR OUTING TODAY?
HMM... WELL...
HOW ARE THEY DIFFERENT...?
MAYBE... THE ONE ON THE RIGHT?
THE ONE ON THE RIGHT IT IS, THEN!
UGH!
TCH!
WHAT IS HE, A GIRL?!

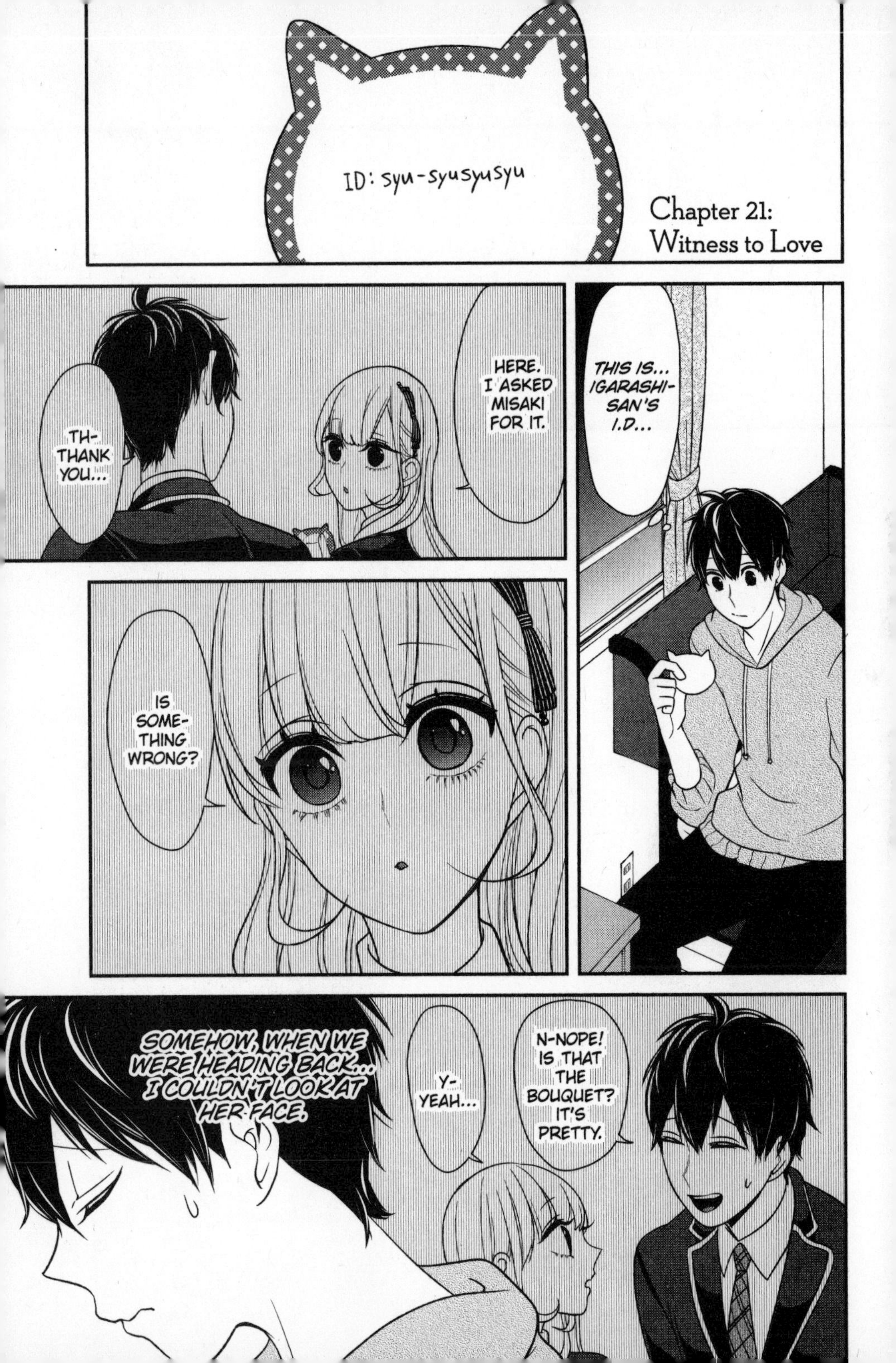
ID: syu-syusyusyu
Chapter 21: Witness to Love
THIS IS... IGARASHI-SAN'S I.D...
HERE. I ASKED MISAKI FOR IT.
TH-THANK YOU...
IS SOMETHING WRONG?
N-NOPE! IS THAT THE BOUQUET? IT'S PRETTY.
Y-YEAH...
SOMEHOW, WHEN WE WERE HEADING BACK... I COULDN'T LOOK AT HER FACE.

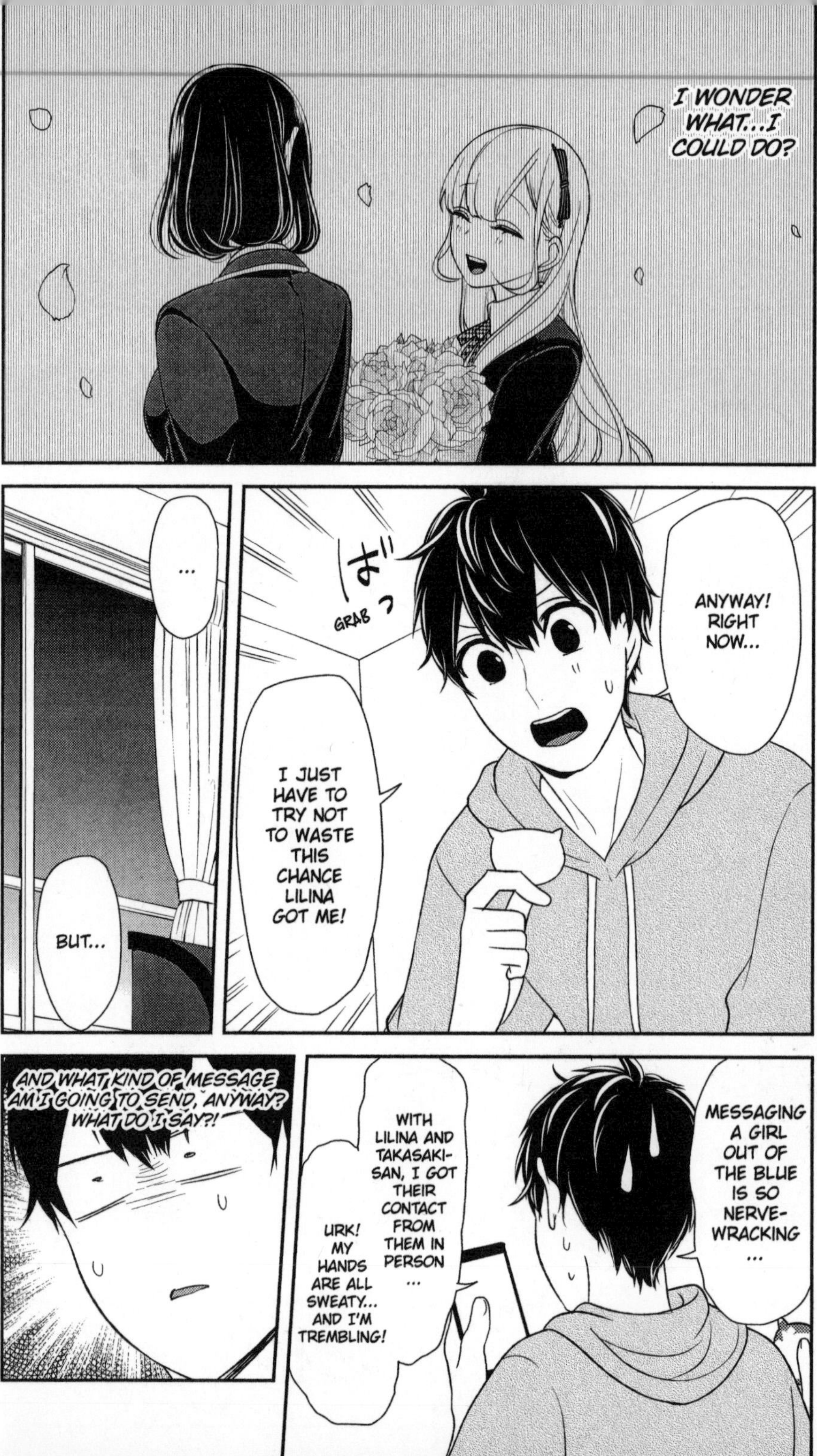

I WONDER WHAT...I COULD DO?
ANYWAY! RIGHT NOW...
GRAB
I JUST HAVE TO TRY NOT TO WASTE THIS CHANCE LILINA GOT ME!
...
BUT...
MESSAGING A GIRL OUT OF THE BLUE IS SO NERVE-WRACKING ...
WITH LILINA AND TAKASAKI-SAN, I GOT THEIR CONTACT FROM THEM IN PERSON ...
URK! MY HANDS ARE ALL SWEATY... AND I'M TREMBLING!
AND WHAT KIND OF MESSAGE AM I GOING TO SEND, ANYWAY? WHAT DO I SAY?!

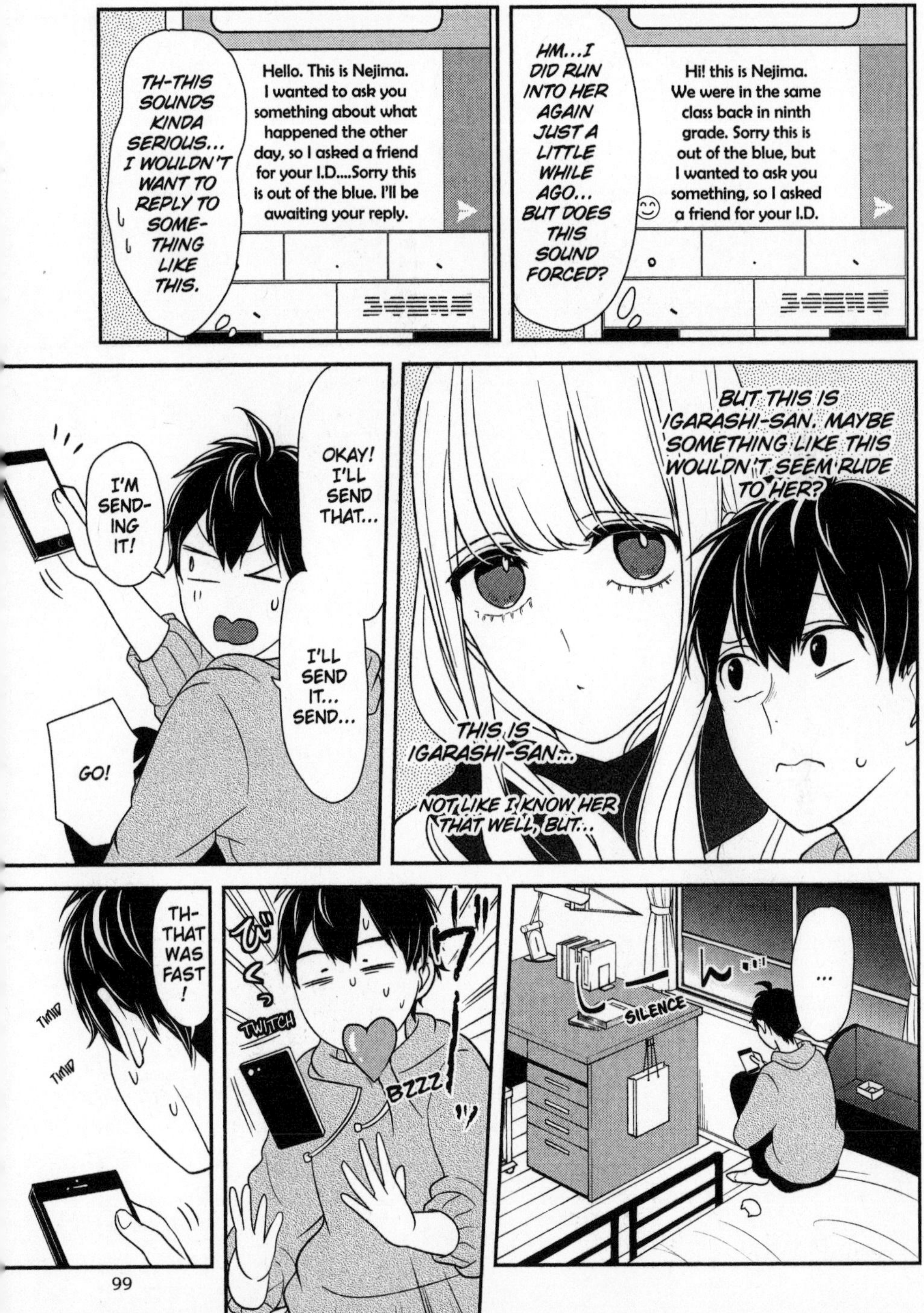
Hi! this is Nejima. We were in the same class back in ninth grade. Sorry this is out of the blue, but I wanted to ask you something, so I asked a friend for your I.D.
HM...I DID RUN INTO HER AGAIN JUST A LITTLE WHILE AGO... BUT DOES THIS SOUND FORCED?
Hello. This is Nejima. I wanted to ask you something about what happened the other day, so I asked a friend for your I.D....Sorry this is out of the blue. I'll be awaiting your reply.
TH-THIS SOUNDS KINDA SERIOUS... I WOULDN'T WANT TO REPLY TO SOMETHING LIKE THIS.
BUT THIS IS IGARASHI-SAN. MAYBE SOMETHING LIKE THIS WOULDN'T SEEM RUDE TO HER?
THIS IS IGARASHI-SAN...
NOT LIKE I KNOW HER THAT WELL, BUT...
OKAY! I'LL SEND THAT...
I'LL SEND IT... SEND...
I'M SENDING IT!
GO!
...
SILENCE
BZZZ
TWITCH
TH-THAT WAS FAST!

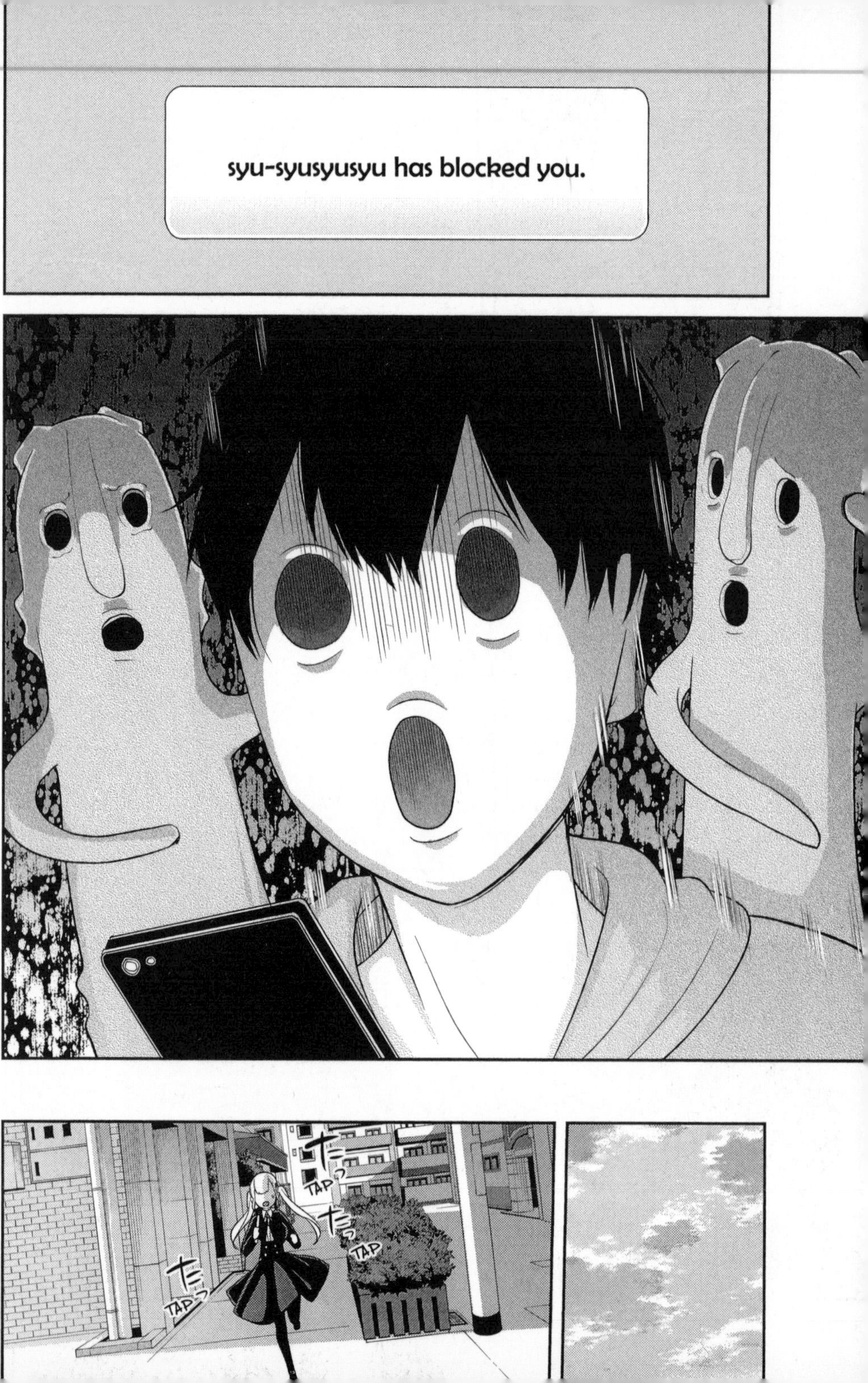
syu-syusyusyu has blocked you.
TAP
TAP
TAP

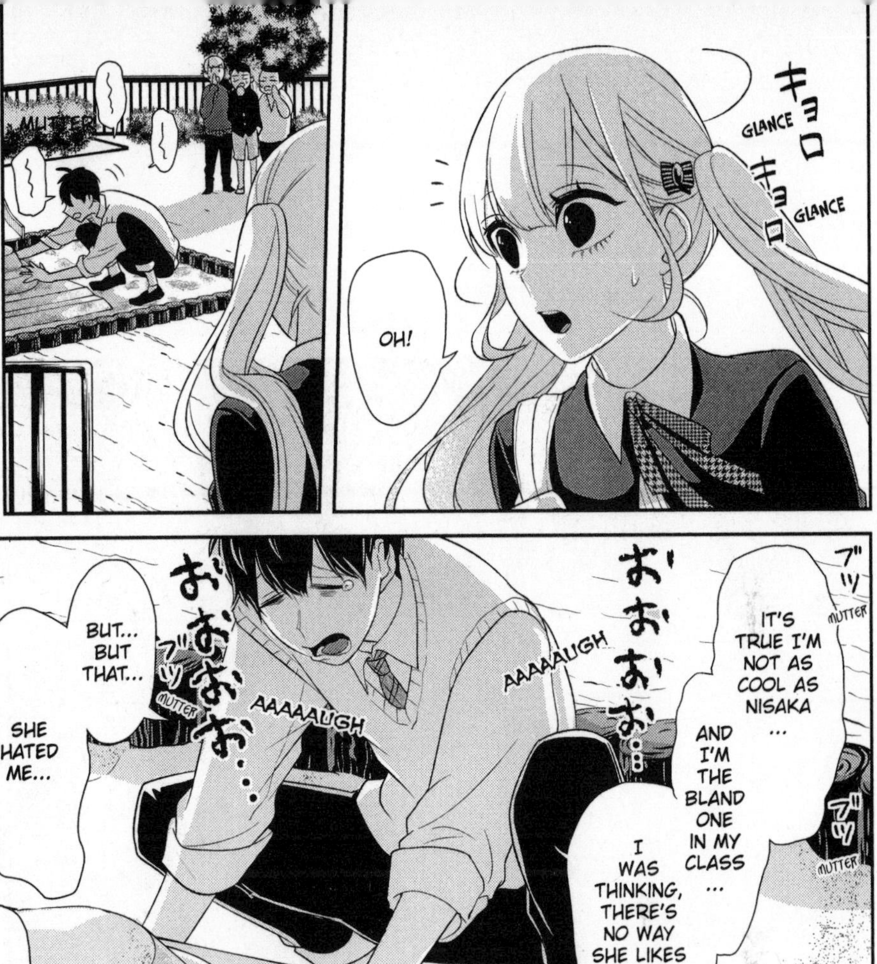
キョロ
GLANCE
キョロ
GLANCE
OH!
MUTTER
ブツ
MUTTER
IT'S TRUE I'M NOT AS COOL AS NISAKA ...
AND I'M THE BLAND ONE IN MY CLASS ...
I WAS THINKING, THERE'S NO WAY SHE LIKES ME, YOU KNOW?
ブツ
MUTTER
おおおお...
AAAAAUGH
AAAAAUGH
おおおお...
BUT... BUT THAT...
ブツ
MUTTER
SHE HATED ME...
ブツ
MUTTER
THAT MUCH?

*KOFUN SHAPED WITH A SQUARED BASE AND A CIRCULAR MOUND ON TOP.

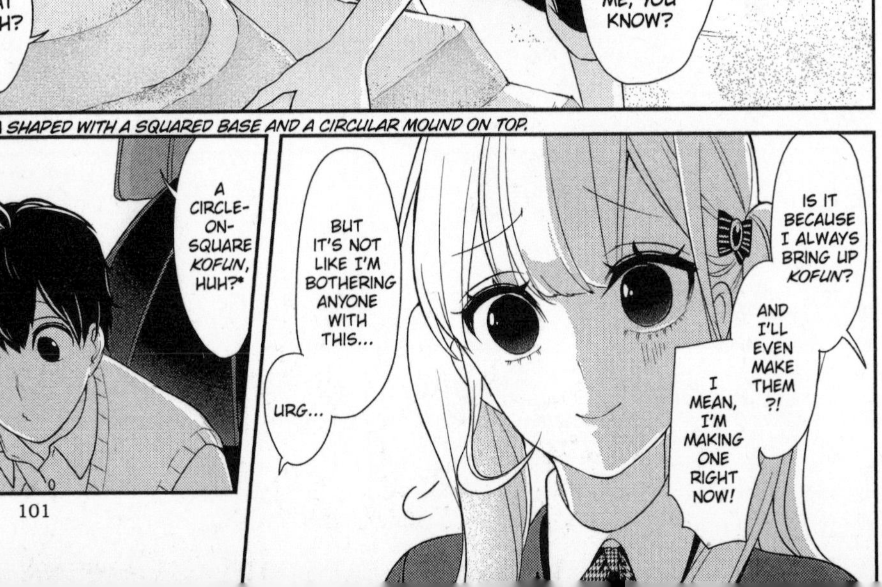
IS IT BECAUSE I ALWAYS BRING UP KOFUN?
AND I'LL EVEN MAKE THEM ?!
I MEAN, I'M MAKING ONE RIGHT NOW!
BUT IT'S NOT LIKE I'M BOTHERING ANYONE WITH THIS...
URG...
A CIRCLE-ON-SQUARE KOFUN, HUH?*

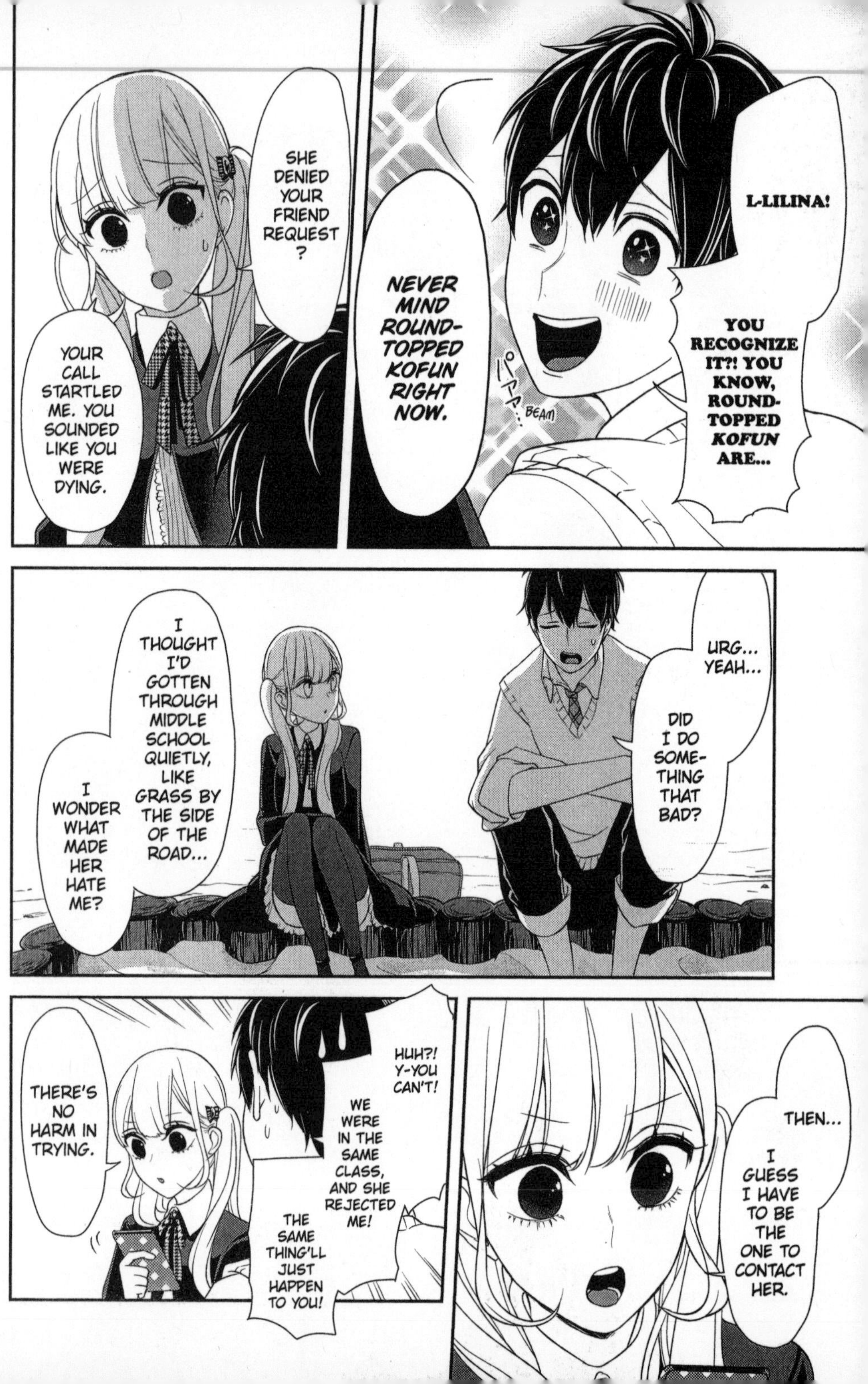
L-LILINA!
YOU RECOGNIZE IT?! YOU KNOW, ROUND-TOPPED KOFUN ARE...
BEAM
NEVER MIND ROUND-TOPPED KOFUN RIGHT NOW.
SHE DENIED YOUR FRIEND REQUEST?
YOUR CALL STARTLED ME. YOU SOUNDED LIKE YOU WERE DYING.
URG... YEAH...
DID I DO SOMETHING THAT BAD?
I THOUGHT I'D GOTTEN THROUGH MIDDLE SCHOOL QUIETLY, LIKE GRASS BY THE SIDE OF THE ROAD...
I WONDER WHAT MADE HER HATE ME?
THEN...
I GUESS I HAVE TO BE THE ONE TO CONTACT HER.
THERE'S NO HARM IN TRYING.
HUH?! Y-YOU CAN'T!
WE WERE IN THE SAME CLASS, AND SHE REJECTED ME!
THE SAME THING'LL JUST HAPPEN TO YOU!

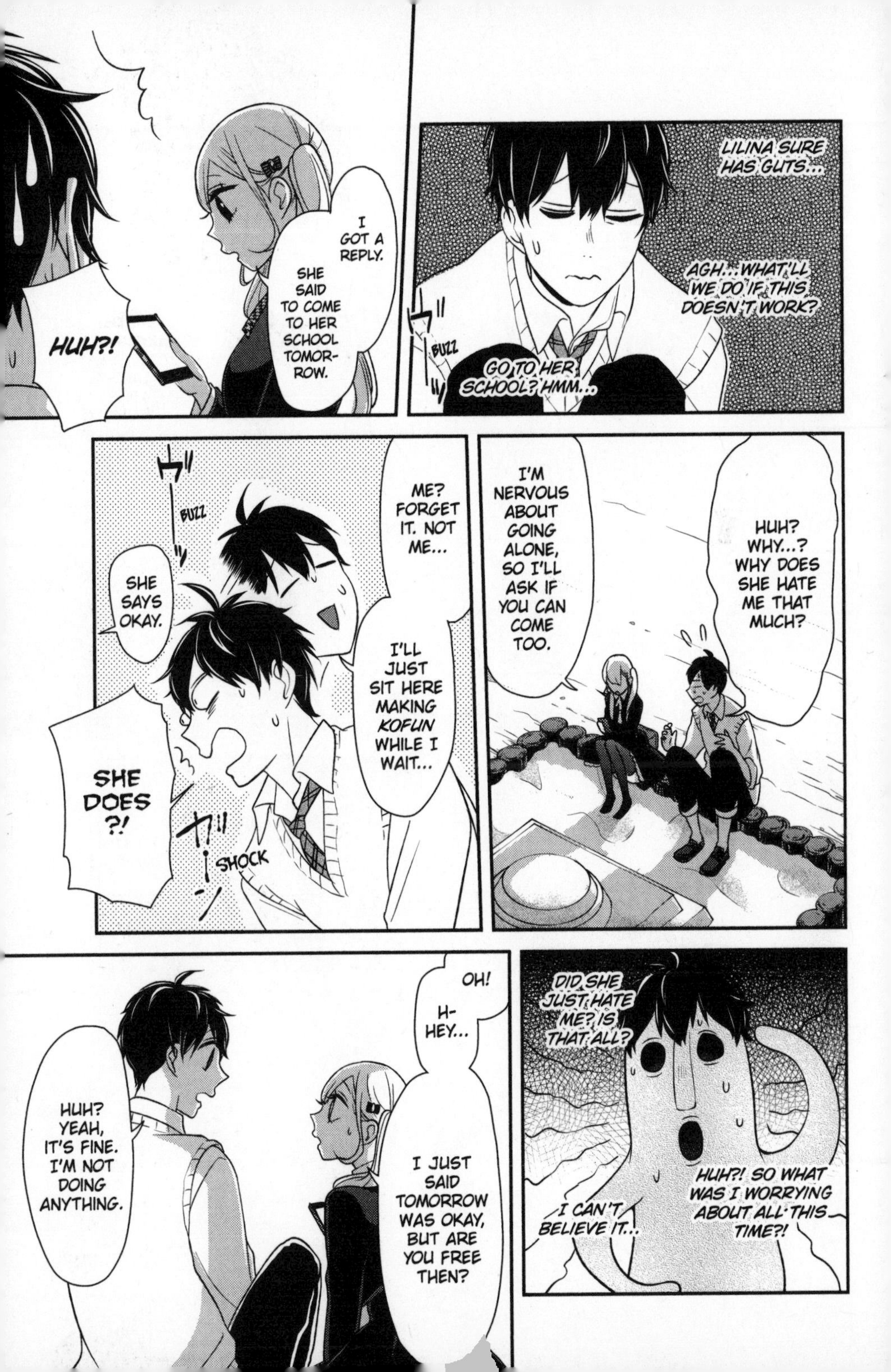
LILINA SURE HAS GUTS...
AGH... WHAT'LL WE DO IF THIS DOESN'T WORK?
BUZZ
GO TO HER SCHOOL? HMM...
I GOT A REPLY.
SHE SAID TO COME TO HER SCHOOL TOMORROW.
HUH?!
HUH? WHY...? WHY DOES SHE HATE ME THAT MUCH?
I'M NERVOUS ABOUT GOING ALONE, SO I'LL ASK IF YOU CAN COME TOO.
ME? FORGET IT. NOT ME...
I'LL JUST SIT HERE MAKING *KOFUN* WHILE I WAIT...
BUZZ
SHE SAYS OKAY.
SHE DOES?!
SHOCK
DID SHE JUST HATE ME? IS THAT ALL?
HUH?! SO WHAT WAS I WORRYING ABOUT ALL THIS TIME?!
I CAN'T BELIEVE IT...
OH!
H-HEY...
I JUST SAID TOMORROW WAS OKAY, BUT ARE YOU FREE THEN?
HUH? YEAH, IT'S FINE. I'M NOT DOING ANYTHING.

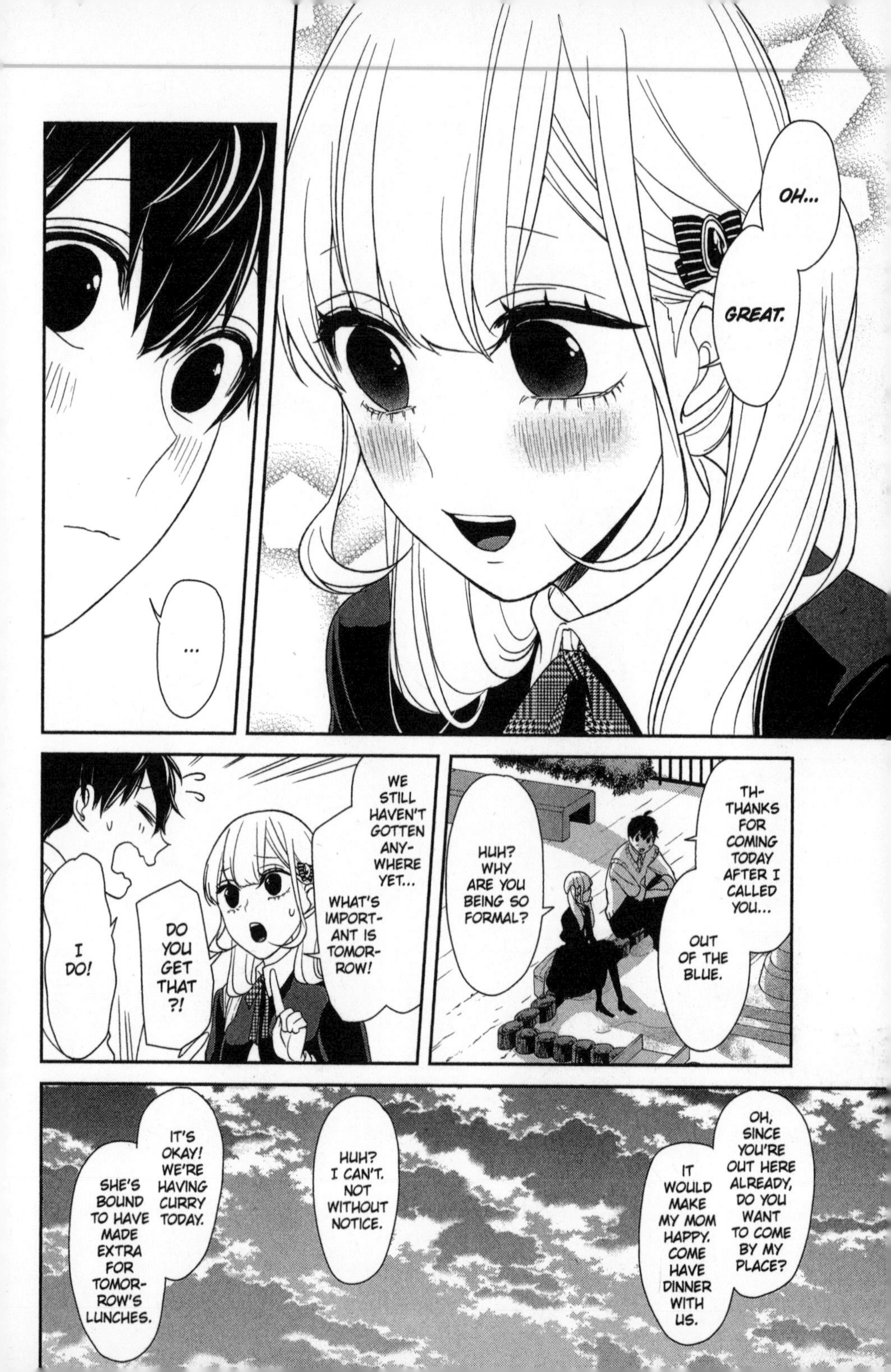
OH...
GREAT.
...
TH-THANKS FOR COMING TODAY AFTER I CALLED YOU...
OUT OF THE BLUE.
HUH? WHY ARE YOU BEING SO FORMAL?
WE STILL HAVEN'T GOTTEN ANYWHERE YET...
WHAT'S IMPORTANT IS TOMORROW!
DO YOU GET THAT?!
I DO!
OH, SINCE YOU'RE OUT HERE ALREADY, DO YOU WANT TO COME BY MY PLACE?
IT WOULD MAKE MY MOM HAPPY. COME HAVE DINNER WITH US.
HUH? I CAN'T. NOT WITHOUT NOTICE.
IT'S OKAY! WE'RE HAVING CURRY TODAY.
SHE'S BOUND TO HAVE MADE EXTRA FOR TOMORROW'S LUNCHES.

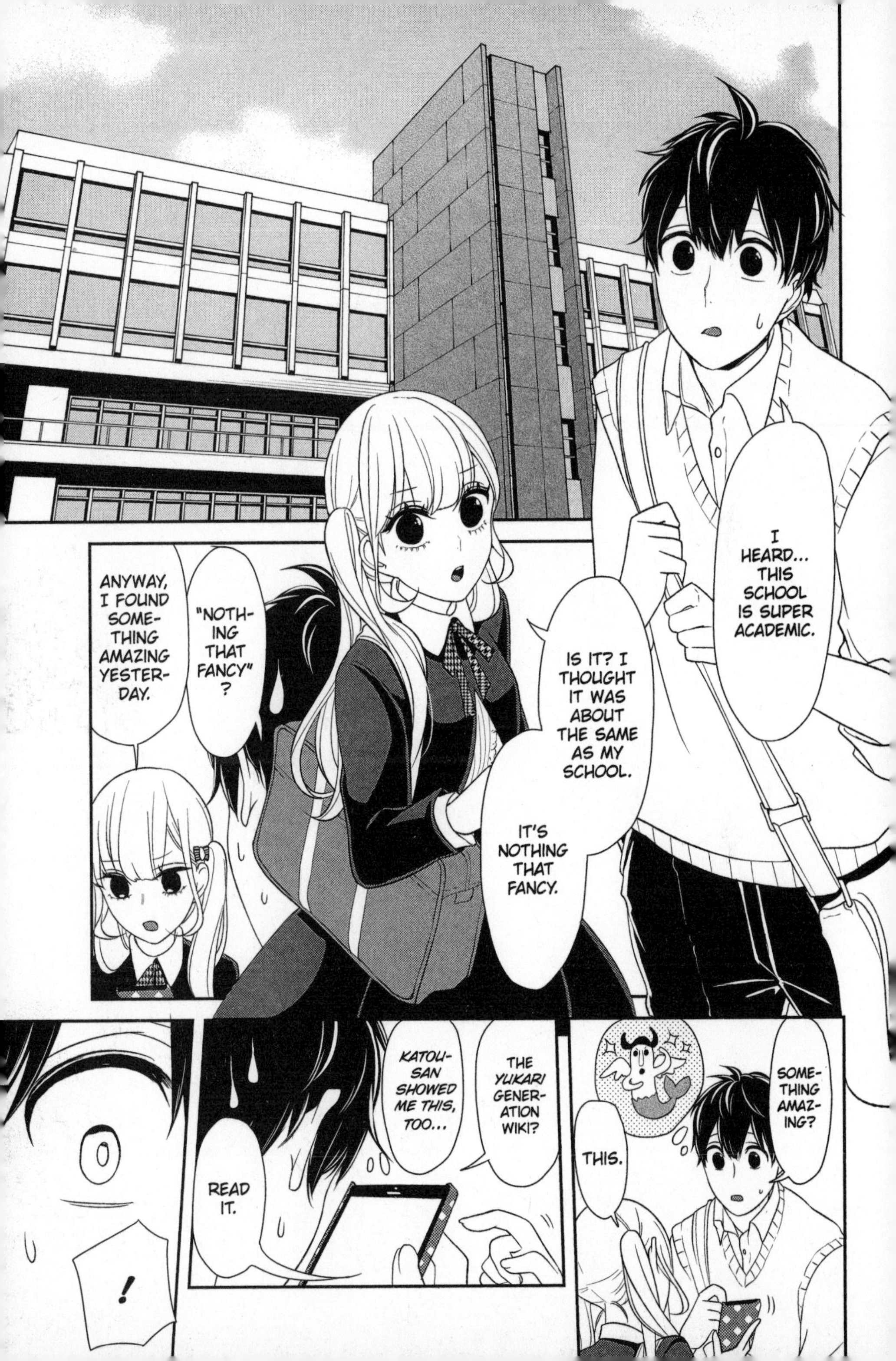

I HEARD... THIS SCHOOL IS SUPER ACADEMIC.
IS IT? I THOUGHT IT WAS ABOUT THE SAME AS MY SCHOOL.
IT'S NOTHING THAT FANCY.
"NOTHING THAT FANCY"?
ANYWAY, I FOUND SOMETHING AMAZING YESTERDAY.
SOMETHING AMAZING?
THIS.
THE YUKARI GENERATION WIKI?
KATOU-SAN SHOWED ME THIS, TOO...
READ IT.
!

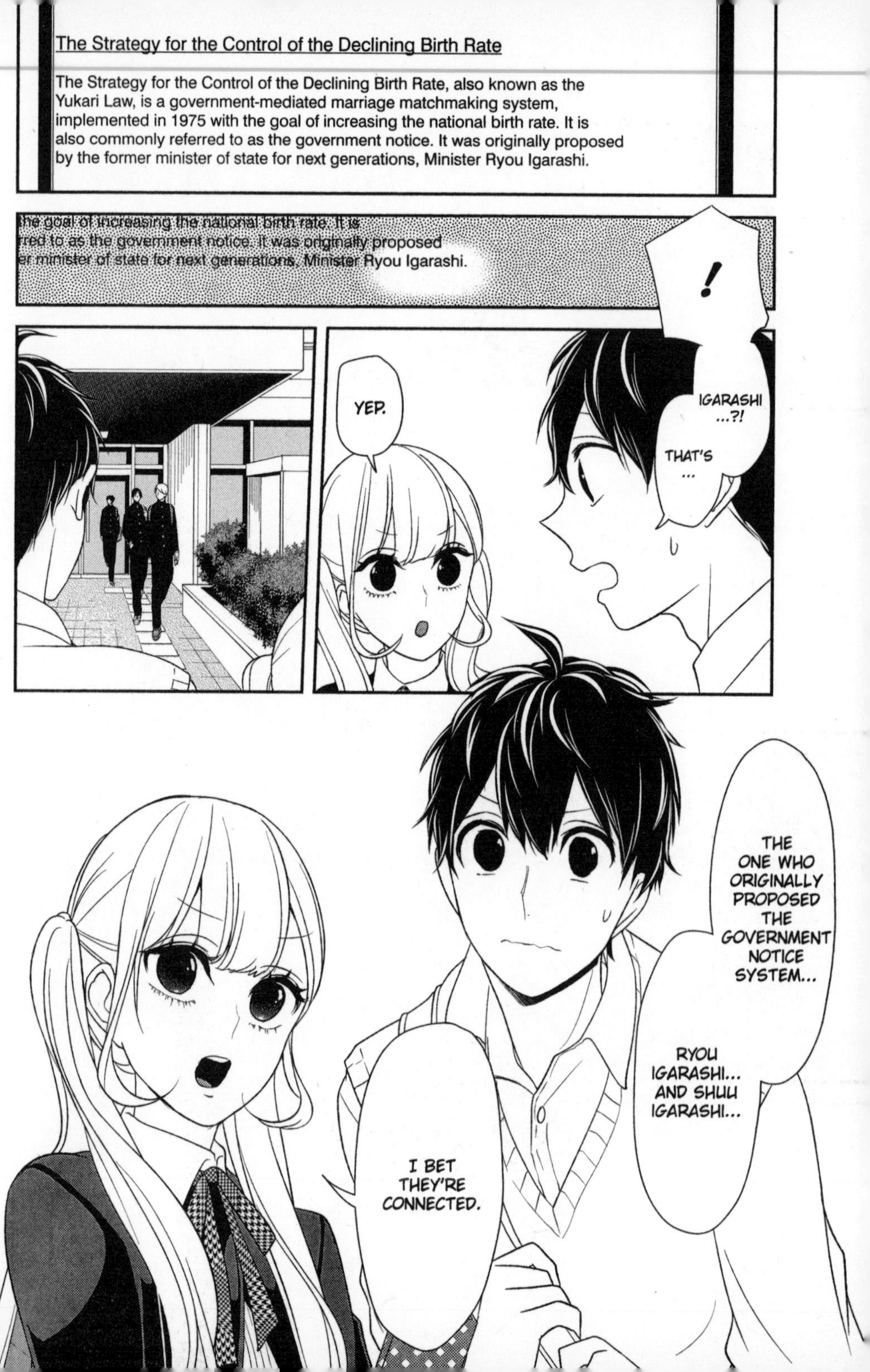
The Strategy for the Control of the Declining Birth Rate
The Strategy for the Control of the Declining Birth Rate, also known as the Yukari Law, is a government-mediated marriage matchmaking system, implemented in 1975 with the goal of increasing the national birth rate. It is also commonly referred to as the government notice. It was originally proposed by the former minister of state for next generations, Minister Ryou Igarashi.
he goal of increasing the national birth rate. It is
rred to as the government notice. It was originally proposed
er minister of state for next generations, Minister Ryou Igarashi.
!
IGARASHI...?!
THAT'S...
YEP.
THE ONE WHO ORIGINALLY PROPOSED THE GOVERNMENT NOTICE SYSTEM...
RYOU IGARASHI... AND SHUU IGARASHI...
I BET THEY'RE CONNECTED.

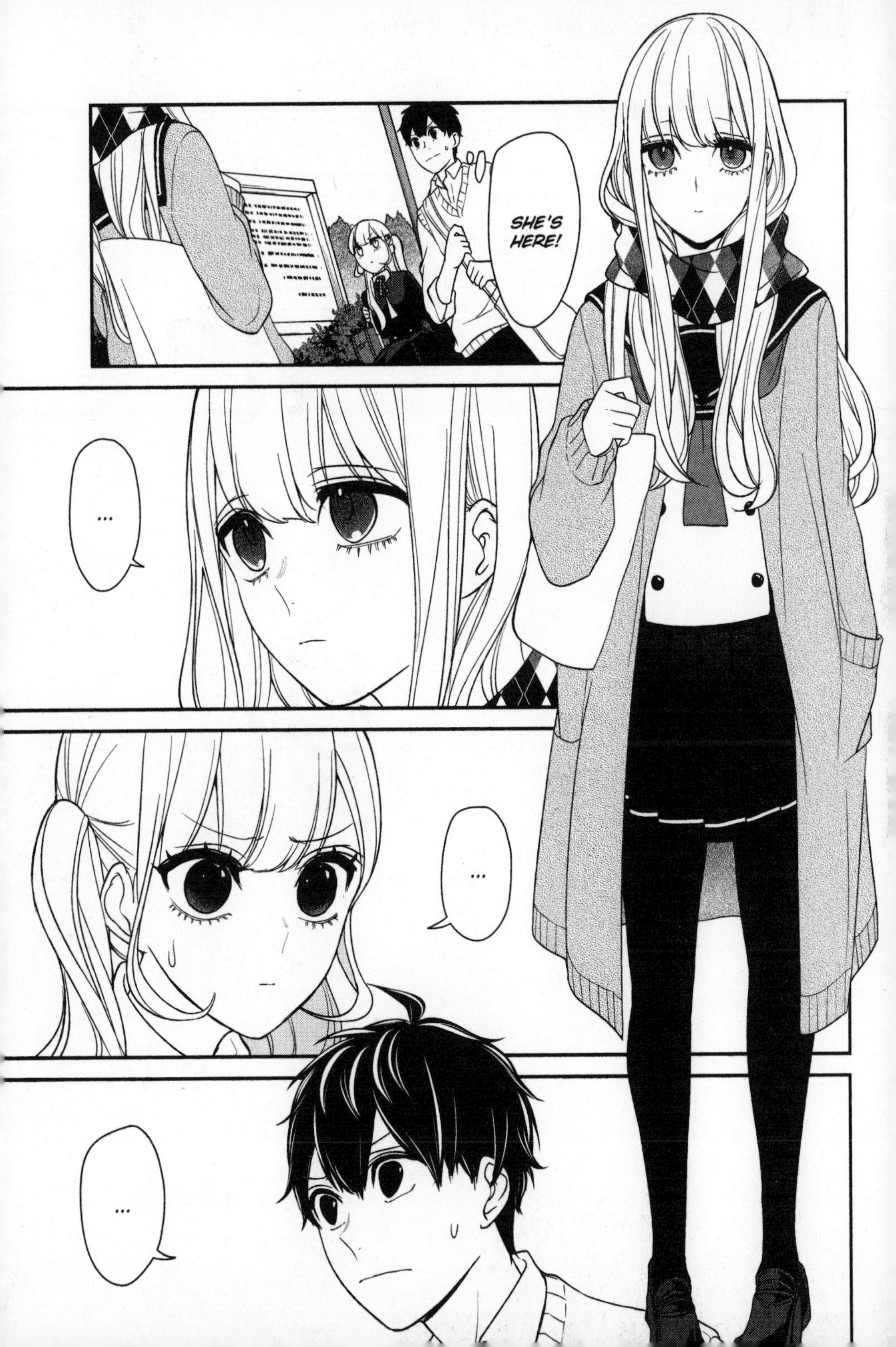

SHE'S HERE!
...
...
...

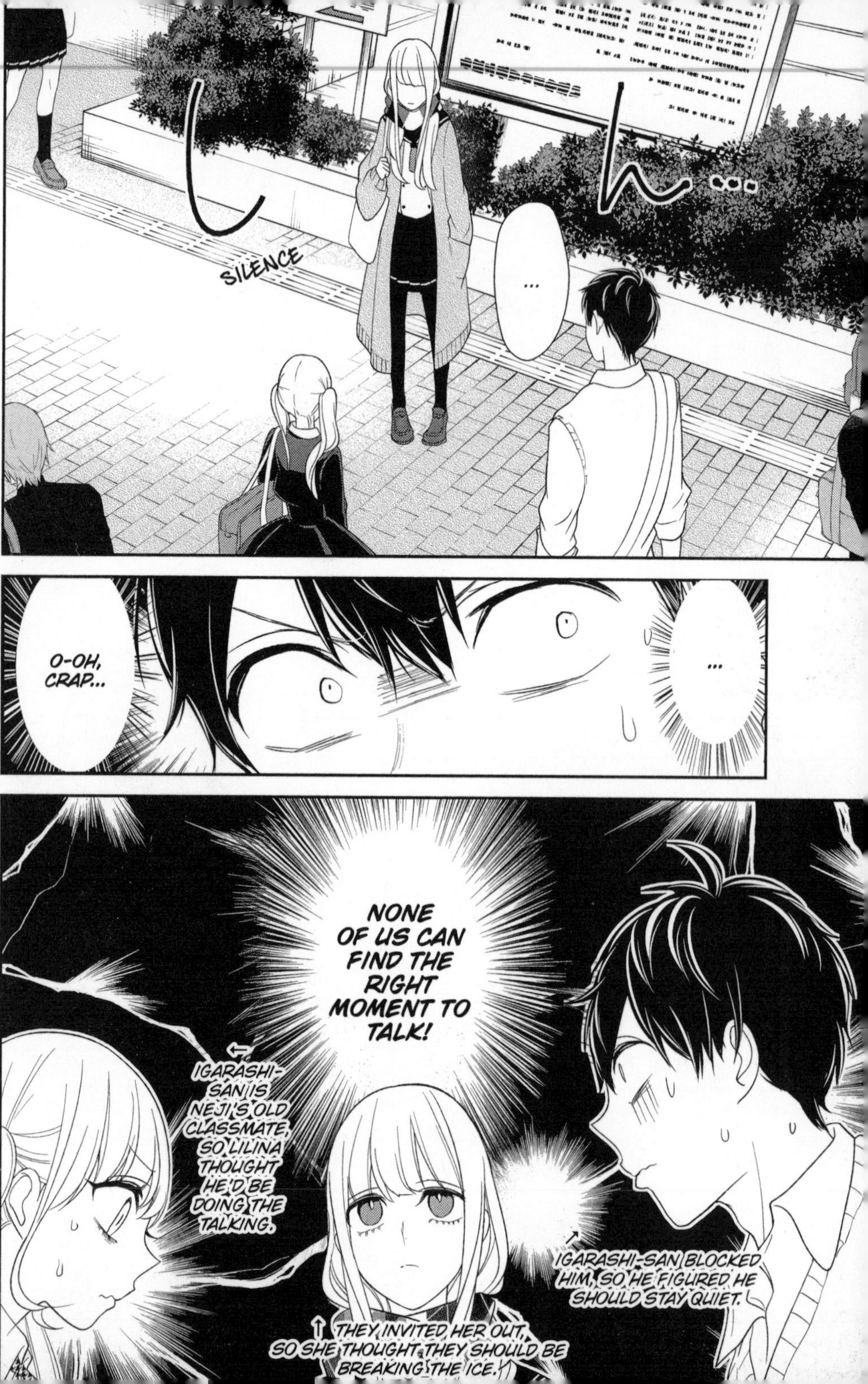

しん...
SILENCE
...
...
O-OH, CRAP...
NONE OF US CAN FIND THE RIGHT MOMENT TO TALK!
IGARASHI-SAN BLOCKED HIM, SO HE FIGURED HE SHOULD STAY QUIET.
THEY INVITED HER OUT, SO SHE THOUGHT THEY SHOULD BE BREAKING THE ICE.
IGARASHI-SAN IS NEJI'S OLD CLASSMATE, SO LILINA THOUGHT HE'D BE DOING THE TALKING.

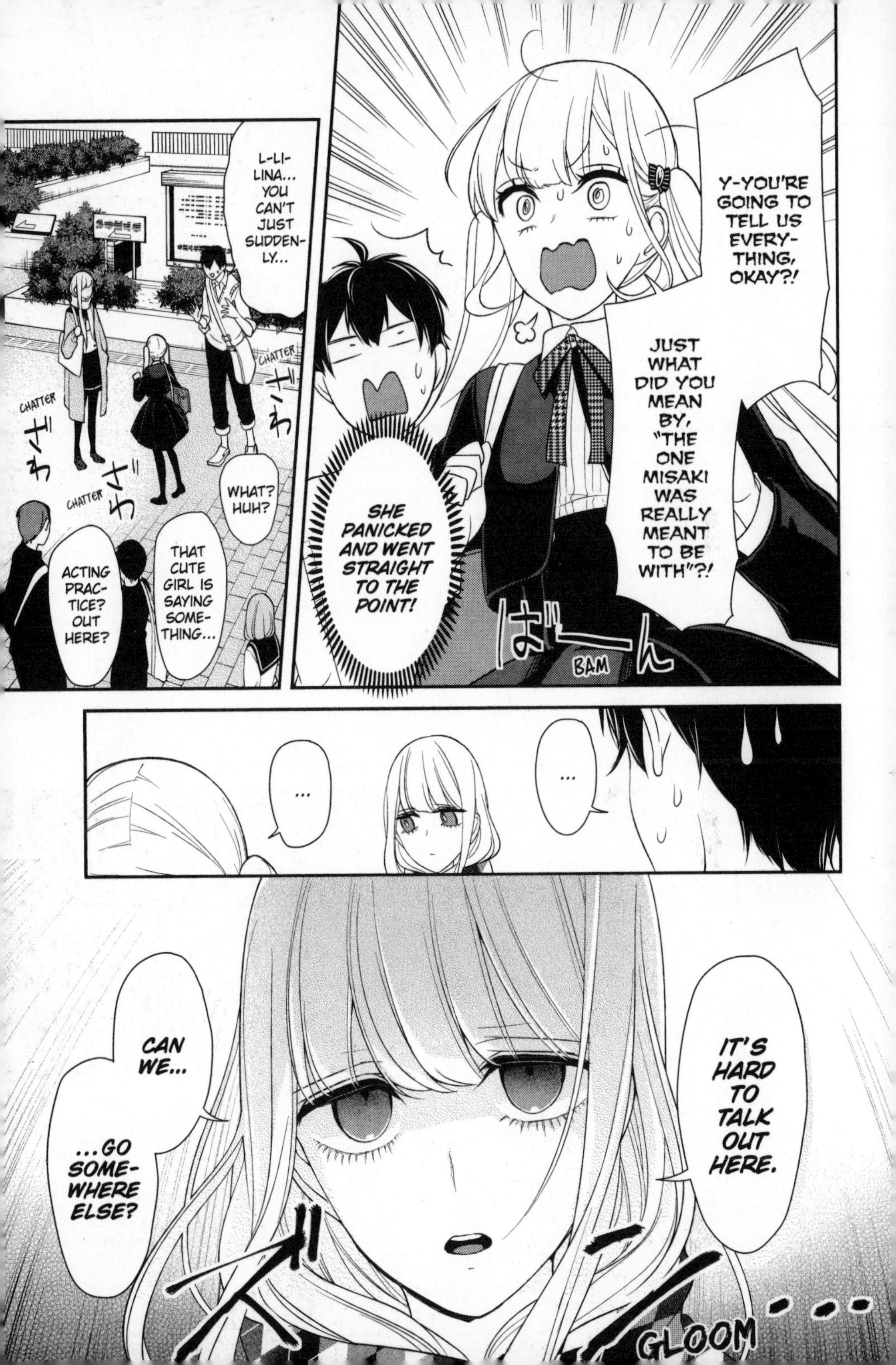

Y-YOU'RE GOING TO TELL US EVERYTHING, OKAY?!
JUST WHAT DID YOU MEAN BY, "THE ONE MISAKI WAS REALLY MEANT TO BE WITH"?!
SHE PANICKED AND WENT STRAIGHT TO THE POINT!
BAM
L-LI-LINA... YOU CAN'T JUST SUDDENLY...
CHATTER
CHATTER
CHATTER
WHAT? HUH?
THAT CUTE GIRL IS SAYING SOMETHING...
ACTING PRACTICE? OUT HERE?
...
...
IT'S HARD TO TALK OUT HERE.
CAN WE...
...GO SOMEWHERE ELSE?
GLOOM

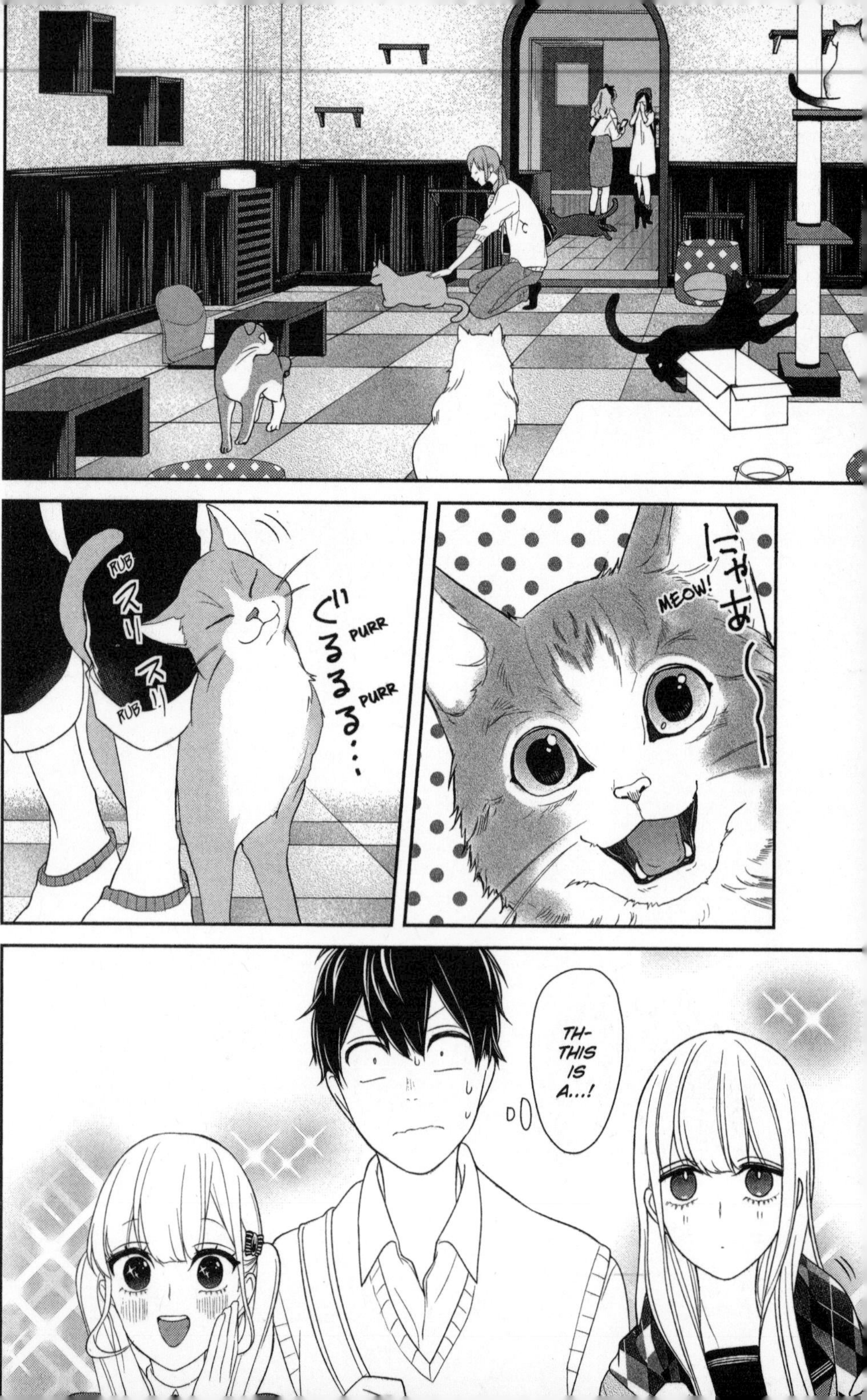
にゃあ〜
MEOW!
スリスリ
RUB RUB
ごろろろ…
PURR PURR
TH-THIS IS A...!

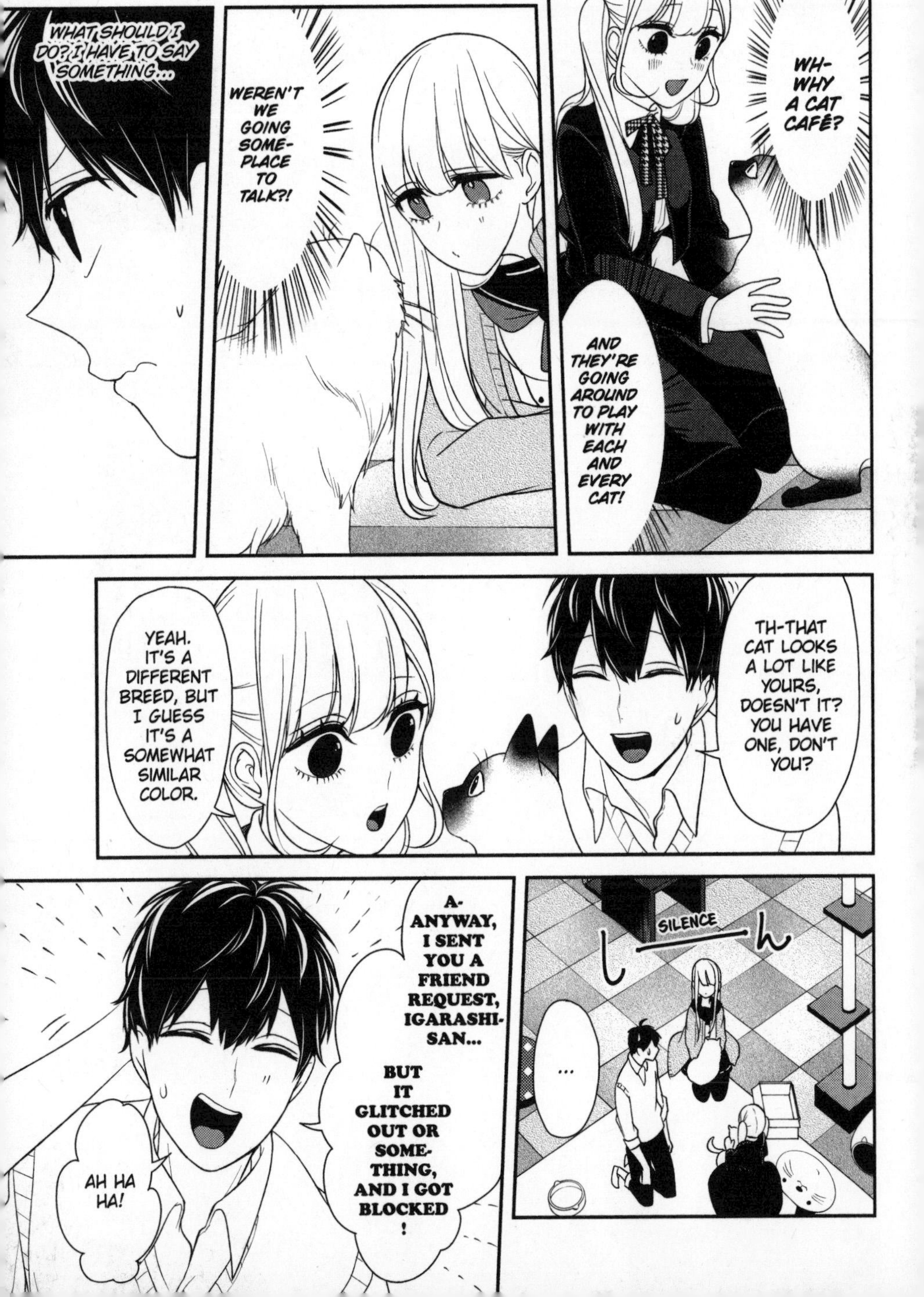
WH-WHY A CAT CAFÉ?
AND THEY'RE GOING AROUND TO PLAY WITH EACH AND EVERY CAT!
WEREN'T WE GOING SOME-PLACE TO TALK?!
WHAT SHOULD I DO? I HAVE TO SAY SOMETHING...
TH-THAT CAT LOOKS A LOT LIKE YOURS, DOESN'T IT? YOU HAVE ONE, DON'T YOU?
YEAH. IT'S A DIFFERENT BREED, BUT I GUESS IT'S A SOMEWHAT SIMILAR COLOR.
SILENCE
し——ん
...
A-ANYWAY, I SENT YOU A FRIEND REQUEST, IGARASHI-SAN...
BUT IT GLITCHED OUT OR SOME-THING, AND I GOT BLOCKED!
AH HA HA!

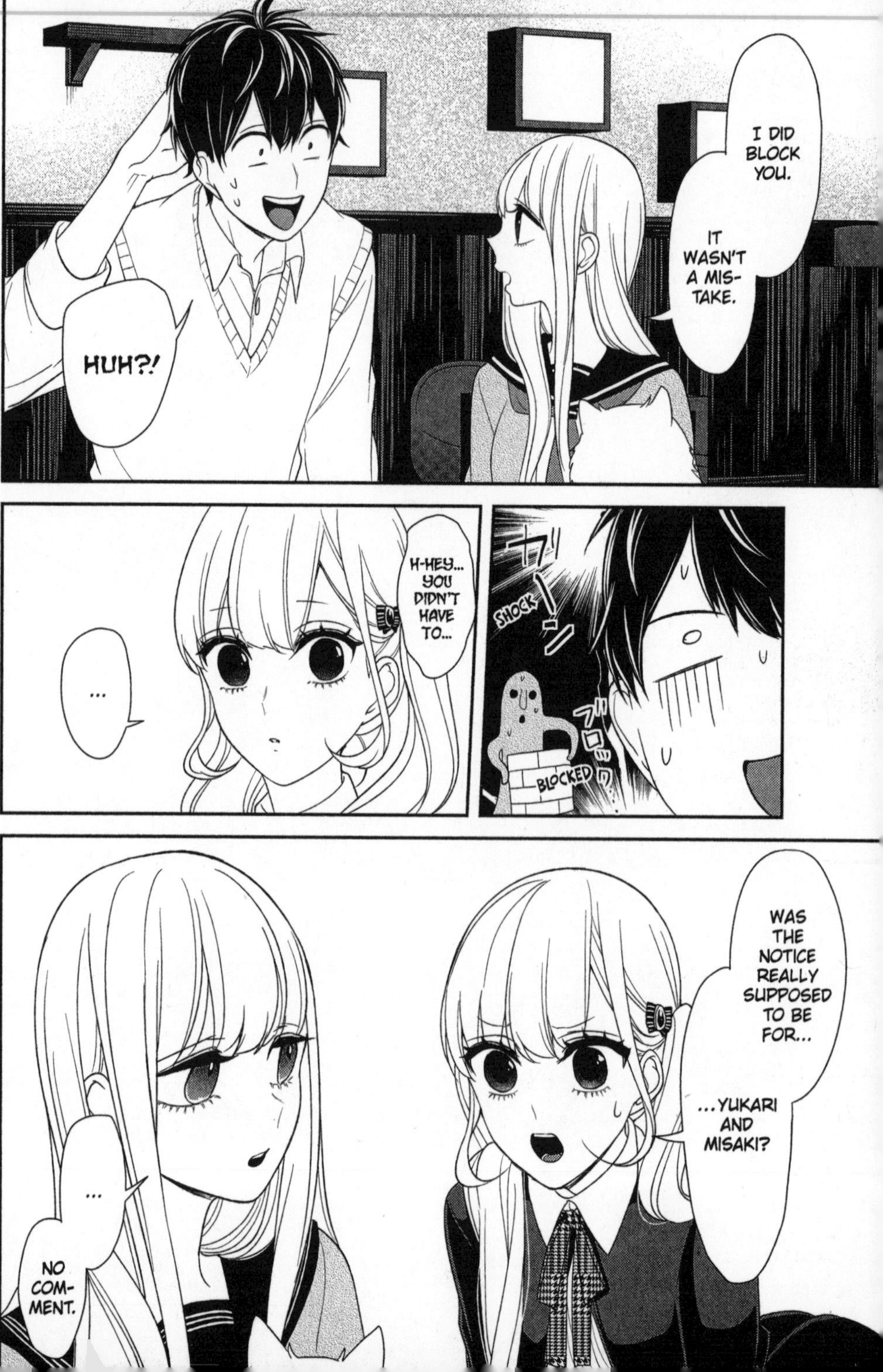
I DID BLOCK YOU.
IT WASN'T A MIS-TAKE.
HUH?!
SHOCK
BLOCKED
H-HEY... YOU DIDN'T HAVE TO...
...
WAS THE NOTICE REALLY SUPPOSED TO BE FOR...
...YUKARI AND MISAKI?
...
NO COM-MENT.

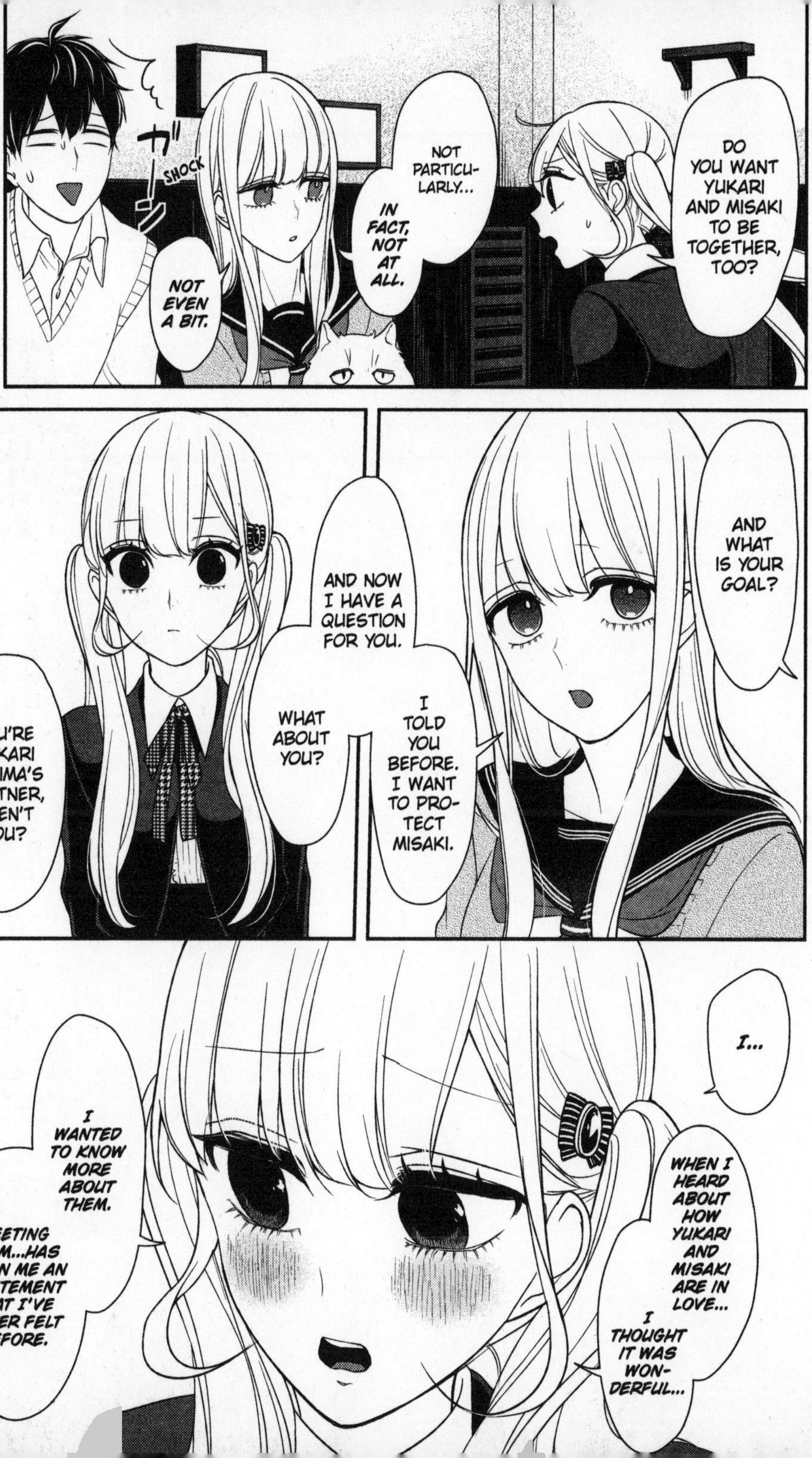

DO YOU WANT YUKARI AND MISAKI TO BE TOGETHER, TOO?
NOT PARTICULARLY...
IN FACT, NOT AT ALL.
NOT EVEN A BIT.
SHOCK
AND WHAT IS YOUR GOAL?
I TOLD YOU BEFORE. I WANT TO PROTECT MISAKI.
WHAT ABOUT YOU?
AND NOW I HAVE A QUESTION FOR YOU.
YOU'RE YUKARI NEJIMA'S PARTNER, AREN'T YOU?
I...
WHEN I HEARD ABOUT HOW YUKARI AND MISAKI ARE IN LOVE...
I THOUGHT IT WAS WONDERFUL...
I WANTED TO KNOW MORE ABOUT THEM.
MEETING THEM...HAS GIVEN ME AN EXCITEMENT THAT I'VE NEVER FELT BEFORE.

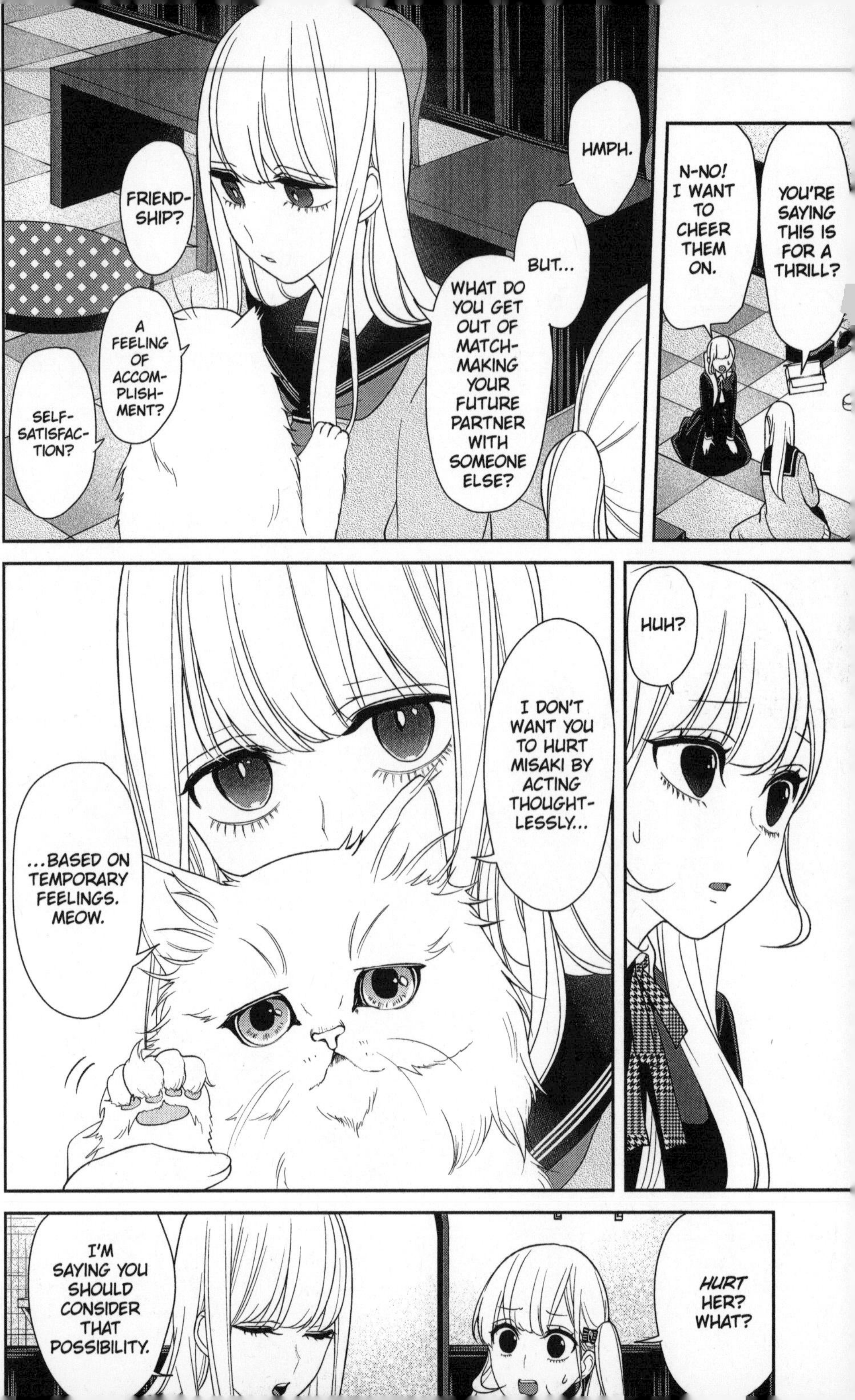
YOU'RE SAYING THIS IS FOR A THRILL?
N-NO! I WANT TO CHEER THEM ON.
HMPH.
BUT... WHAT DO YOU GET OUT OF MATCH-MAKING YOUR FUTURE PARTNER WITH SOMEONE ELSE?
FRIEND-SHIP?
A FEELING OF ACCOM-PLISH-MENT?
SELF-SATISFAC-TION?
HUH?
I DON'T WANT YOU TO HURT MISAKI BY ACTING THOUGHT-LESSLY...
...BASED ON TEMPORARY FEELINGS. MEOW.
HURT HER? WHAT?
I'M SAYING YOU SHOULD CONSIDER THAT POSSIBILITY.

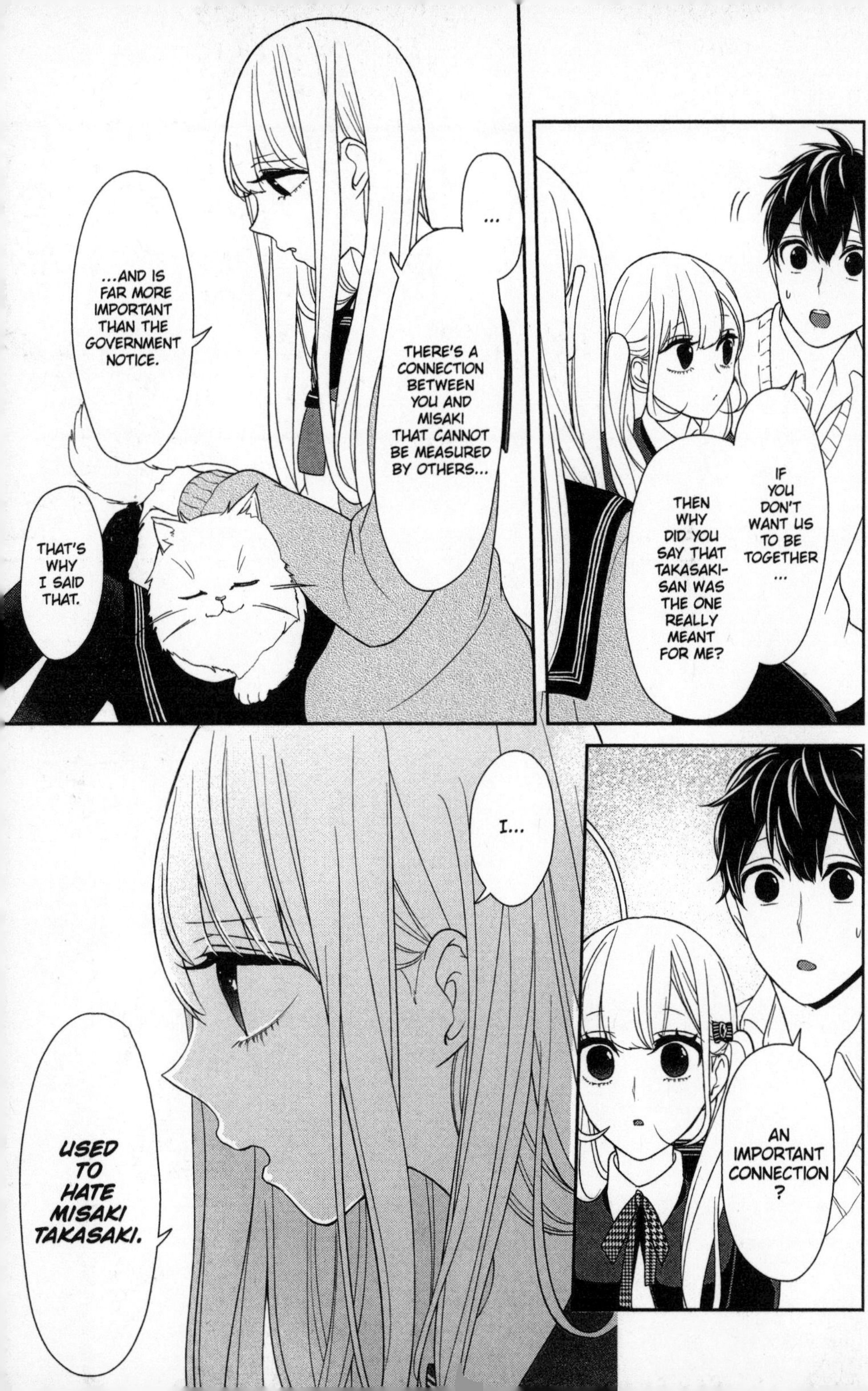
IF YOU DON'T WANT US TO BE TOGETHER...
THEN WHY DID YOU SAY THAT TAKASAKI-SAN WAS THE ONE REALLY MEANT FOR ME?
...
THERE'S A CONNECTION BETWEEN YOU AND MISAKI THAT CANNOT BE MEASURED BY OTHERS...
...AND IS FAR MORE IMPORTANT THAN THE GOVERNMENT NOTICE.
THAT'S WHY I SAID THAT.
AN IMPORTANT CONNECTION?
I...
USED TO HATE MISAKI TAKASAKI.

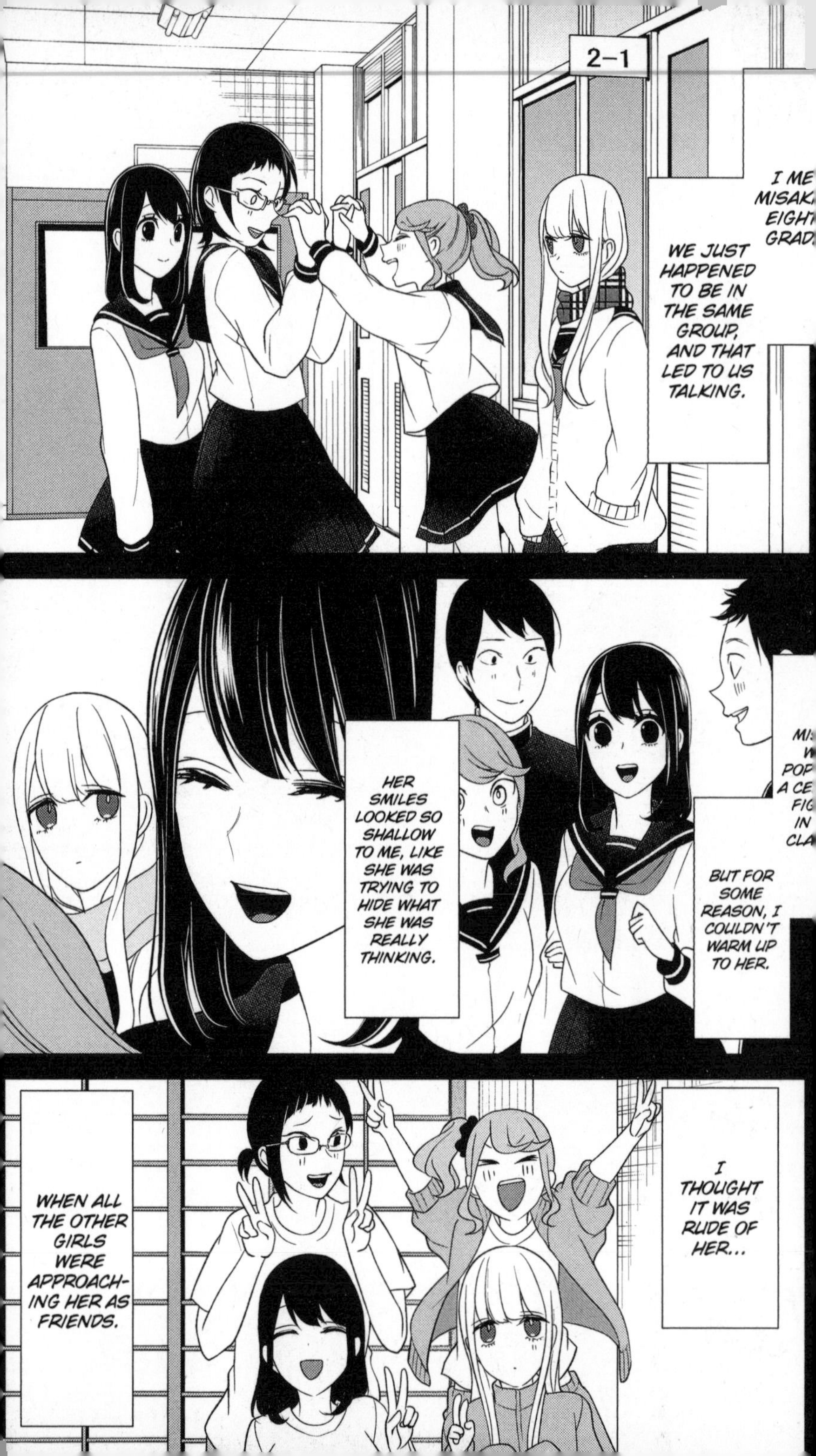
2-1
WE JUST HAPPENED TO BE IN THE SAME GROUP, AND THAT LED TO US TALKING.
BUT FOR SOME REASON, I COULDN'T WARM UP TO HER.
HER SMILES LOOKED SO SHALLOW TO ME, LIKE SHE WAS TRYING TO HIDE WHAT SHE WAS REALLY THINKING.
I THOUGHT IT WAS RUDE OF HER...
WHEN ALL THE OTHER GIRLS WERE APPROACH-ING HER AS FRIENDS.

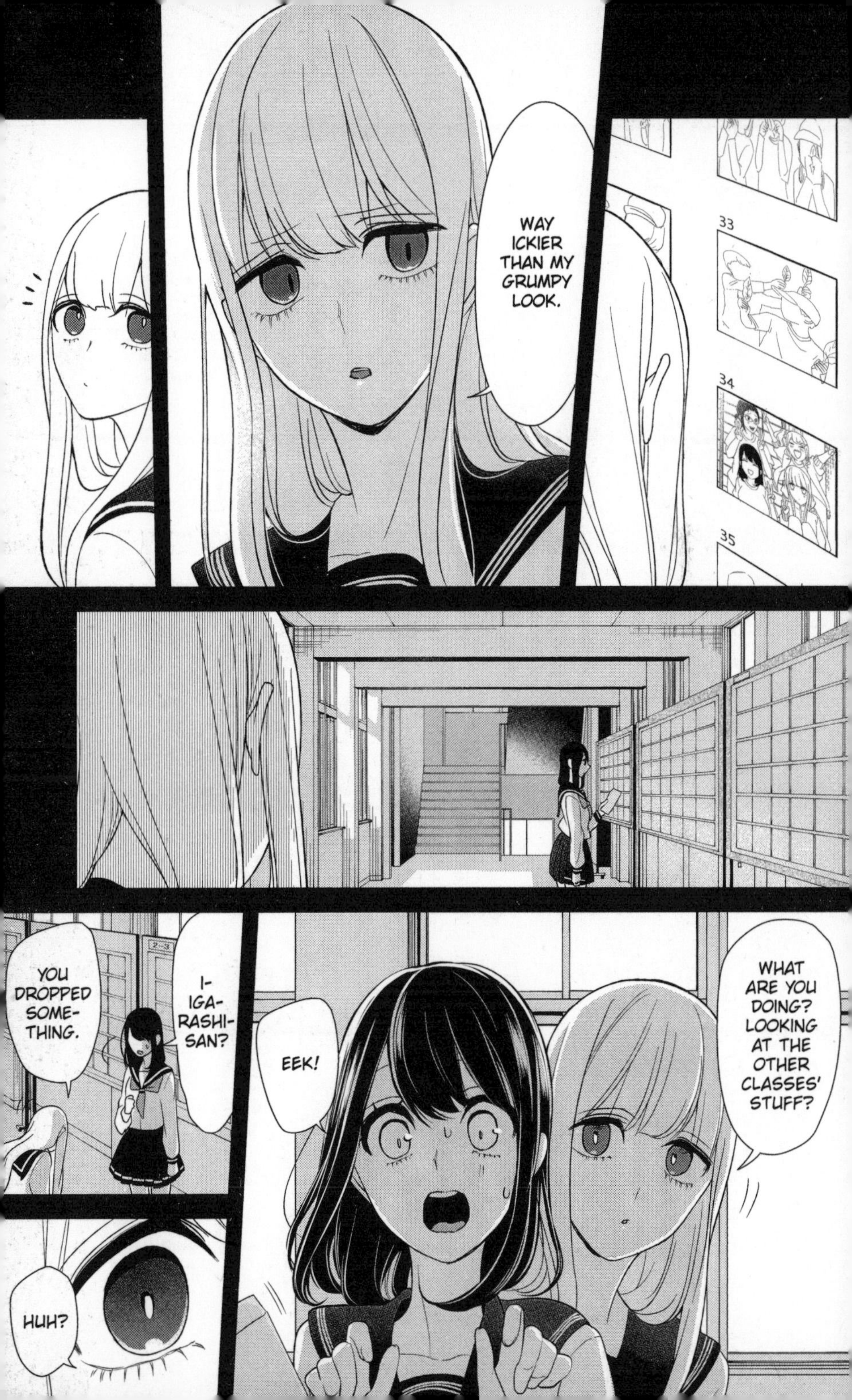
33
34
35
WAY ICKIER THAN MY GRUMPY LOOK.
WHAT ARE YOU DOING? LOOKING AT THE OTHER CLASSES' STUFF?
EEK!
I-IGARASHI-SAN?
YOU DROPPED SOME-THING.
HUH?

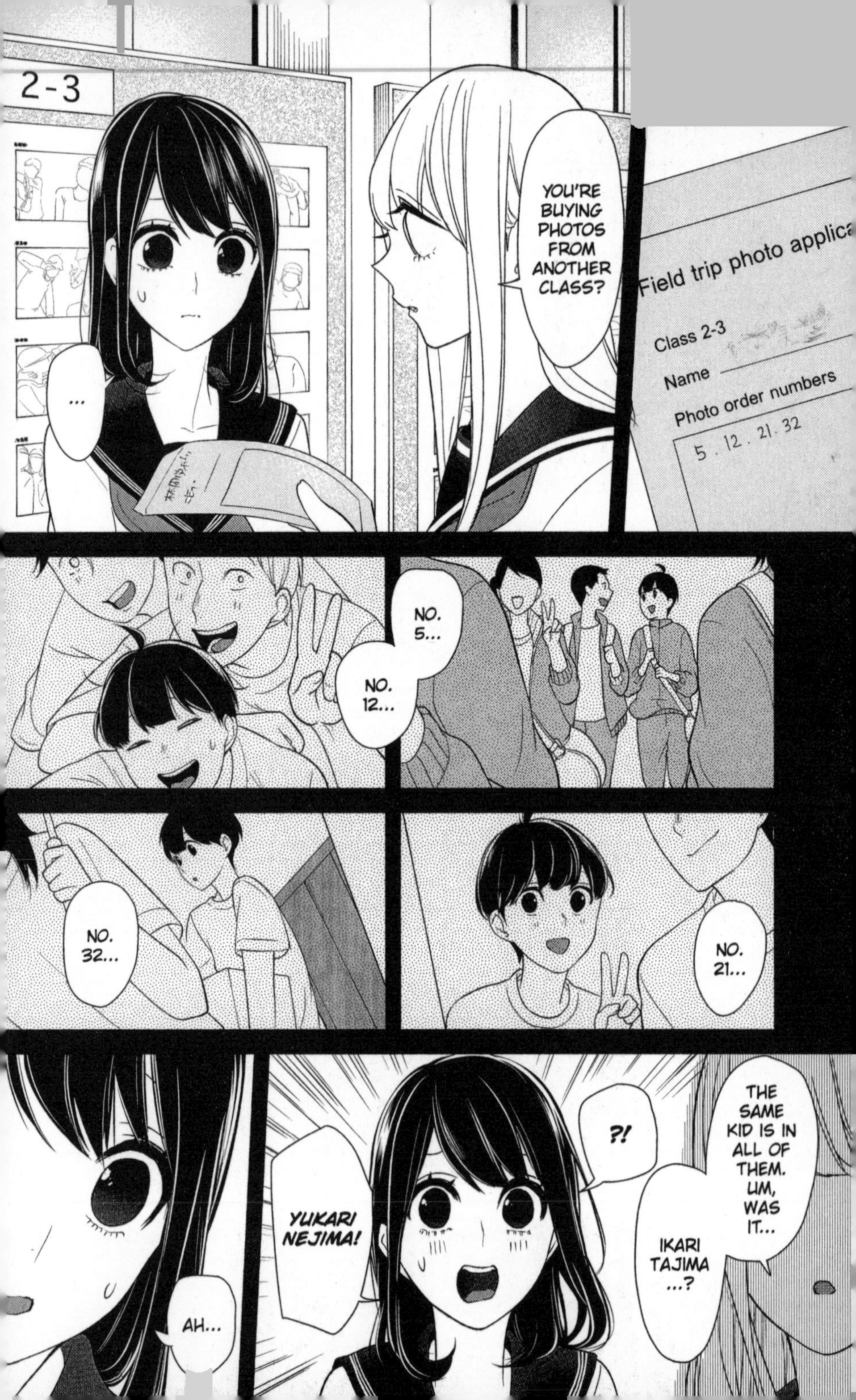
Field trip photo applica
Class 2-3
Name
Photo order numbers
5 . 12 . 21 . 32
2-3
YOU'RE BUYING PHOTOS FROM ANOTHER CLASS?
...
NO. 5...
NO. 12...
NO. 21...
NO. 32...
THE SAME KID IS IN ALL OF THEM. UM, WAS IT...
IKARI TAJIMA ...?
?!
YUKARI NEJIMA!
AH...

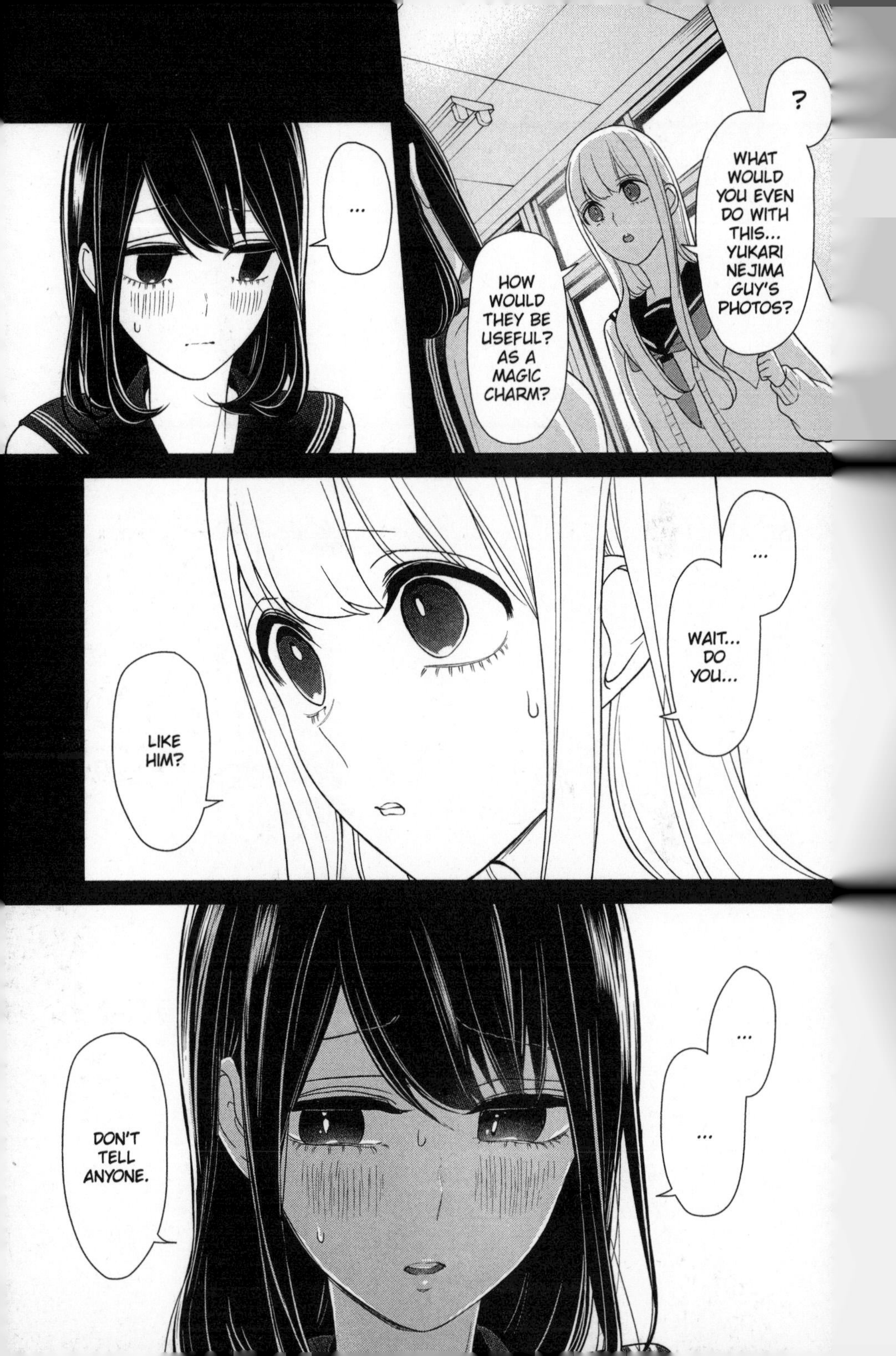
?
WHAT WOULD YOU EVEN DO WITH THIS... YUKARI NEJIMA GUY'S PHOTOS?
HOW WOULD THEY BE USEFUL? AS A MAGIC CHARM?
...
...
WAIT... DO YOU...
LIKE HIM?
...
...
DON'T TELL ANYONE.

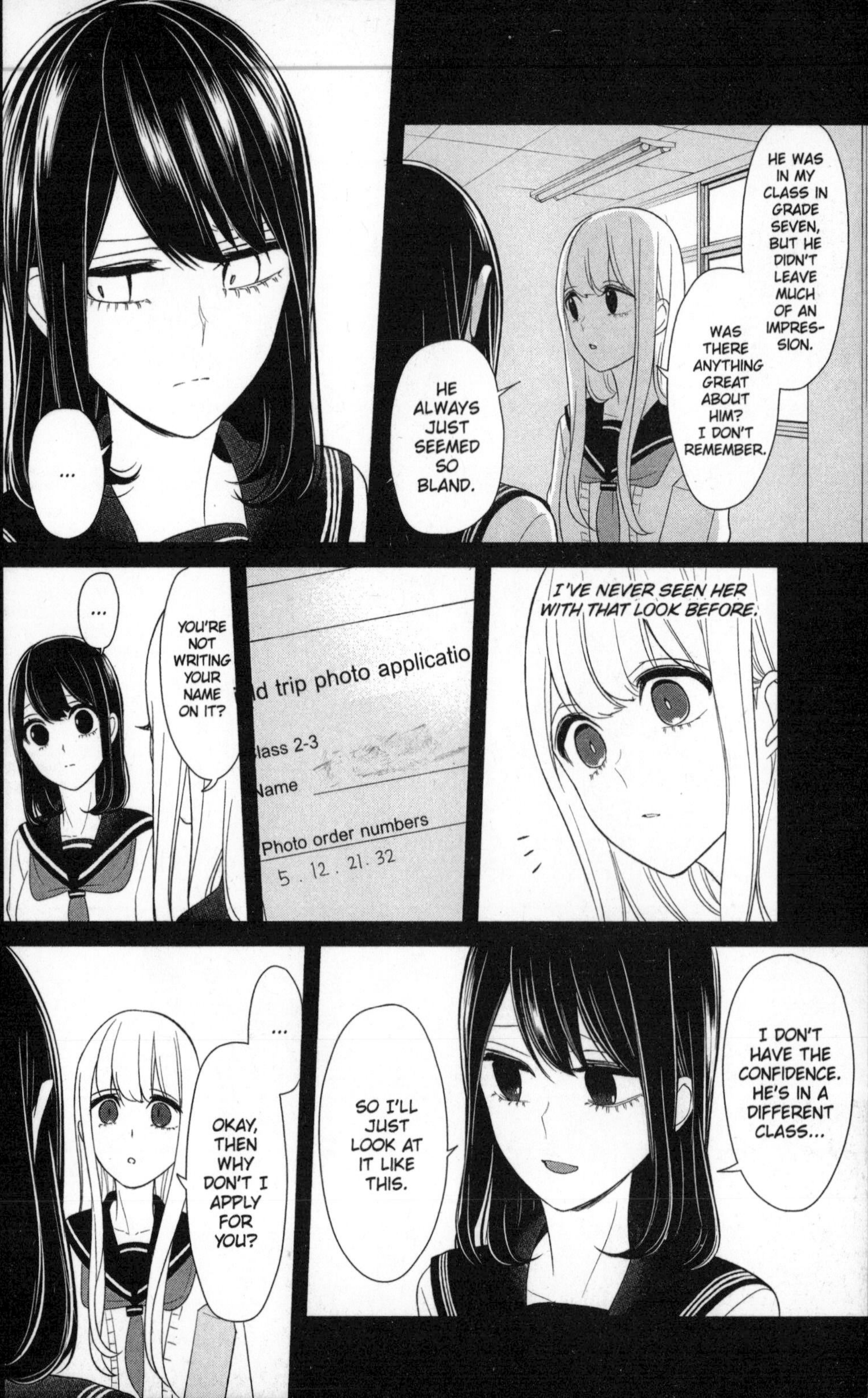
HE WAS IN MY CLASS IN GRADE SEVEN, BUT HE DIDN'T LEAVE MUCH OF AN IMPRESSION.
WAS THERE ANYTHING GREAT ABOUT HIM? I DON'T REMEMBER.
HE ALWAYS JUST SEEMED SO BLAND.
...
I'VE NEVER SEEN HER WITH THAT LOOK BEFORE.
d trip photo applicatio
lass 2-3
Name
Photo order numbers
5 . 12 . 21 . 32
YOU'RE NOT WRITING YOUR NAME ON IT?
...
I DON'T HAVE THE CONFIDENCE. HE'S IN A DIFFERENT CLASS...
SO I'LL JUST LOOK AT IT LIKE THIS.
...
OKAY, THEN WHY DON'T I APPLY FOR YOU?

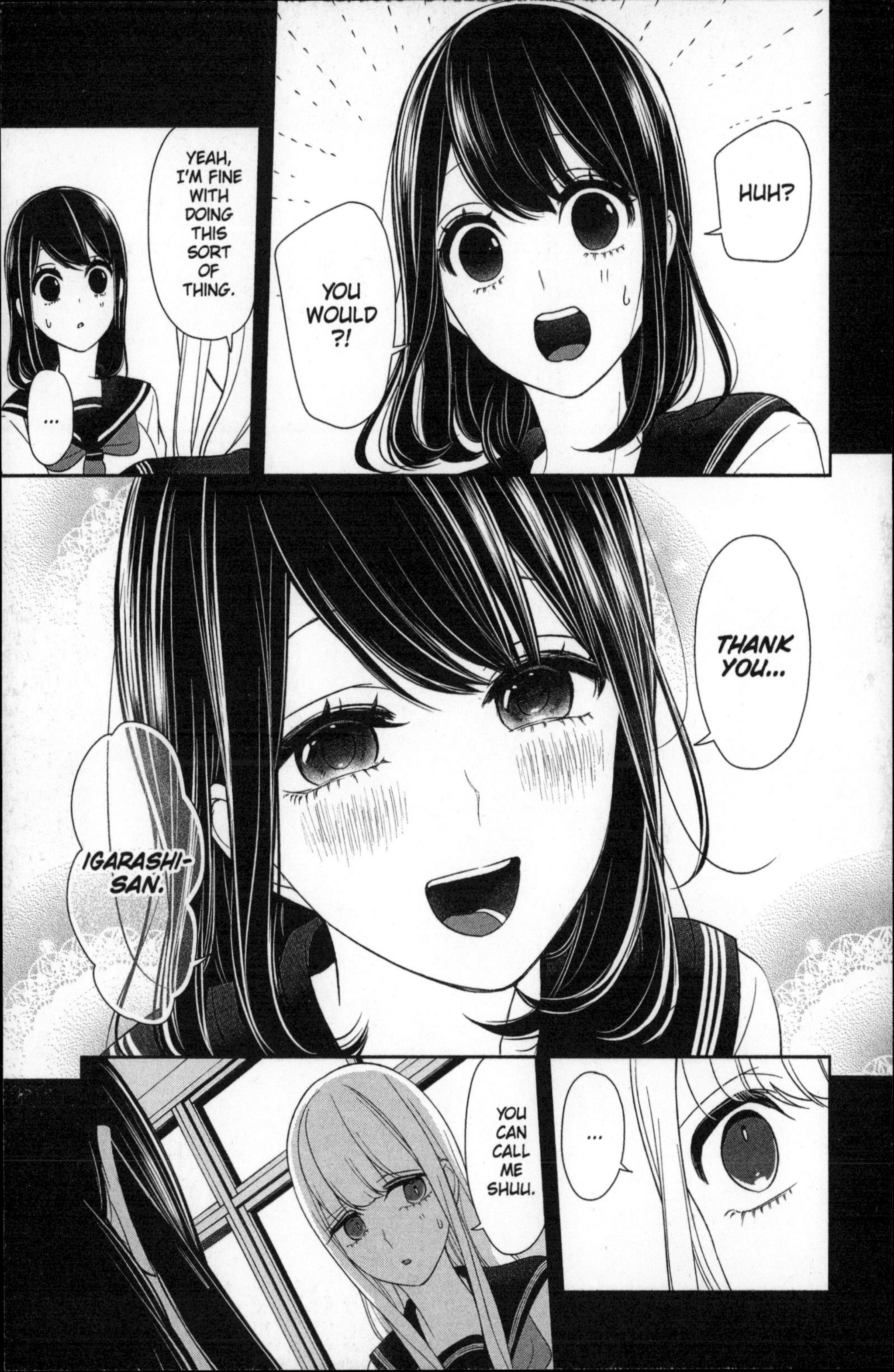
HUH?
YOU WOULD ?!
YEAH, I'M FINE WITH DOING THIS SORT OF THING.
...
THANK YOU...
IGARASHI-SAN.
...
YOU CAN CALL ME SHUU.

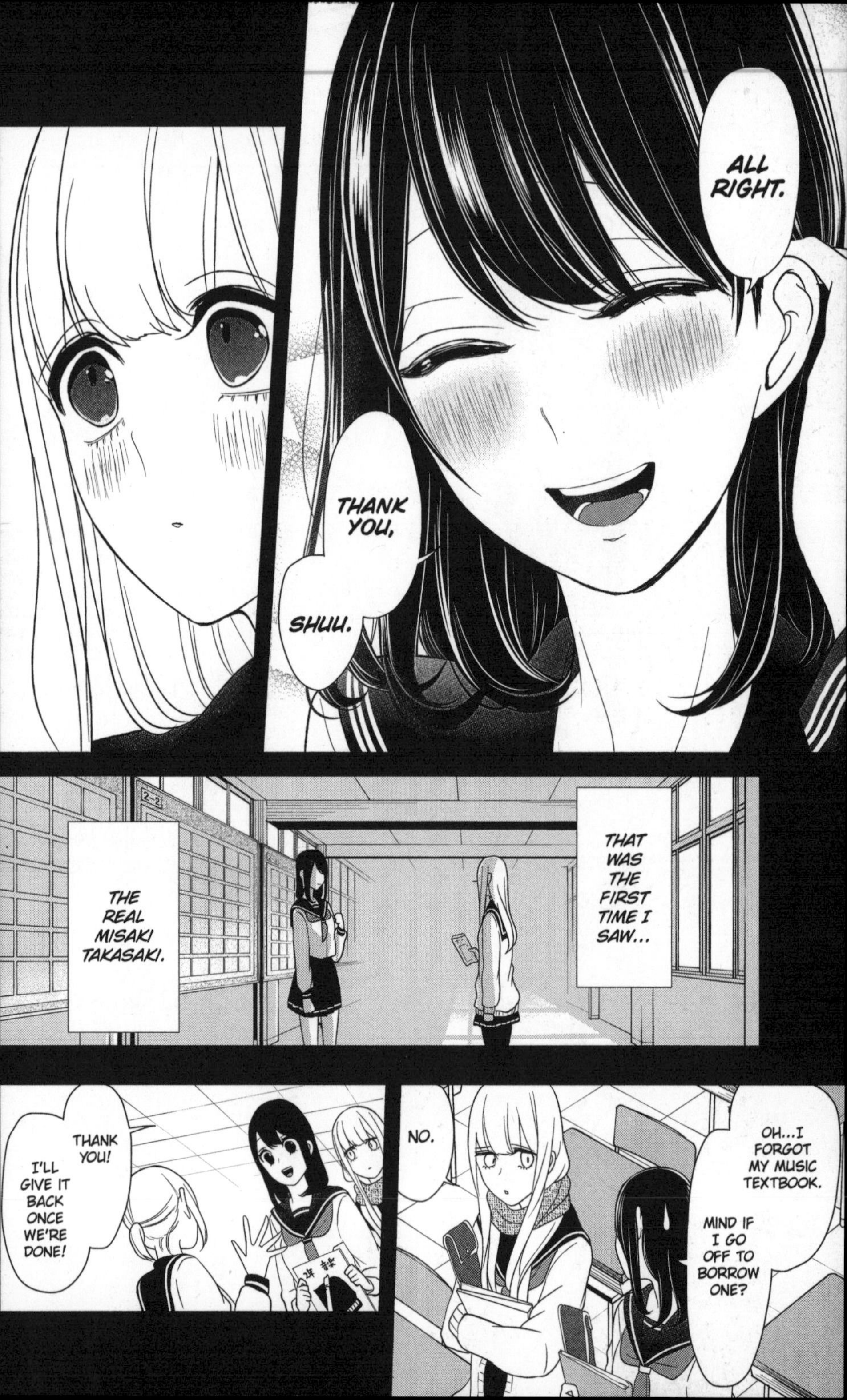
ALL RIGHT.
THANK YOU,
SHUU.
THAT WAS THE FIRST TIME I SAW...
THE REAL MISAKI TAKASAKI.
OH...I FORGOT MY MUSIC TEXTBOOK.
MIND IF I GO OFF TO BORROW ONE?
NO.
THANK YOU!
I'LL GIVE IT BACK ONCE WE'RE DONE!

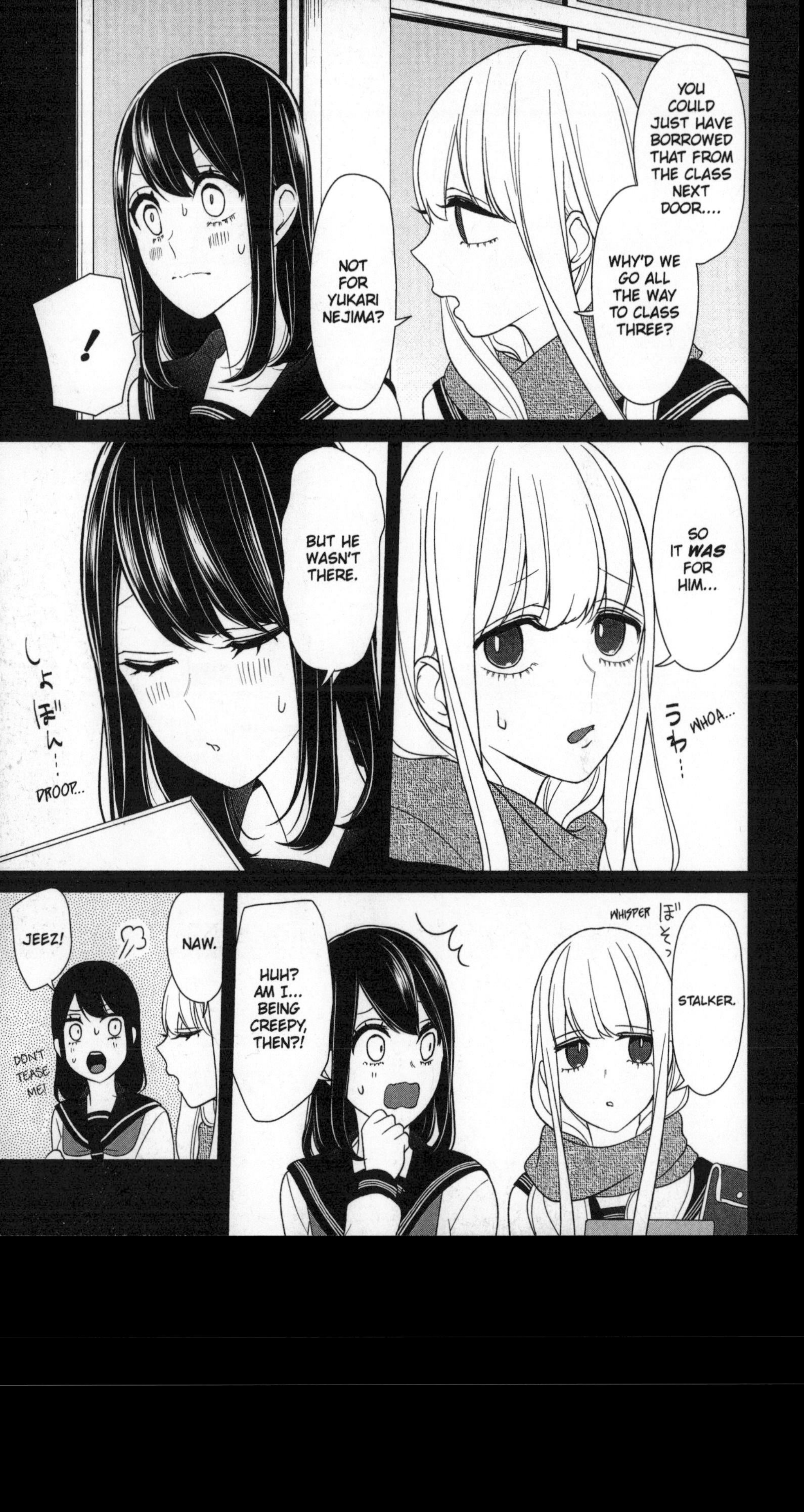
YOU COULD JUST HAVE BORROWED THAT FROM THE CLASS NEXT DOOR....
WHY'D WE GO ALL THE WAY TO CLASS THREE?
NOT FOR YUKARI NEJIMA?
!
SO IT **WAS** FOR HIM...
うわ…
WHOA...
BUT HE WASN'T THERE.
しょぼん…
DROOP...
ぼそっ
WHISPER
STALKER.
HUH? AM I... BEING CREEPY, THEN?!
NAW.
JEEZ!
DON'T TEASE ME!

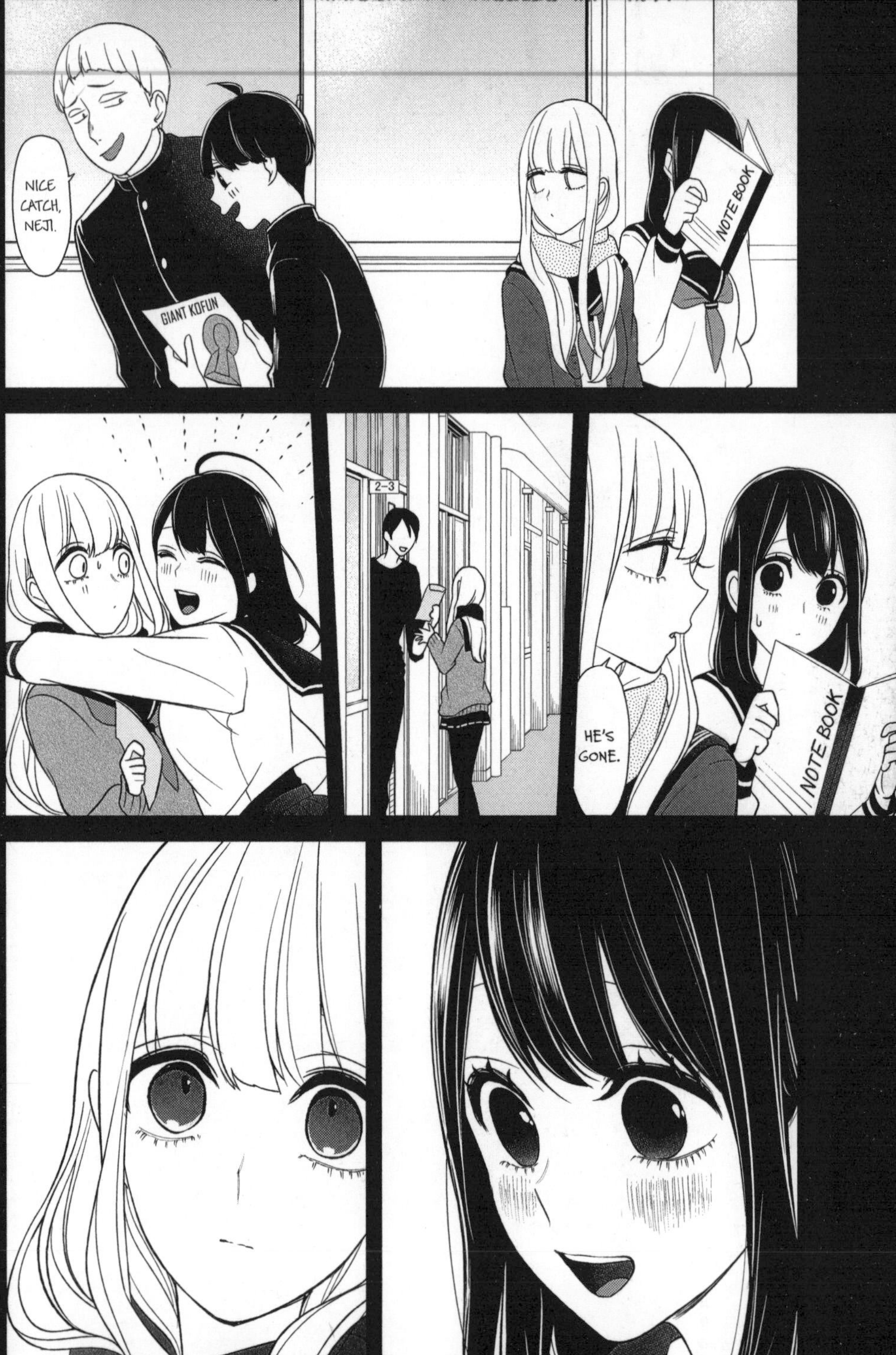
NOTE BOOK
NICE CATCH, NEJI.
GIANT KOFUN
HE'S GONE.
NOTE BOOK
2-3

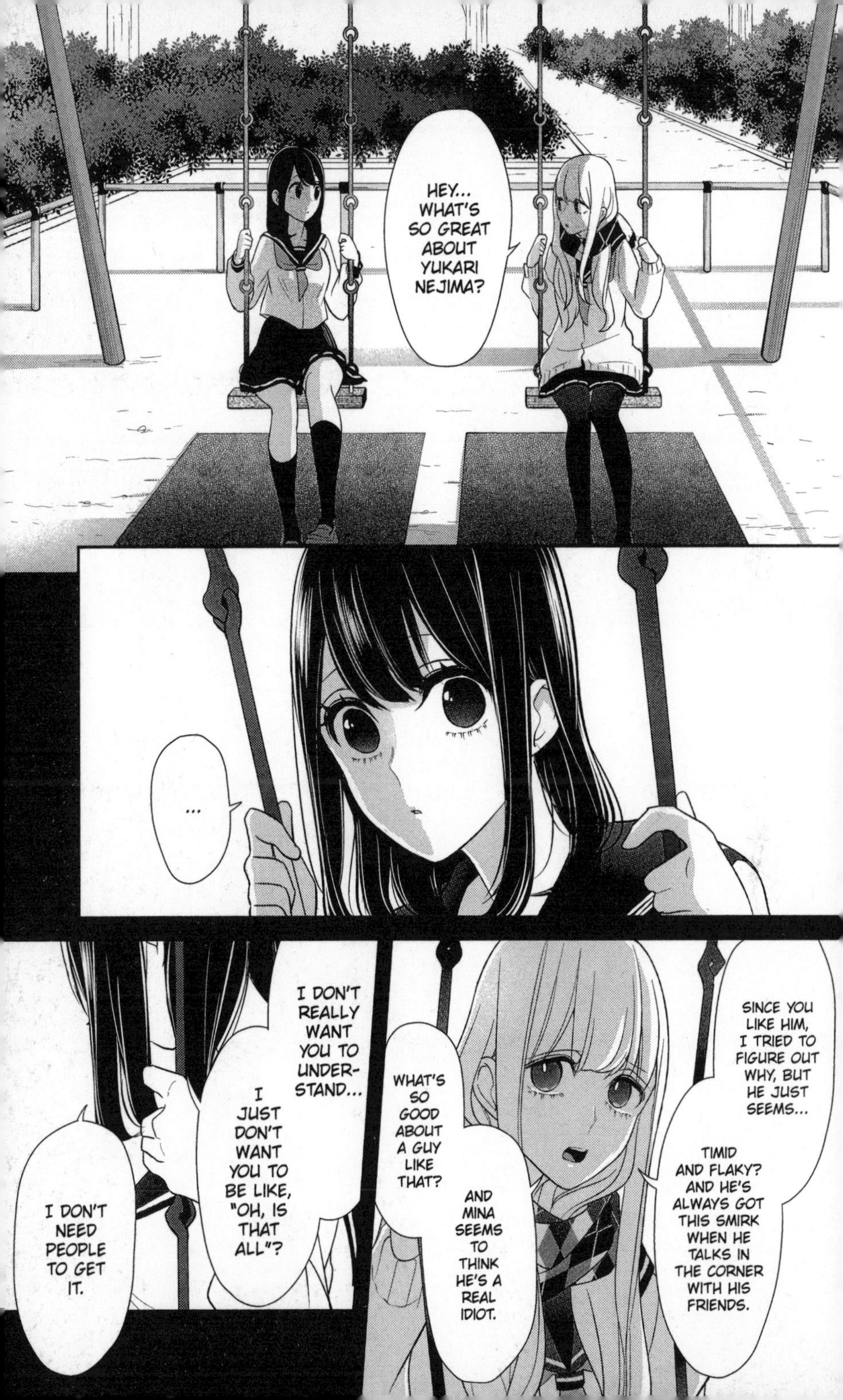
HEY... WHAT'S SO GREAT ABOUT YUKARI NEJIMA?
...
SINCE YOU LIKE HIM, I TRIED TO FIGURE OUT WHY, BUT HE JUST SEEMS...
TIMID AND FLAKY? AND HE'S ALWAYS GOT THIS SMIRK WHEN HE TALKS IN THE CORNER WITH HIS FRIENDS.
AND MINA SEEMS TO THINK HE'S A REAL IDIOT.
WHAT'S SO GOOD ABOUT A GUY LIKE THAT?
I DON'T REALLY WANT YOU TO UNDER-STAND...
I JUST DON'T WANT YOU TO BE LIKE, "OH, IS THAT ALL"?
I DON'T NEED PEOPLE TO GET IT.

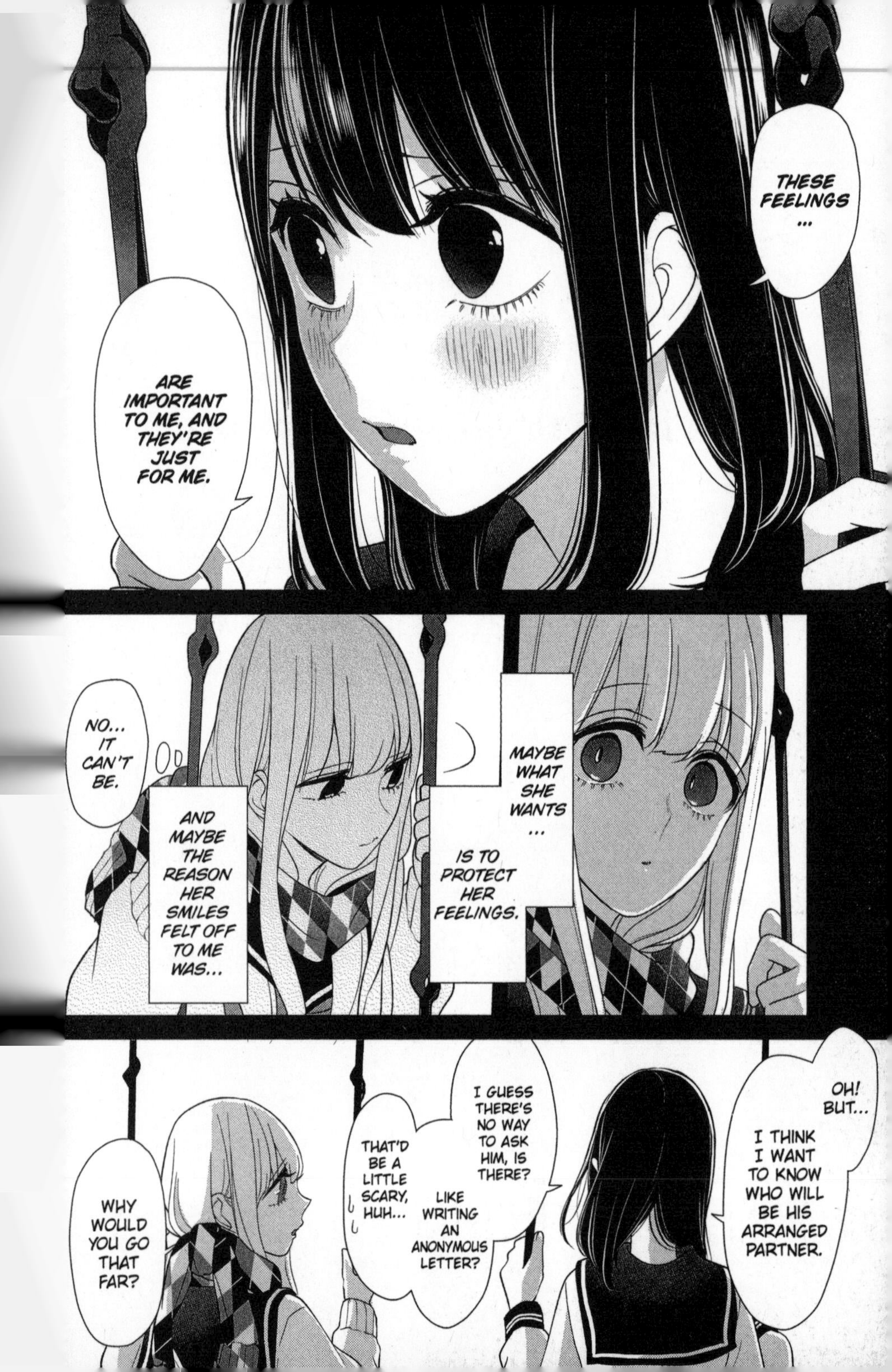
THESE FEELINGS ...
ARE IMPORTANT TO ME, AND THEY'RE JUST FOR ME.
MAYBE WHAT SHE WANTS ...
IS TO PROTECT HER FEELINGS.
AND MAYBE THE REASON HER SMILES FELT OFF TO ME WAS...
NO... IT CAN'T BE.
OH! BUT...
I THINK I WANT TO KNOW WHO WILL BE HIS ARRANGED PARTNER.
I GUESS THERE'S NO WAY TO ASK HIM, IS THERE?
LIKE WRITING AN ANONYMOUS LETTER?
THAT'D BE A LITTLE SCARY, HUH...
WHY WOULD YOU GO THAT FAR?

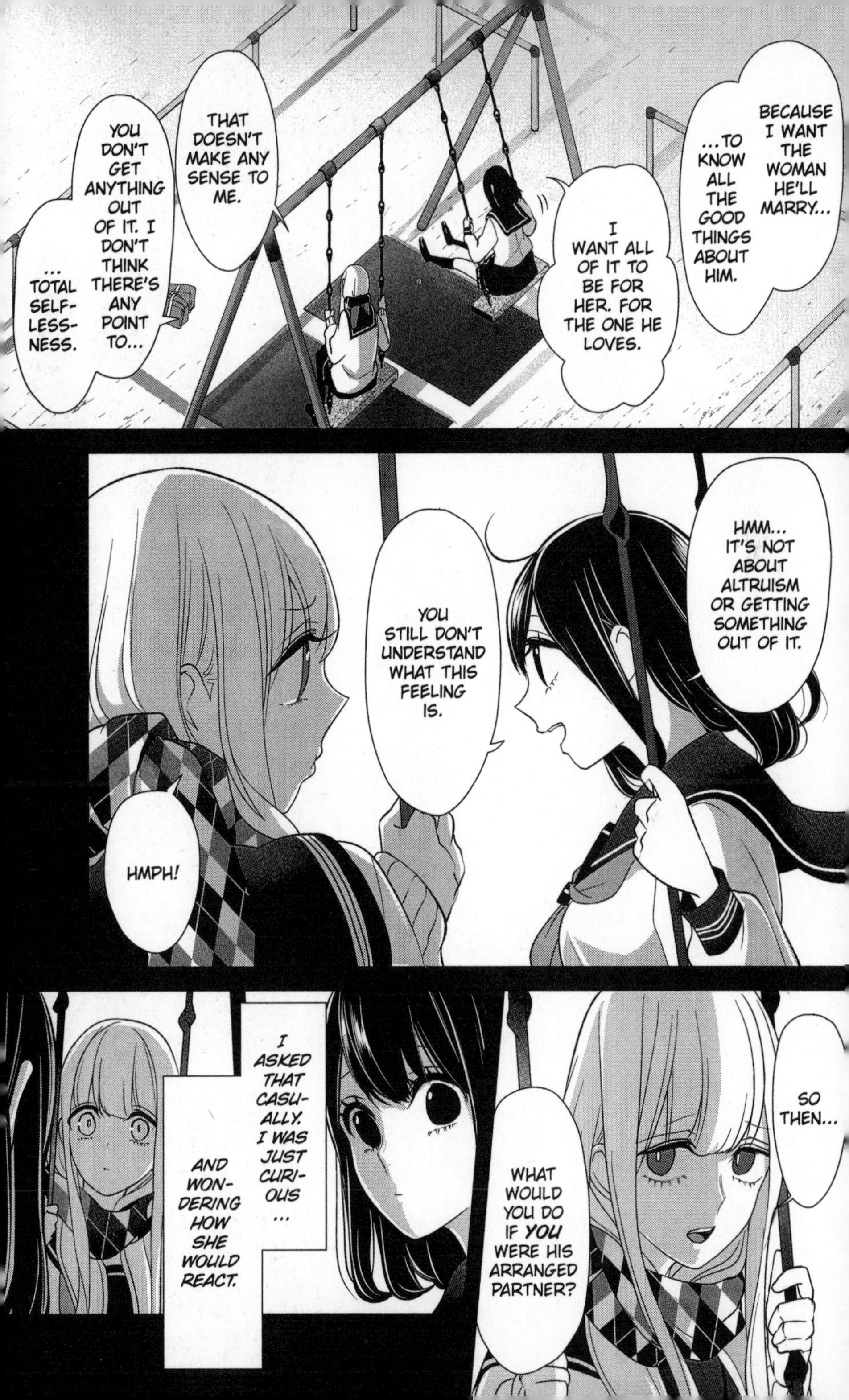

BECAUSE I WANT THE WOMAN HE'LL MARRY...
...TO KNOW ALL THE GOOD THINGS ABOUT HIM.
I WANT ALL OF IT TO BE FOR HER. FOR THE ONE HE LOVES.
THAT DOESN'T MAKE ANY SENSE TO ME.
YOU DON'T GET ANYTHING OUT OF IT. I DON'T THINK THERE'S ANY POINT TO...
...TOTAL SELF-LESS-NESS.
HMM... IT'S NOT ABOUT ALTRUISM OR GETTING SOMETHING OUT OF IT.
YOU STILL DON'T UNDERSTAND WHAT THIS FEELING IS.
HMPH!
SO THEN...
WHAT WOULD YOU DO IF *YOU* WERE HIS ARRANGED PARTNER?
I ASKED THAT CASU-ALLY. I WAS JUST CURI-OUS...
AND WON-DERING HOW SHE WOULD REACT.

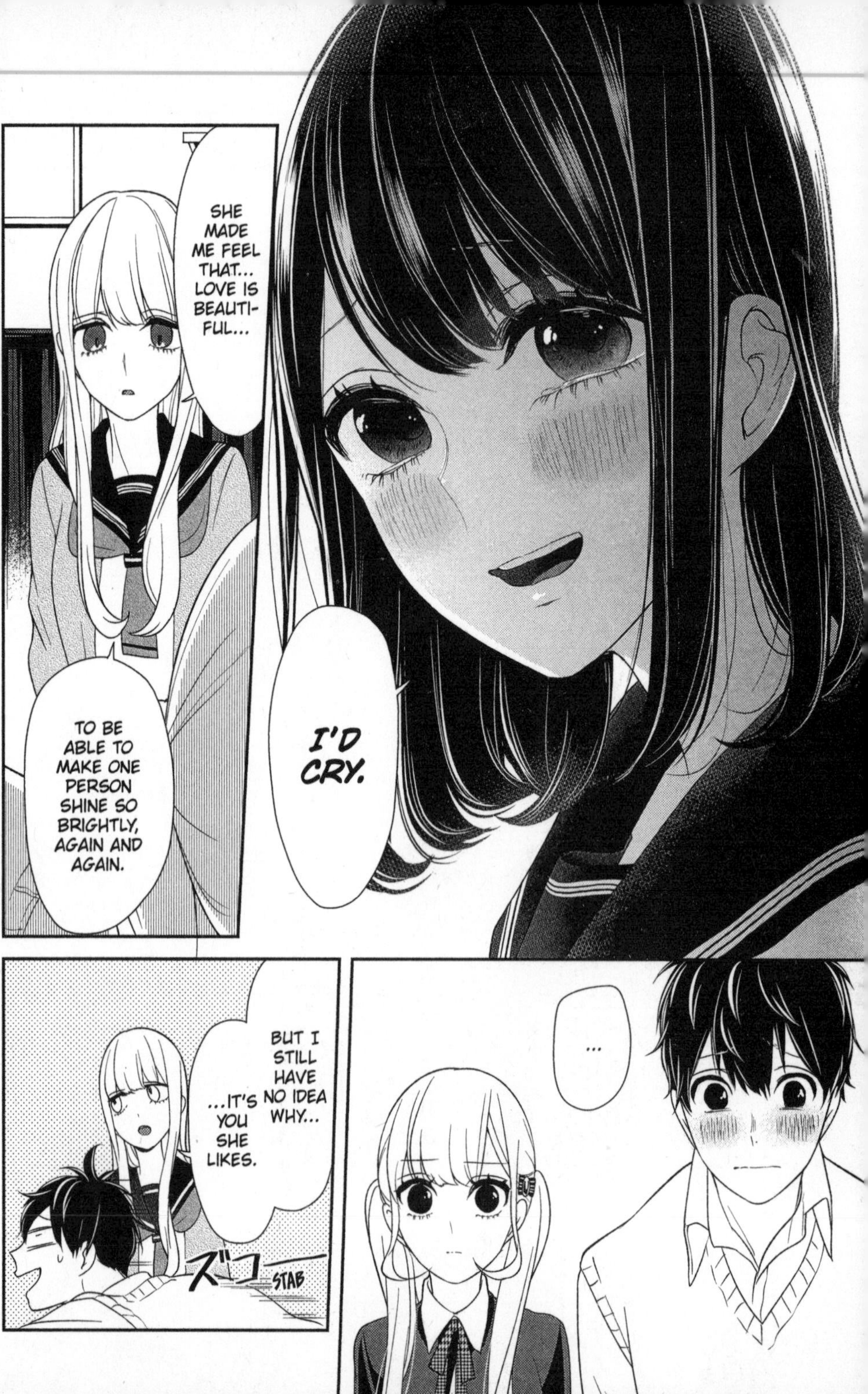
I'D CRY.
SHE MADE ME FEEL THAT... LOVE IS BEAUTIFUL...
TO BE ABLE TO MAKE ONE PERSON SHINE SO BRIGHTLY, AGAIN AND AGAIN.
...
BUT I STILL HAVE NO IDEA WHY...
...IT'S YOU SHE LIKES.
ズコー
STAB

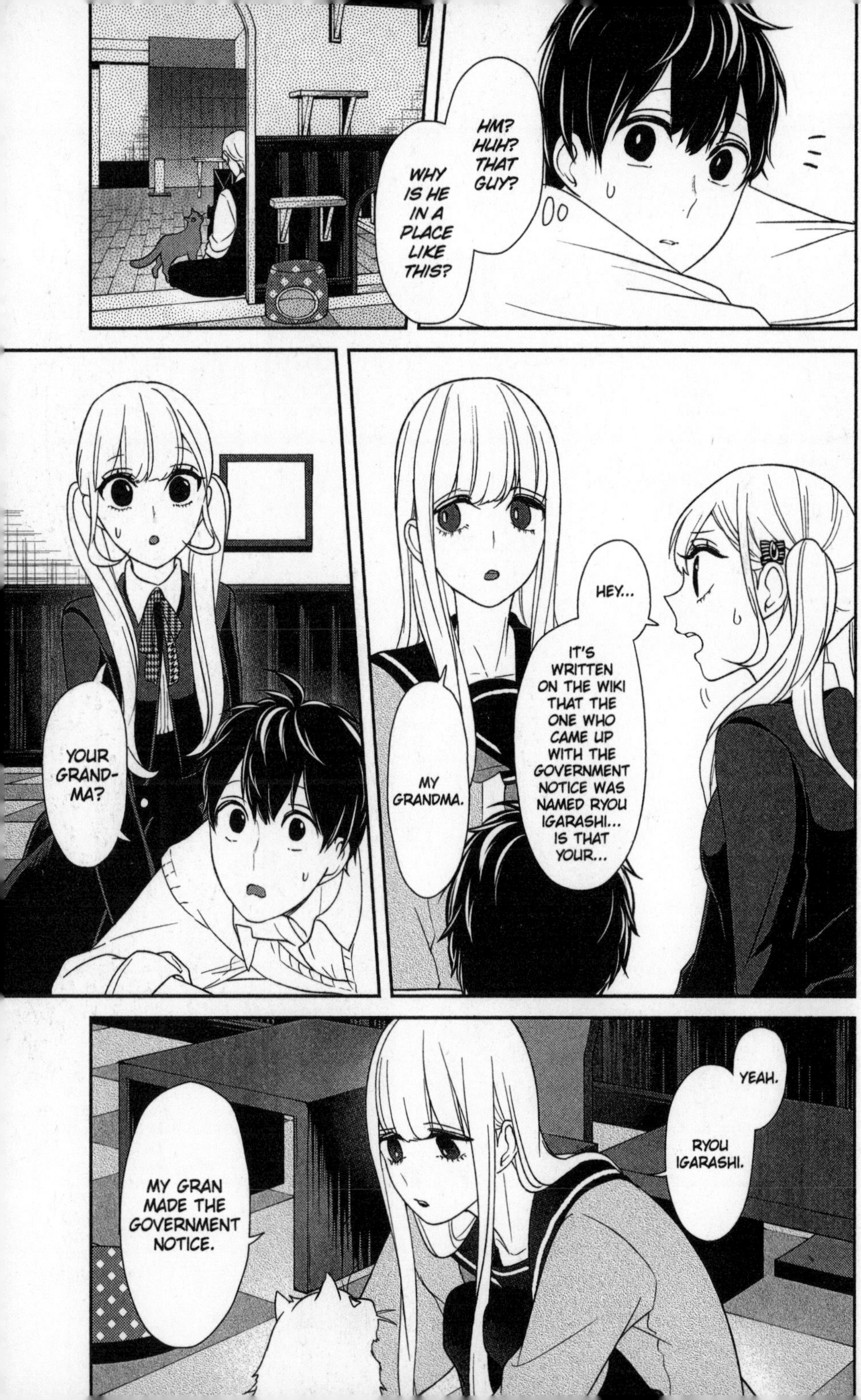
HM? HUH? THAT GUY?
WHY IS HE IN A PLACE LIKE THIS?
HEY...
IT'S WRITTEN ON THE WIKI THAT THE ONE WHO CAME UP WITH THE GOVERNMENT NOTICE WAS NAMED RYOU IGARASHI... IS THAT YOUR...
MY GRANDMA.
YOUR GRAND-MA?
YEAH.
RYOU IGARASHI.
MY GRAN MADE THE GOVERNMENT NOTICE.

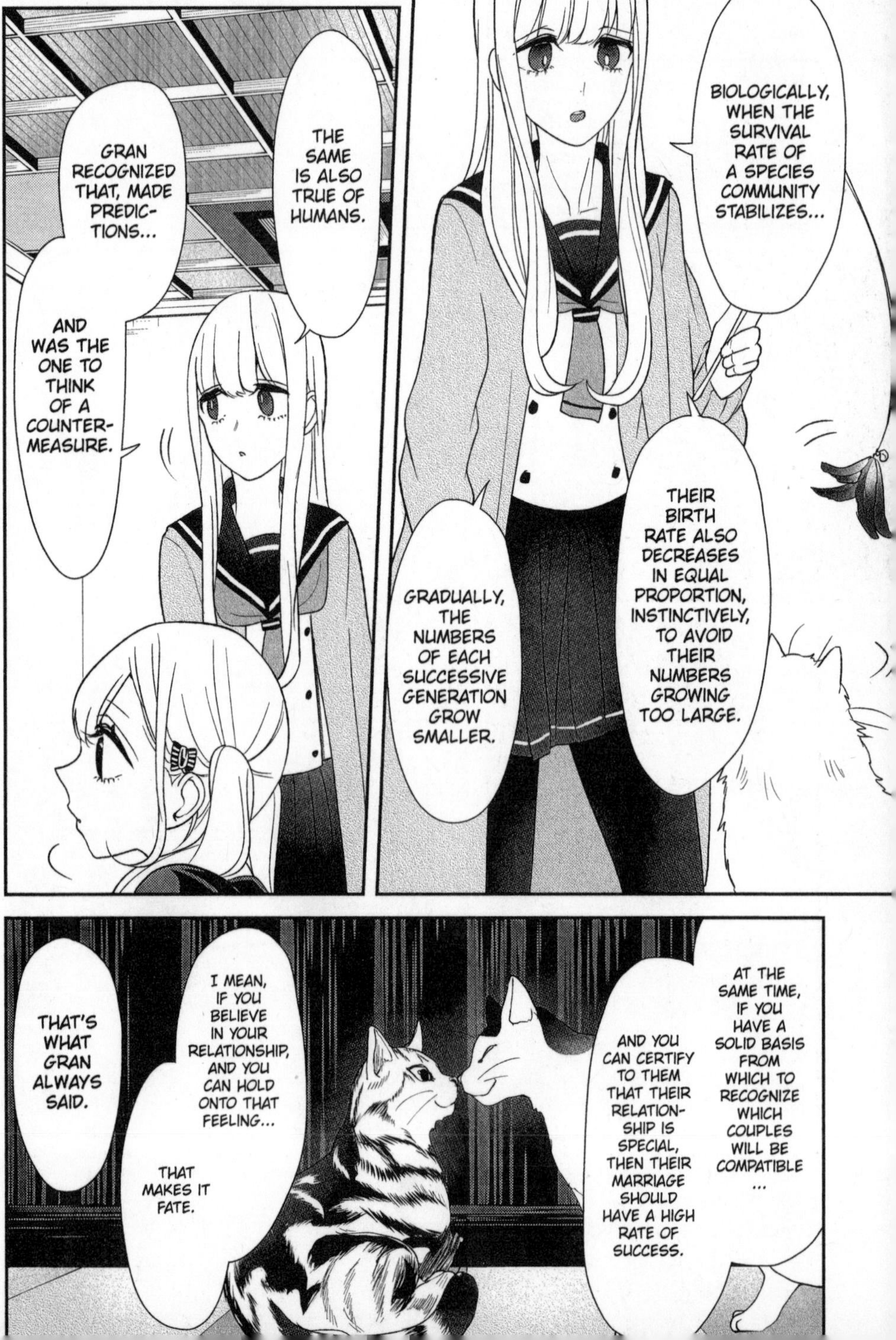
BIOLOGICALLY, WHEN THE SURVIVAL RATE OF A SPECIES COMMUNITY STABILIZES...
THEIR BIRTH RATE ALSO DECREASES IN EQUAL PROPORTION, INSTINCTIVELY, TO AVOID THEIR NUMBERS GROWING TOO LARGE.
GRADUALLY, THE NUMBERS OF EACH SUCCESSIVE GENERATION GROW SMALLER.
THE SAME IS ALSO TRUE OF HUMANS.
GRAN RECOGNIZED THAT, MADE PREDIC-TIONS...
AND WAS THE ONE TO THINK OF A COUNTER-MEASURE.
AT THE SAME TIME, IF YOU HAVE A SOLID BASIS FROM WHICH TO RECOGNIZE WHICH COUPLES WILL BE COMPATIBLE...
AND YOU CAN CERTIFY TO THEM THAT THEIR RELATION-SHIP IS SPECIAL, THEN THEIR MARRIAGE SHOULD HAVE A HIGH RATE OF SUCCESS.
I MEAN, IF YOU BELIEVE IN YOUR RELATIONSHIP, AND YOU CAN HOLD ONTO THAT FEELING...
THAT MAKES IT FATE.
THAT'S WHAT GRAN ALWAYS SAID.

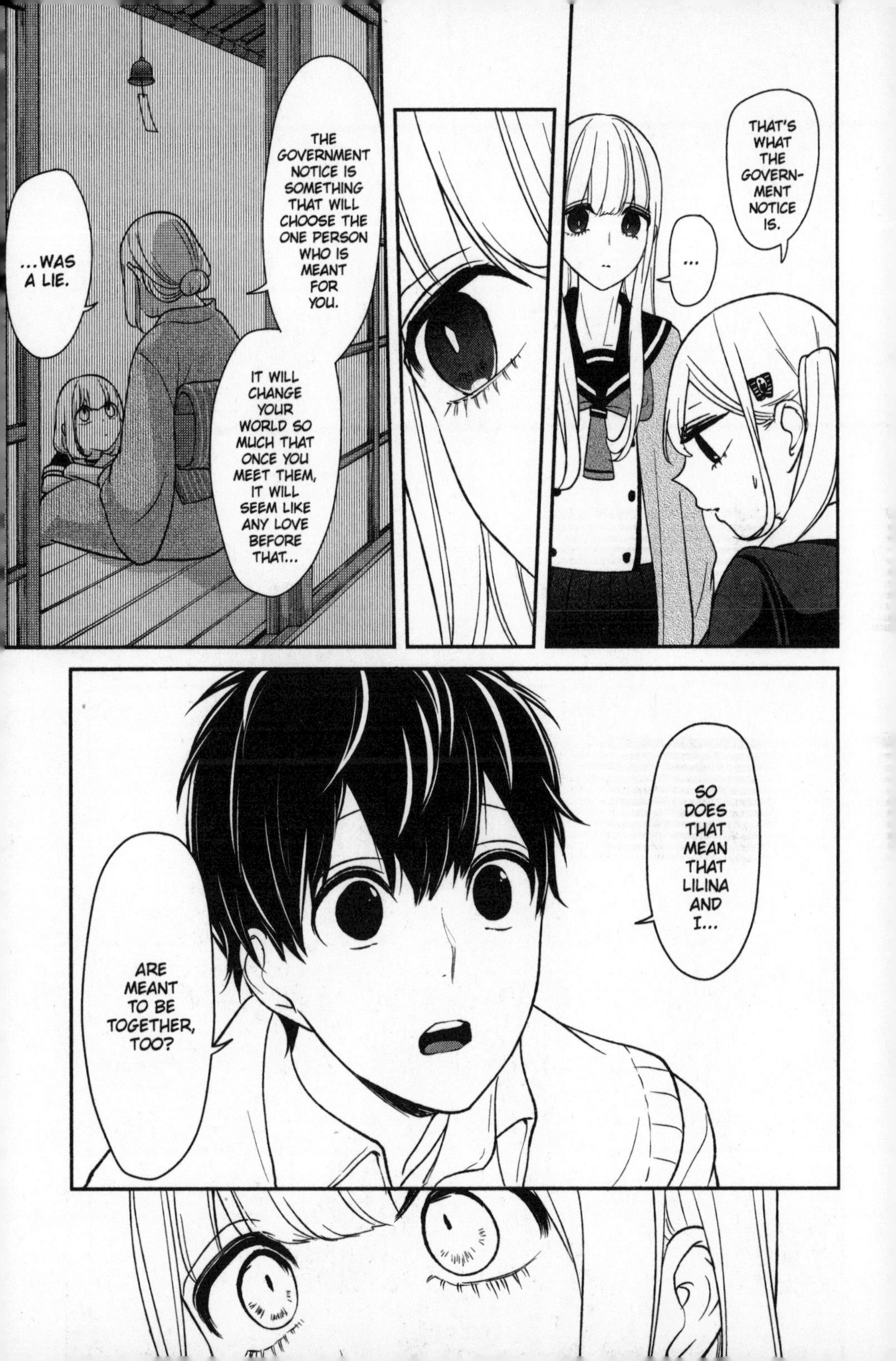
THAT'S WHAT THE GOVERNMENT NOTICE IS.
...
THE GOVERNMENT NOTICE IS SOMETHING THAT WILL CHOOSE THE ONE PERSON WHO IS MEANT FOR YOU.
IT WILL CHANGE YOUR WORLD SO MUCH THAT ONCE YOU MEET THEM, IT WILL SEEM LIKE ANY LOVE BEFORE THAT...
...WAS A LIE.
SO DOES THAT MEAN THAT LILINA AND I...
ARE MEANT TO BE TOGETHER, TOO?

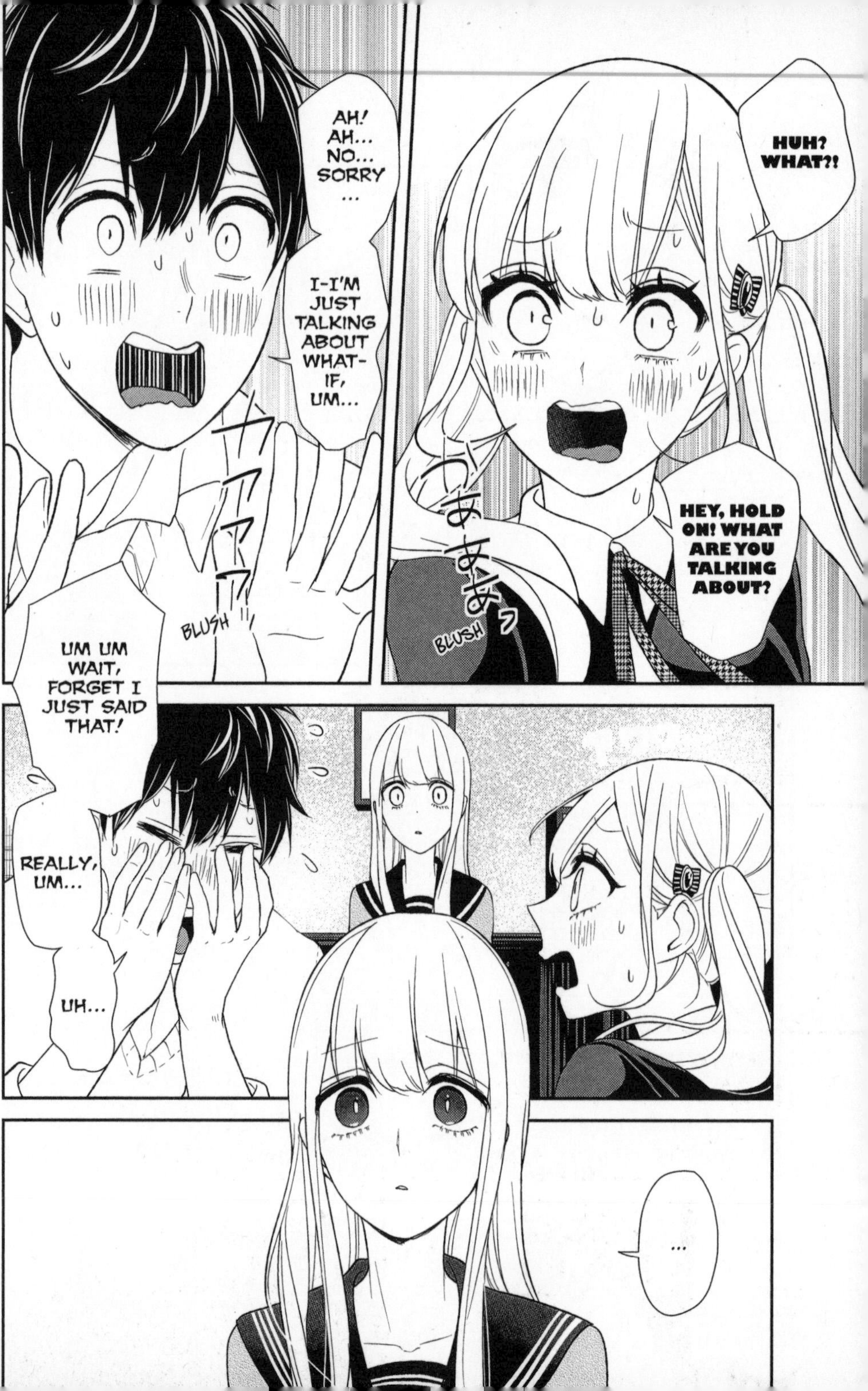
HUH? WHAT?!
HEY, HOLD ON! WHAT ARE YOU TALKING ABOUT?
BLUSH
AH! AH... NO... SORRY ...
I-I'M JUST TALKING ABOUT WHAT-IF, UM...
BLUSH
UM UM WAIT, FORGET I JUST SAID THAT!
REALLY, UM...
UH...
...

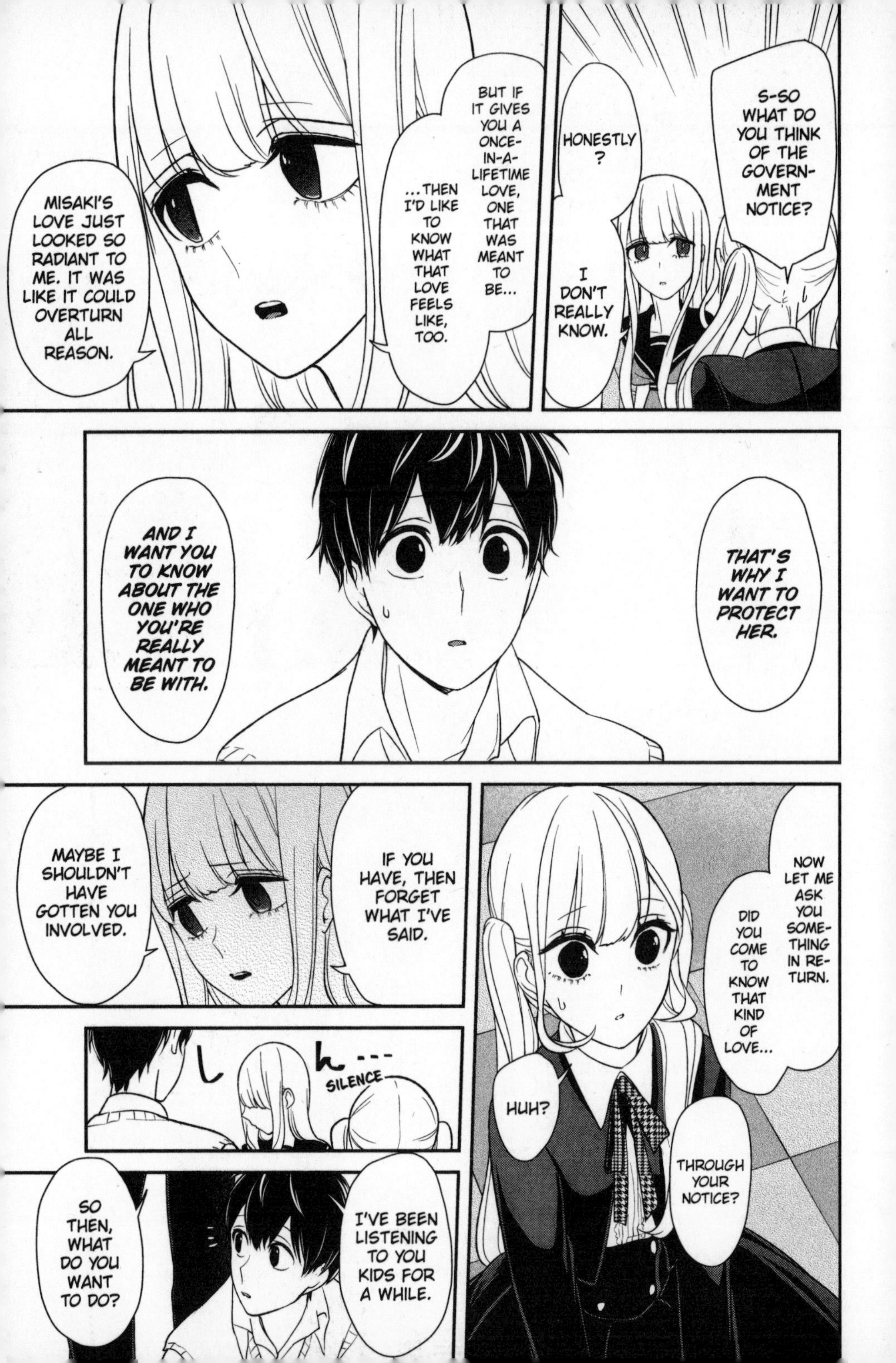
S-SO WHAT DO YOU THINK OF THE GOVERNMENT NOTICE?
HONESTLY?
I DON'T REALLY KNOW.
BUT IF IT GIVES YOU A ONCE-IN-A-LIFETIME LOVE, ONE THAT WAS MEANT TO BE...
...THEN I'D LIKE TO KNOW WHAT THAT LOVE FEELS LIKE, TOO.
MISAKI'S LOVE JUST LOOKED SO RADIANT TO ME. IT WAS LIKE IT COULD OVERTURN ALL REASON.
THAT'S WHY I WANT TO PROTECT HER.
AND I WANT YOU TO KNOW ABOUT THE ONE WHO YOU'RE REALLY MEANT TO BE WITH.
NOW LET ME ASK YOU SOMETHING IN RETURN.
DID YOU COME TO KNOW THAT KIND OF LOVE...
HUH?
THROUGH YOUR NOTICE?
IF YOU HAVE, THEN FORGET WHAT I'VE SAID.
MAYBE I SHOULDN'T HAVE GOTTEN YOU INVOLVED.
しん---
SILENCE
I'VE BEEN LISTENING TO YOU KIDS FOR A WHILE.
SO THEN, WHAT DO YOU WANT TO DO?

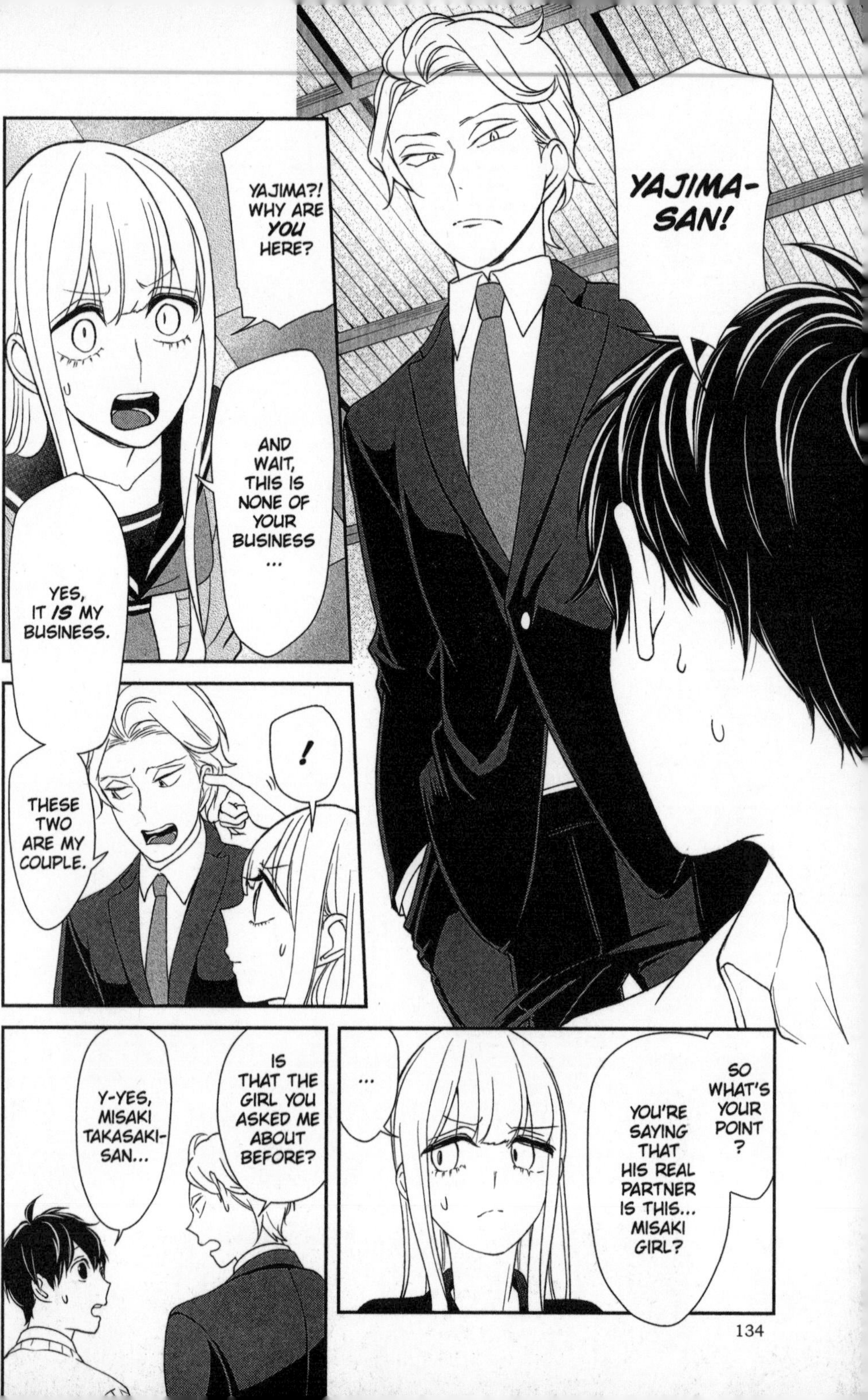
YAJIMA-SAN!
YAJIMA?! WHY ARE *YOU* HERE?
AND WAIT, THIS IS NONE OF YOUR BUSINESS ...
YES, IT *IS* MY BUSINESS.
!
THESE TWO ARE MY COUPLE.
SO WHAT'S YOUR POINT?
YOU'RE SAYING THAT HIS REAL PARTNER IS THIS... MISAKI GIRL?
...
IS THAT THE GIRL YOU ASKED ME ABOUT BEFORE?
Y-YES, MISAKI TAKASAKI-SAN...

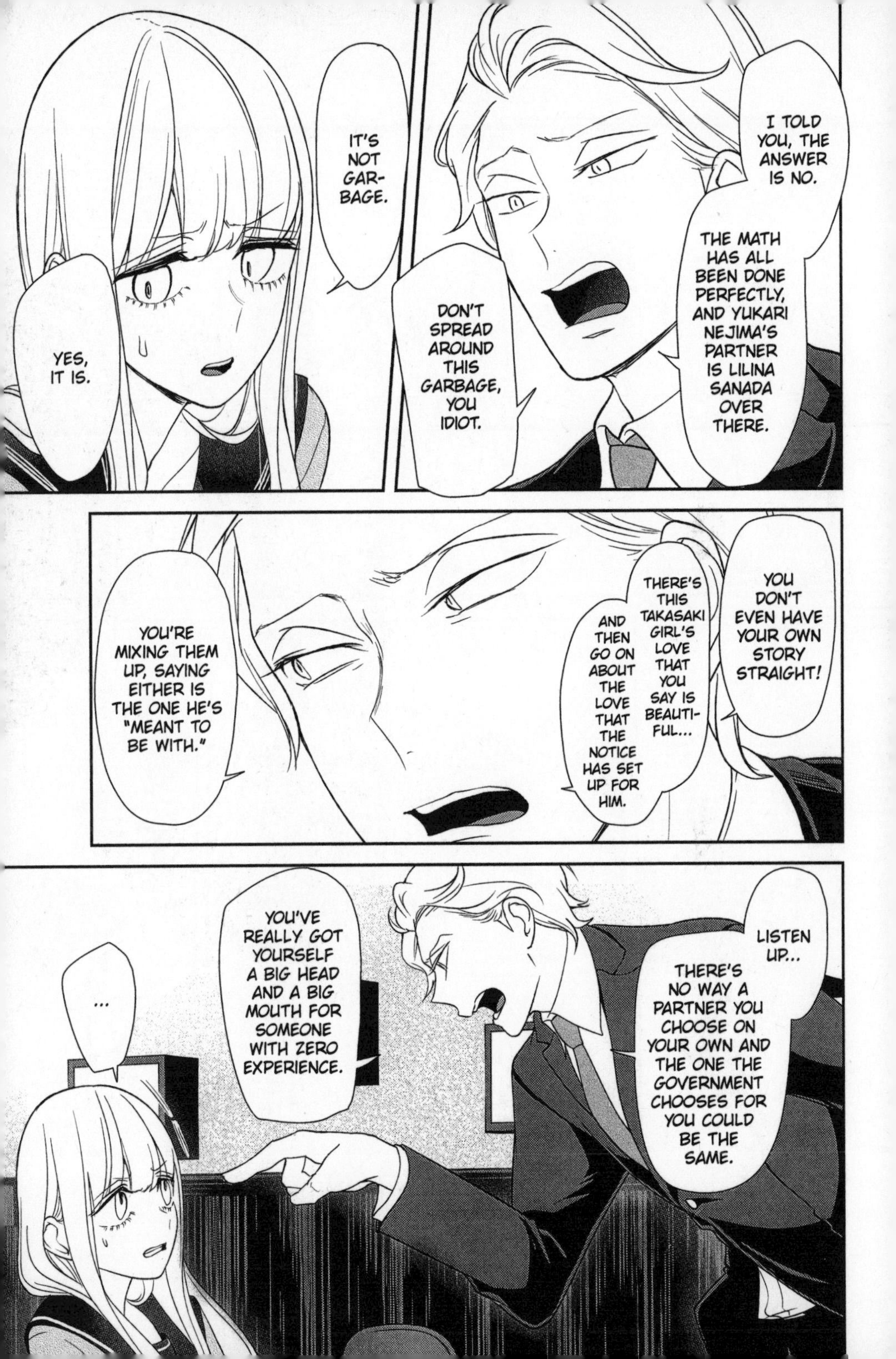
I TOLD YOU, THE ANSWER IS NO.
THE MATH HAS ALL BEEN DONE PERFECTLY, AND YUKARI NEJIMA'S PARTNER IS LILINA SANADA OVER THERE.
DON'T SPREAD AROUND THIS GARBAGE, YOU IDIOT.
IT'S NOT GARBAGE.
YES, IT IS.
YOU DON'T EVEN HAVE YOUR OWN STORY STRAIGHT!
THERE'S THIS TAKASAKI GIRL'S LOVE THAT YOU SAY IS BEAUTIFUL...
AND THEN GO ON ABOUT THE LOVE THAT THE NOTICE HAS SET UP FOR HIM.
YOU'RE MIXING THEM UP, SAYING EITHER IS THE ONE HE'S "MEANT TO BE WITH."
LISTEN UP...
THERE'S NO WAY A PARTNER YOU CHOOSE ON YOUR OWN AND THE ONE THE GOVERNMENT CHOOSES FOR YOU COULD BE THE SAME.
YOU'VE REALLY GOT YOURSELF A BIG HEAD AND A BIG MOUTH FOR SOMEONE WITH ZERO EXPERIENCE.
...

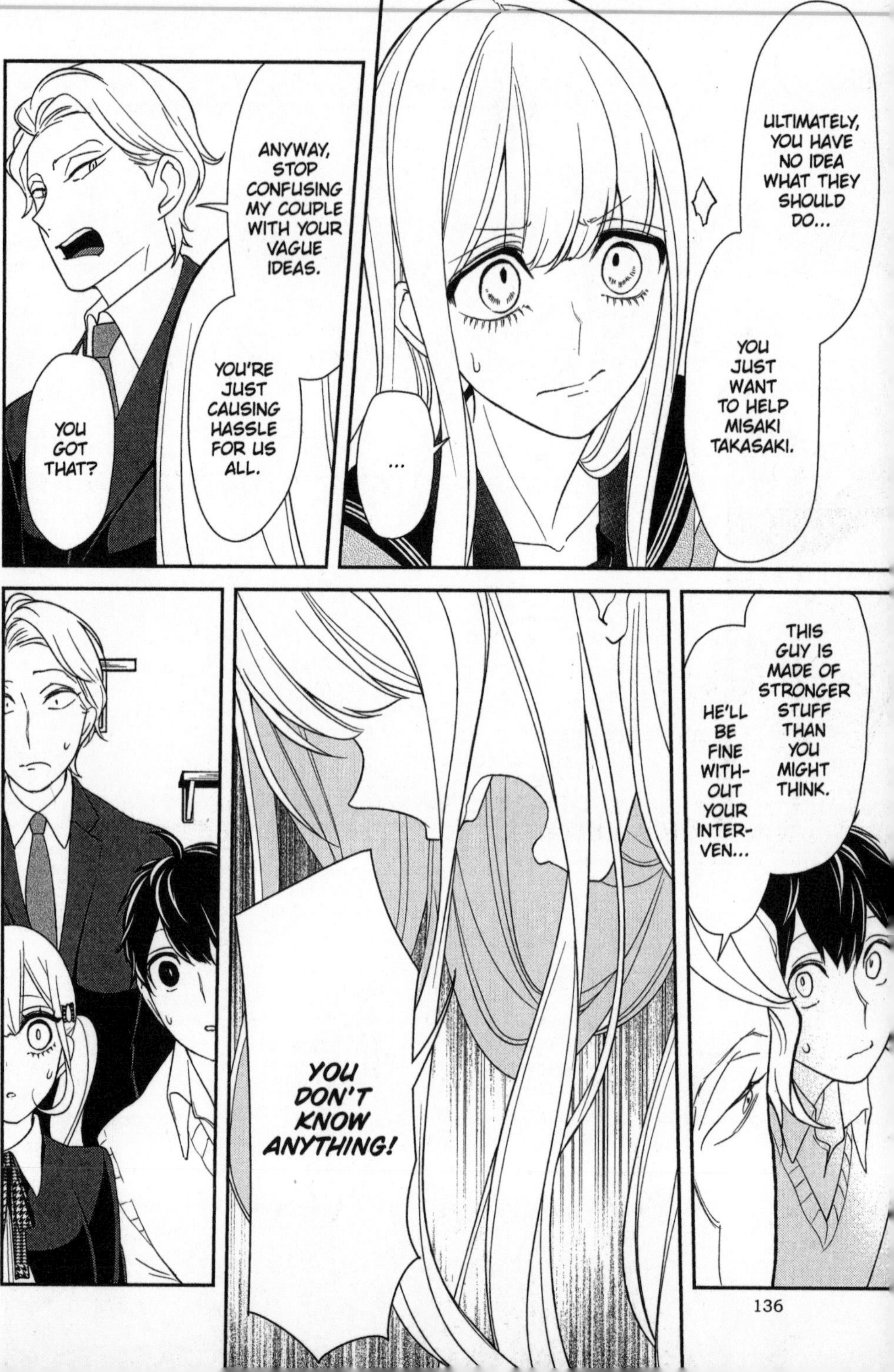
ULTIMATELY, YOU HAVE NO IDEA WHAT THEY SHOULD DO...
YOU JUST WANT TO HELP MISAKI TAKASAKI.
...
ANYWAY, STOP CONFUSING MY COUPLE WITH YOUR VAGUE IDEAS.
YOU'RE JUST CAUSING HASSLE FOR US ALL.
YOU GOT THAT?
THIS GUY IS MADE OF STRONGER STUFF THAN YOU MIGHT THINK.
HE'LL BE FINE WITHOUT YOUR INTERVEN...
YOU DON'T KNOW ANYTHING!

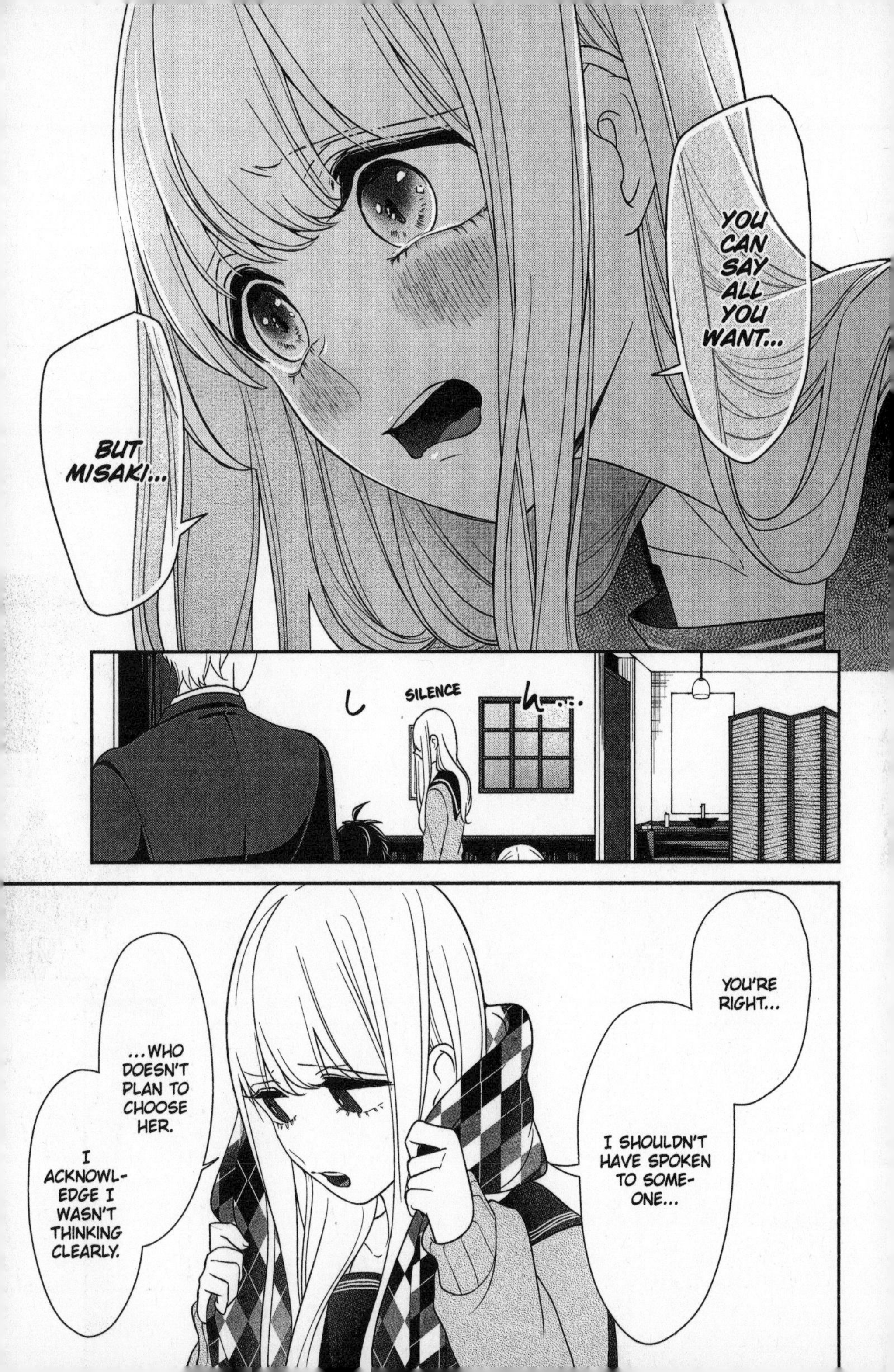
YOU CAN SAY ALL YOU WANT...
BUT MISAKI...
し
SILENCE
ん...
YOU'RE RIGHT...
I SHOULDN'T HAVE SPOKEN TO SOME-ONE...
...WHO DOESN'T PLAN TO CHOOSE HER.
I ACKNOWL-EDGE I WASN'T THINKING CLEARLY.

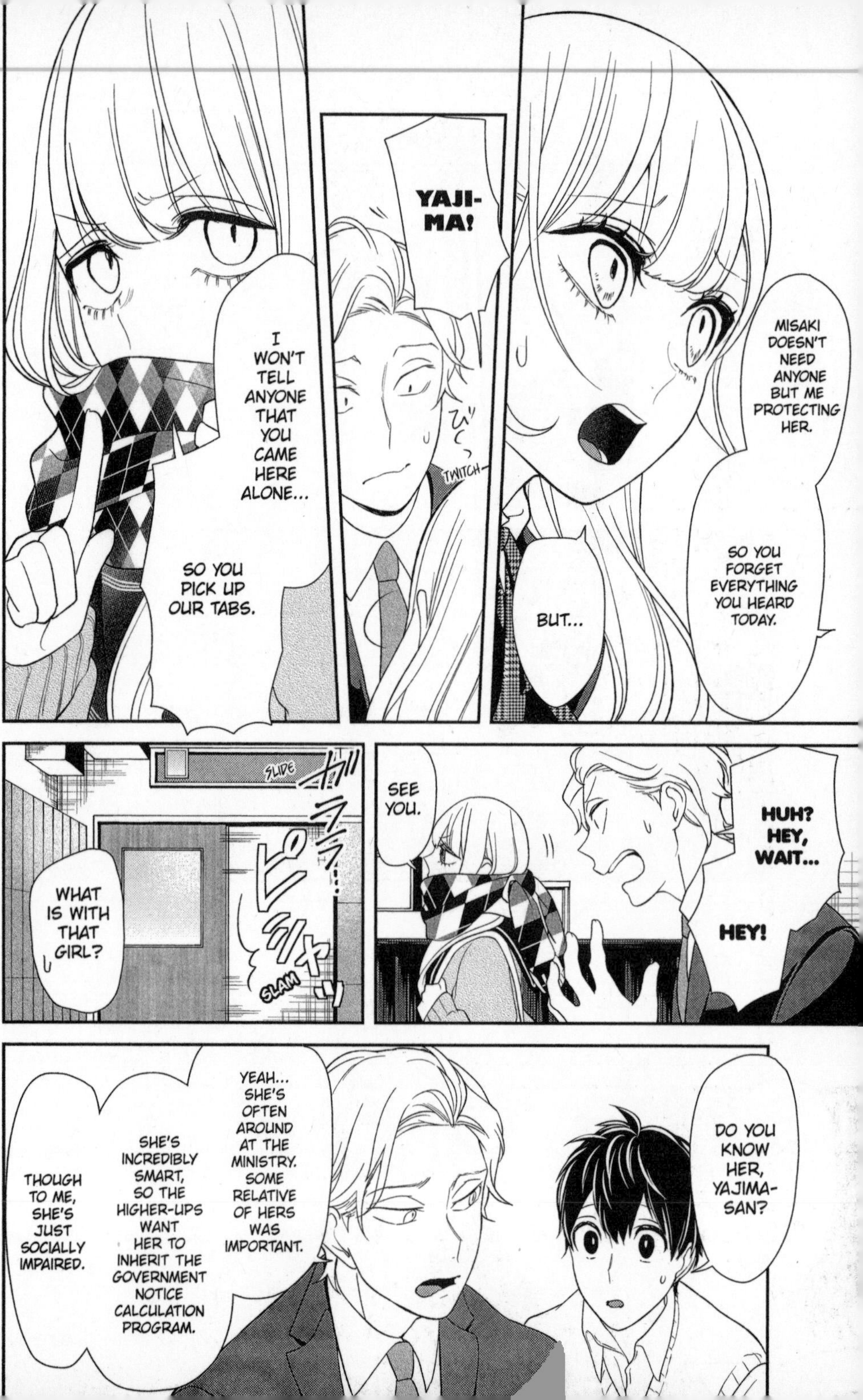
MISAKI DOESN'T NEED ANYONE BUT ME PROTECTING HER.
SO YOU FORGET EVERYTHING YOU HEARD TODAY.
BUT...
YAJI-MA!
TWITCH
I WON'T TELL ANYONE THAT YOU CAME HERE ALONE...
SO YOU PICK UP OUR TABS.
HUH? HEY, WAIT...
HEY!
SEE YOU.
SLIDE
SLAM
WHAT IS WITH THAT GIRL?
DO YOU KNOW HER, YAJIMA-SAN?
YEAH... SHE'S OFTEN AROUND AT THE MINISTRY. SOME RELATIVE OF HERS WAS IMPORTANT.
SHE'S INCREDIBLY SMART, SO THE HIGHER-UPS WANT HER TO INHERIT THE GOVERNMENT NOTICE CALCULATION PROGRAM.
THOUGH TO ME, SHE'S JUST SOCIALLY IMPAIRED.

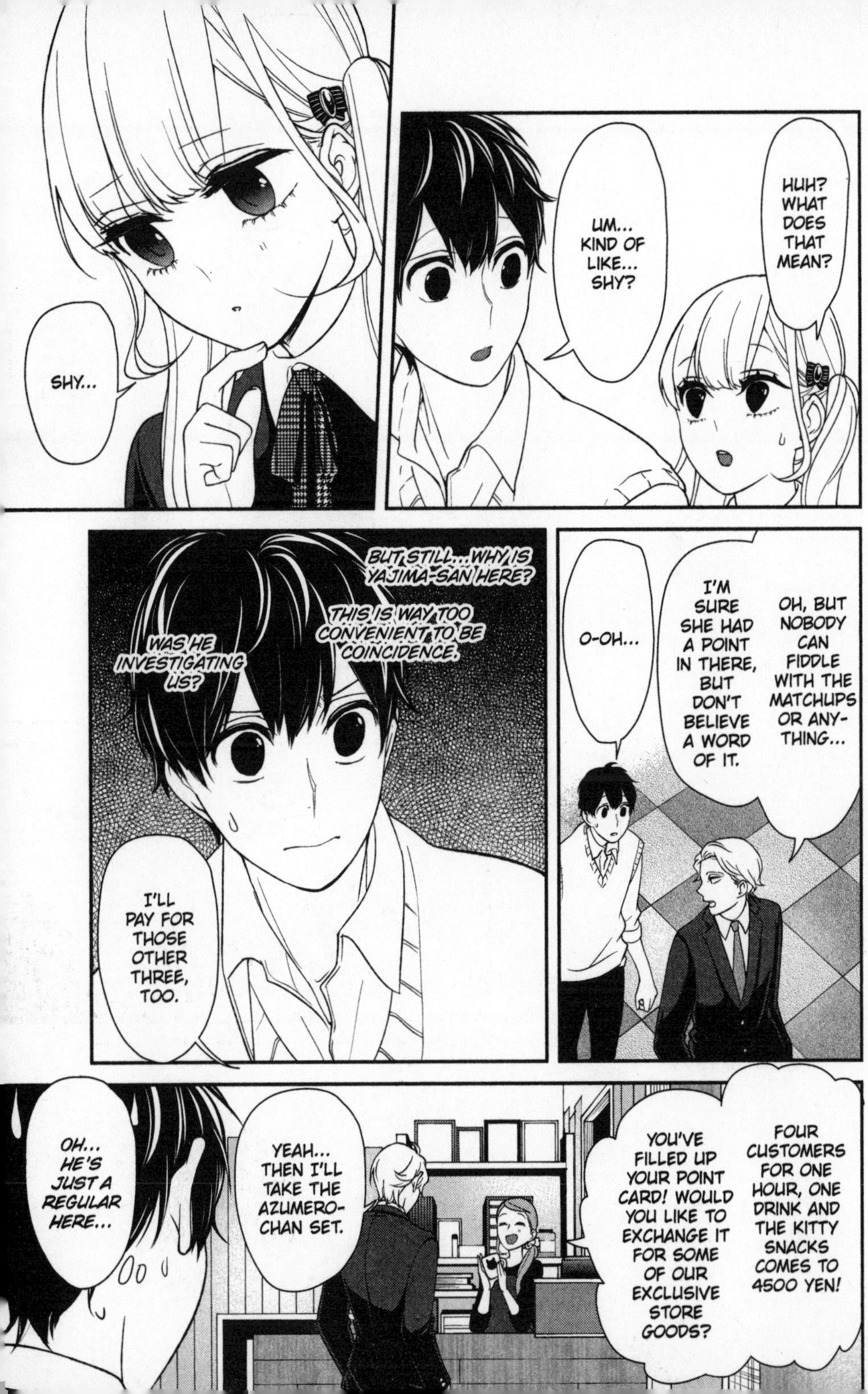
HUH? WHAT DOES THAT MEAN?
UM... KIND OF LIKE... SHY?
SHY...
OH, BUT NOBODY CAN FIDDLE WITH THE MATCHUPS OR ANY-THING...
I'M SURE SHE HAD A POINT IN THERE, BUT DON'T BELIEVE A WORD OF IT.
O-OH...
BUT STILL... WHY IS YAJIMA-SAN HERE?
THIS IS WAY TOO CONVENIENT TO BE COINCIDENCE.
WAS HE INVESTIGATING US?
I'LL PAY FOR THOSE OTHER THREE, TOO.
FOUR CUSTOMERS FOR ONE HOUR, ONE DRINK AND THE KITTY SNACKS COMES TO 4500 YEN!
YOU'VE FILLED UP YOUR POINT CARD! WOULD YOU LIKE TO EXCHANGE IT FOR SOME OF OUR EXCLUSIVE STORE GOODS?
YEAH... THEN I'LL TAKE THE AZUMERO-CHAN SET.
OH... HE'S JUST A REGULAR HERE...

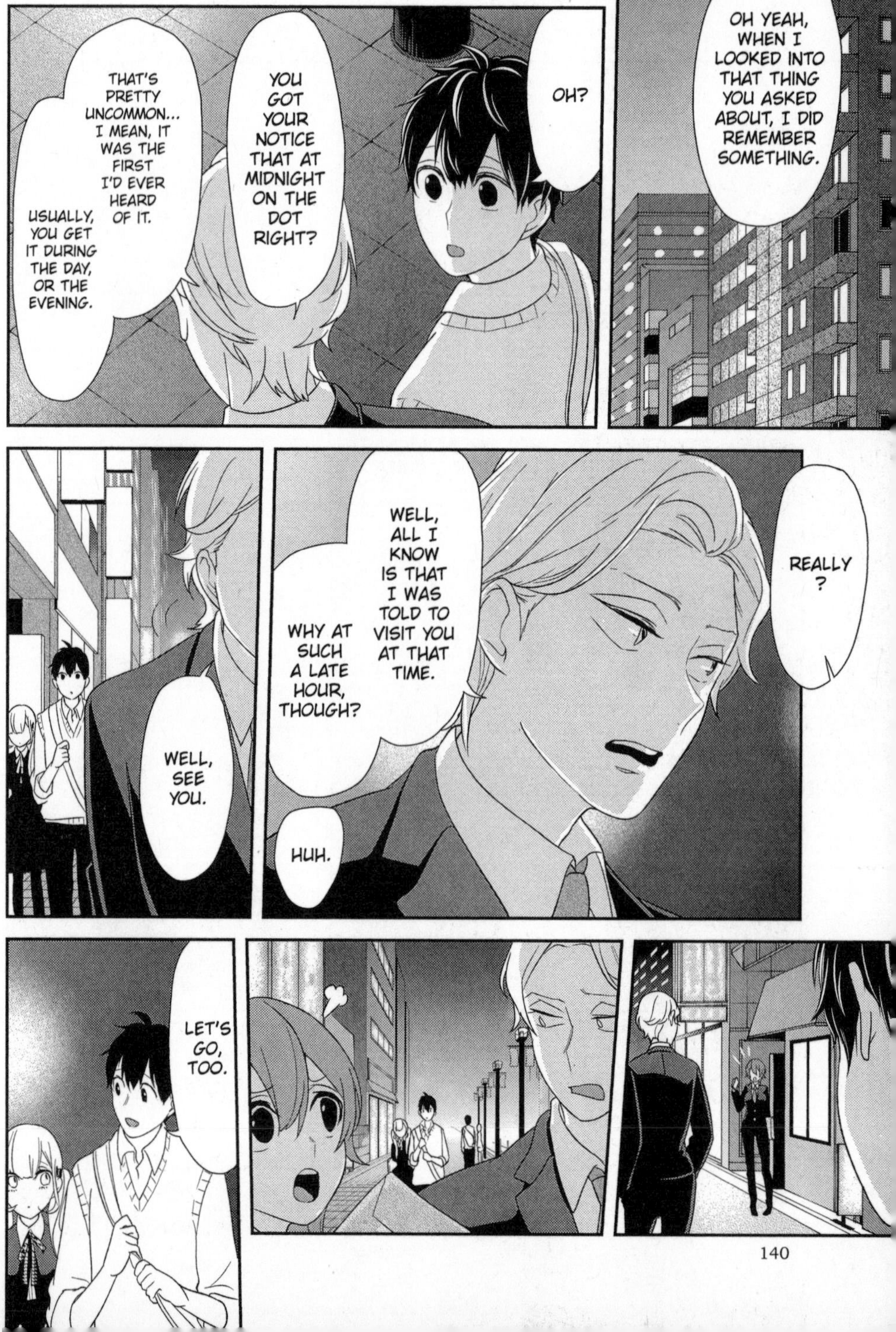
OH YEAH, WHEN I LOOKED INTO THAT THING YOU ASKED ABOUT, I DID REMEMBER SOMETHING.
OH?
YOU GOT YOUR NOTICE THAT AT MIDNIGHT ON THE DOT RIGHT?
THAT'S PRETTY UNCOMMON... I MEAN, IT WAS THE FIRST I'D EVER HEARD OF IT.
USUALLY, YOU GET IT DURING THE DAY, OR THE EVENING.
REALLY?
WELL, ALL I KNOW IS THAT I WAS TOLD TO VISIT YOU AT THAT TIME.
WHY AT SUCH A LATE HOUR, THOUGH?
HUH.
WELL, SEE YOU.
LET'S GO, TOO.

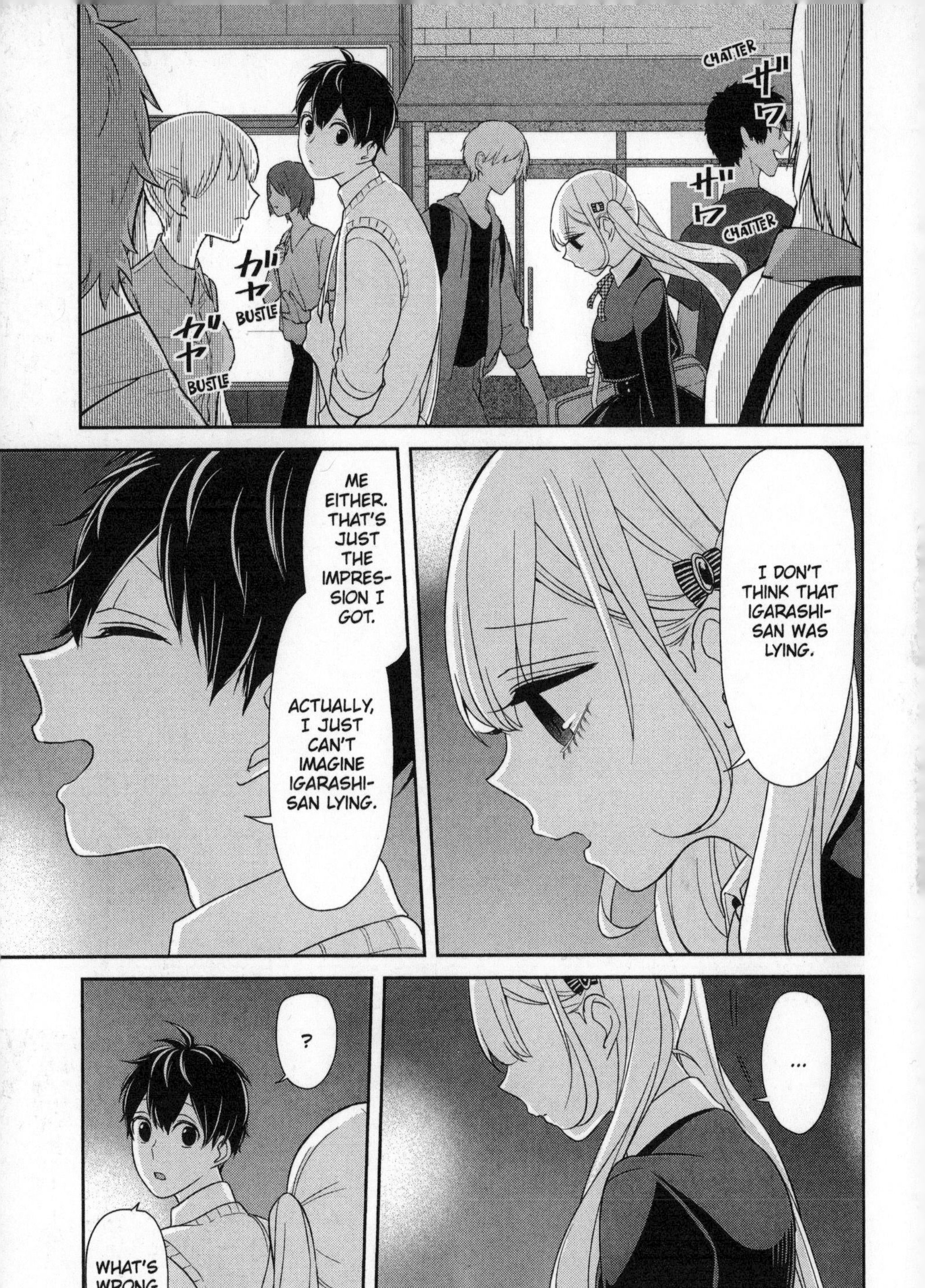
CHATTER
ザワ
ザワ
CHATTER
ガヤ
BUSTLE
ガヤ
BUSTLE
I DON'T THINK THAT IGARASHI-SAN WAS LYING.
ME EITHER. THAT'S JUST THE IMPRESSION I GOT.
ACTUALLY, I JUST CAN'T IMAGINE IGARASHI-SAN LYING.
...
?
WHAT'S WRONG?

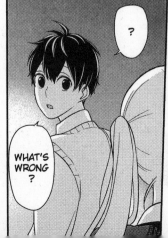

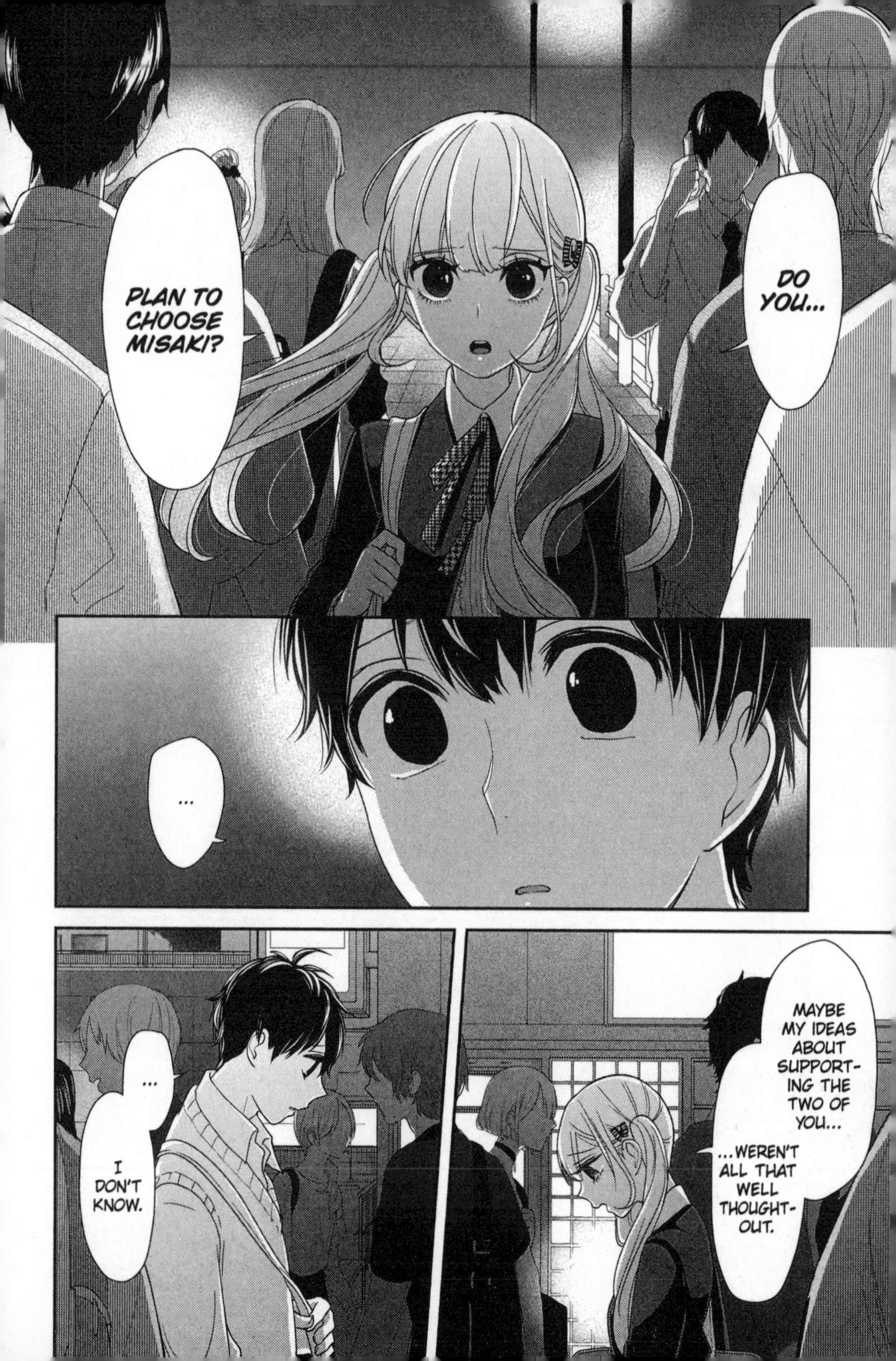
DO YOU...
PLAN TO CHOOSE MISAKI?
...
MAYBE MY IDEAS ABOUT SUPPORTING THE TWO OF YOU...
...WEREN'T ALL THAT WELL THOUGHT-OUT.
...
I DON'T KNOW.

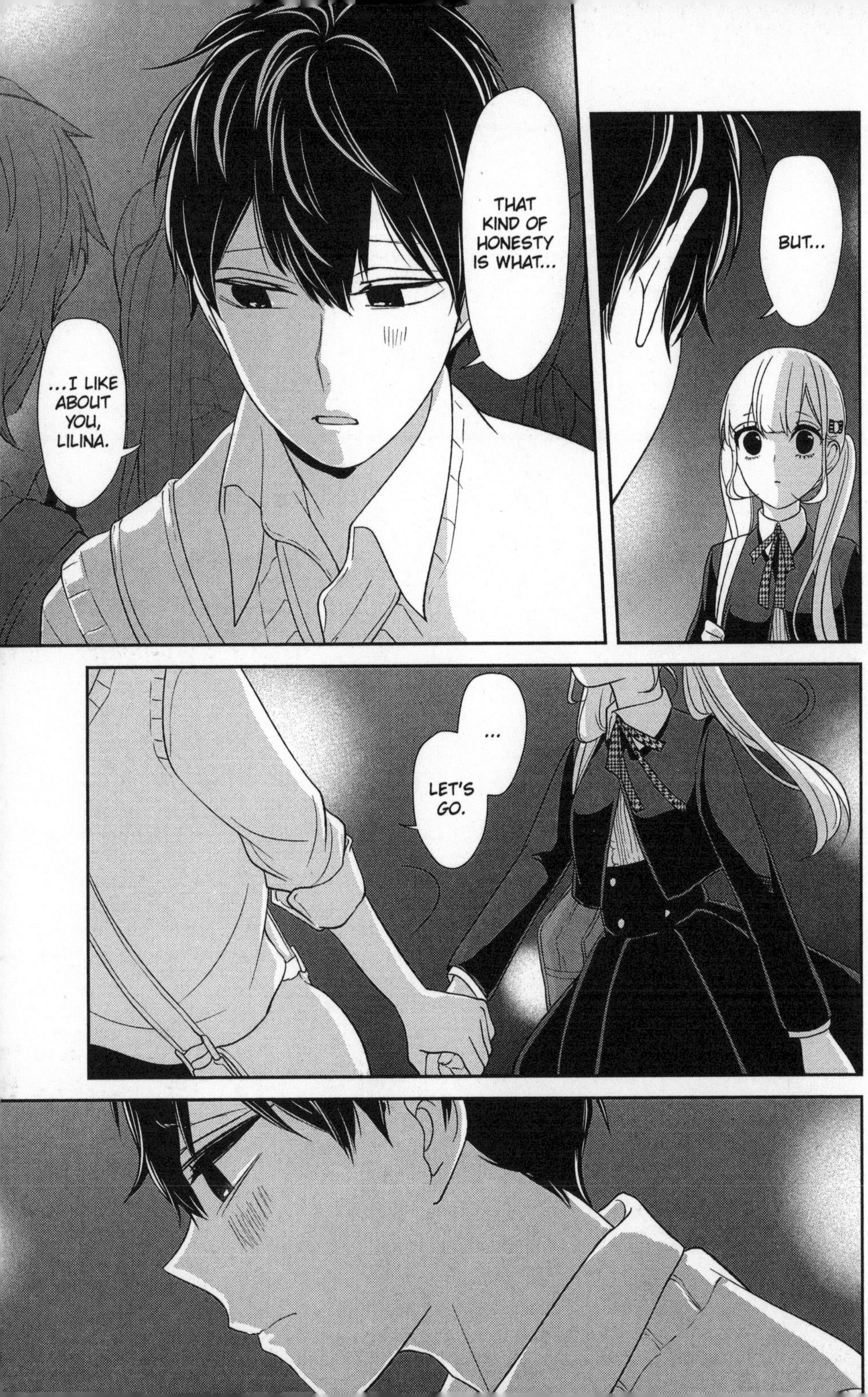
BUT...
THAT KIND OF HONESTY IS WHAT...
...I LIKE ABOUT YOU, LILINA.
...
LET'S GO.

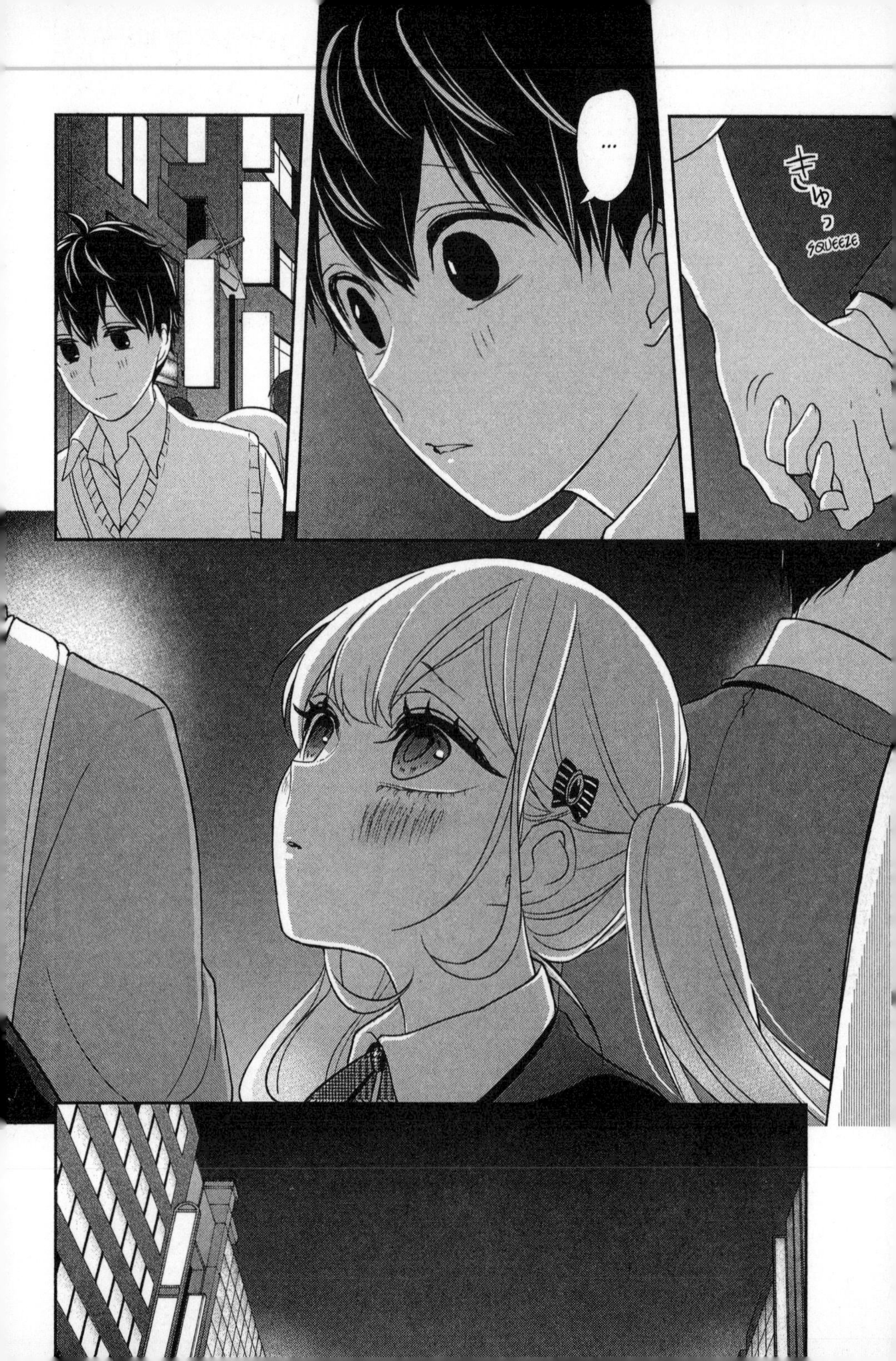
きゅっ
SQUEEZE
...

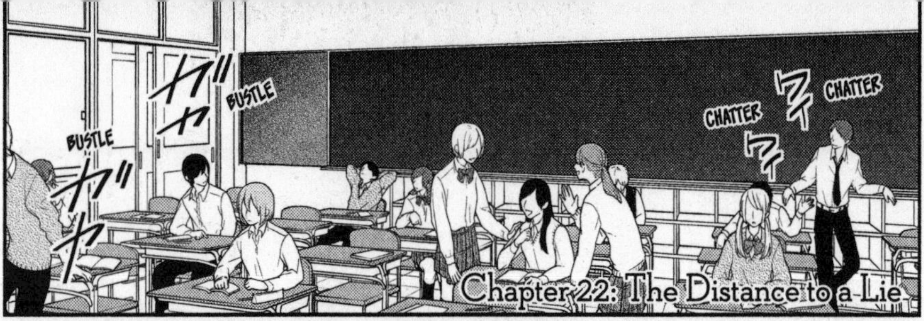
BUSTLE
BUSTLE
CHATTER
CHATTER

Chapter 22: The Distance to a Lie

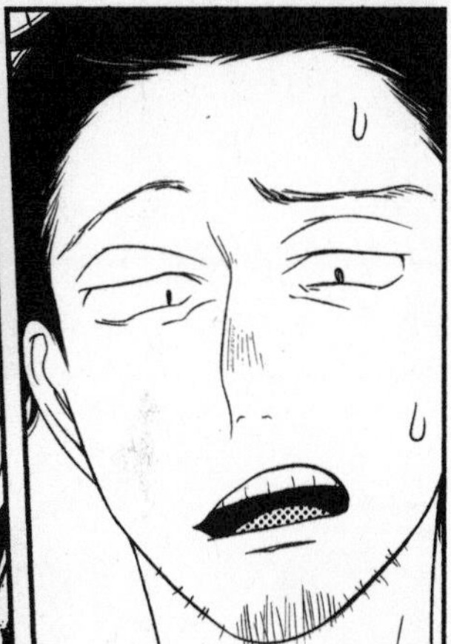
NEJIMA... YOU'RE...
IN TROUBLE.

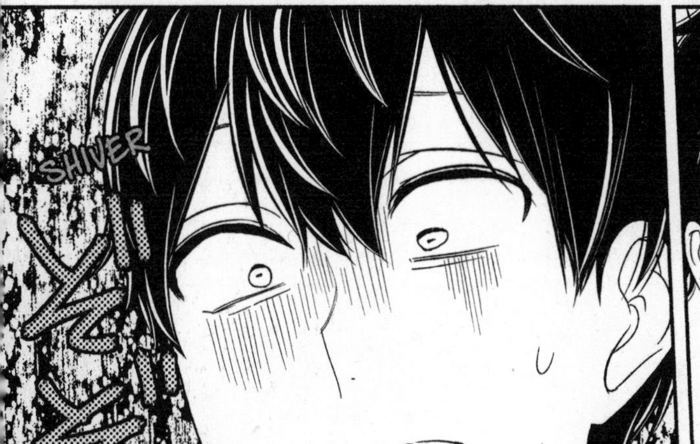
SHIVER
SHIVER
SHIVER

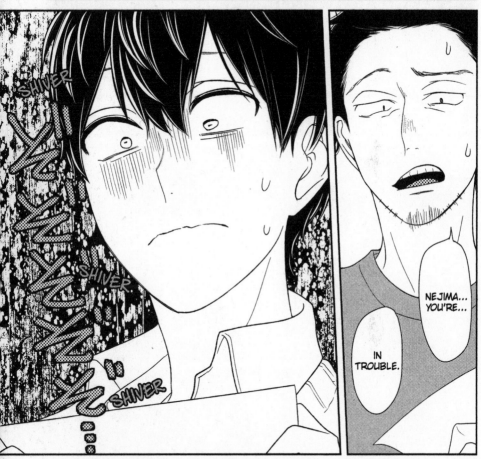

Year: 1 Class: 4 No. 11 Yukari Nejima

Subject	Score	Average	High Score	Subject	Score
Japanese	61	58	98	English 1	36
Classical Japanese	42	46	95	OC	33
World History A	70	58	83	Social Studies	51
History A	76	55	88	Science A	29
Math 1	32	56	85	Science B	54
Math A	37	60	83	Information 1	51
Elective A	65	65	85	Elective B	58

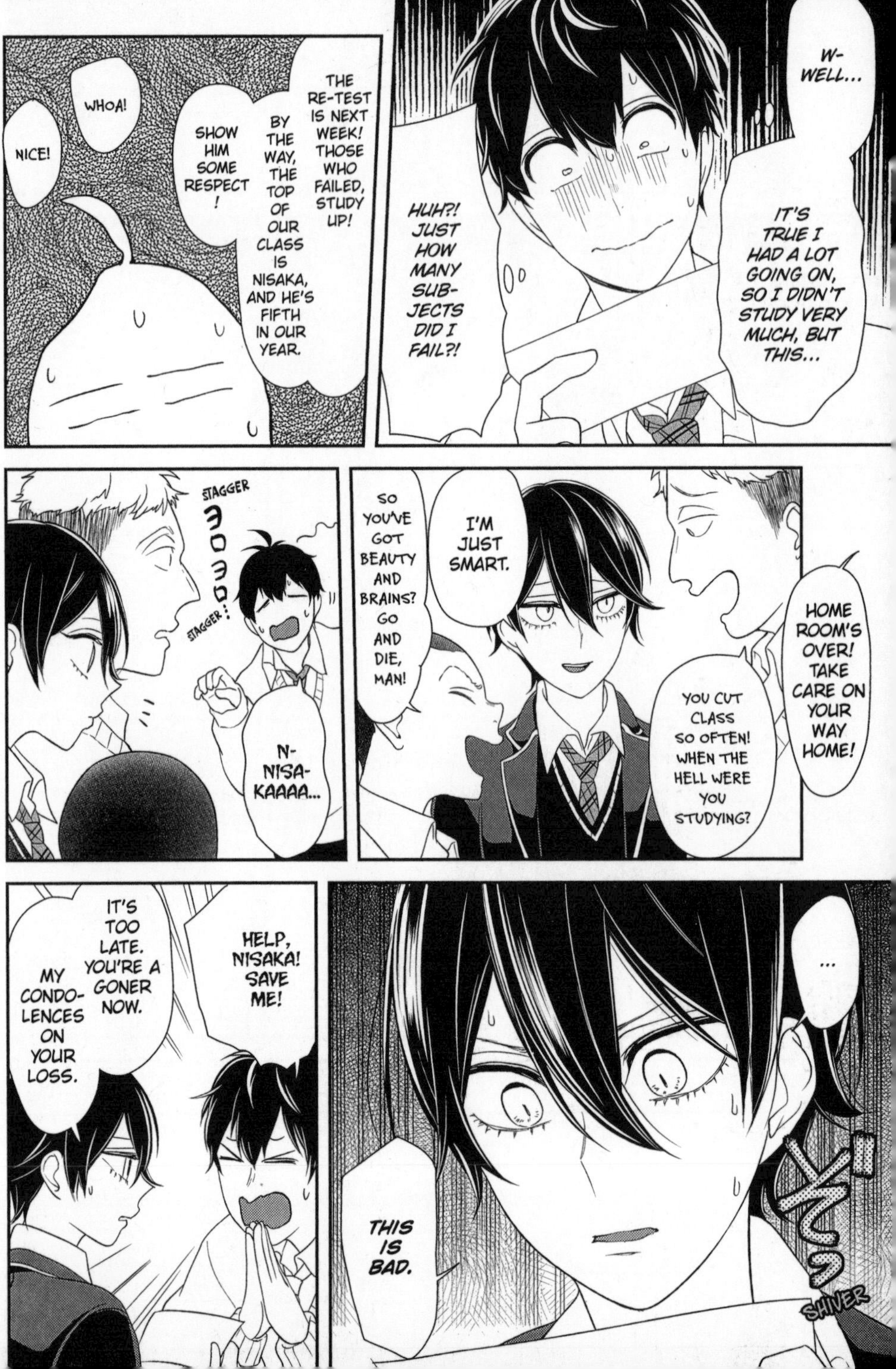

W-WELL...
IT'S TRUE I HAD A LOT GOING ON, SO I DIDN'T STUDY VERY MUCH, BUT THIS...
HUH?! JUST HOW MANY SUB-JECTS DID I FAIL?!
THE RE-TEST IS NEXT WEEK! THOSE WHO FAILED, STUDY UP!
BY THE WAY, THE TOP OF OUR CLASS IS NISAKA, AND HE'S FIFTH IN OUR YEAR.
SHOW HIM SOME RESPECT!
WHOA!
NICE!
HOME ROOM'S OVER! TAKE CARE ON YOUR WAY HOME!
I'M JUST SMART.
YOU CUT CLASS SO OFTEN! WHEN THE HELL WERE YOU STUDYING?
SO YOU'VE GOT BEAUTY AND BRAINS? GO AND DIE, MAN!
STAGGER
STAGGER
N-NISA-KAAAA...
...
THIS IS BAD.
SHIVER
HELP, NISAKA! SAVE ME!
IT'S TOO LATE. YOU'RE A GONER NOW.
MY CONDO-LENCES ON YOUR LOSS.

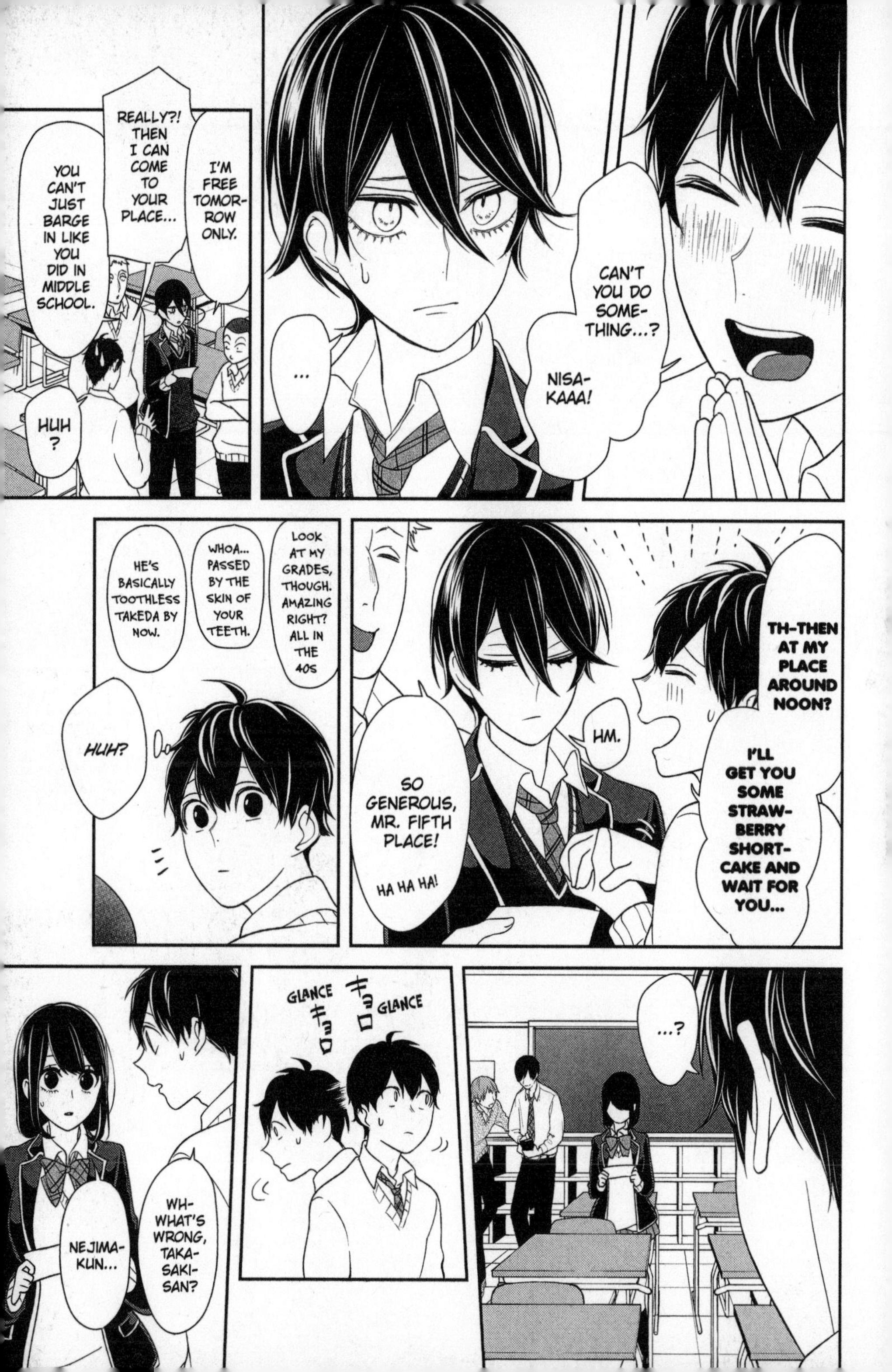
CAN'T YOU DO SOME-THING...?
NISA-KAAA!
...
I'M FREE TOMOR-ROW ONLY.
REALLY?! THEN I CAN COME TO YOUR PLACE...
YOU CAN'T JUST BARGE IN LIKE YOU DID IN MIDDLE SCHOOL.
HUH?
TH-THEN AT MY PLACE AROUND NOON?
I'LL GET YOU SOME STRAW-BERRY SHORT-CAKE AND WAIT FOR YOU...
HM.
SO GENEROUS, MR. FIFTH PLACE!
HA HA HA!
LOOK AT MY GRADES, THOUGH. AMAZING RIGHT? ALL IN THE 40S
WHOA... PASSED BY THE SKIN OF YOUR TEETH.
HE'S BASICALLY TOOTHLESS TAKEDA BY NOW.
HUH?
...?
GLANCE キョロ GLANCE キョロ
WH-WHAT'S WRONG, TAKA-SAKI-SAN?
NEJIMA-KUN...

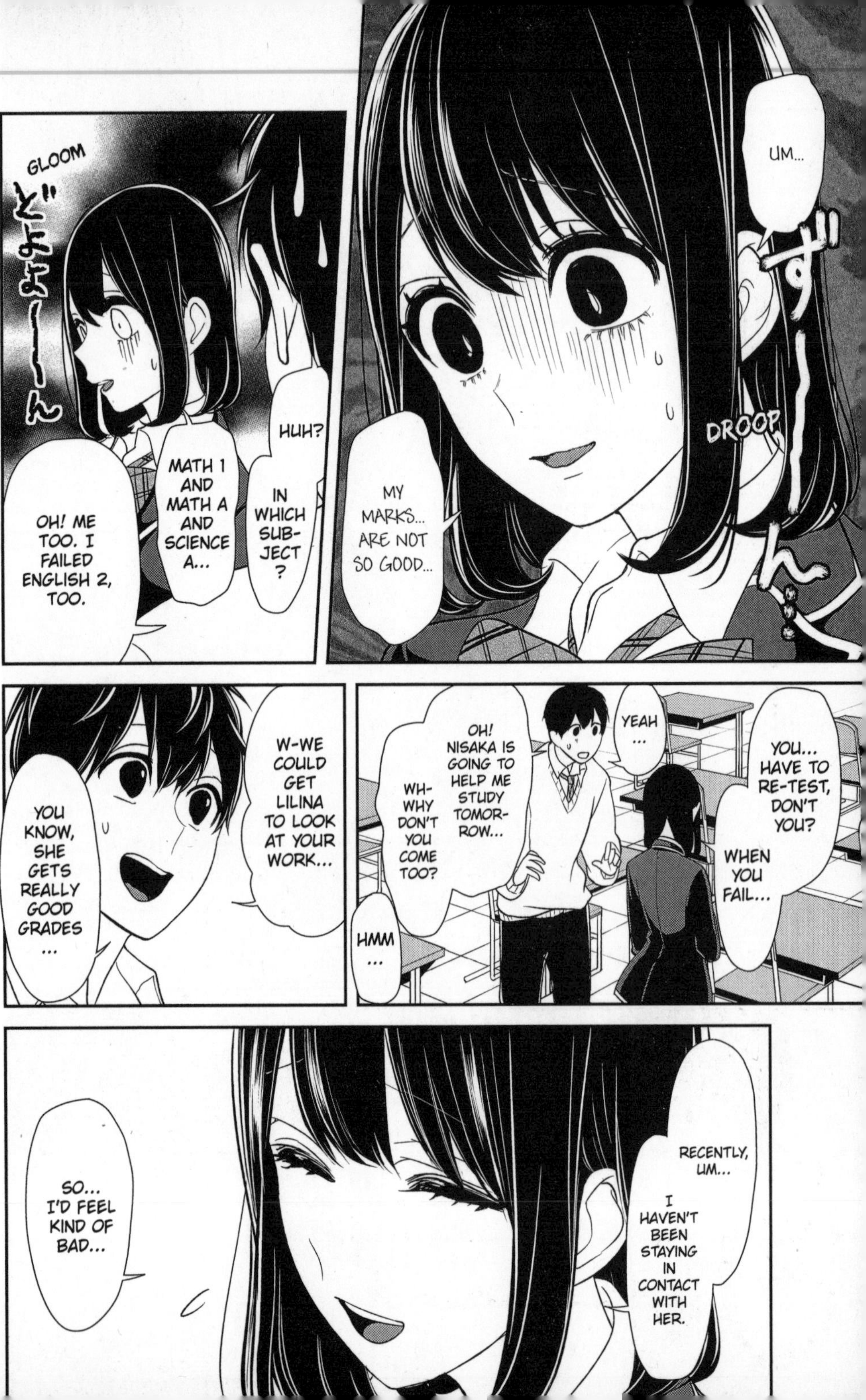
UM...
ずーん
DROOP
MY MARKS... ARE NOT SO GOOD...
HUH?
IN WHICH SUB-JECT?
MATH 1 AND MATH A AND SCIENCE A...
OH! ME TOO. I FAILED ENGLISH 2, TOO.
GLOOM
どよよーーん
YOU... HAVE TO RE-TEST, DON'T YOU?
WHEN YOU FAIL...
YEAH ...
OH! NISAKA IS GOING TO HELP ME STUDY TOMOR-ROW...
WH-WHY DON'T YOU COME TOO?
HMM ...
W-WE COULD GET LILINA TO LOOK AT YOUR WORK...
YOU KNOW, SHE GETS REALLY GOOD GRADES ...
RECENTLY, UM...
I HAVEN'T BEEN STAYING IN CONTACT WITH HER.
SO... I'D FEEL KIND OF BAD...

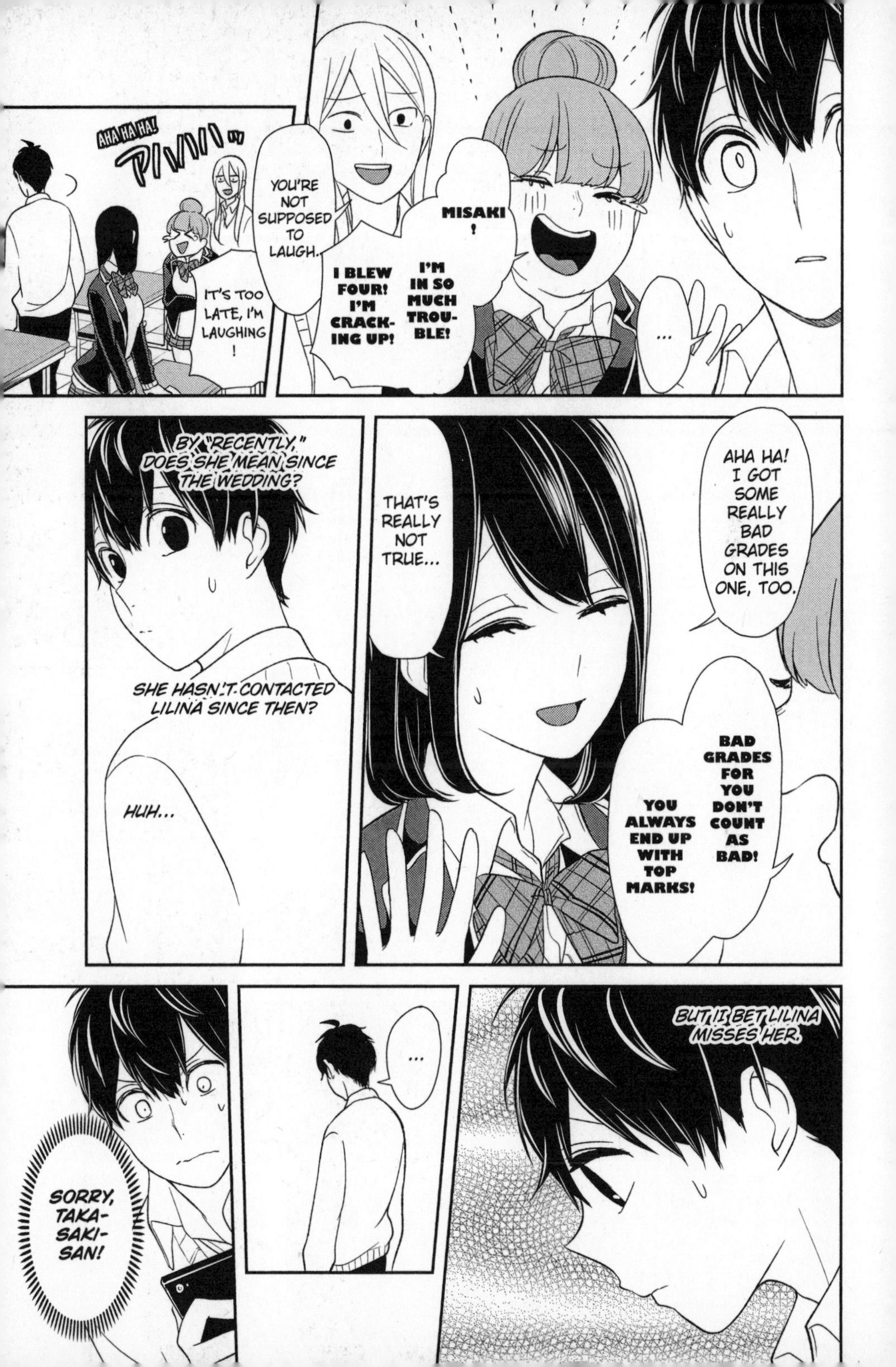
...
MISAKI!
I'M IN SO MUCH TROUBLE!
I BLEW FOUR! I'M CRACKING UP!
YOU'RE NOT SUPPOSED TO LAUGH.
AHA HA HA!
IT'S TOO LATE, I'M LAUGHING!
AHA HA! I GOT SOME REALLY BAD GRADES ON THIS ONE, TOO.
THAT'S REALLY NOT TRUE...
BAD GRADES FOR YOU DON'T COUNT AS BAD!
YOU ALWAYS END UP WITH TOP MARKS!
BY "RECENTLY," DOES SHE MEAN SINCE THE WEDDING?
SHE HASN'T CONTACTED LILINA SINCE THEN?
HUH...
BUT I BET LILINA MISSES HER.
...
SORRY, TAKASAKI-SAN!

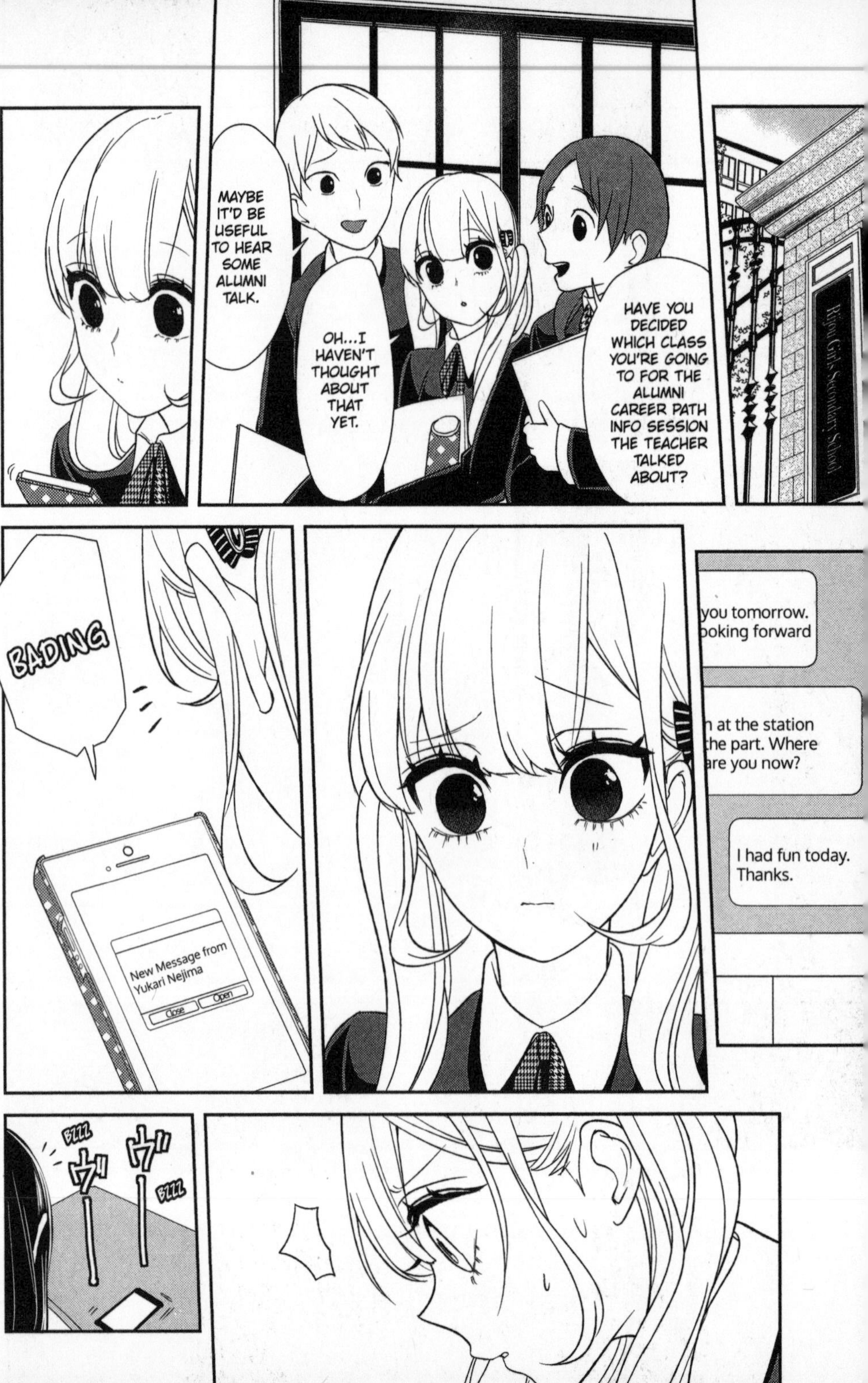
Rijou Girls Secondary School
HAVE YOU DECIDED WHICH CLASS YOU'RE GOING TO FOR THE ALUMNI CAREER PATH INFO SESSION THE TEACHER TALKED ABOUT?
OH...I HAVEN'T THOUGHT ABOUT THAT YET.
MAYBE IT'D BE USEFUL TO HEAR SOME ALUMNI TALK.
you tomorrow. ooking forward
n at the station the part. Where are you now?
I had fun today. Thanks.
BADING
New Message from Yukari Nejima
Close
Open
BZZZ
ヴー
ヴー
BZZZ

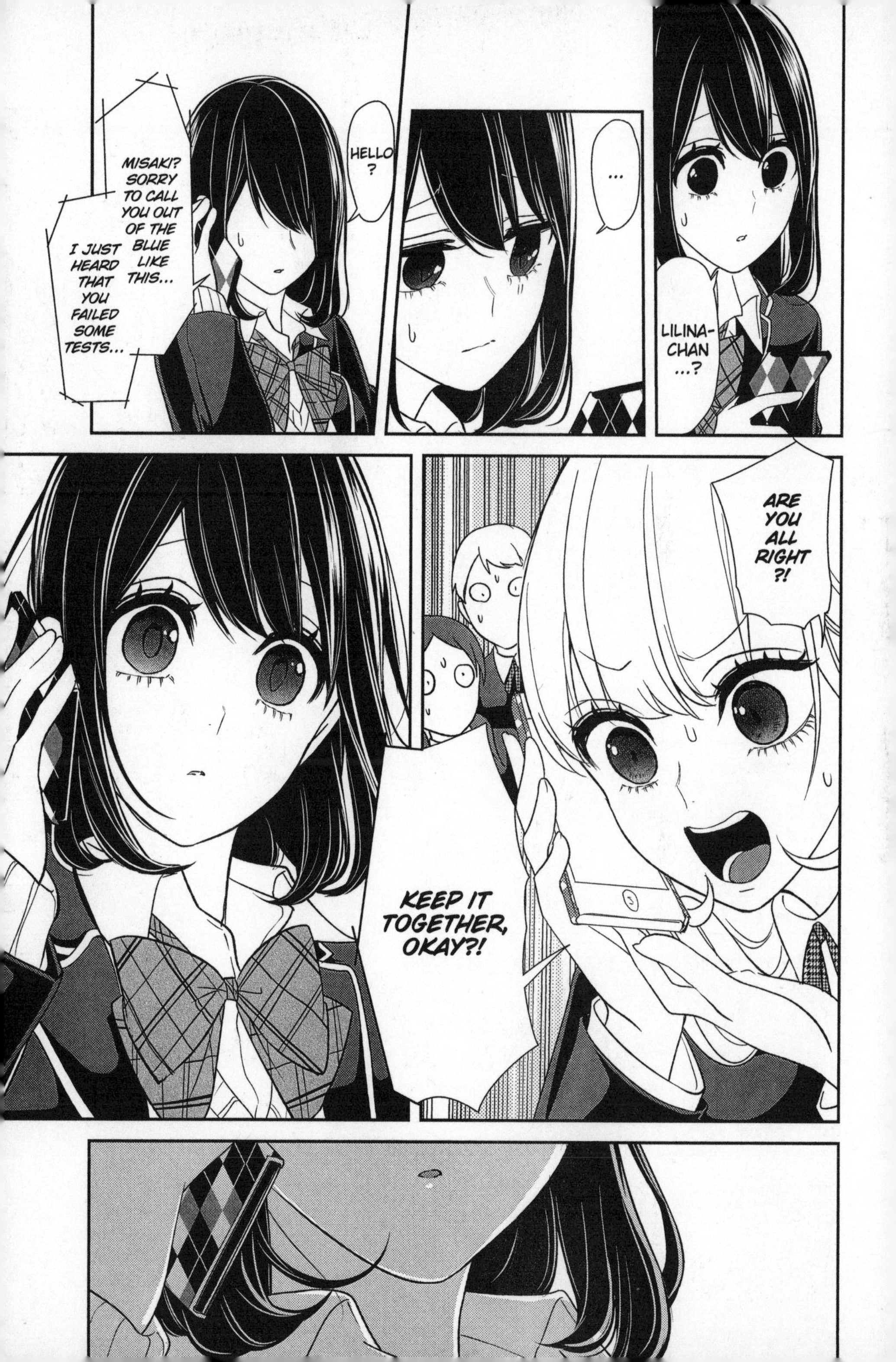
LILINA-CHAN...?
...
HELLO?
MISAKI? SORRY TO CALL YOU OUT OF THE BLUE LIKE THIS...
I JUST HEARD THAT YOU FAILED SOME TESTS...
ARE YOU ALL RIGHT?!
KEEP IT TOGETHER, OKAY?!

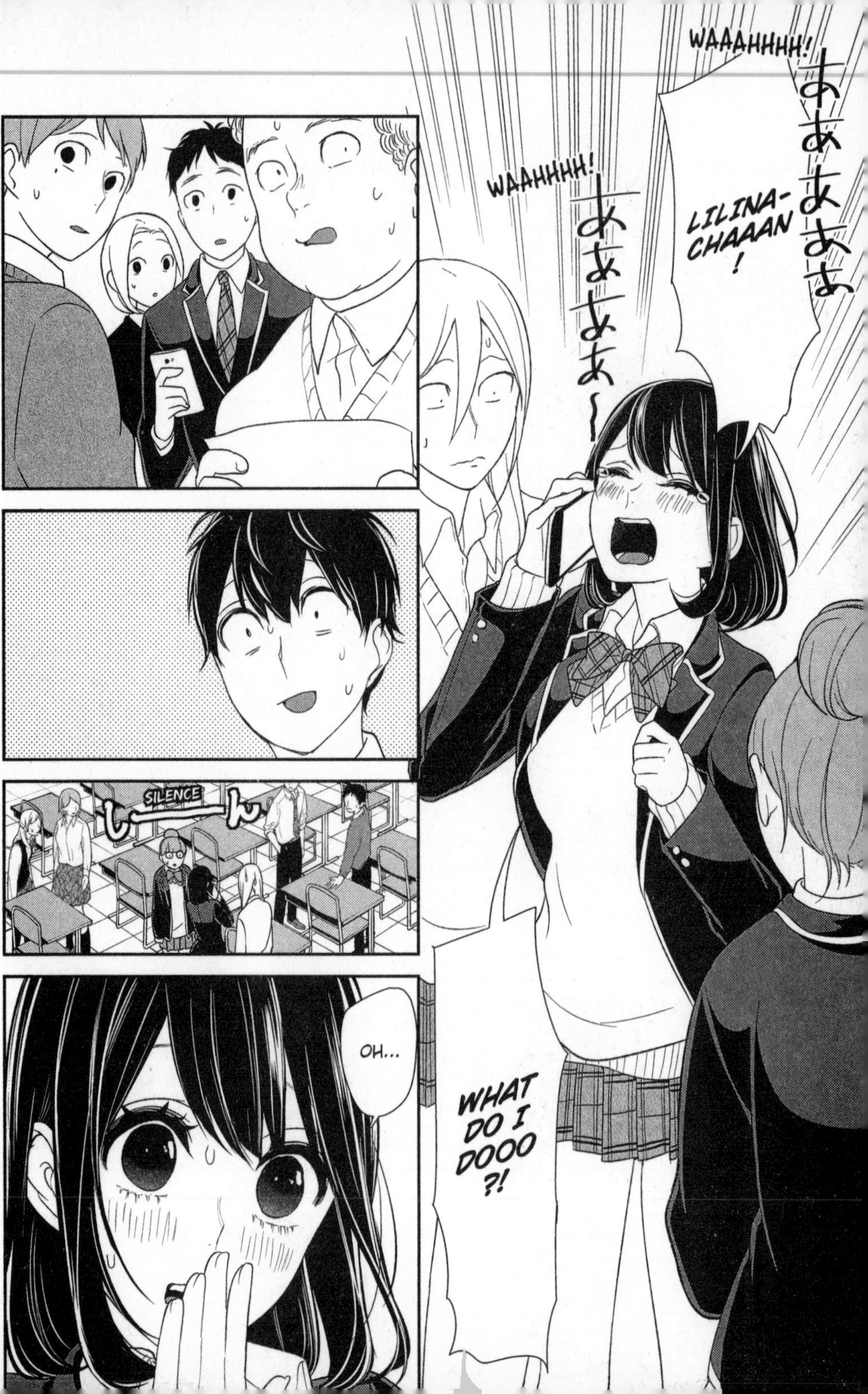
WAAAHHHH!
あああぁ
LILINA-CHAAAN!
WAAHHHH!
あぁあぁ〜!
WHAT DO I DOOO?!
SILENCE
し——ん
OH...

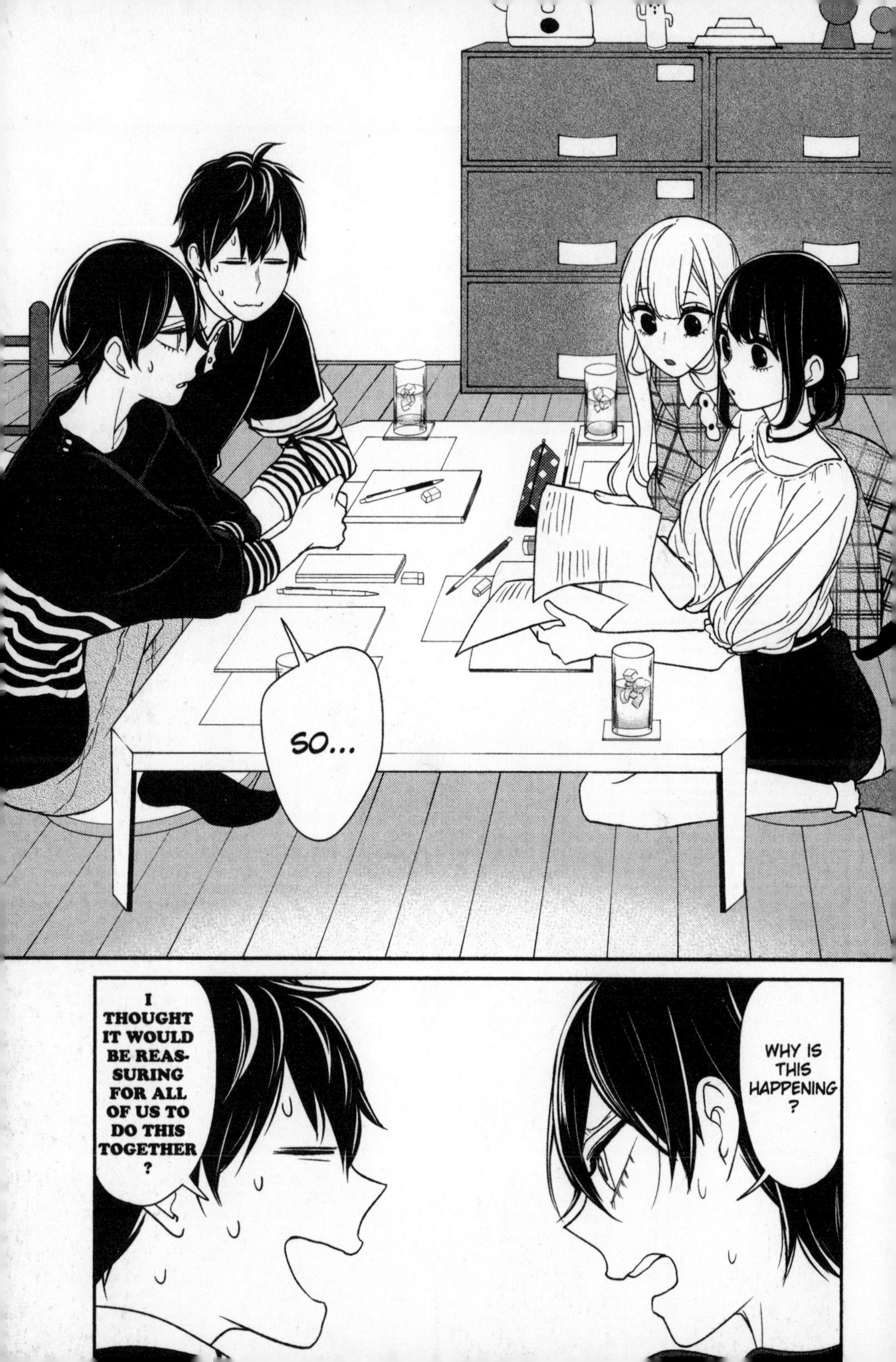
SO...
WHY IS THIS HAPPENING?
I THOUGHT IT WOULD BE REAS-SURING FOR ALL OF US TO DO THIS TOGETHER?

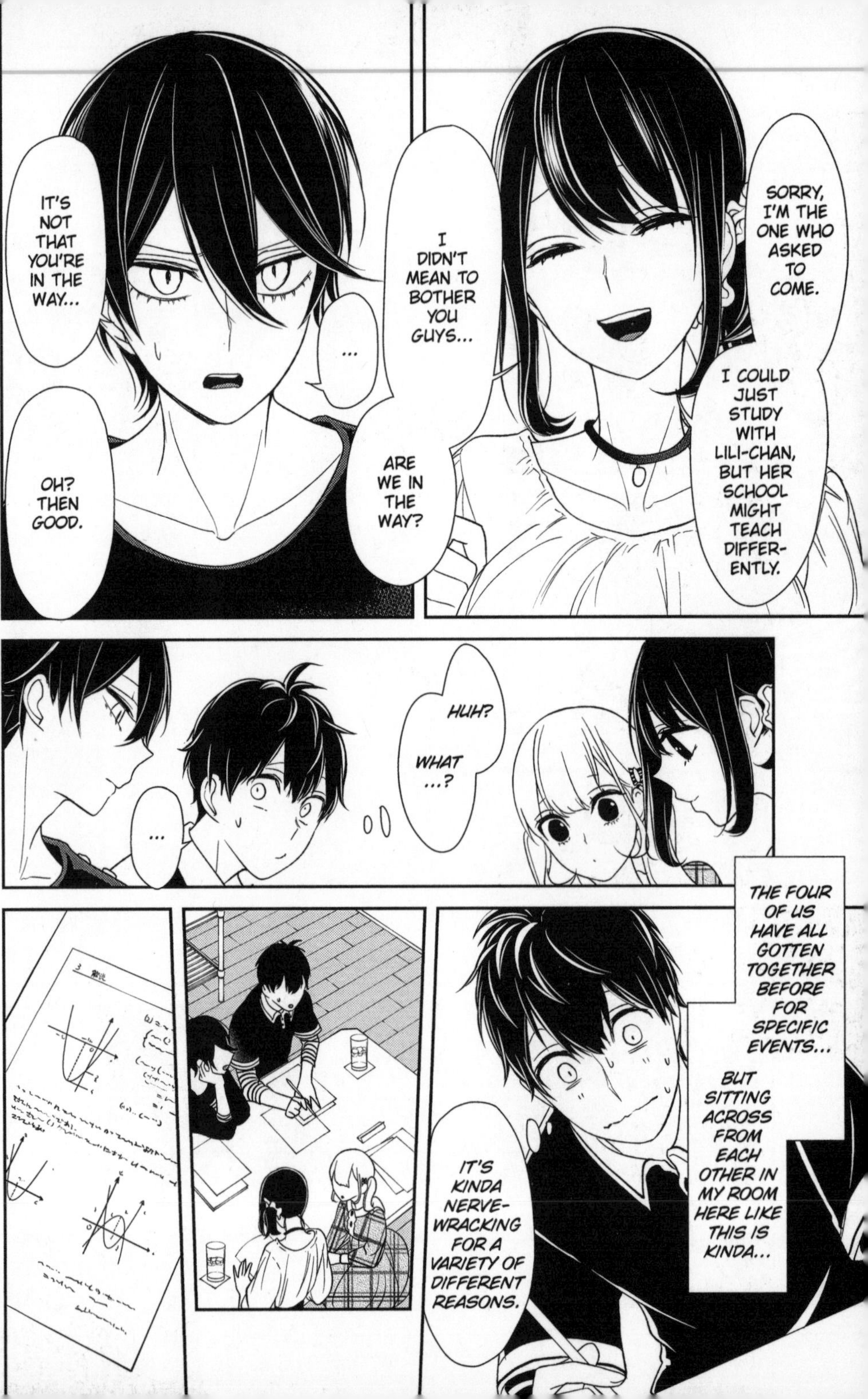
SORRY, I'M THE ONE WHO ASKED TO COME.
I COULD JUST STUDY WITH LILI-CHAN, BUT HER SCHOOL MIGHT TEACH DIFFER-ENTLY.
I DIDN'T MEAN TO BOTHER YOU GUYS...
ARE WE IN THE WAY?
...
IT'S NOT THAT YOU'RE IN THE WAY...
OH? THEN GOOD.
HUH?
WHAT ...?
...
THE FOUR OF US HAVE ALL GOTTEN TOGETHER BEFORE FOR SPECIFIC EVENTS...
BUT SITTING ACROSS FROM EACH OTHER IN MY ROOM HERE LIKE THIS IS KINDA...
IT'S KINDA NERVE-WRACKING FOR A VARIETY OF DIFFERENT REASONS.

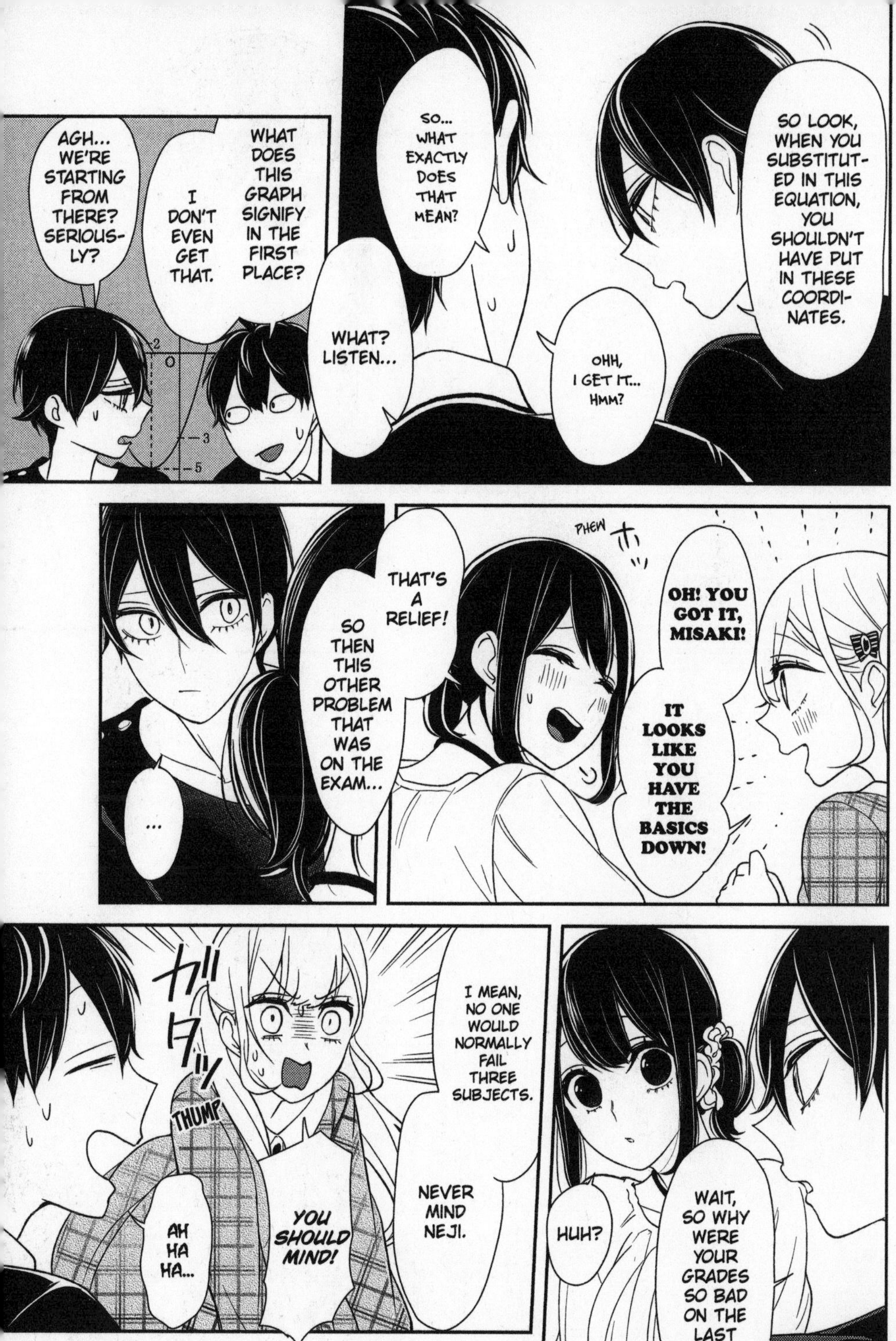
SO LOOK, WHEN YOU SUBSTITUTED IN THIS EQUATION, YOU SHOULDN'T HAVE PUT IN THESE COORDINATES.
OHH, I GET IT... HMM?
SO... WHAT EXACTLY DOES THAT MEAN?
WHAT? LISTEN...
WHAT DOES THIS GRAPH SIGNIFY IN THE FIRST PLACE?
I DON'T EVEN GET THAT.
AGH... WE'RE STARTING FROM THERE? SERIOUSLY?
OH! YOU GOT IT, MISAKI!
IT LOOKS LIKE YOU HAVE THE BASICS DOWN!
PHEW
THAT'S A RELIEF!
SO THEN THIS OTHER PROBLEM THAT WAS ON THE EXAM...
...
WAIT, SO WHY WERE YOUR GRADES SO BAD ON THE LAST EXAM?
HUH?
I MEAN, NO ONE WOULD NORMALLY FAIL THREE SUBJECTS.
NEVER MIND NEJI.
YOU SHOULD MIND!
THUMP
AH HA HA...

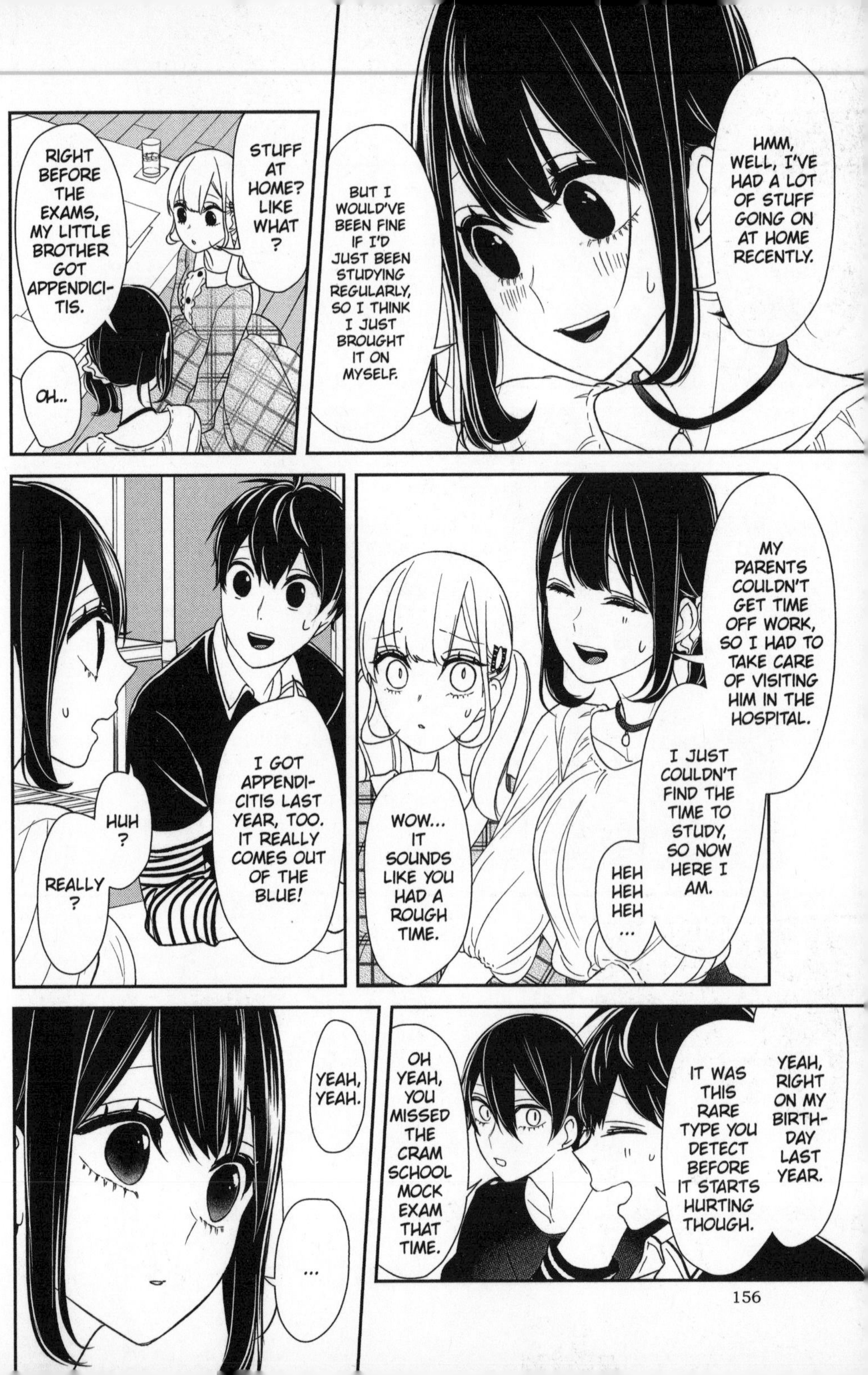
HMM, WELL, I'VE HAD A LOT OF STUFF GOING ON AT HOME RECENTLY.
BUT I WOULD'VE BEEN FINE IF I'D JUST BEEN STUDYING REGULARLY, SO I THINK I JUST BROUGHT IT ON MYSELF.
STUFF AT HOME? LIKE WHAT?
RIGHT BEFORE THE EXAMS, MY LITTLE BROTHER GOT APPENDICI-TIS.
OH...
MY PARENTS COULDN'T GET TIME OFF WORK, SO I HAD TO TAKE CARE OF VISITING HIM IN THE HOSPITAL.
I JUST COULDN'T FIND THE TIME TO STUDY, SO NOW HERE I AM.
HEH HEH HEH...
WOW... IT SOUNDS LIKE YOU HAD A ROUGH TIME.
I GOT APPENDI-CITIS LAST YEAR, TOO. IT REALLY COMES OUT OF THE BLUE!
HUH? REALLY?
YEAH, RIGHT ON MY BIRTH-DAY LAST YEAR.
IT WAS THIS RARE TYPE YOU DETECT BEFORE IT STARTS HURTING THOUGH.
OH YEAH, YOU MISSED THE CRAM SCHOOL MOCK EXAM THAT TIME.
YEAH, YEAH.
...

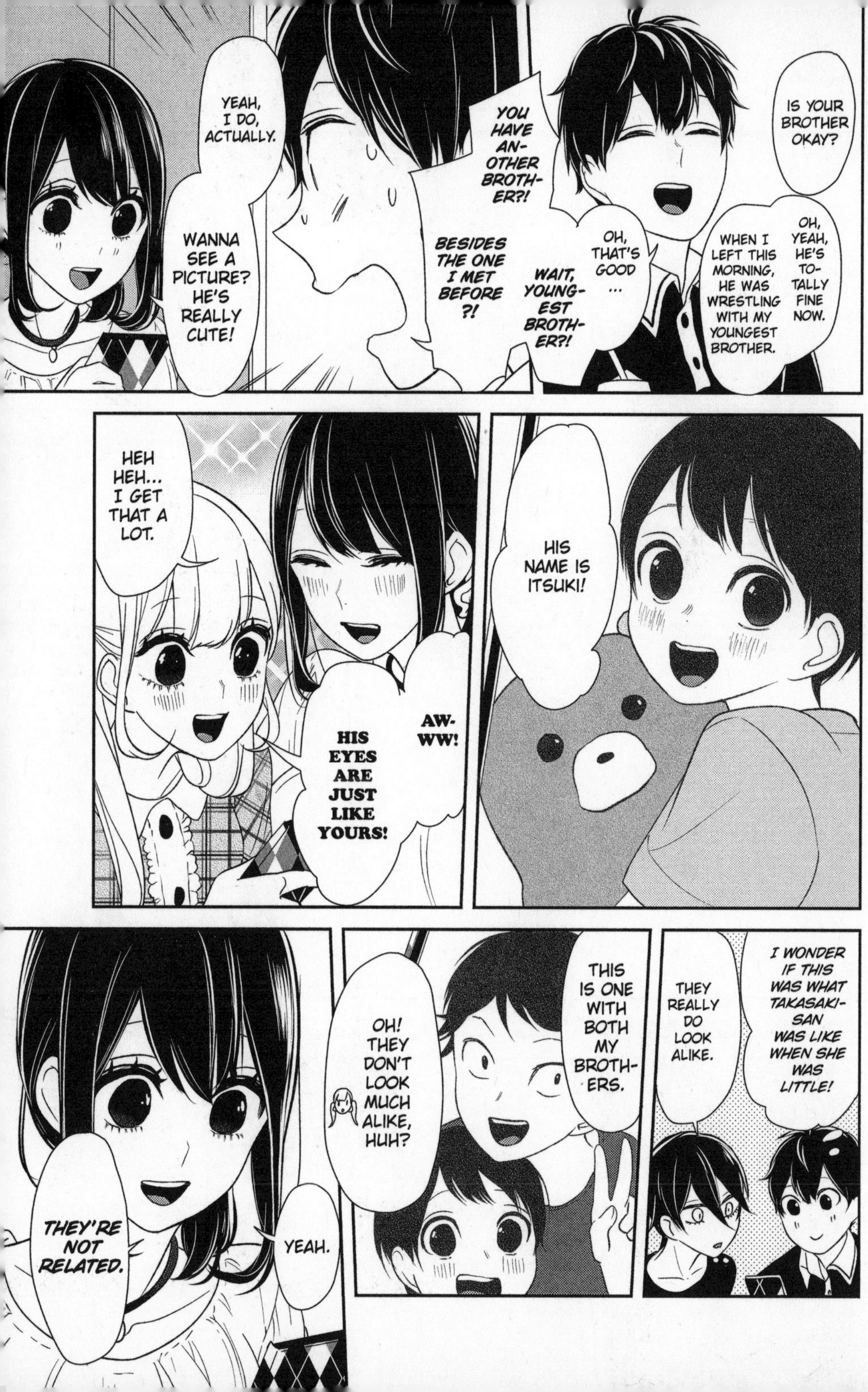
IS YOUR BROTHER OKAY?
OH, YEAH, HE'S TO-TALLY FINE NOW.
WHEN I LEFT THIS MORNING, HE WAS WRESTLING WITH MY YOUNGEST BROTHER.
OH, THAT'S GOOD ...
WAIT, YOUNG-EST BROTH-ER?!
YOU HAVE AN-OTHER BROTH-ER?!
BESIDES THE ONE I MET BEFORE ?!
YEAH, I DO, ACTUALLY.
WANNA SEE A PICTURE? HE'S REALLY CUTE!
HIS NAME IS ITSUKI!
AW-WW!
HIS EYES ARE JUST LIKE YOURS!
HEH HEH... I GET THAT A LOT.
I WONDER IF THIS WAS WHAT TAKASAKI-SAN WAS LIKE WHEN SHE WAS LITTLE!
THEY REALLY DO LOOK ALIKE.
THIS IS ONE WITH BOTH MY BROTH-ERS.
OH! THEY DON'T LOOK MUCH ALIKE, HUH?
YEAH.
THEY'RE NOT RELATED.

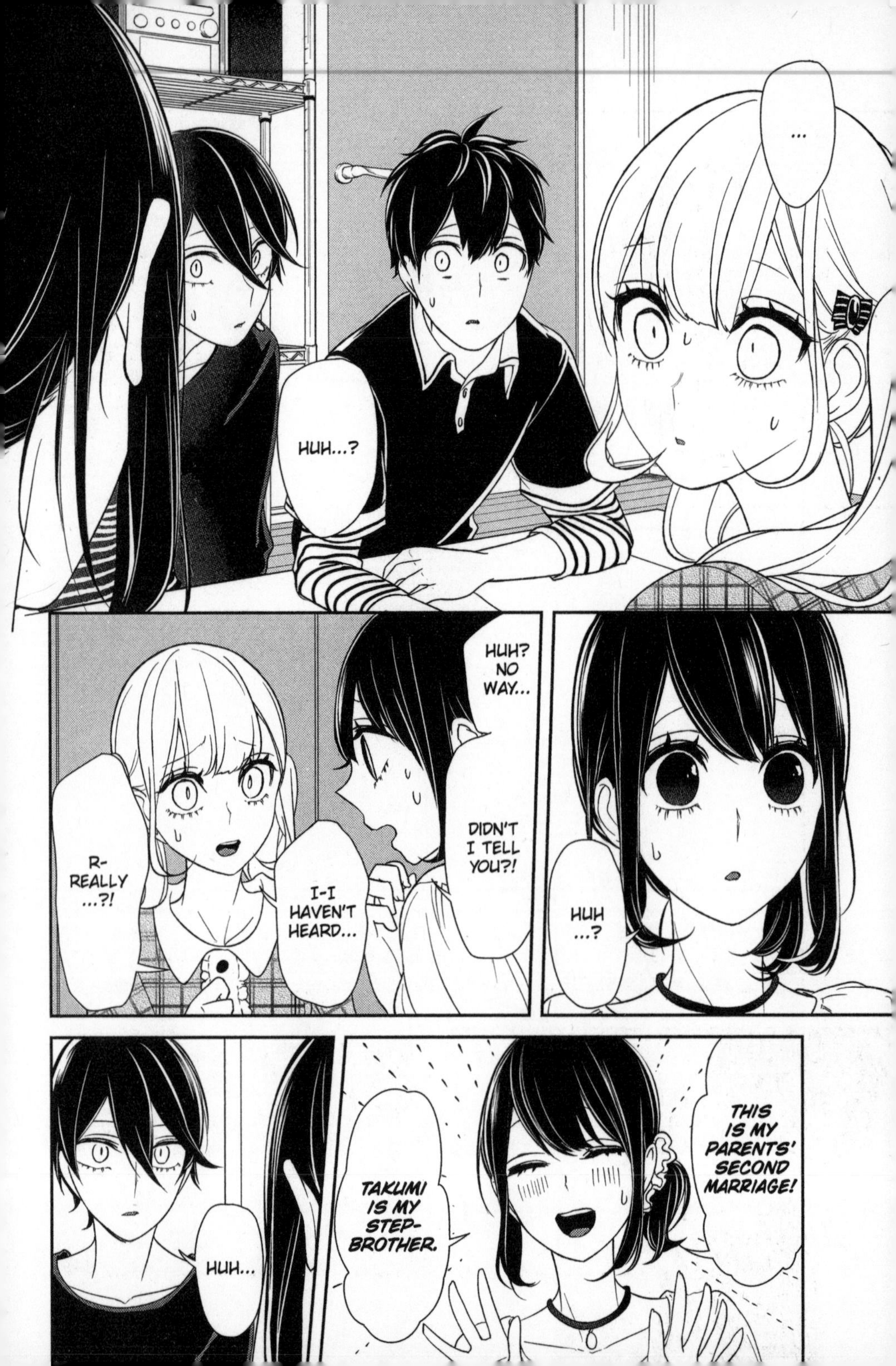
...
HUH...?
HUH ...?
HUH? NO WAY...
DIDN'T I TELL YOU?!
I-I HAVEN'T HEARD...
R- REALLY ...?!
THIS IS MY PARENTS' SECOND MARRIAGE!
TAKUMI IS MY STEP-BROTHER.
HUH...

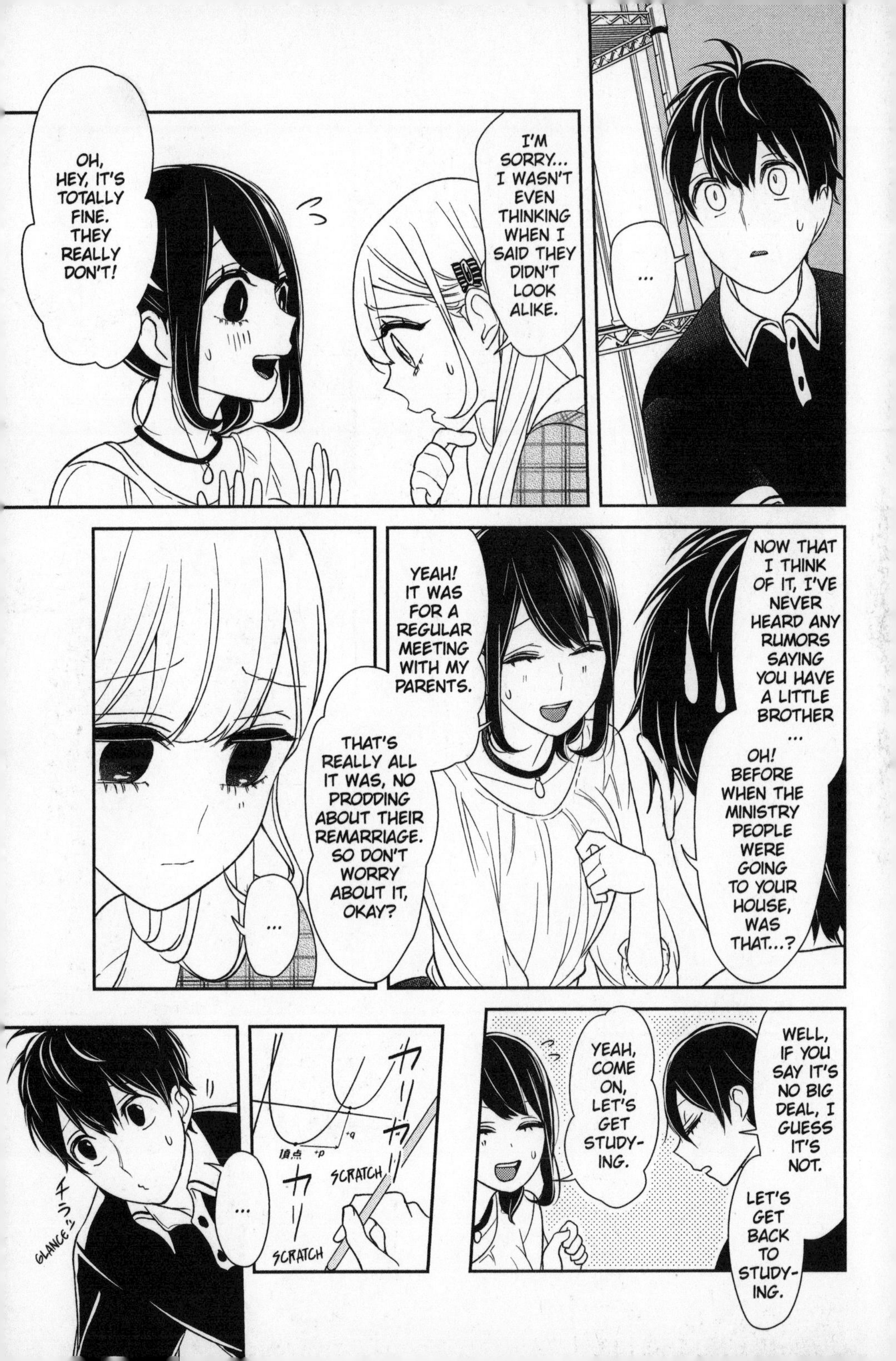
...
I'M SORRY... I WASN'T EVEN THINKING WHEN I SAID THEY DIDN'T LOOK ALIKE.
OH, HEY, IT'S TOTALLY FINE. THEY REALLY DON'T!
NOW THAT I THINK OF IT, I'VE NEVER HEARD ANY RUMORS SAYING YOU HAVE A LITTLE BROTHER...
OH! BEFORE WHEN THE MINISTRY PEOPLE WERE GOING TO YOUR HOUSE, WAS THAT...?
YEAH! IT WAS FOR A REGULAR MEETING WITH MY PARENTS.
THAT'S REALLY ALL IT WAS, NO PRODDING ABOUT THEIR REMARRIAGE. SO DON'T WORRY ABOUT IT, OKAY?
...
WELL, IF YOU SAY IT'S NO BIG DEAL, I GUESS IT'S NOT.
LET'S GET BACK TO STUDY-ING.
YEAH, COME ON, LET'S GET STUDY-ING.
カリカリ
SCRATCH
頂点 +p +q
カリ
SCRATCH
...
チラッ
GLANCE

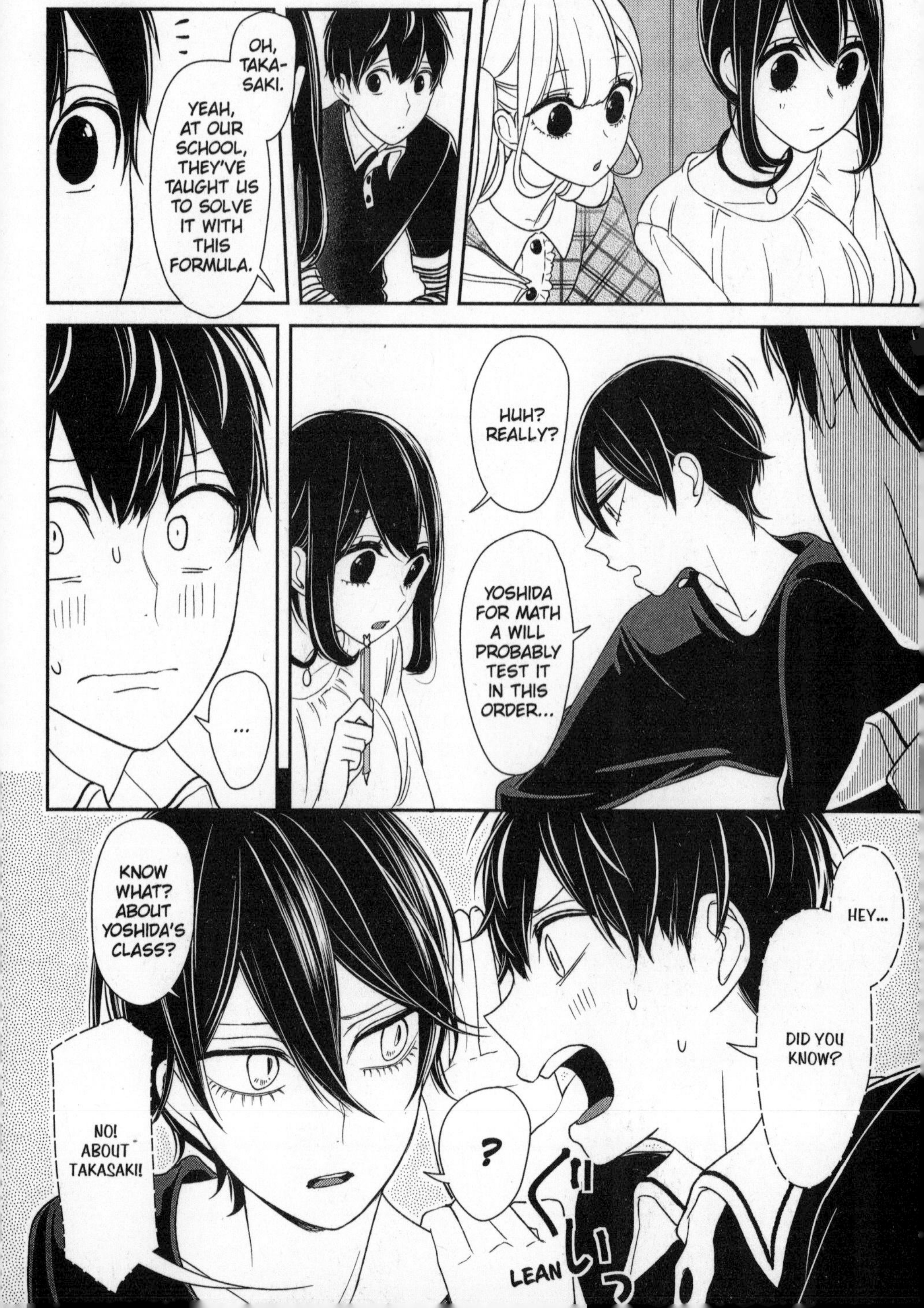
OH, TAKA-SAKI.
YEAH, AT OUR SCHOOL, THEY'VE TAUGHT US TO SOLVE IT WITH THIS FORMULA.
HUH? REALLY?
YOSHIDA FOR MATH A WILL PROBABLY TEST IT IN THIS ORDER...
...
HEY...
DID YOU KNOW?
KNOW WHAT? ABOUT YOSHIDA'S CLASS?
?
NO! ABOUT TAKASAKI!
LEAN

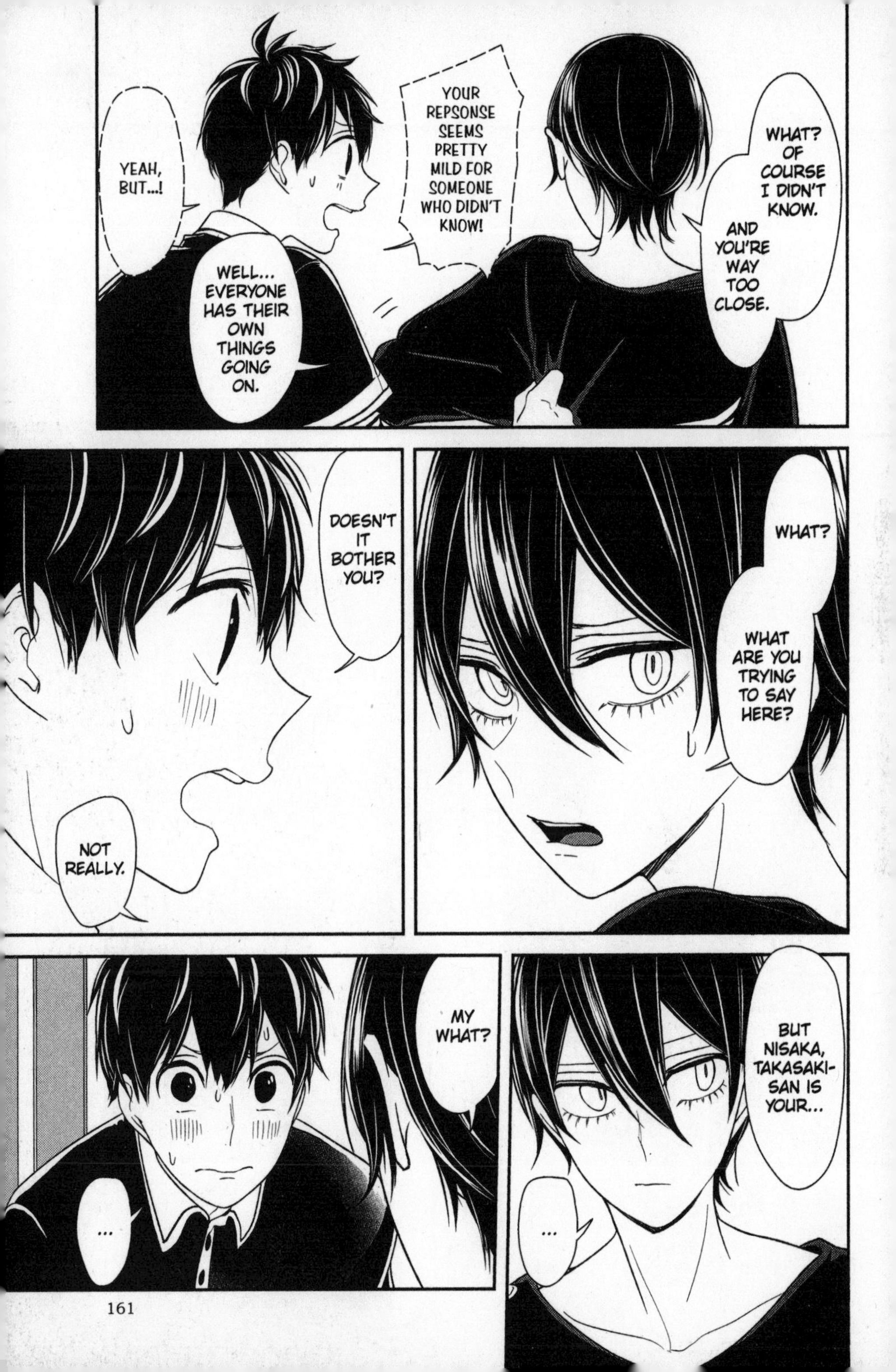
WHAT? OF COURSE I DIDN'T KNOW.
AND YOU'RE WAY TOO CLOSE.
YOUR REPSONSE SEEMS PRETTY MILD FOR SOMEONE WHO DIDN'T KNOW!
YEAH, BUT...!
WELL... EVERYONE HAS THEIR OWN THINGS GOING ON.
WHAT?
WHAT ARE YOU TRYING TO SAY HERE?
DOESN'T IT BOTHER YOU?
NOT REALLY.
BUT NISAKA, TAKASAKI-SAN IS YOUR...
...
MY WHAT?
...

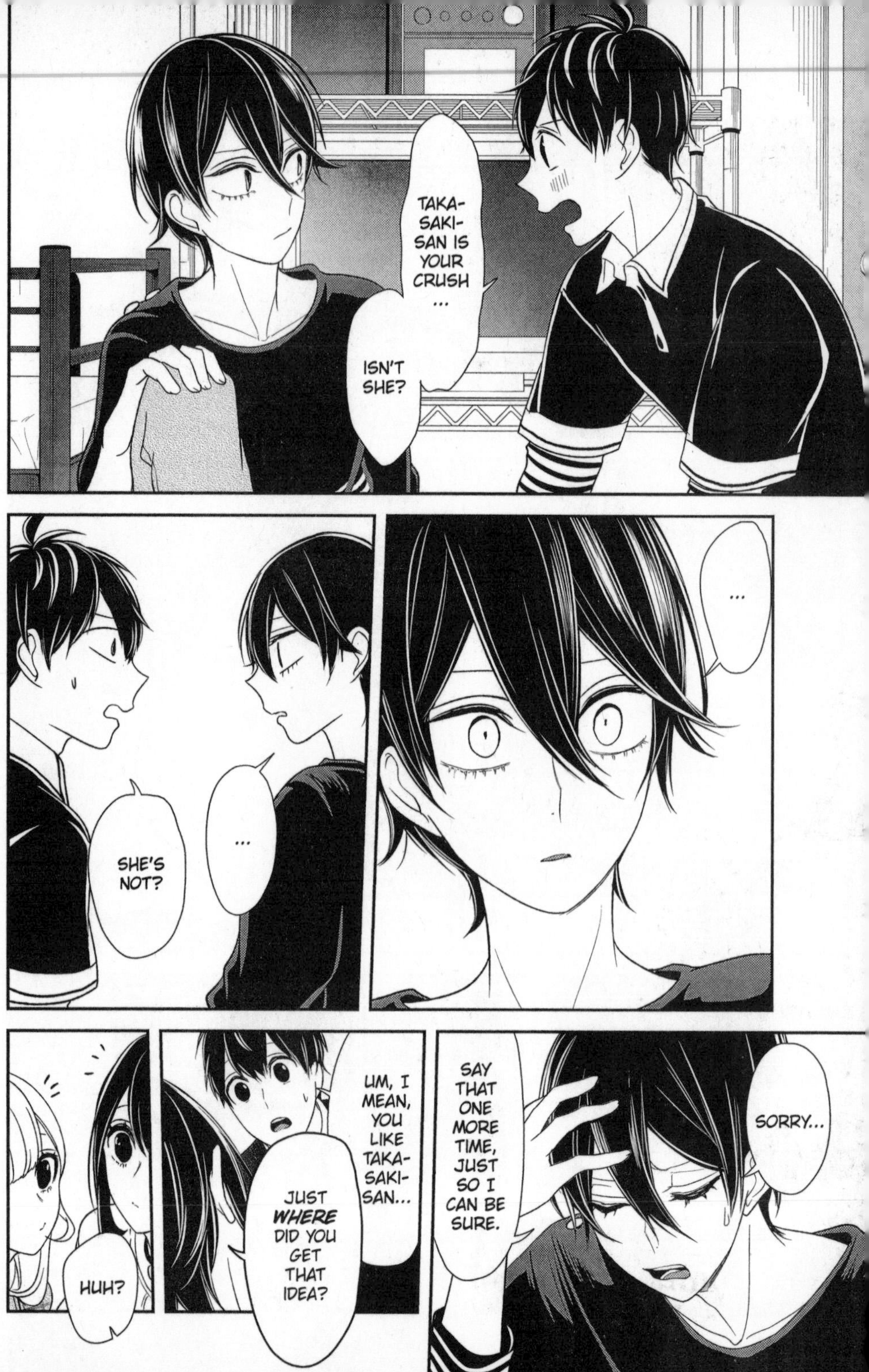
TAKA-SAKI-SAN IS YOUR CRUSH ...
ISN'T SHE?
...
...
SHE'S NOT?
SORRY...
SAY THAT ONE MORE TIME, JUST SO I CAN BE SURE.
UM, I MEAN, YOU LIKE TAKA-SAKI-SAN...
JUST *WHERE* DID YOU GET THAT IDEA?
HUH?

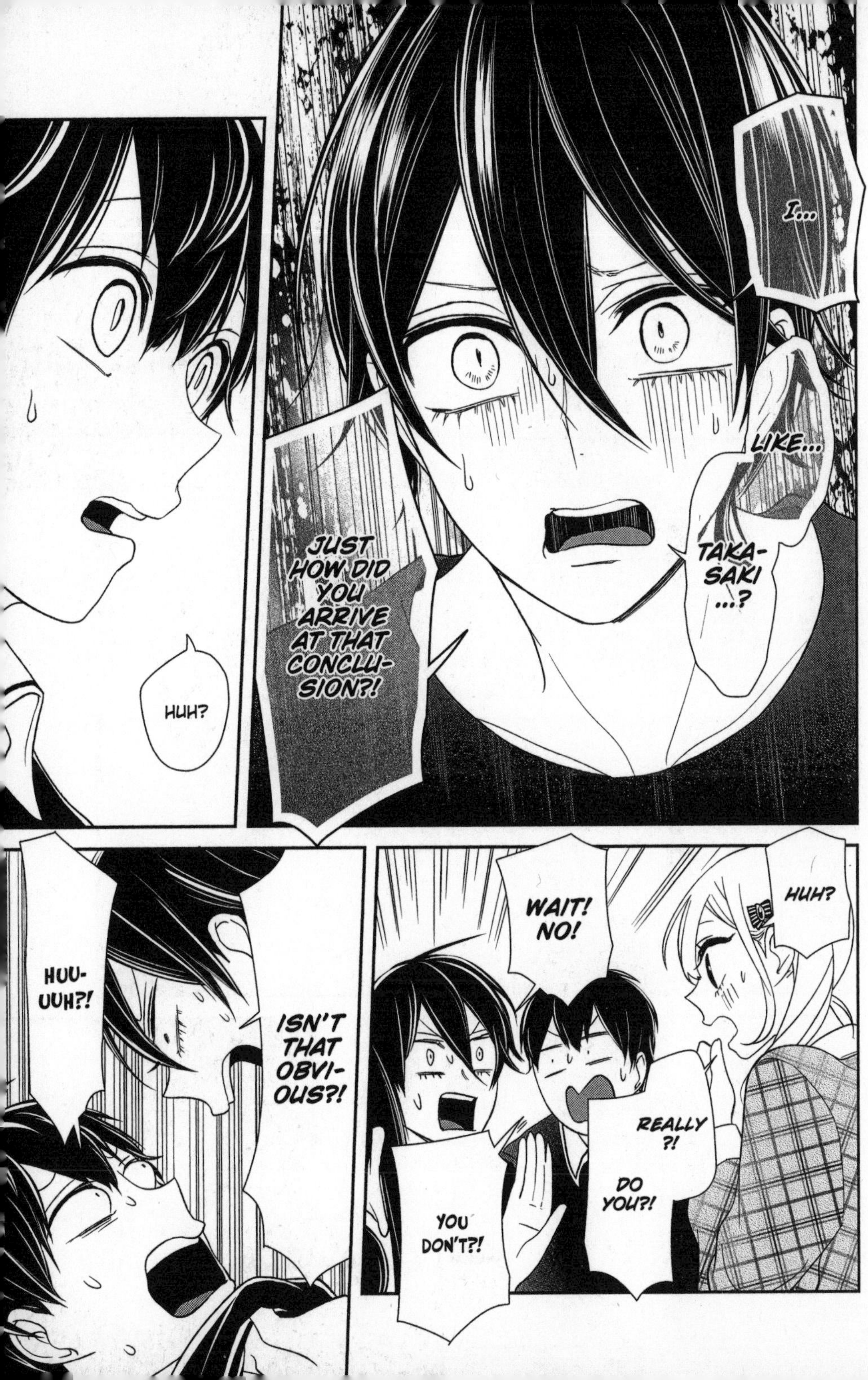
I...
LIKE...
TAKA-SAKI ...?
JUST HOW DID YOU ARRIVE AT THAT CONCLU-SION?!
HUH?
HUH?
WAIT! NO!
REALLY?!
DO YOU?!
YOU DON'T?!
ISN'T THAT OBVI-OUS?!
HUU-UUH?!

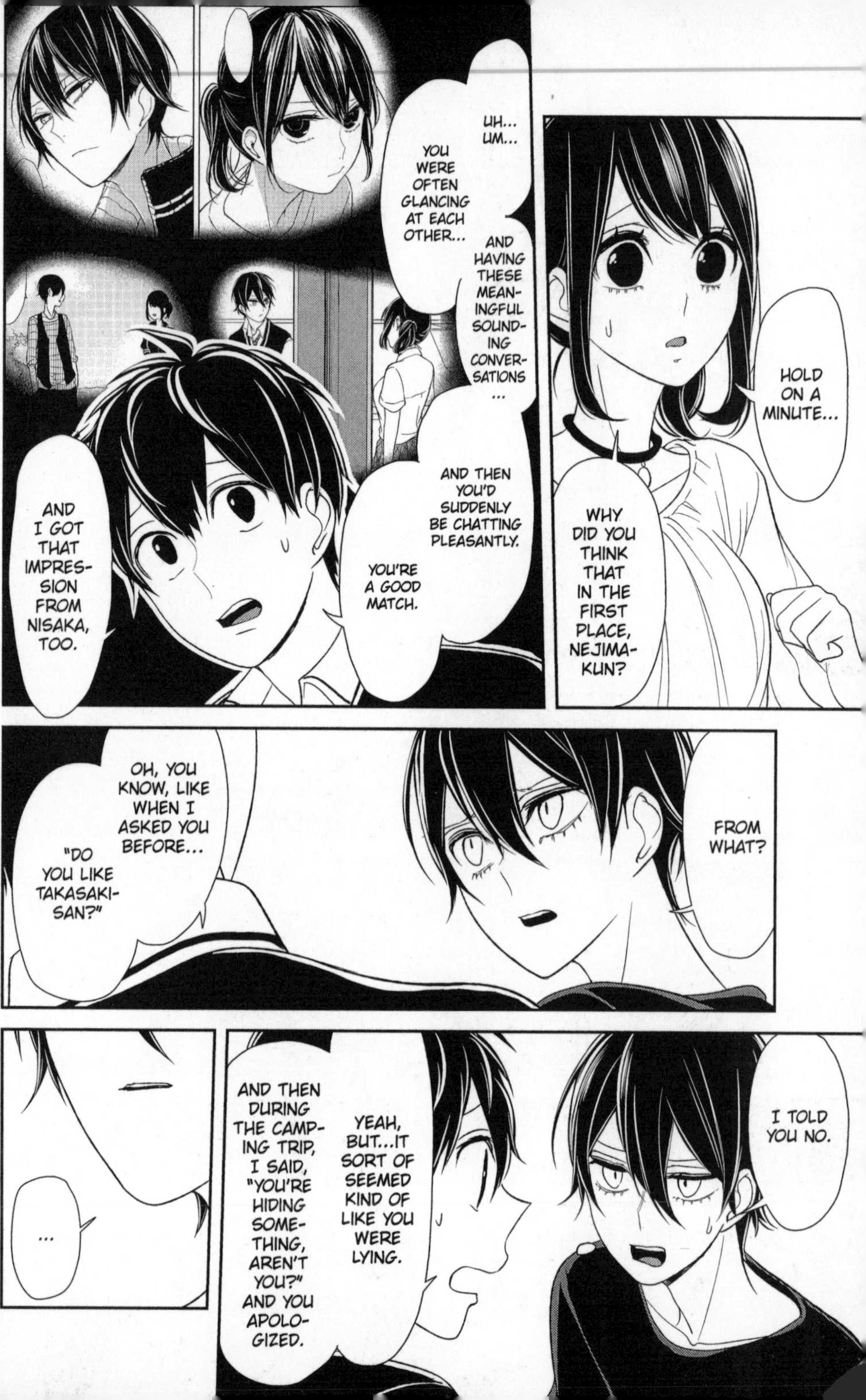
HOLD ON A MINUTE...
WHY DID YOU THINK THAT IN THE FIRST PLACE, NEJIMA-KUN?
UH... UM...
YOU WERE OFTEN GLANCING AT EACH OTHER...
AND HAVING THESE MEANINGFUL SOUNDING CONVERSATIONS...
AND THEN YOU'D SUDDENLY BE CHATTING PLEASANTLY.
YOU'RE A GOOD MATCH.
AND I GOT THAT IMPRESSION FROM NISAKA, TOO.
FROM WHAT?
OH, YOU KNOW, LIKE WHEN I ASKED YOU BEFORE...
"DO YOU LIKE TAKASAKI-SAN?"
I TOLD YOU NO.
YEAH, BUT...IT SORT OF SEEMED KIND OF LIKE YOU WERE LYING.
AND THEN DURING THE CAMPING TRIP, I SAID, "YOU'RE HIDING SOMETHING, AREN'T YOU?" AND YOU APOLOGIZED.
...

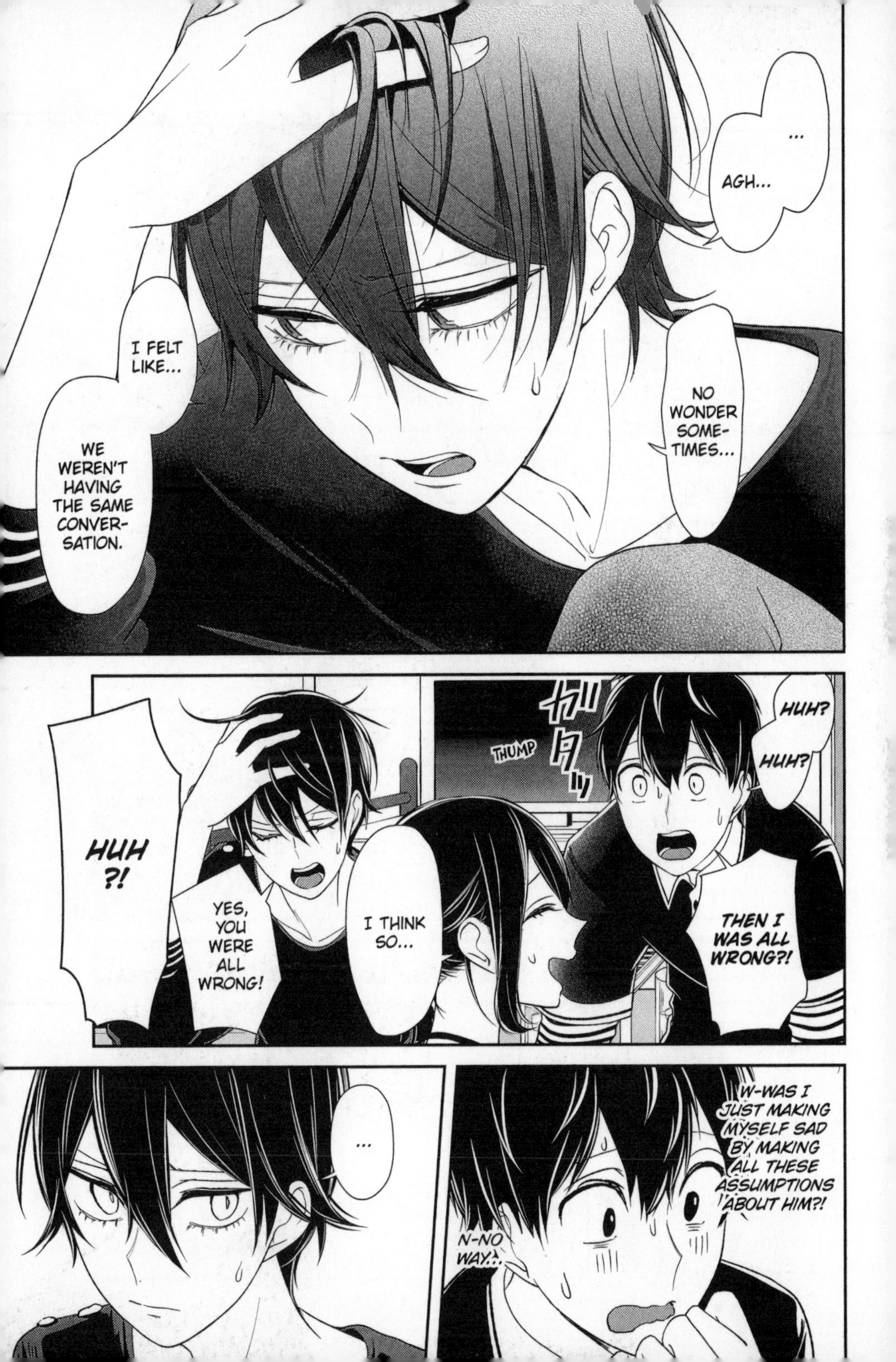
...
AGH...
NO WONDER SOMETIMES...
I FELT LIKE...
WE WEREN'T HAVING THE SAME CONVERSATION.
HUH?
HUH?
THUMP
THEN I WAS ALL WRONG?!
I THINK SO...
YES, YOU WERE ALL WRONG!
HUH ?!
W-WAS I JUST MAKING MYSELF SAD BY MAKING ALL THESE ASSUMPTIONS ABOUT HIM?!
N-NO WAY...
...

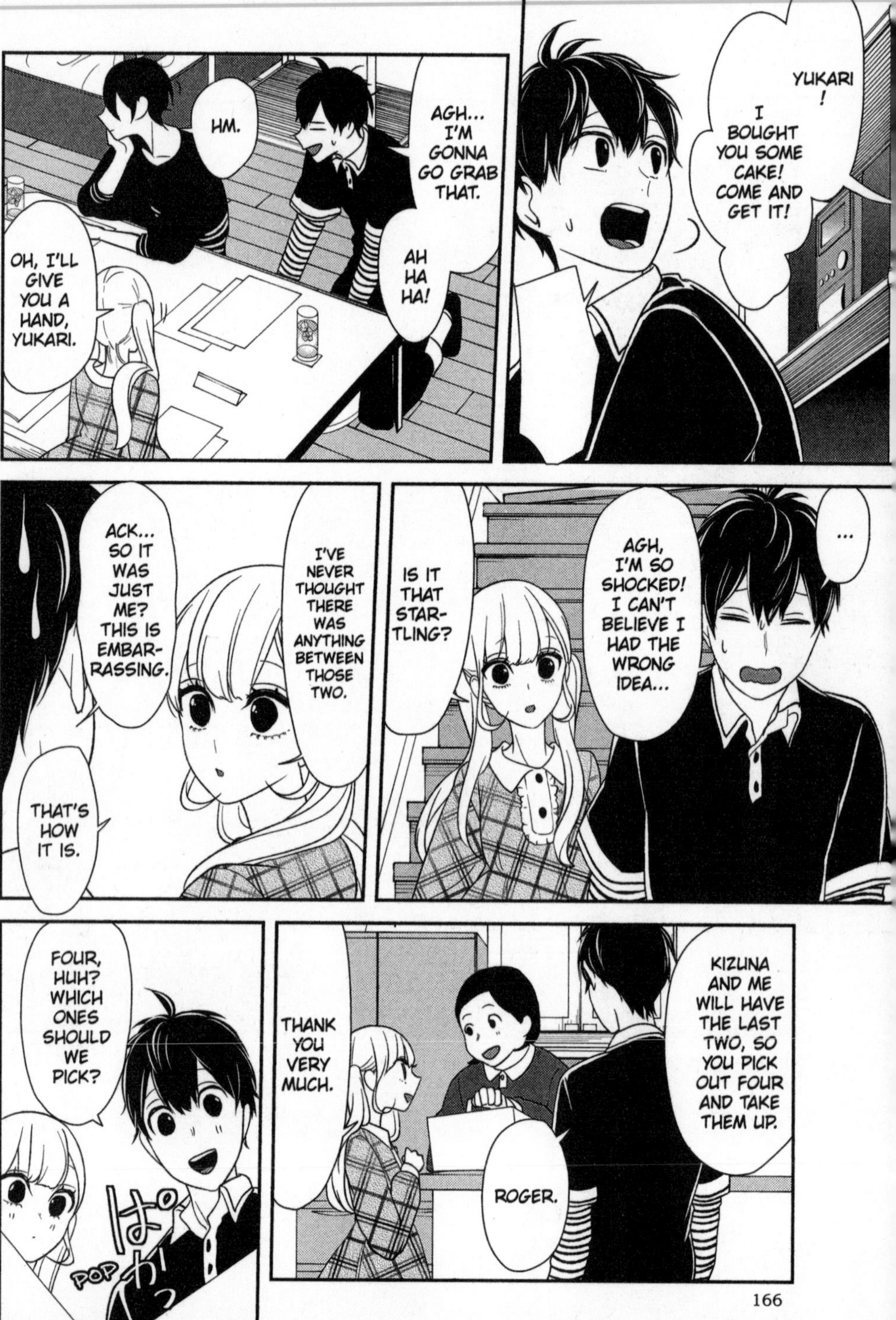
YUKARI! I BOUGHT YOU SOME CAKE! COME AND GET IT!
AGH... I'M GONNA GO GRAB THAT.
HM.
AH HA HA!
OH, I'LL GIVE YOU A HAND, YUKARI.
...
AGH, I'M SO SHOCKED! I CAN'T BELIEVE I HAD THE WRONG IDEA...
IS IT THAT STAR-TLING?
I'VE NEVER THOUGHT THERE WAS ANYTHING BETWEEN THOSE TWO.
ACK... SO IT WAS JUST ME? THIS IS EMBAR-RASSING.
THAT'S HOW IT IS.
KIZUNA AND ME WILL HAVE THE LAST TWO, SO YOU PICK OUT FOUR AND TAKE THEM UP.
ROGER.
THANK YOU VERY MUCH.
FOUR, HUH? WHICH ONES SHOULD WE PICK?
ぱっ
POP

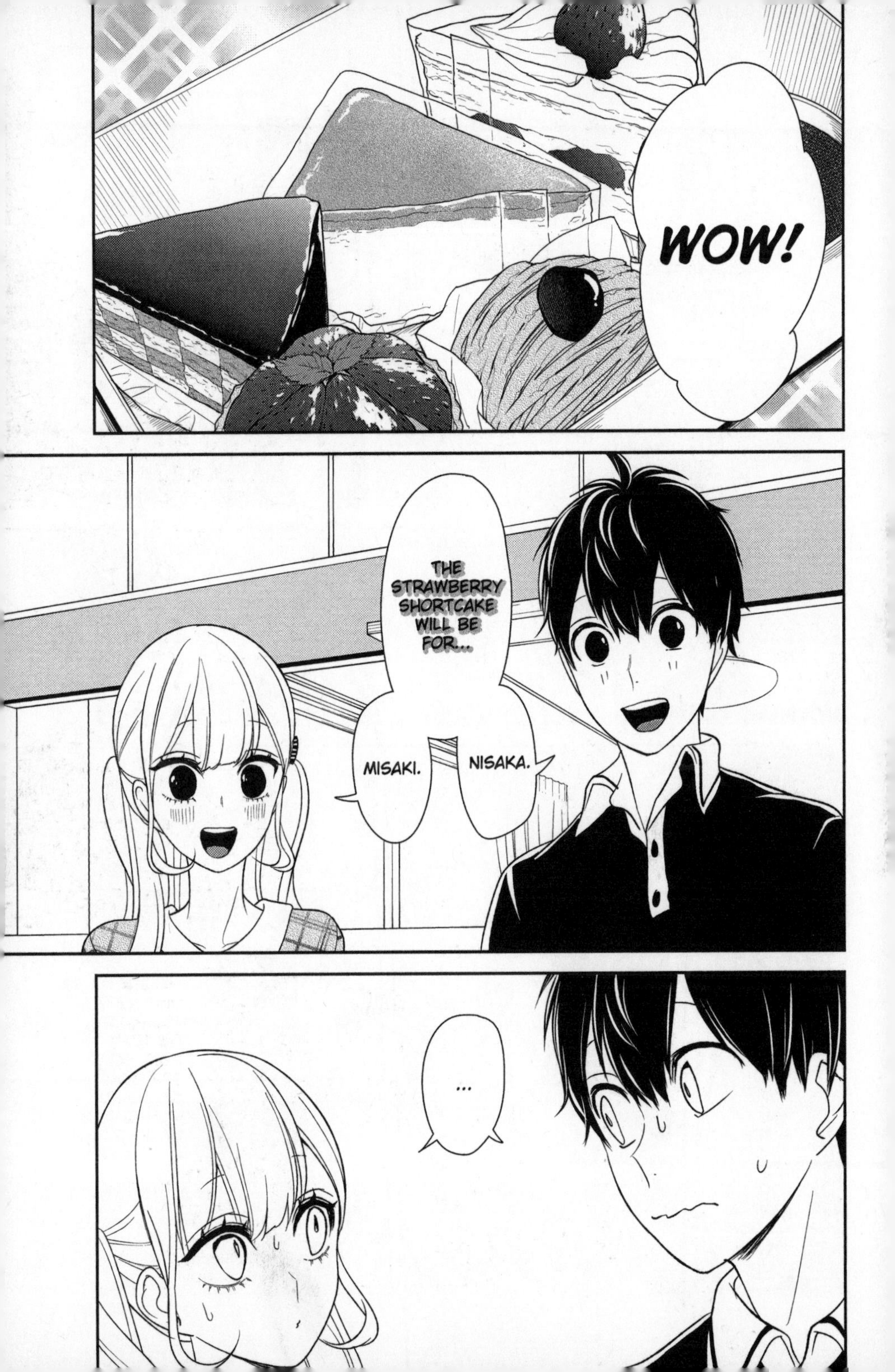
WOW!
THE STRAWBERRY SHORTCAKE WILL BE FOR...
NISAKA.
MISAKI.
...

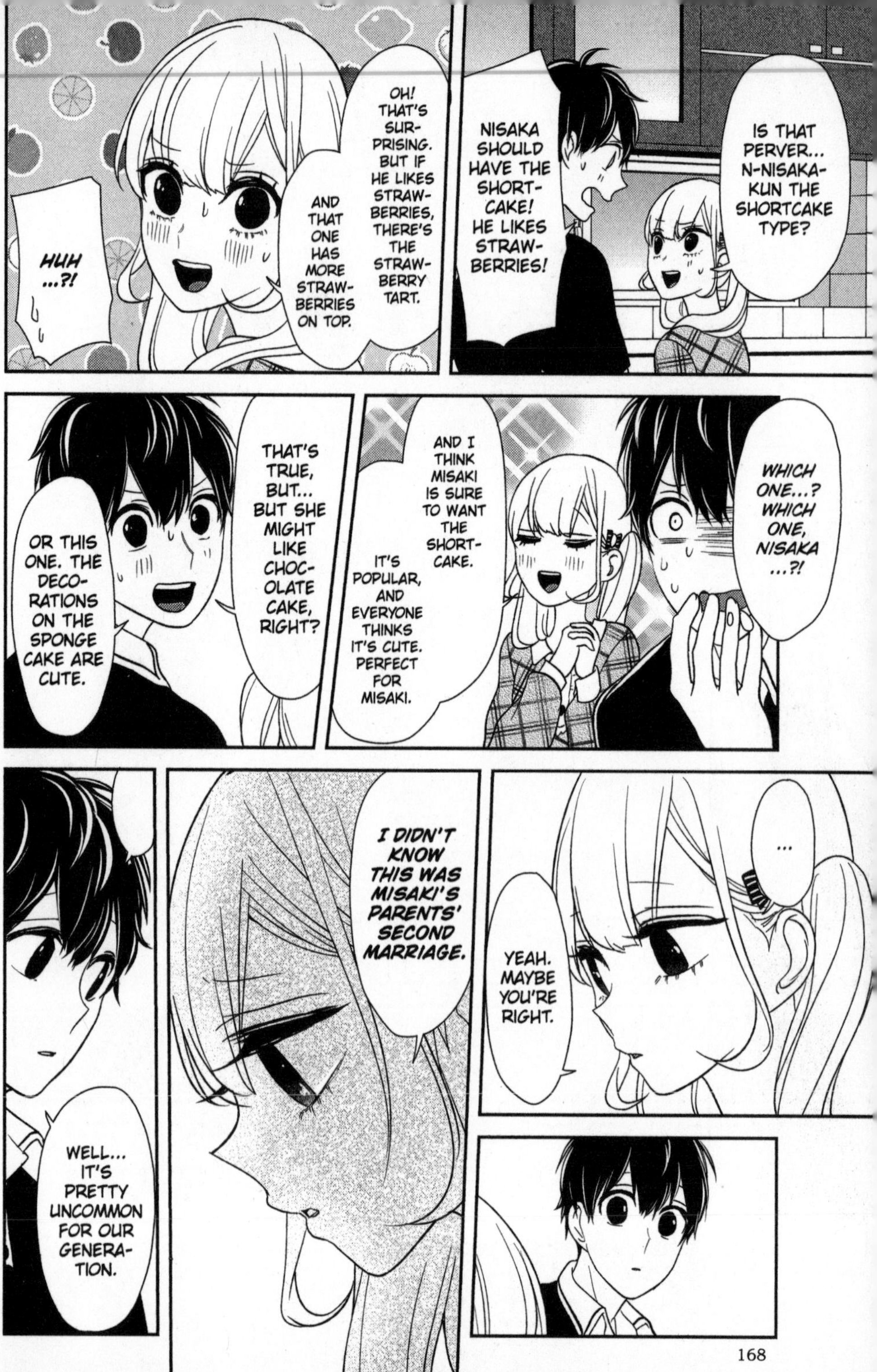
IS THAT PERVER... N-NISAKA-KUN THE SHORTCAKE TYPE?
NISAKA SHOULD HAVE THE SHORTCAKE! HE LIKES STRAWBERRIES!
OH! THAT'S SURPRISING. BUT IF HE LIKES STRAWBERRIES, THERE'S THE STRAWBERRY TART.
AND THAT ONE HAS MORE STRAWBERRIES ON TOP.
HUH ...?!
WHICH ONE...? WHICH ONE, NISAKA ...?!
AND I THINK MISAKI IS SURE TO WANT THE SHORTCAKE.
IT'S POPULAR, AND EVERYONE THINKS IT'S CUTE. PERFECT FOR MISAKI.
THAT'S TRUE, BUT... BUT SHE MIGHT LIKE CHOCOLATE CAKE, RIGHT?
OR THIS ONE. THE DECORATIONS ON THE SPONGE CAKE ARE CUTE.
...
YEAH. MAYBE YOU'RE RIGHT.
I DIDN'T KNOW THIS WAS MISAKI'S PARENTS' SECOND MARRIAGE.
WELL... IT'S PRETTY UNCOMMON FOR OUR GENERATION.

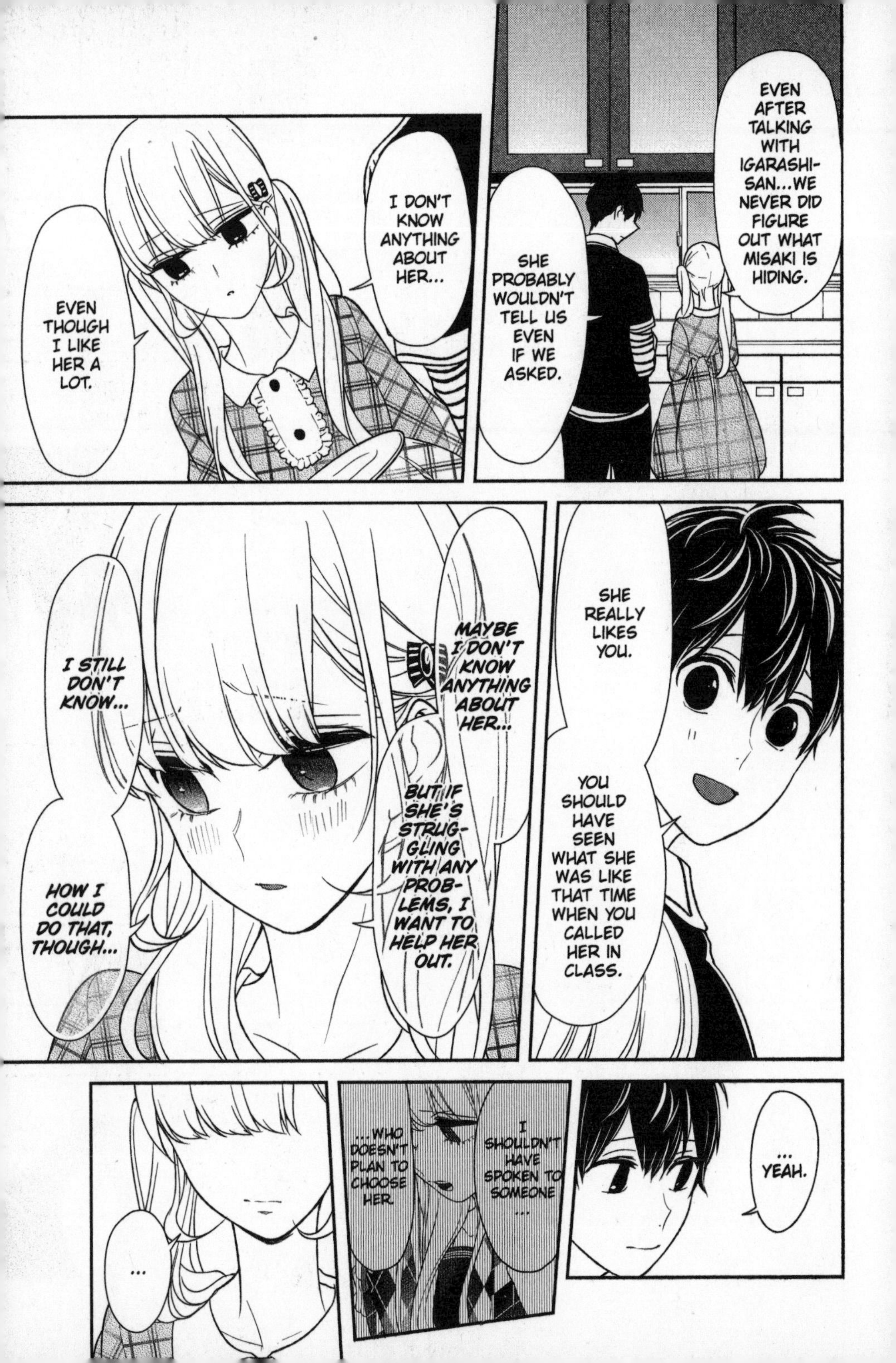
EVEN AFTER TALKING WITH IGARASHI-SAN...WE NEVER DID FIGURE OUT WHAT MISAKI IS HIDING.
SHE PROBABLY WOULDN'T TELL US EVEN IF WE ASKED.
I DON'T KNOW ANYTHING ABOUT HER...
EVEN THOUGH I LIKE HER A LOT.
SHE REALLY LIKES YOU.
YOU SHOULD HAVE SEEN WHAT SHE WAS LIKE THAT TIME WHEN YOU CALLED HER IN CLASS.
MAYBE I DON'T KNOW ANYTHING ABOUT HER...
BUT IF SHE'S STRUGGLING WITH ANY PROBLEMS, I WANT TO HELP HER OUT.
I STILL DON'T KNOW...
HOW I COULD DO THAT, THOUGH...
...YEAH.
I SHOULDN'T HAVE SPOKEN TO SOMEONE...
...WHO DOESN'T PLAN TO CHOOSE HER.
...

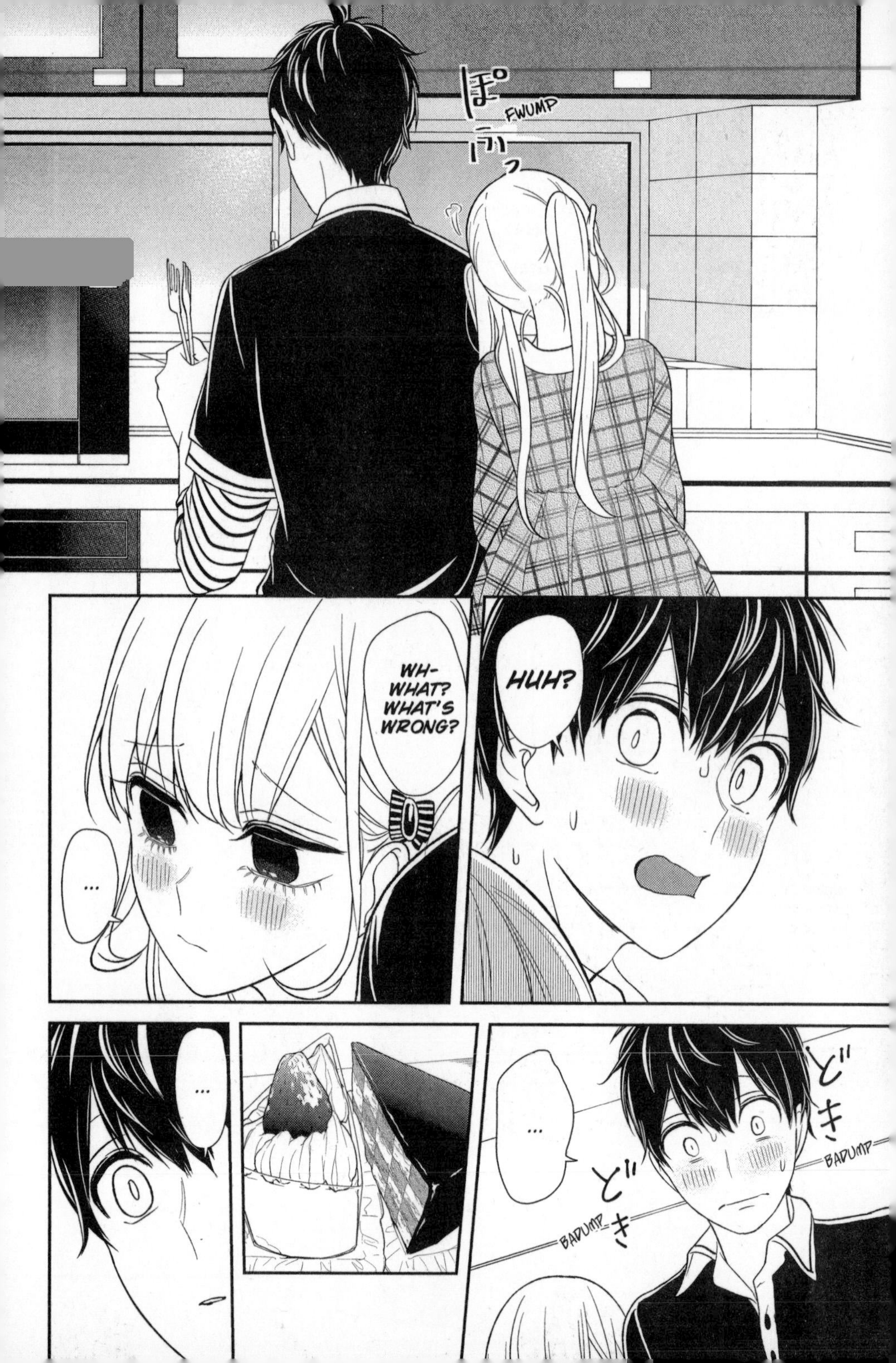
ぽふっ
FWUMP
HUH?
WH-
WHAT?
WHAT'S
WRONG?
...
...
どきどき
BADUMP
BADUMP
...

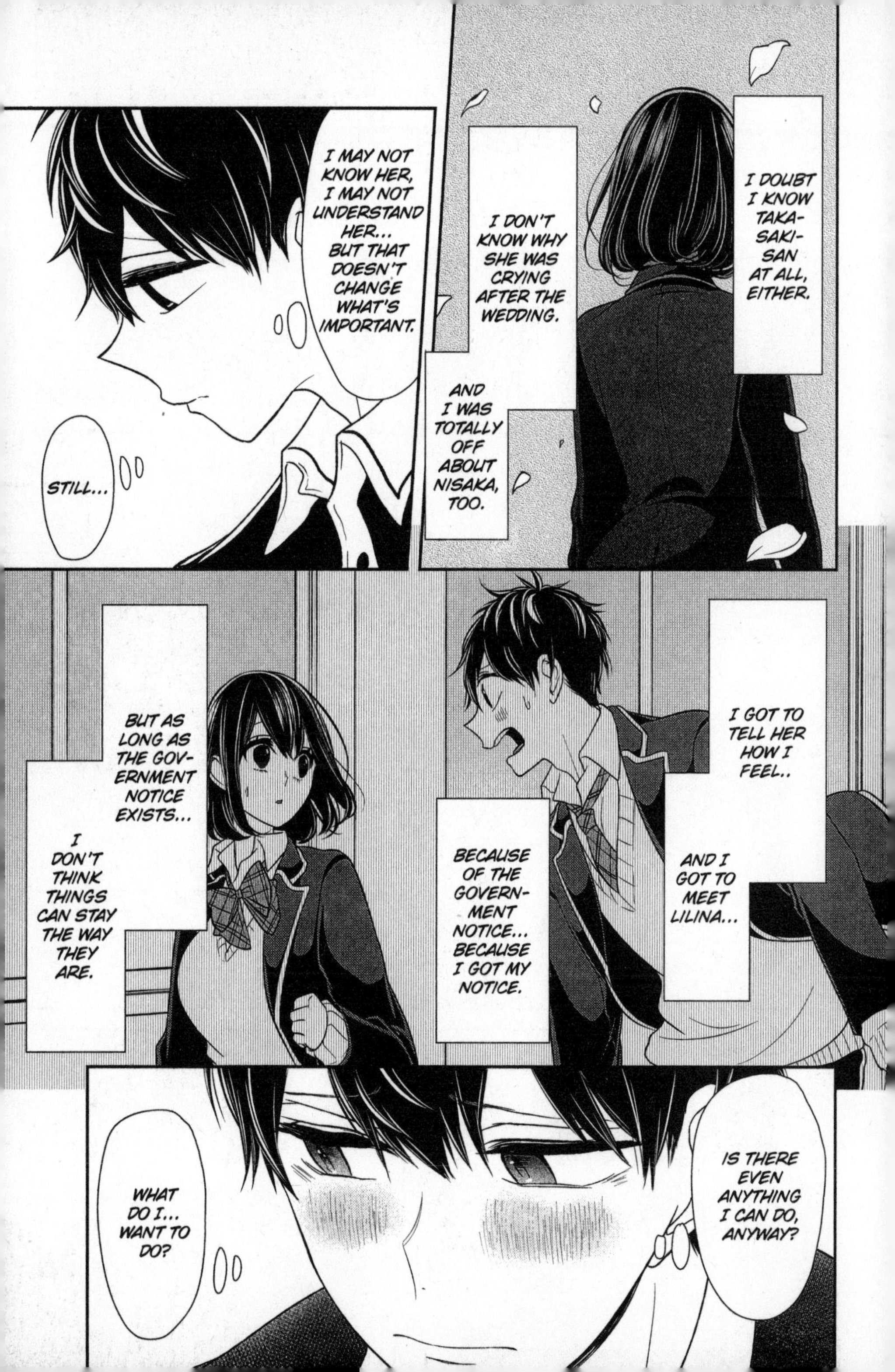
I DOUBT I KNOW TAKASAKI-SAN AT ALL, EITHER.
I DON'T KNOW WHY SHE WAS CRYING AFTER THE WEDDING.
AND I WAS TOTALLY OFF ABOUT NISAKA, TOO.
I MAY NOT KNOW HER, I MAY NOT UNDERSTAND HER... BUT THAT DOESN'T CHANGE WHAT'S IMPORTANT.
STILL...
I GOT TO TELL HER HOW I FEEL..
AND I GOT TO MEET LILINA...
BECAUSE OF THE GOVERNMENT NOTICE... BECAUSE I GOT MY NOTICE.
BUT AS LONG AS THE GOVERNMENT NOTICE EXISTS...
I DON'T THINK THINGS CAN STAY THE WAY THEY ARE.
IS THERE EVEN ANYTHING I CAN DO, ANYWAY?
WHAT DO I... WANT TO DO?

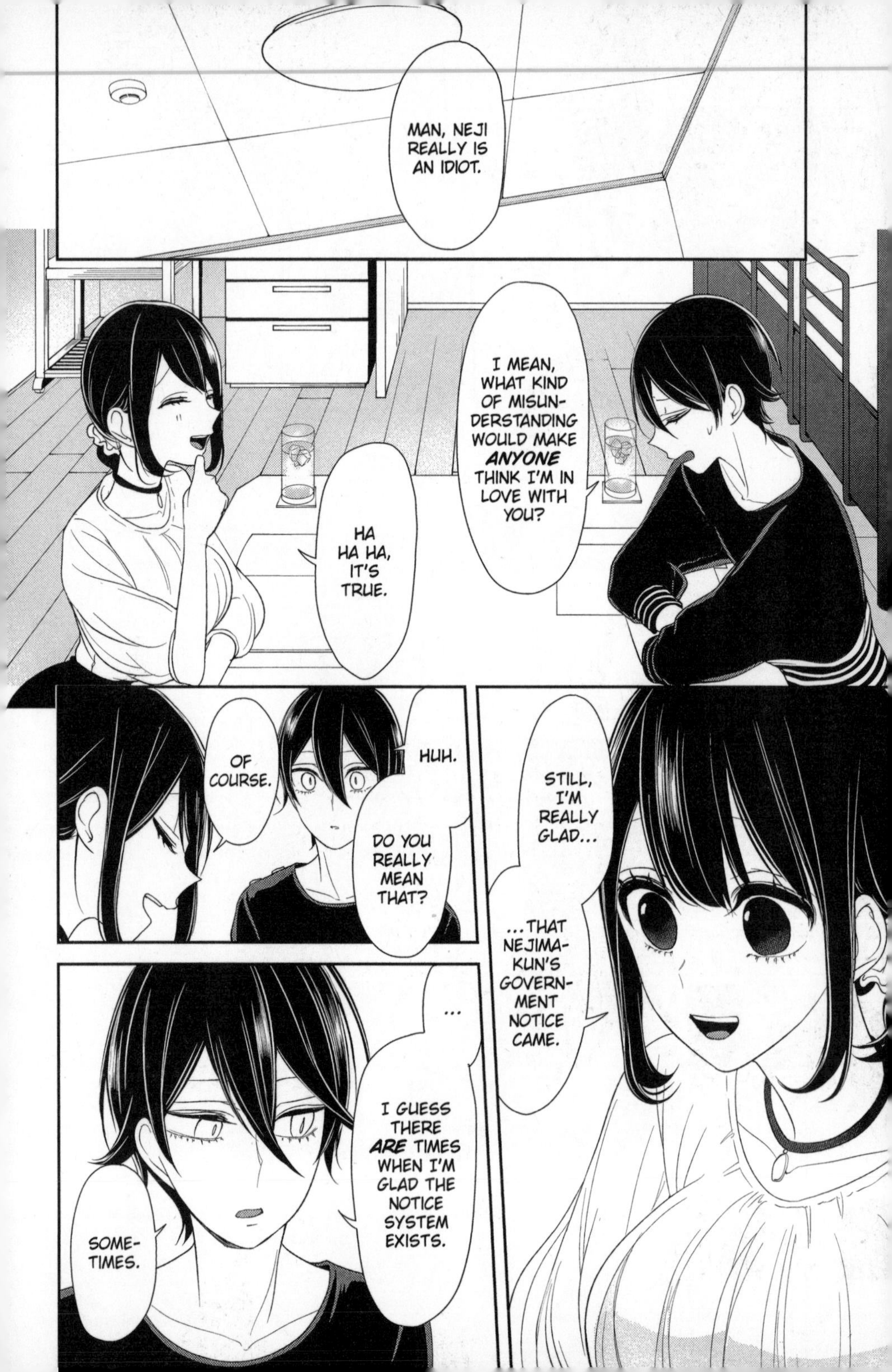
MAN, NEJI REALLY IS AN IDIOT.
I MEAN, WHAT KIND OF MISUNDERSTANDING WOULD MAKE *ANYONE* THINK I'M IN LOVE WITH YOU?
HA HA HA, IT'S TRUE.
STILL, I'M REALLY GLAD...
...THAT NEJIMA-KUN'S GOVERNMENT NOTICE CAME.
HUH.
DO YOU REALLY MEAN THAT?
OF COURSE.
...
I GUESS THERE *ARE* TIMES WHEN I'M GLAD THE NOTICE SYSTEM EXISTS.
SOMETIMES.

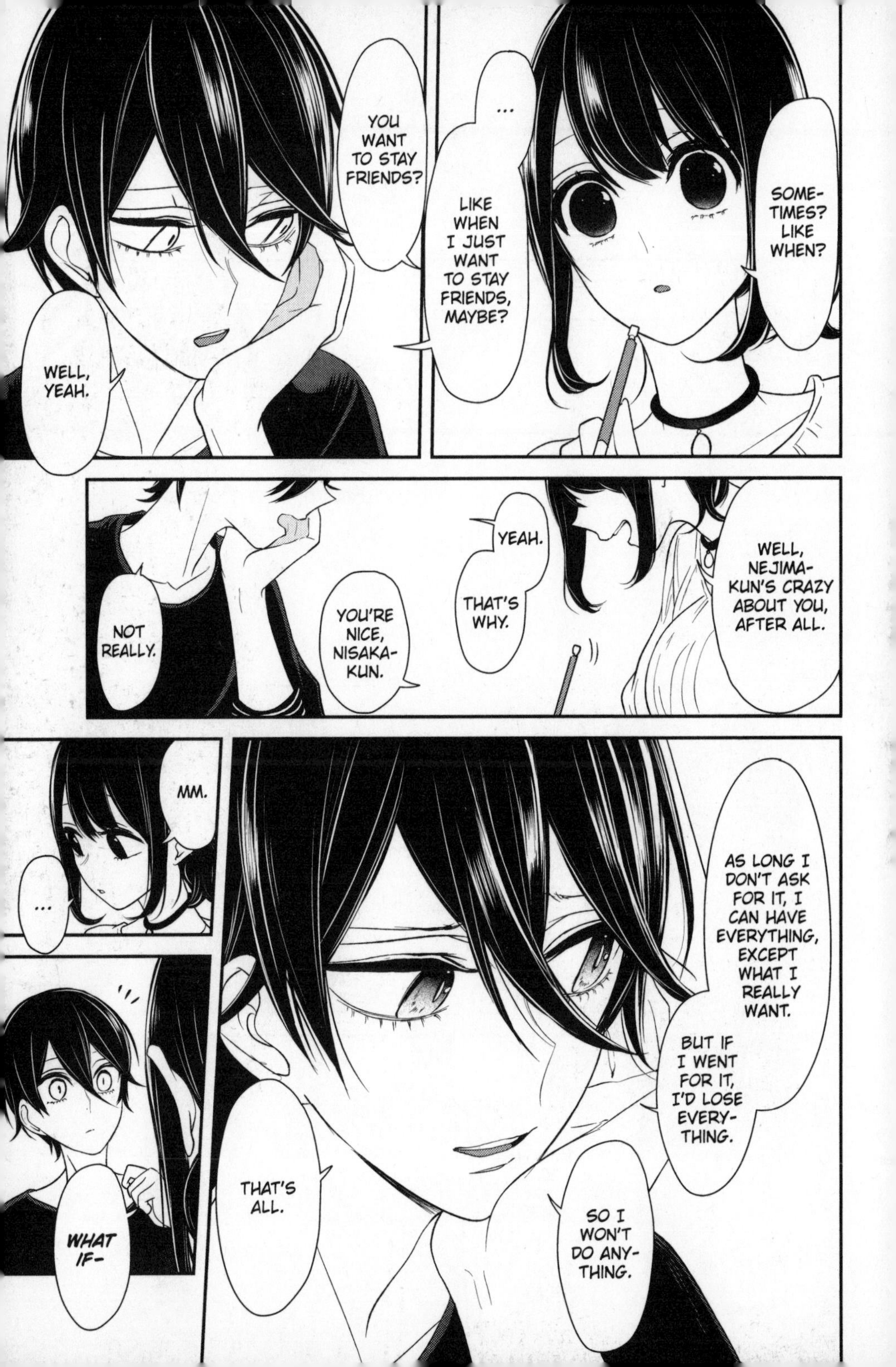
SOME-TIMES? LIKE WHEN?
...
LIKE WHEN I JUST WANT TO STAY FRIENDS, MAYBE?
YOU WANT TO STAY FRIENDS?
WELL, YEAH.
WELL, NEJIMA-KUN'S CRAZY ABOUT YOU, AFTER ALL.
YEAH.
THAT'S WHY.
YOU'RE NICE, NISAKA-KUN.
NOT REALLY.
AS LONG I DON'T ASK FOR IT, I CAN HAVE EVERYTHING, EXCEPT WHAT I REALLY WANT.
BUT IF I WENT FOR IT, I'D LOSE EVERY-THING.
SO I WON'T DO ANY-THING.
THAT'S ALL.
MM.
...
WHAT IF-

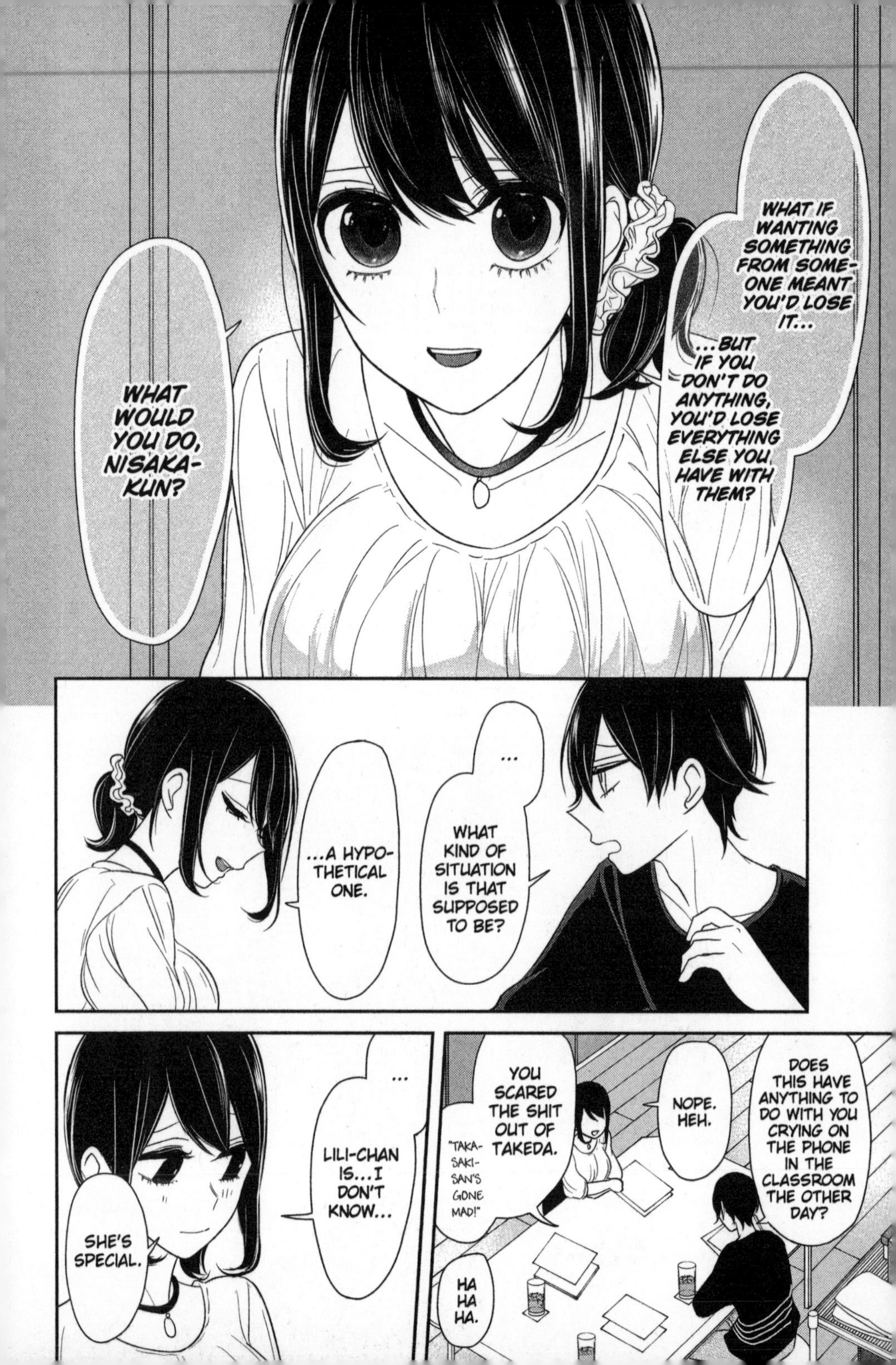
WHAT IF WANTING SOMETHING FROM SOME-ONE MEANT YOU'D LOSE IT...
...BUT IF YOU DON'T DO ANYTHING, YOU'D LOSE EVERYTHING ELSE YOU HAVE WITH THEM?
WHAT WOULD YOU DO, NISAKA-KUN?
...
WHAT KIND OF SITUATION IS THAT SUPPOSED TO BE?
...A HYPO-THETICAL ONE.
DOES THIS HAVE ANYTHING TO DO WITH YOU CRYING ON THE PHONE IN THE CLASSROOM THE OTHER DAY?
NOPE. HEH.
YOU SCARED THE SHIT OUT OF TAKEDA.
"TAKA-SAKI-SAN'S GONE MAD!"
HA HA HA HA.
...
LILI-CHAN IS...I DON'T KNOW...
SHE'S SPECIAL.

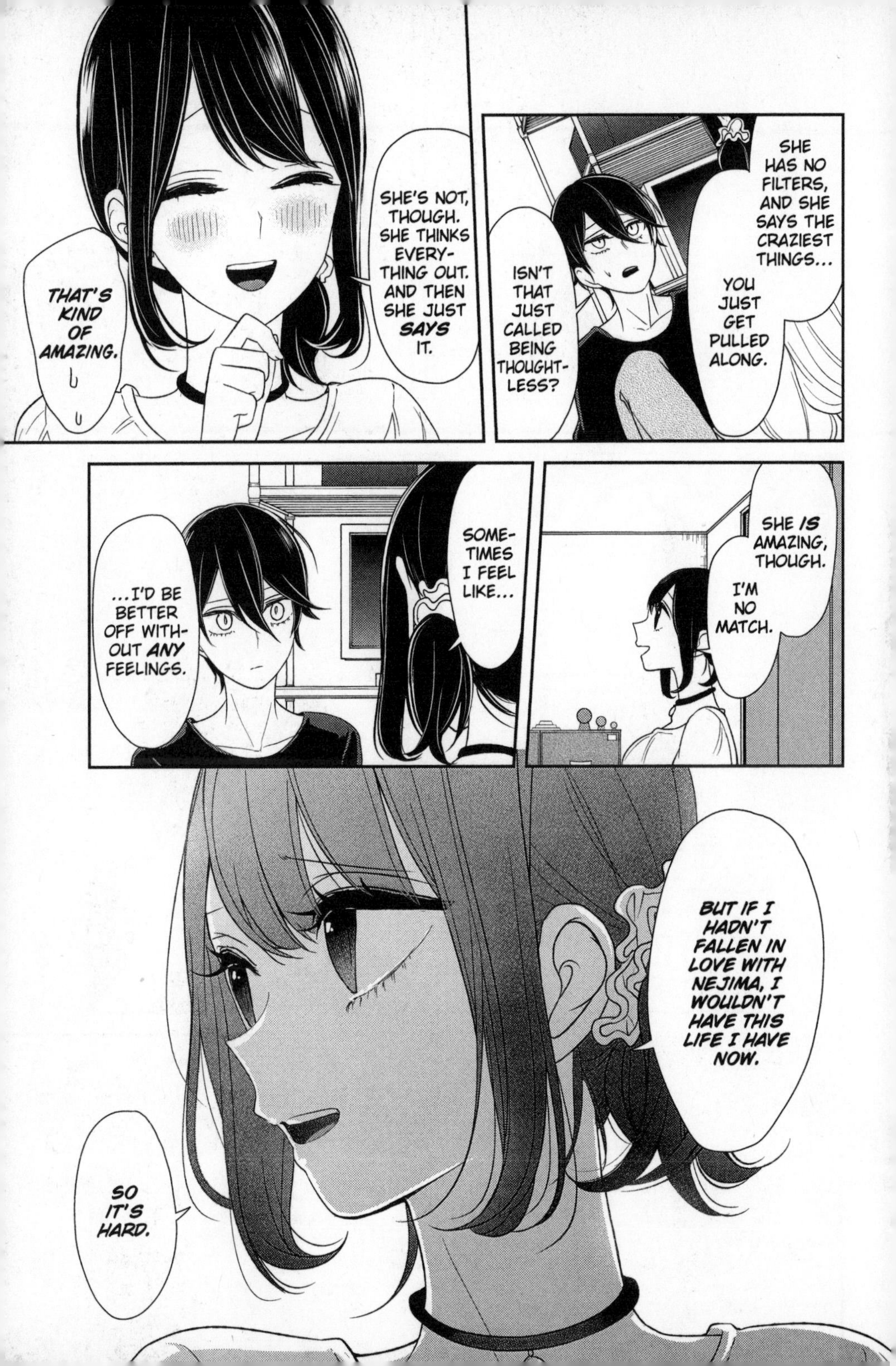
SHE HAS NO FILTERS, AND SHE SAYS THE CRAZIEST THINGS...
YOU JUST GET PULLED ALONG.
ISN'T THAT JUST CALLED BEING THOUGHT-LESS?
SHE'S NOT, THOUGH. SHE THINKS EVERY-THING OUT. AND THEN SHE JUST *SAYS* IT.
THAT'S KIND OF AMAZING.
SHE *IS* AMAZING, THOUGH.
I'M NO MATCH.
SOME-TIMES I FEEL LIKE...
...I'D BE BETTER OFF WITH-OUT *ANY* FEELINGS.
BUT IF I HADN'T FALLEN IN LOVE WITH NEJIMA, I WOULDN'T HAVE THIS LIFE I HAVE NOW.
SO IT'S HARD.

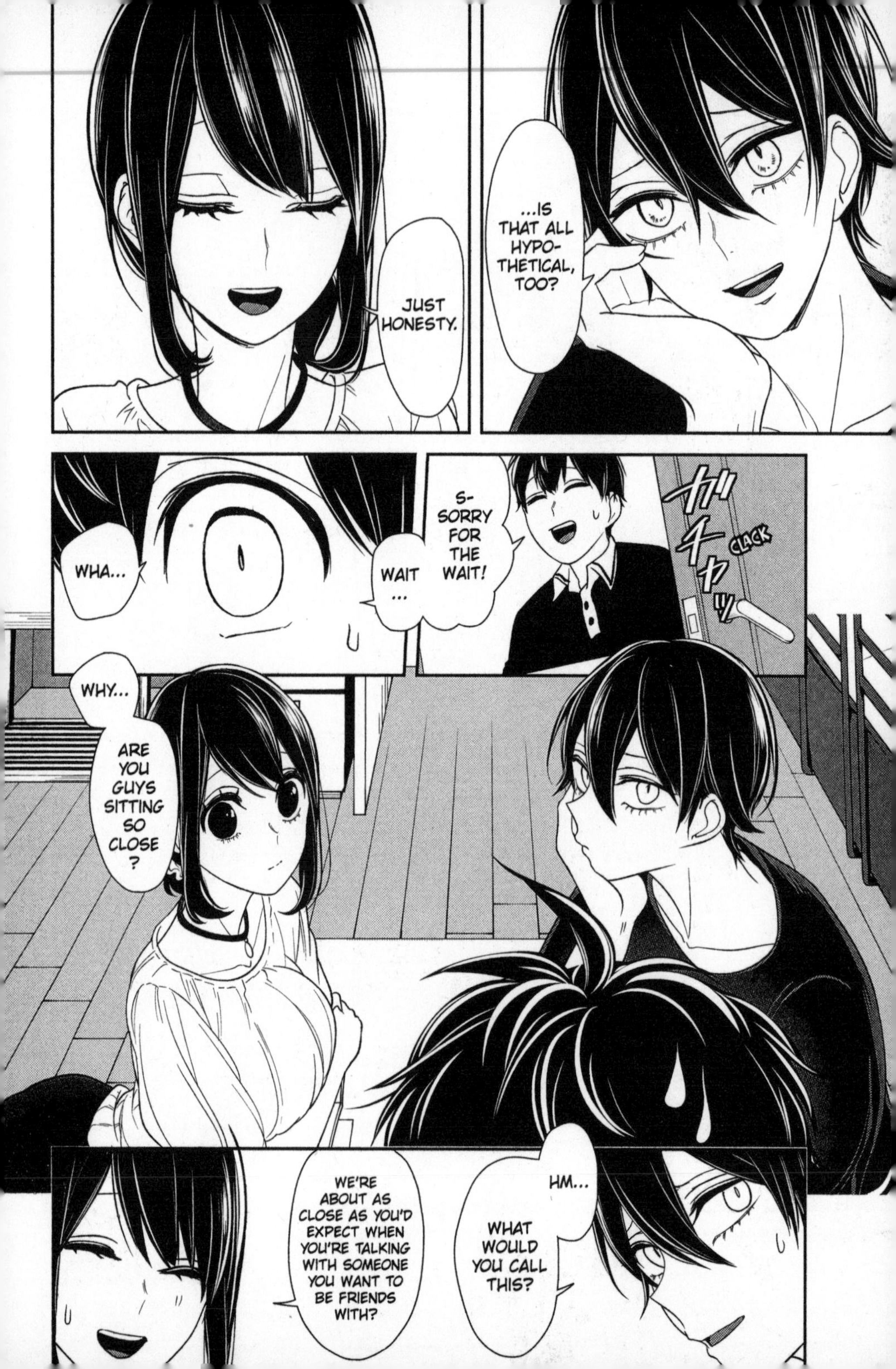
...IS THAT ALL HYPO-THETICAL, TOO?
JUST HONESTY.
S-SORRY FOR THE WAIT!
ガチャッ
CLACK
WAIT...
WHA...
WHY...
ARE YOU GUYS SITTING SO CLOSE?
HM...
WHAT WOULD YOU CALL THIS?
WE'RE ABOUT AS CLOSE AS YOU'D EXPECT WHEN YOU'RE TALKING WITH SOMEONE YOU WANT TO BE FRIENDS WITH?

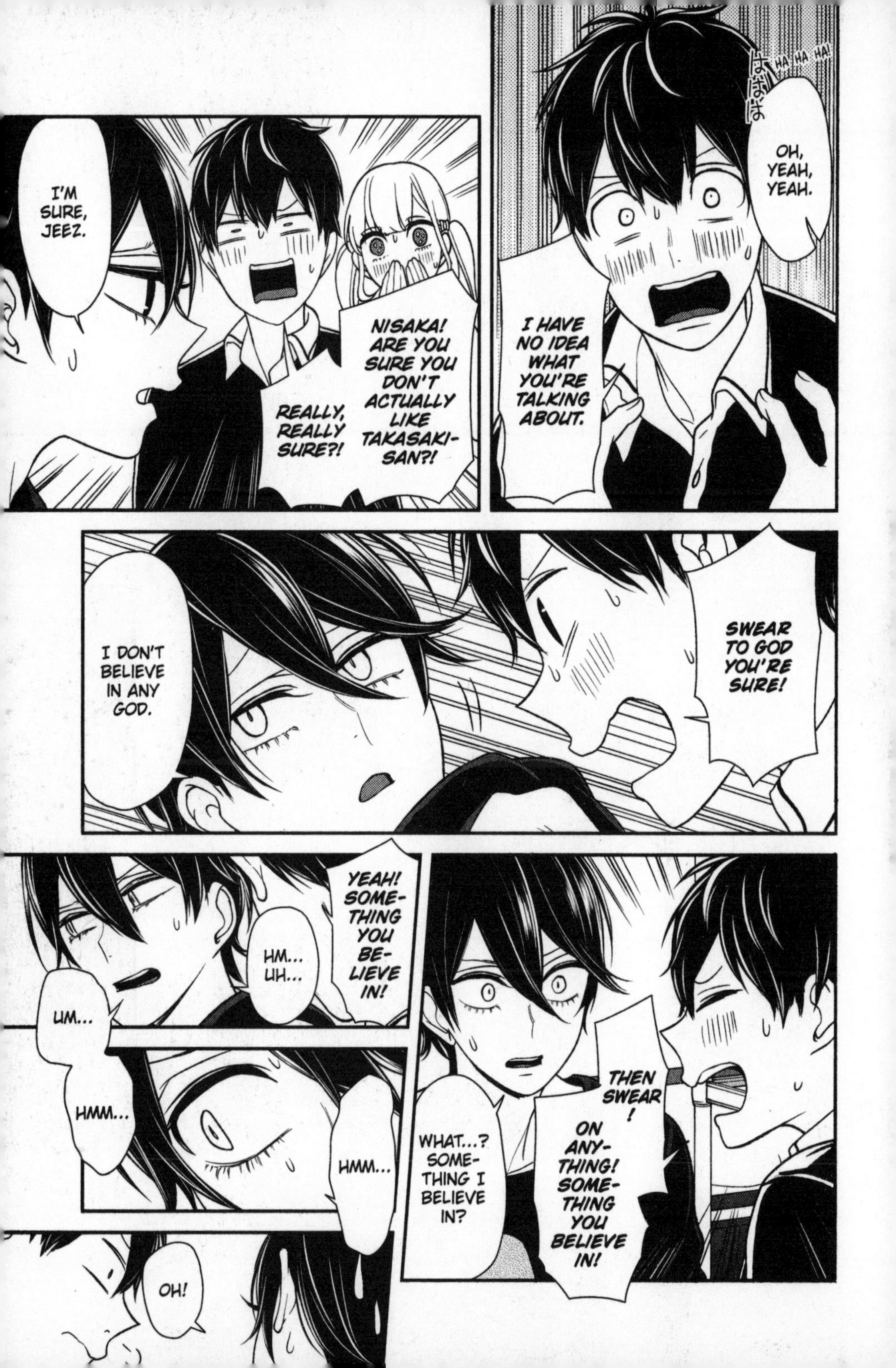
HA HA HA!
ははは
OH, YEAH, YEAH.
I HAVE NO IDEA WHAT YOU'RE TALKING ABOUT.
NISAKA! ARE YOU SURE YOU DON'T ACTUALLY LIKE TAKASAKI-SAN?!
REALLY, REALLY SURE?!
I'M SURE, JEEZ.
SWEAR TO GOD YOU'RE SURE!
I DON'T BELIEVE IN ANY GOD.
THEN SWEAR! ON ANYTHING! SOMETHING YOU BELIEVE IN!
WHAT...? SOMETHING I BELIEVE IN?
YEAH! SOMETHING YOU BELIEVE IN!
HM... UH...
UM...
HMM...
HMM...
OH!

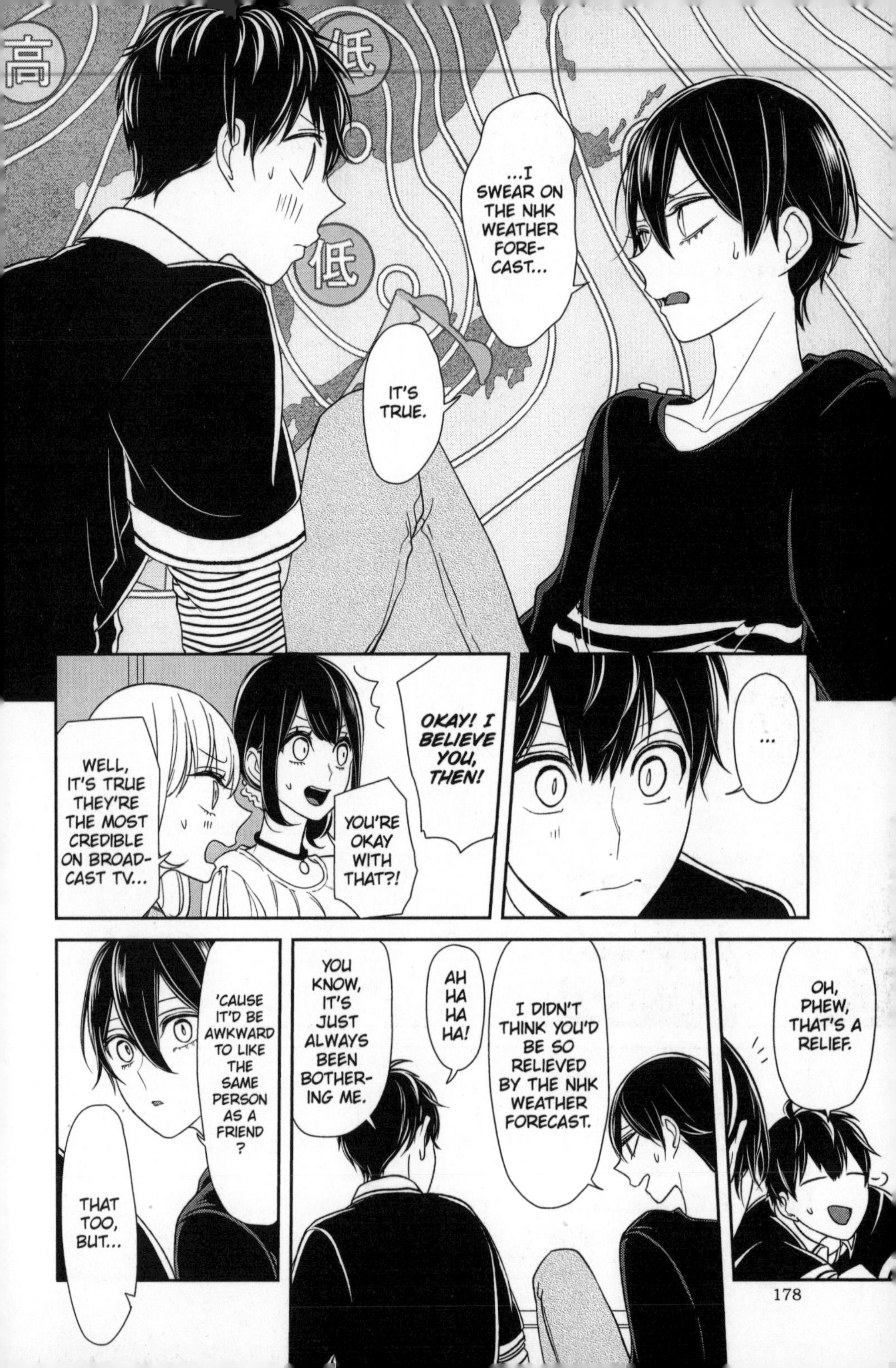

高
低
低
...I SWEAR ON THE NHK WEATHER FORE-CAST...
IT'S TRUE.
...
OKAY! I BELIEVE YOU, THEN!
YOU'RE OKAY WITH THAT?!
WELL, IT'S TRUE THEY'RE THE MOST CREDIBLE ON BROAD-CAST TV...
OH, PHEW, THAT'S A RELIEF.
I DIDN'T THINK YOU'D BE SO RELIEVED BY THE NHK WEATHER FORECAST.
AH HA HA HA!
YOU KNOW, IT'S JUST ALWAYS BEEN BOTHER-ING ME.
'CAUSE IT'D BE AWKWARD TO LIKE THE SAME PERSON AS A FRIEND?
THAT TOO, BUT...

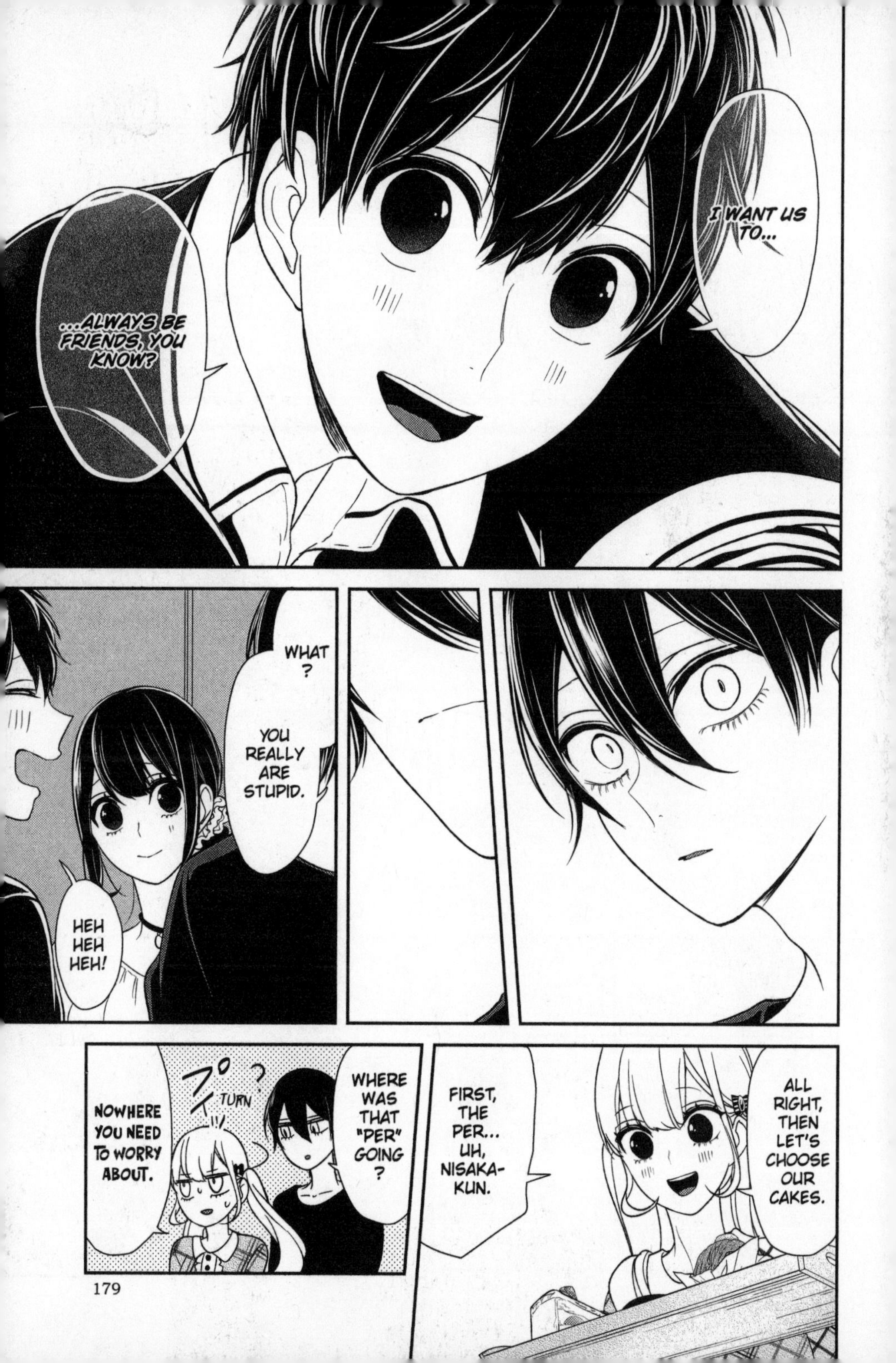
I WANT US TO...
...ALWAYS BE FRIENDS, YOU KNOW?
WHAT?
YOU REALLY ARE STUPID.
HEH HEH HEH!
ALL RIGHT, THEN LET'S CHOOSE OUR CAKES.
FIRST, THE PER... UH, NISAKA-KUN.
WHERE WAS THAT "PER" GOING?
TURN
NOWHERE YOU NEED TO WORRY ABOUT.

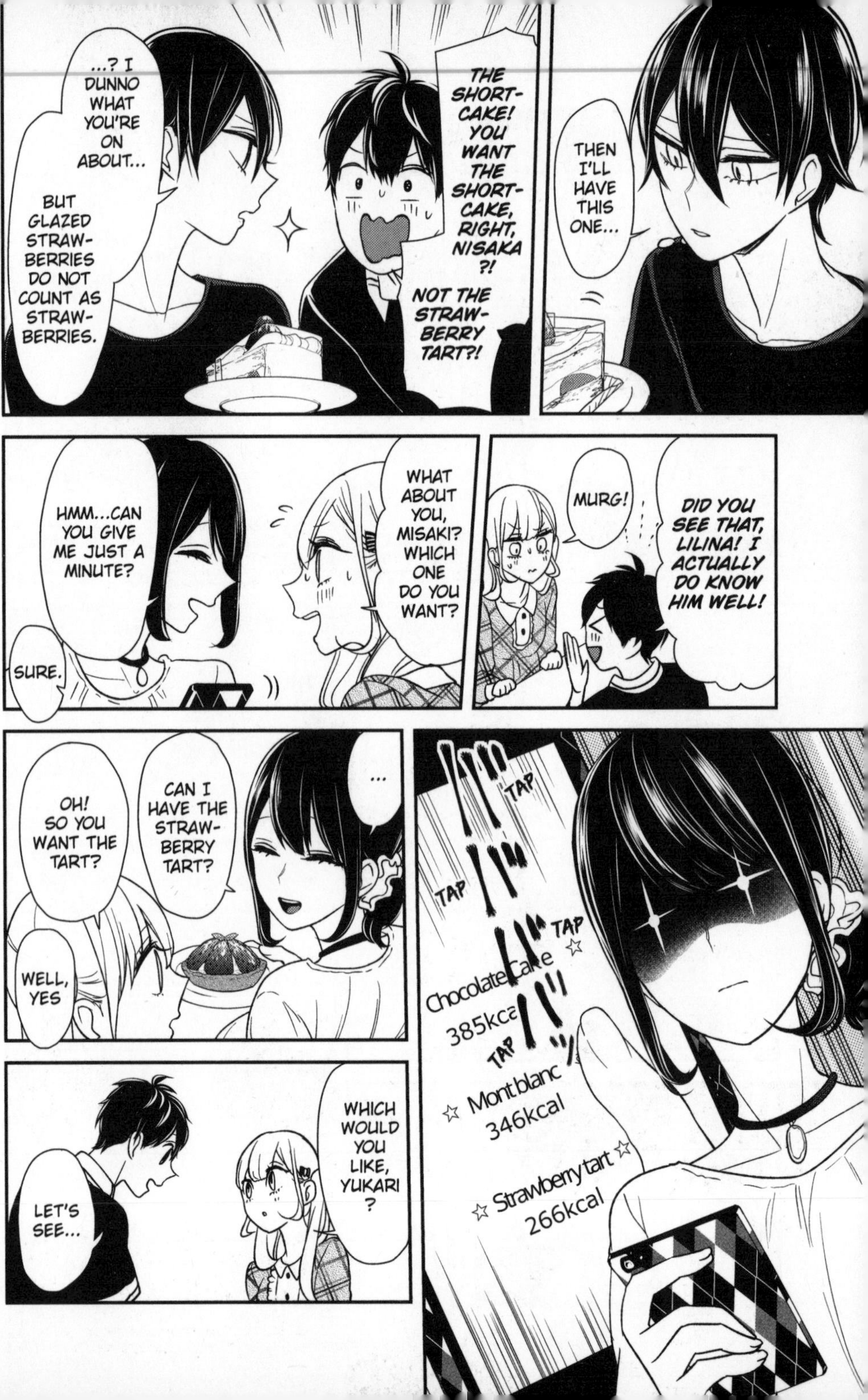
THEN I'LL HAVE THIS ONE...
THE SHORT-CAKE! YOU WANT THE SHORT-CAKE, RIGHT, NISAKA?!
NOT THE STRAW-BERRY TART?!
...? I DUNNO WHAT YOU'RE ON ABOUT...
BUT GLAZED STRAW-BERRIES DO NOT COUNT AS STRAW-BERRIES.
DID YOU SEE THAT, LILINA! I ACTUALLY DO KNOW HIM WELL!
MURG!
WHAT ABOUT YOU, MISAKI? WHICH ONE DO YOU WANT?
HMM...CAN YOU GIVE ME JUST A MINUTE?
SURE.
TAP
TAP
TAP
TAP
Chocolate Cake 385kca
☆ Mont blanc 346kcal ☆
☆ Strawberry tart 266kcal
...
CAN I HAVE THE STRAW-BERRY TART?
OH! SO YOU WANT THE TART?
WELL, YES
WHICH WOULD YOU LIKE, YUKARI?
LET'S SEE...

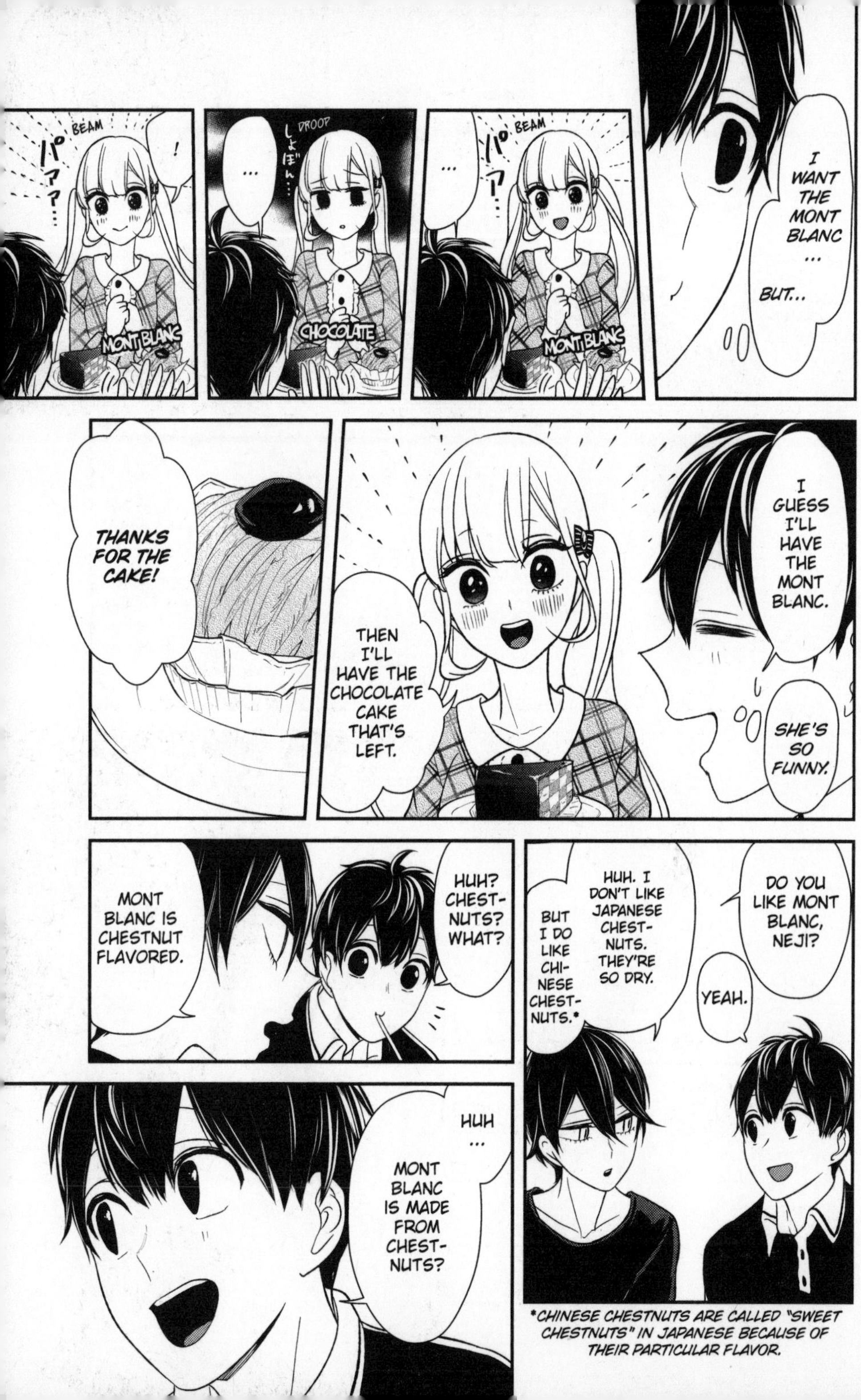

I WANT THE MONT BLANC ...
BUT...
BEAM
パァ...
...
MONT BLANC
DROOP
しょぼん...
...
CHOCOLATE
BEAM
パァァ...
!
MONT BLANC
I GUESS I'LL HAVE THE MONT BLANC.
SHE'S SO FUNNY.
THEN I'LL HAVE THE CHOCOLATE CAKE THAT'S LEFT.
THANKS FOR THE CAKE!
DO YOU LIKE MONT BLANC, NEJI?
YEAH.
HUH. I DON'T LIKE JAPANESE CHESTNUTS. THEY'RE SO DRY.
BUT I DO LIKE CHINESE CHESTNUTS.*
HUH? CHESTNUTS? WHAT?
MONT BLANC IS CHESTNUT FLAVORED.
HUH ...
MONT BLANC IS MADE FROM CHESTNUTS?

*CHINESE CHESTNUTS ARE CALLED "SWEET CHESTNUTS" IN JAPANESE BECAUSE OF THEIR PARTICULAR FLAVOR.

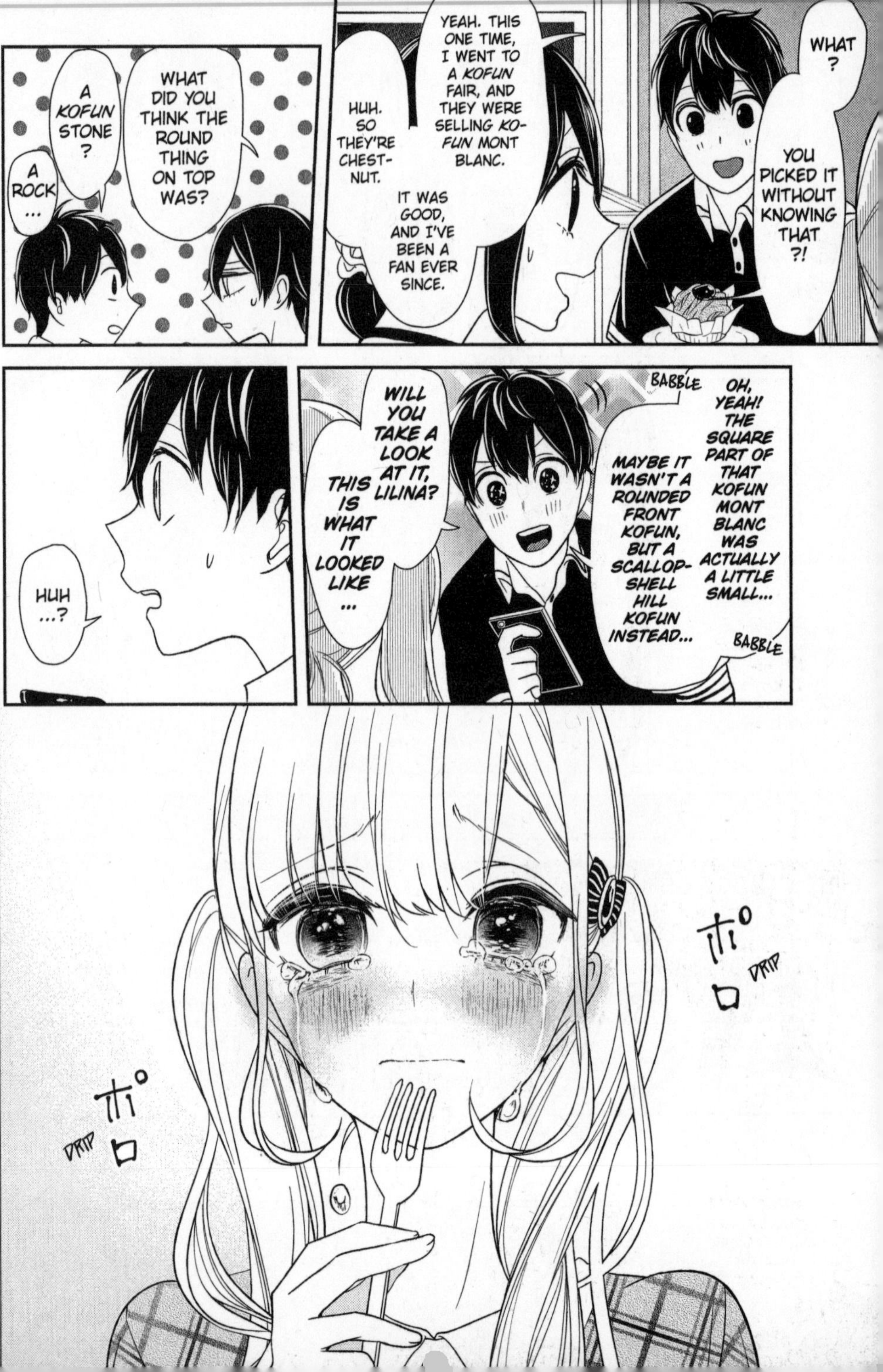
WHAT?
YOU PICKED IT WITHOUT KNOWING THAT?!
YEAH. THIS ONE TIME, I WENT TO A KOFUN FAIR, AND THEY WERE SELLING KOFUN MONT BLANC.
IT WAS GOOD, AND I'VE BEEN A FAN EVER SINCE.
HUH. SO THEY'RE CHESTNUT.
WHAT DID YOU THINK THE ROUND THING ON TOP WAS?
A KOFUN STONE?
A ROCK...
BABBLE
OH, YEAH! THE SQUARE PART OF THAT KOFUN MONT BLANC WAS ACTUALLY A LITTLE SMALL...
MAYBE IT WASN'T A ROUNDED FRONT KOFUN, BUT A SCALLOP-SHELL HILL KOFUN INSTEAD...
BABBLE
WILL YOU TAKE A LOOK AT IT, LILINA?
THIS IS WHAT IT LOOKED LIKE...
HUH...?
ポロ
DRIP
ポロ
DRIP

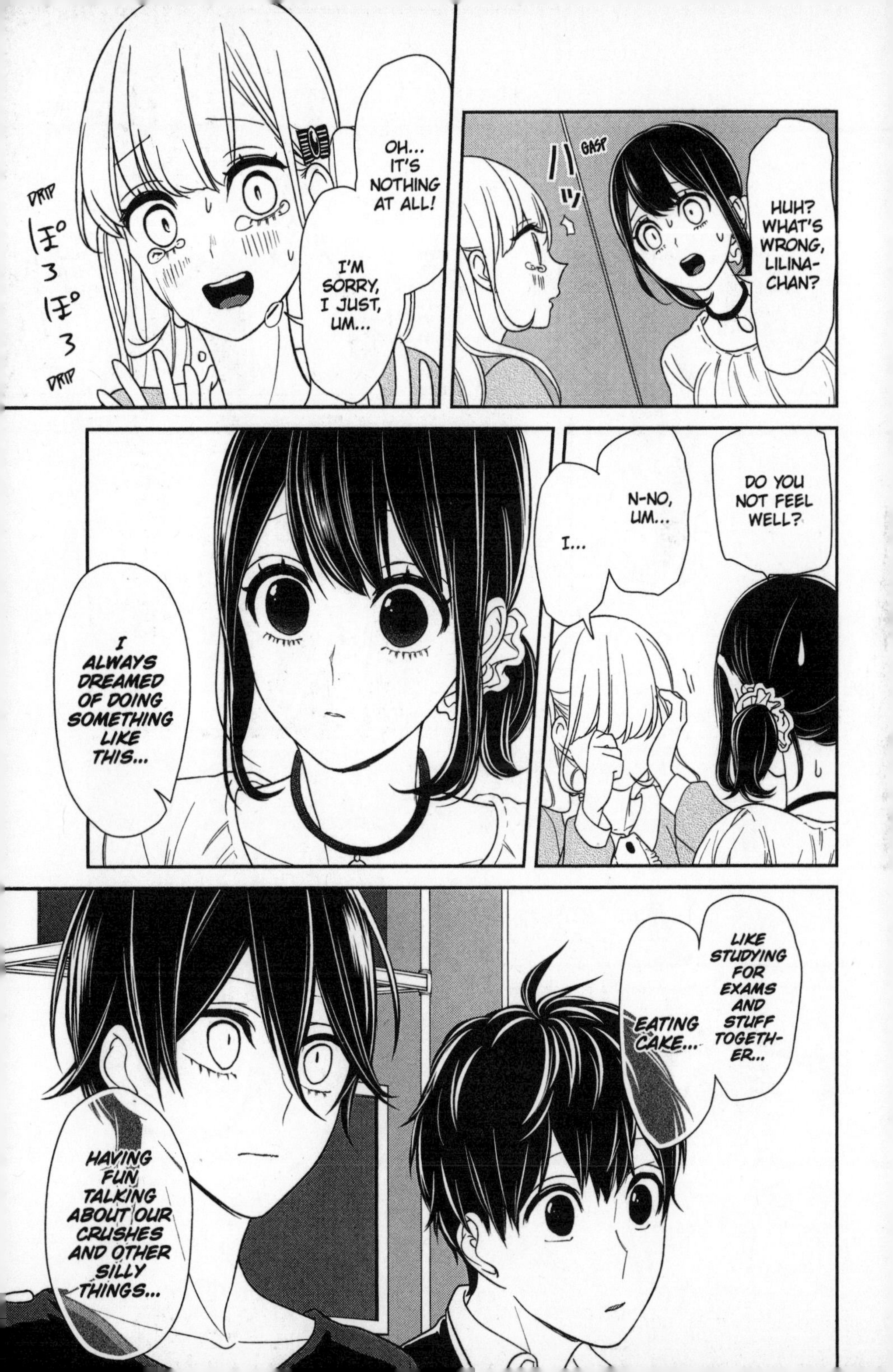

GASP
ハッ
HUH? WHAT'S WRONG, LILINA-CHAN?
OH... IT'S NOTHING AT ALL!
I'M SORRY, I JUST, UM...
DRIP
ポロポロ
DRIP
DO YOU NOT FEEL WELL?
N-NO, UM...
I...
I ALWAYS DREAMED OF DOING SOMETHING LIKE THIS...
LIKE STUDYING FOR EXAMS AND STUFF TOGETHER...
EATING CAKE...
HAVING FUN TALKING ABOUT OUR CRUSHES AND OTHER SILLY THINGS...

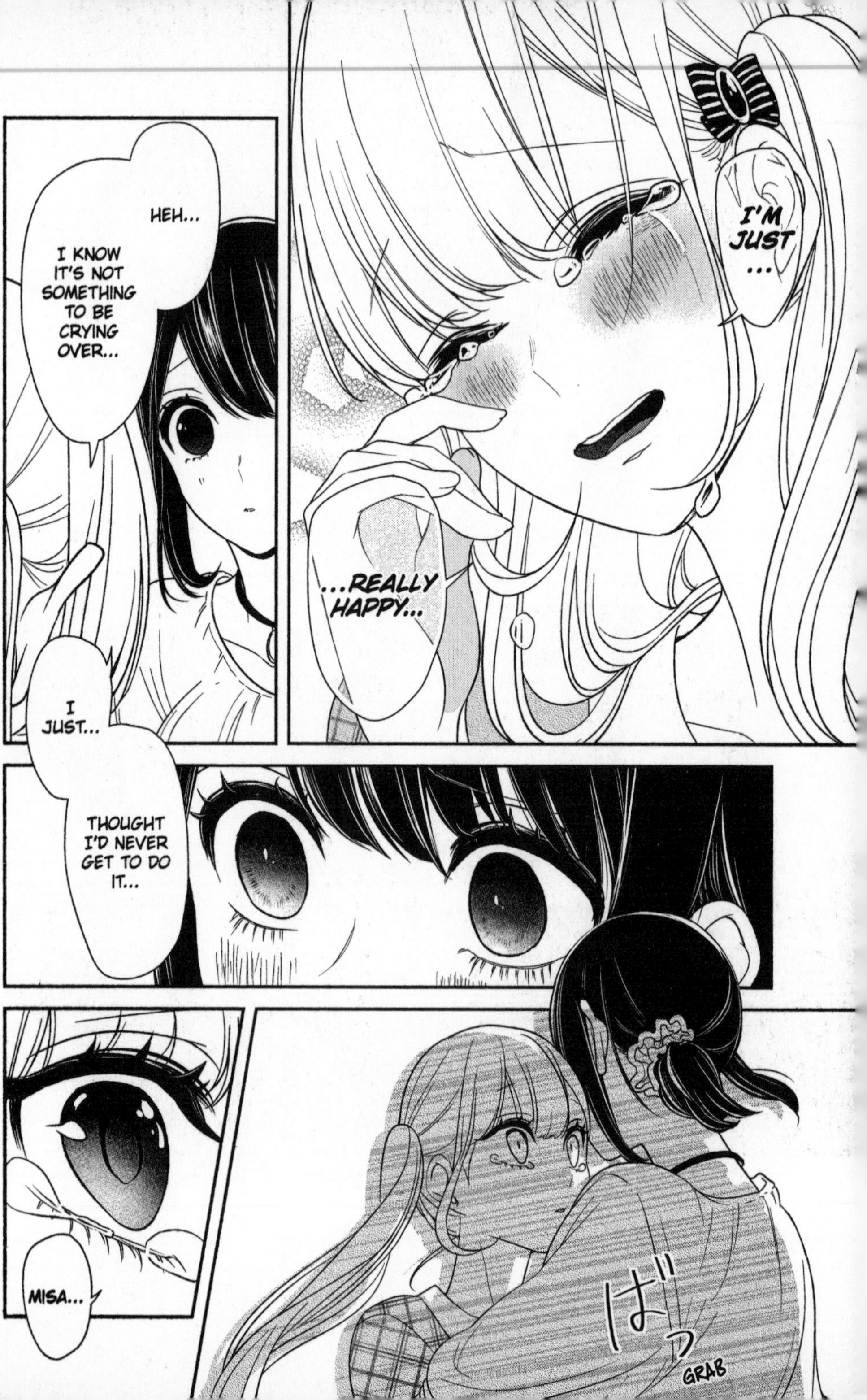
I'M JUST...
...REALLY HAPPY...
HEH...
I KNOW IT'S NOT SOMETHING TO BE CRYING OVER...
I JUST...
THOUGHT I'D NEVER GET TO DO IT...
ぱっ
GRAB
MISA...

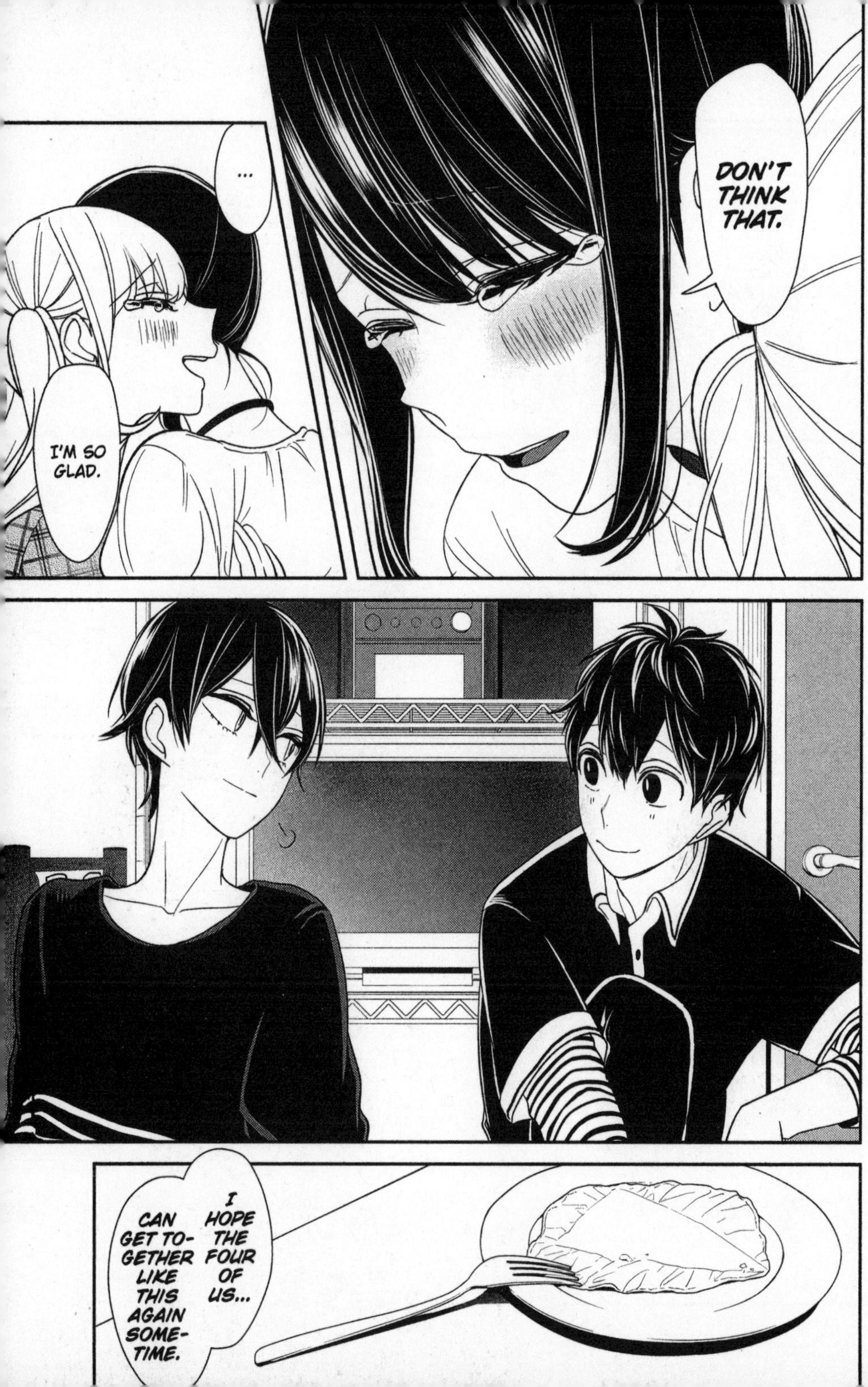
DON'T THINK THAT.
...
I'M SO GLAD.
I HOPE THE FOUR OF US... CAN GET TOGETHER LIKE THIS AGAIN SOMETIME.

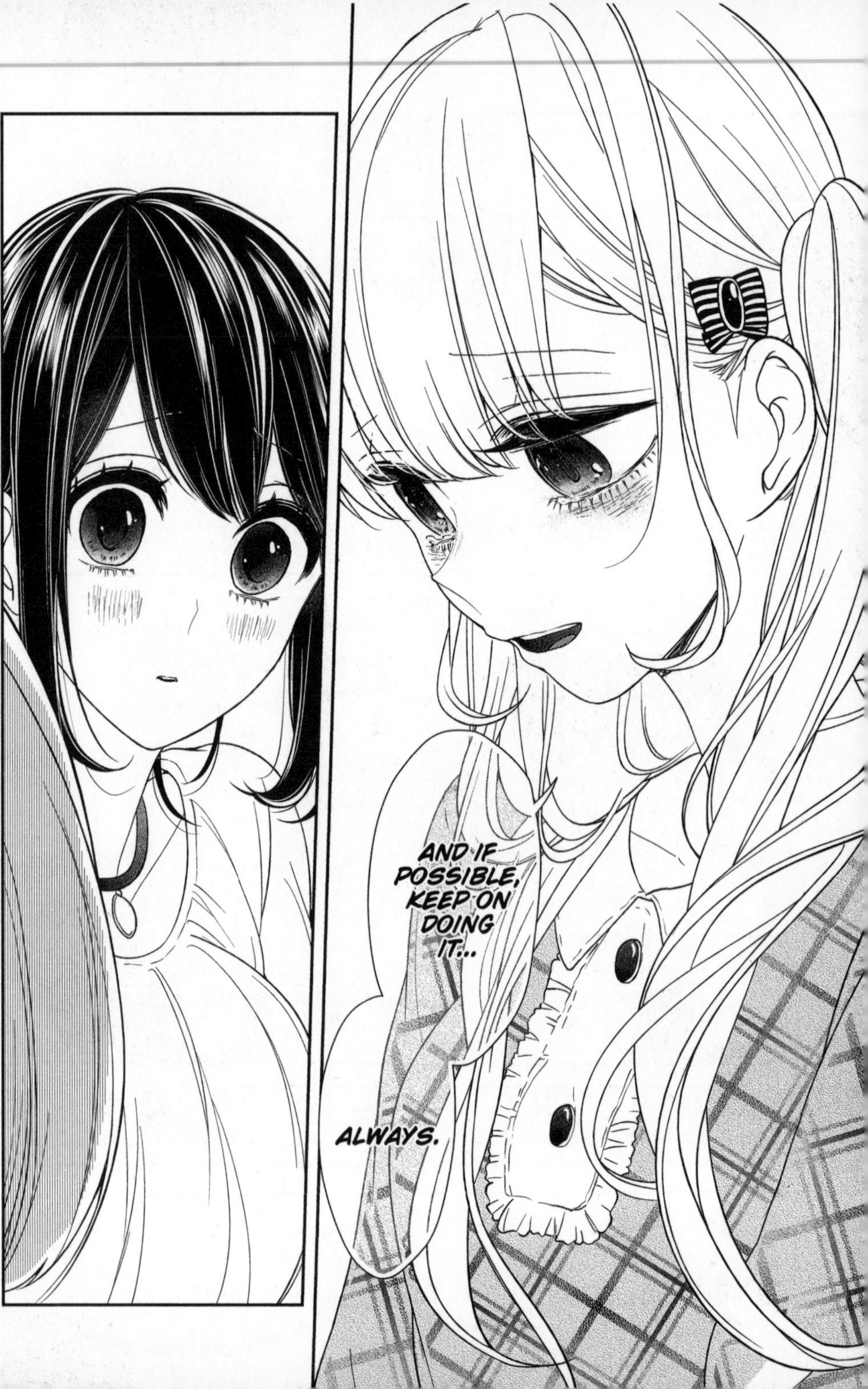
AND IF POSSIBLE, KEEP ON DOING IT...
ALWAYS.

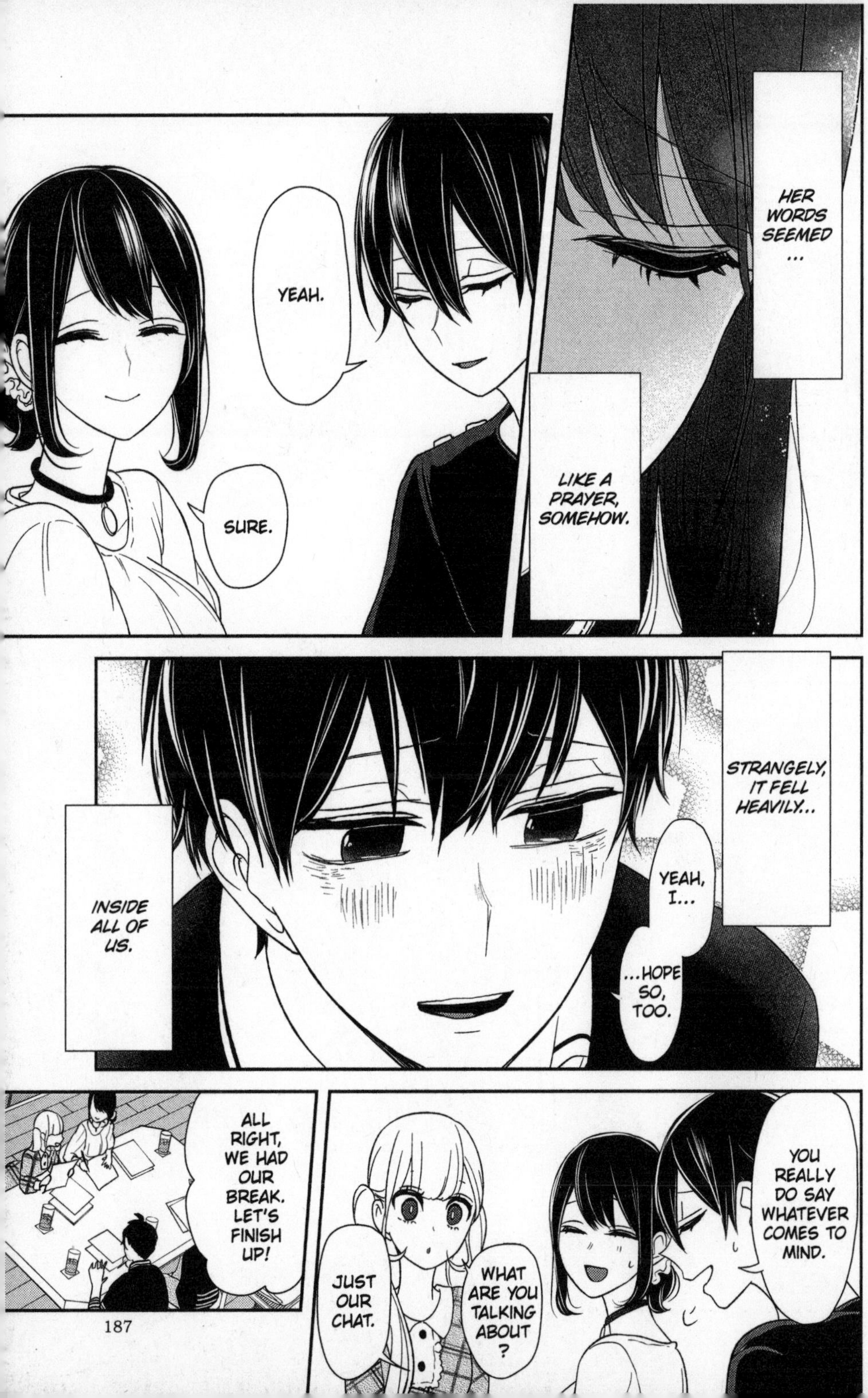
HER WORDS SEEMED...
LIKE A PRAYER, SOMEHOW.
YEAH.
SURE.
STRANGELY, IT FELL HEAVILY...
YEAH, I...
...HOPE SO, TOO.
INSIDE ALL OF US.
YOU REALLY DO SAY WHATEVER COMES TO MIND.
WHAT ARE YOU TALKING ABOUT?
JUST OUR CHAT.
ALL RIGHT, WE HAD OUR BREAK. LET'S FINISH UP!

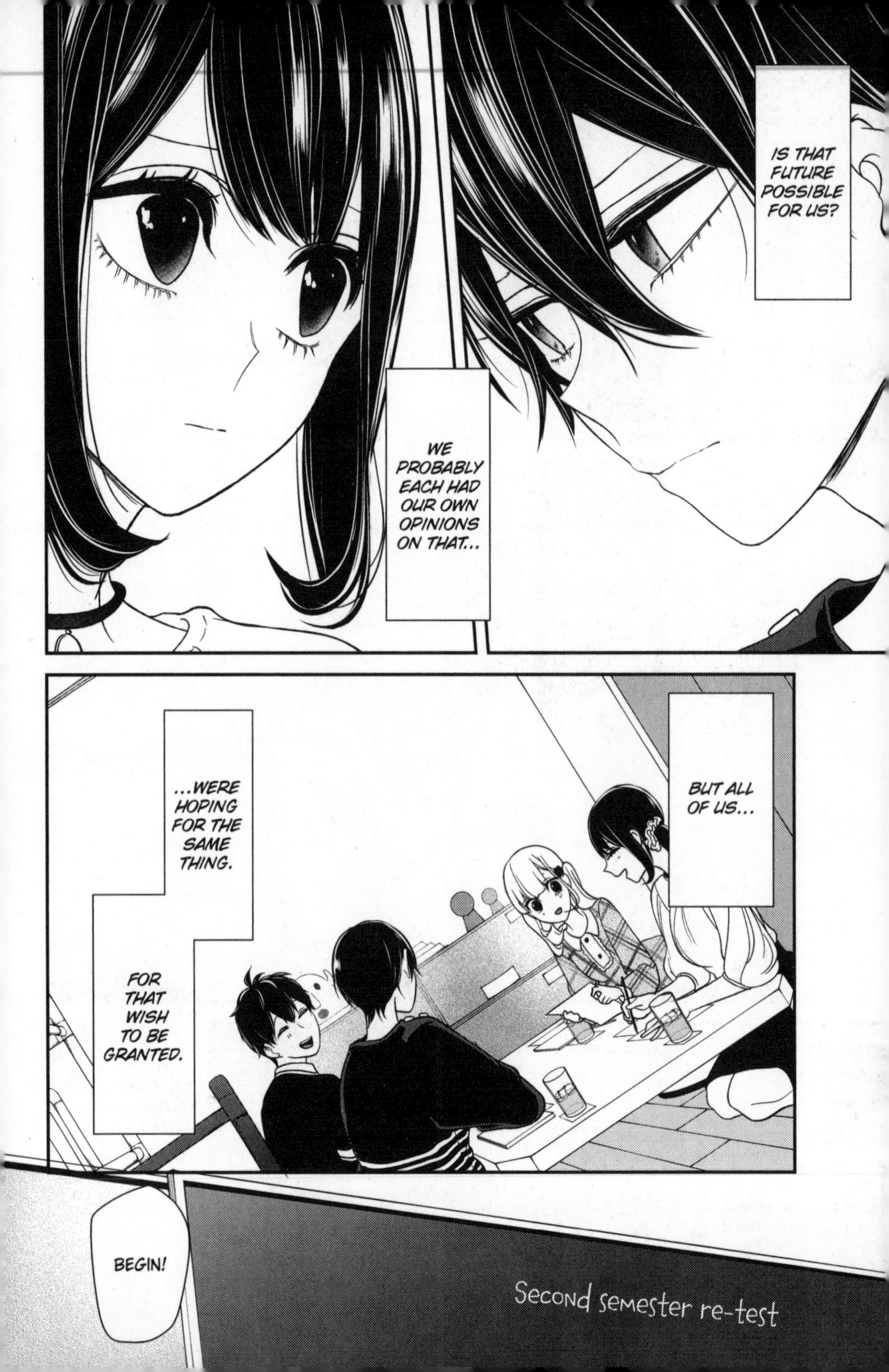
IS THAT FUTURE POSSIBLE FOR US?
WE PROBABLY EACH HAD OUR OWN OPINIONS ON THAT...
BUT ALL OF US...
...WERE HOPING FOR THE SAME THING.
FOR THAT WISH TO BE GRANTED.
Second semester re-test
BEGIN!

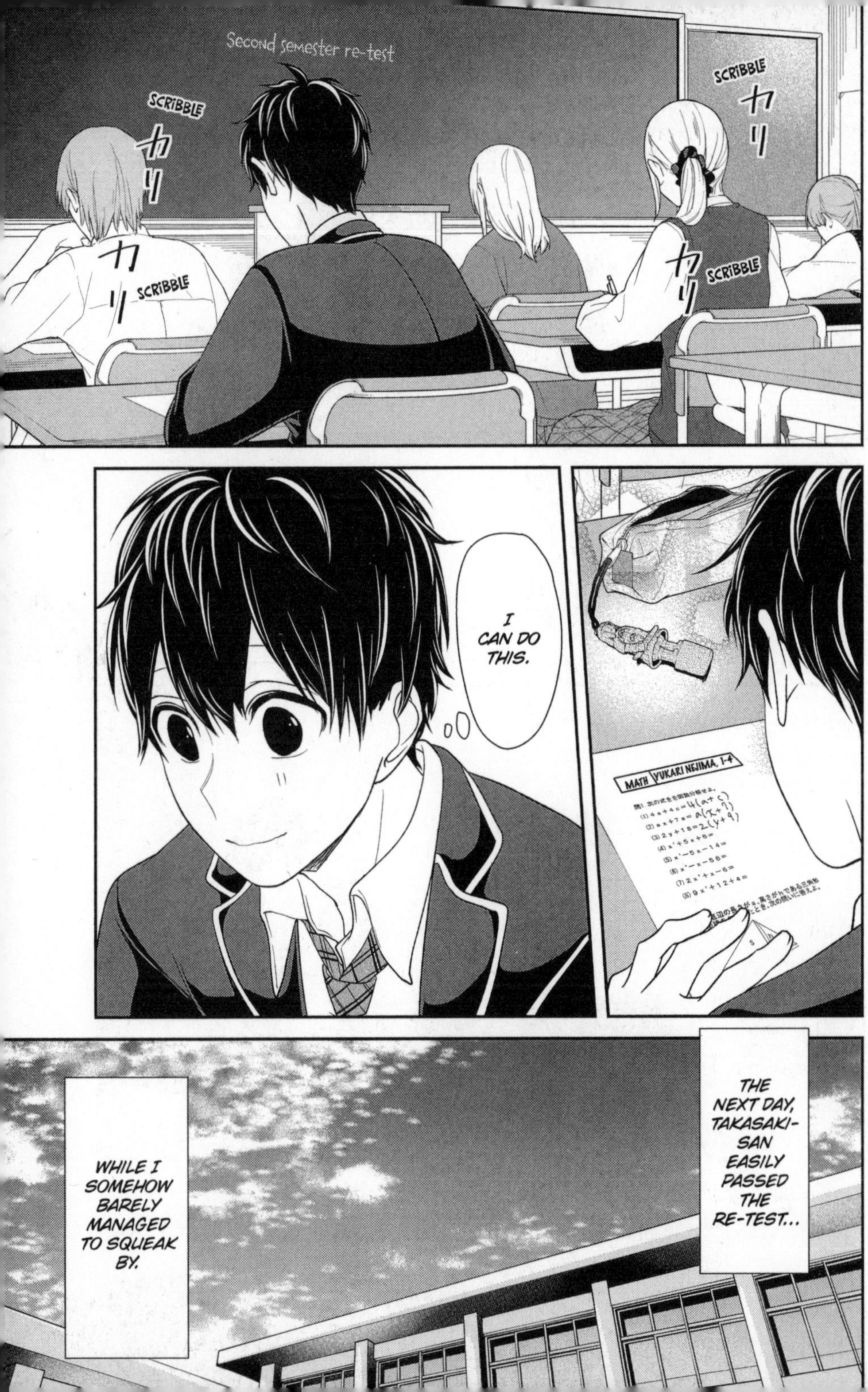
Second semester re-test
SCRIBBLE
カリ
SCRIBBLE
カリ
SCRIBBLE
カリ
SCRIBBLE
カリ
MATH YUKARI NEJIMA, 1-4
I CAN DO THIS.
THE NEXT DAY, TAKASAKI-SAN EASILY PASSED THE RE-TEST...
WHILE I SOMEHOW BARELY MANAGED TO SQUEAK BY.

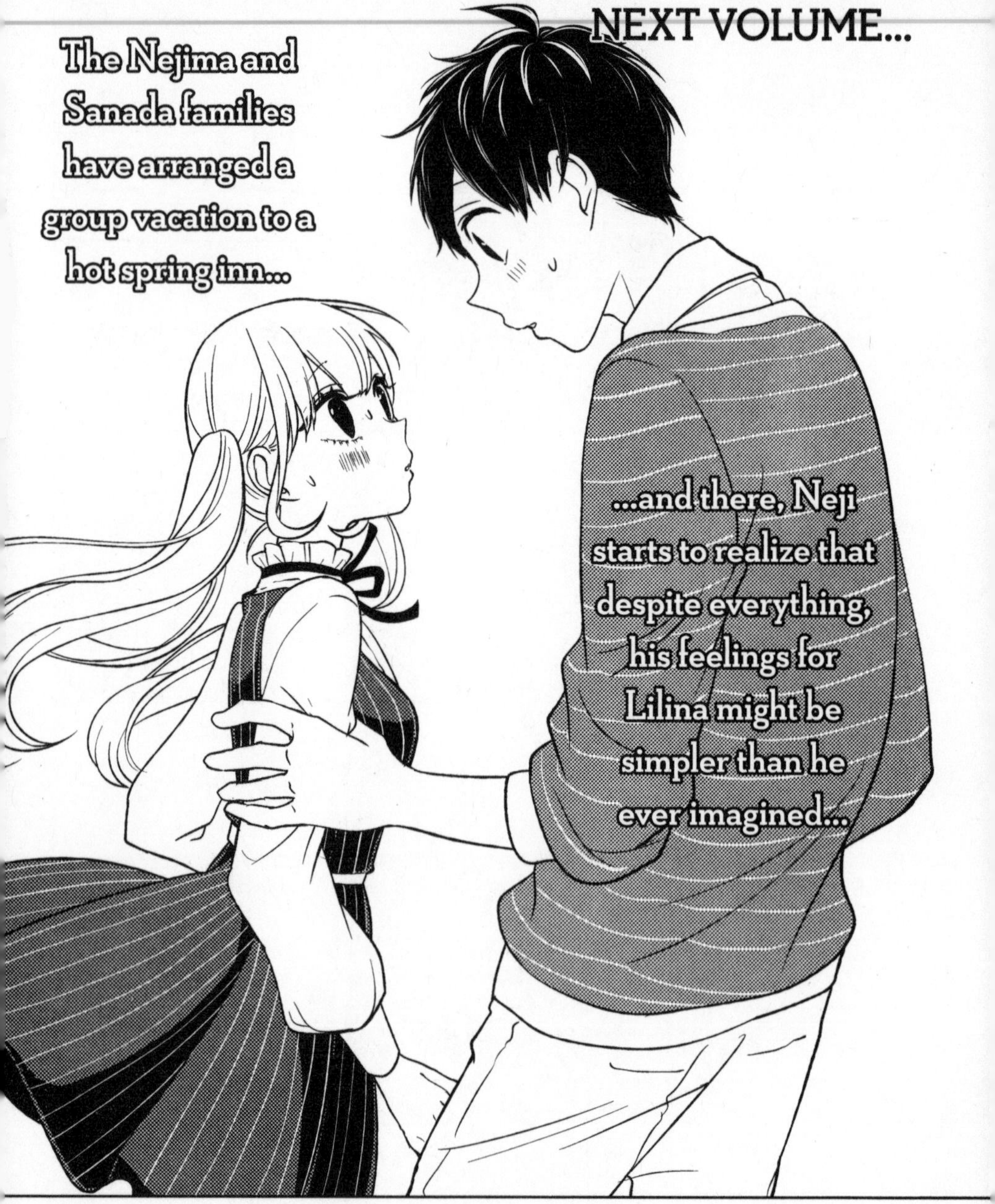
NEXT VOLUME...
The Nejima and Sanada families have arranged a group vacation to a hot spring inn...
...and there, Neji starts to realize that despite everything, his feelings for Lilina might be simpler than he ever imagined...

THE INEVITABLE, HEART-POUNDING HOT SPRINGS TRIP...

VOLUME 6 IS UNMISSABLE!

Love&Lies

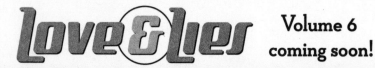

Volume 6
coming soon!

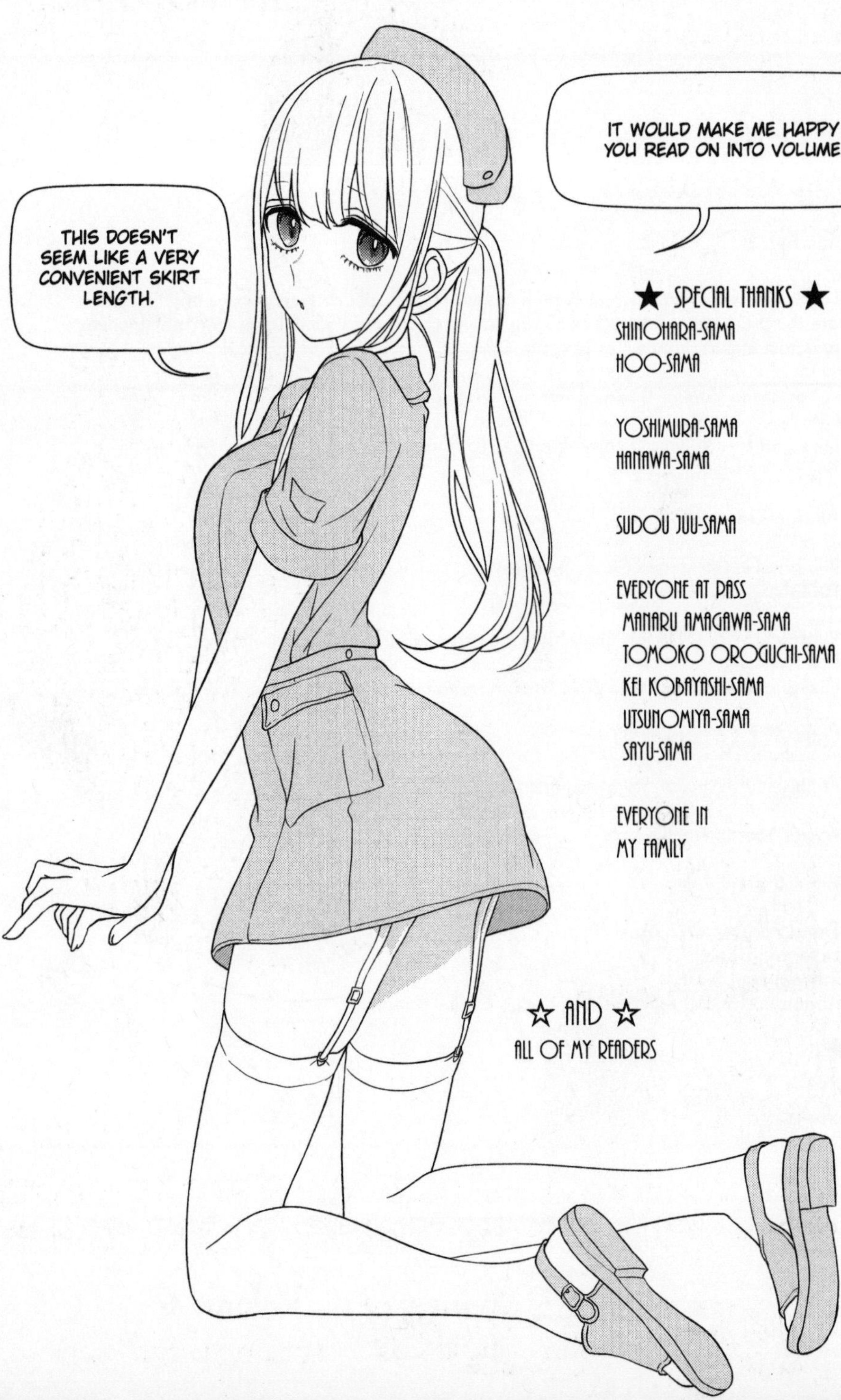
IT WOULD MAKE ME HAPPY IF YOU READ ON INTO VOLUME 6.
THIS DOESN'T SEEM LIKE A VERY CONVENIENT SKIRT LENGTH.

★ SPECIAL THANKS ★

SHINOHARA-SAMA
HOO-SAMA

YOSHIMURA-SAMA
HANAWA-SAMA

SUDOU JUU-SAMA

EVERYONE AT PASS
MANARU AMAGAWA-SAMA
TOMOKO OROGUCHI-SAMA
KEI KOBAYASHI-SAMA
UTSUNOMIYA-SAMA
SAYU-SAMA

EVERYONE IN
MY FAMILY

☆ AND ☆
ALL OF MY READERS

Love and Lies Volume 5 is a work of fiction. Names, characters, places, and incidents are the products of the author's imagination or are used fictitiously. Any resemblance to actual events, locales, or persons, living or dead, is entirely coincidental.

A Kodansha Comics Trade Paperback Original.

Published in the United States by Kodansha Comics, an imprint of Kodansha USA Publishing, LLC, New York.

Publication rights for this English edition arranged through Kodansha Ltd., Tokyo.

First published in Japan in 2016 by Kodansha Ltd., Tokyo, as *Koi to Uso* Volume 5.

ISBN 978-1-63236-561-3

Printed in the United States of America.

www.kodanshacomics.com

9 8 7 6 5 4 3 2 1

Translator: Jennifer Ward
Lettering: Daniel CY
Editing: Paul Starr
Kodansha Comics edition cover design by Phil Balsman